APPLIED BEHAVIOR ANALYSIS and SCHOOL PSYCHOLOGY

APPLIED BEHAVIOR ANALYSIS and SCHOOL PSYCHOLOGY

A Research Guide to Principles and Procedures

H. A. CHRIS NINNESS and
SIGRID S. GLENN

GREENWOOD PRESS
New York • Westport, Connecticut • London

Library of Congress Cataloging-in-Publication Data

Ninness, H. A. Chris.
Applied behavior analysis and school psychology : a research guide to principles and procedures / H. A. Chris Ninness and Sigrid S. Glenn.
p. cm.
Bibliography: p.
Includes index.
ISBN 0-313-24267-4 (lib. bdg. : alk. paper)
1. Behavior modification. 2. Educational psychology. I. Glenn, Sigrid S., 1939- . II. Title.
LB1060.2.N56 1988
371.1'024—dc19 87-29544

British Library Cataloguing in Publication Data is available.

Library of Congress Catalog Card Number: 87-29544
ISBN: 0-313-24267-4

First published in 1988

Greenwood Press, Inc.
88 Post Road West, Westport, Connecticut 06881

Printed in the United States of America

The paper used in this book complies with the Permanent Paper Standard issued by the National Information Standards Organization (Z39.48-1984).

10 9 8 7 6 5 4 3 2 1

In memory of
our teacher, colleague, and friend
Donald Lee Whaley
1934–1983

Contents

Preface

The plight of teachers, struggling daily to carry out the task of educating students in an environment rife with conflicting demands, led us to undertake the writing of this book. Our belief is that most of the demands made on teachers are considered, in the view of the demanding parties, to be consistent with what is best for students and for the culture in which they live. For if a culture does not produce individuals who can and will contribute to their own and its survival, the culture and its practices will fail to survive. And since most individuals could not survive alone, depending as we do on others to carry out many activities required for our survival, most of us wouldn't survive long either. So a great deal is at stake, and we count heavily on the educational system to keep the culture together.

Most people would probably agree that both our culture and its people will be served if the educational process results in healthy, productive, happy, caring, and skilled people. The reader might at this point wonder why, if we have similar goals, there are conflicting and even crippling demands made on the very people who have taken upon themselves the serious and difficult task of realizing these cultural goals.

One reason is that everybody in a position to make demands on the teacher seems to have a different idea of what the teacher needs to do to reach the goals. ''More discipline'' . . . often defined in terms of harsh demands backed up by aversive treatment. ''More love'' . . . often defined in terms of ''sharing problems'' or accepting underachievement and misbehavior as accepting the child ''as he is.'' ''More individualized approach'' . . . often defined as letting the child determine the curriculum. ''More teaching of concepts'' . . . often translated into haphazard programming of educational materials in the name of creative teaching.

We agree that discipline, love, an individualized approach, and the teaching of concepts are important. But we believe that harsh demands, aversive control, long discussions about problems, accepting underachievement and misbehavior, letting children determine the curriculum, and idiosyncratic teaching of complex concepts are part of the problem and certainly are not part of the solution.

Actually, though, our beliefs are quite irrelevant. What is relevant is that there is a growing body of experimental research that *demonstrates* how teachers can produce the behavior that we call productive, happy, caring, healthful, and skillful. This research has resulted from the combined efforts of applied researchers and teachers and other school personnel; it has been and continues to be carried out right in the classroom setting.

The purpose of this book is to provide teachers and other school personnel (as well as graduate students who will someday be teachers, school psychologists, counselors, and administrators) with detailed information about the procedures teachers have used to obtain positive outcomes of many kinds in their classrooms. Experimental research is a complex activity, and carrying it out in natural settings (rather than in a laboratory) makes it even more complicated. The problem is that so many things are going on in the everyday world that an experimental procedure must be extremely powerful to produce a result. Another way of saying this is that the scientific principle underlying the use of the procedure in the natural setting must be quite fundamental and robust if the procedure is to have an effect amid the other events.

Alternative events (other than the experimental procedure) must be ruled out as causing an observed change in behavior if we are to accept the results of the experiment as scientifically valid. This is done in applied behavior analysis through experimental designs of two main kinds. One, the reversal design—sometimes called ABA design—involves three phases. First, data are systematically collected on the behavior of interest, usually under the conditions in which the behavior occurs in the natural setting as it currently is. Second, an experimental procedure is introduced and data collection continues on the same behavior. Finally, the experimental procedure is removed and the behavior continues to be observed and data collected. If the procedure had an effect, the behavior should be pretty much the same in the first and third conditions and different in the second, when the experimental procedure was in operation.

This design has two problems. One is that sometimes once a procedure is implemented and the behavior changes, the behavior stays changed. This is especially true when the procedure is to produce a new behavior that is maintained by the everyday environment once it comes into existence. For example, if a teacher were to teach a child to read phonetically using a particular procedure (or set of procedures), then the child would continue reading after the teacher discontinued the teaching procedure. That is, as long as reading produced useful outcomes for the child, the child would continue reading. And reading almost always is useful, since it allows the child to follow written directions, to read notes his friends or parents write to him, to find out how a story ends, and so on. The other problem with the ABA (reversal) design is that some other event could have been accidentally introduced at the same time as the experimental procedure, and that other event may have been the real source of change. The way researchers get around this problem is to reverse the procedure several times, which makes it unlikely that some other event consistently happens each time the procedure is reinstated and doesn't happen each time the procedure is no longer used.

The way researchers get around the first problem is to use another type of design, most often the multiple-baseline design. There are many versions of the multiple-baseline design, but the basic strategy is to take data on two or more behaviors (of one or more persons) and introduce the experimental procedure with only one behavior. If that behavior changes (and the other behavior or behaviors don't), then the researcher tentatively accepts that the procedure made the difference. To check out that hypothesis, the researchers introduce the procedure on the next behavior on which they are collecting data. If that behavior then changes, there is even stronger support for the hypothesis that the experimental procedure was responsible for the changes.

Researchers don't usually stop there, though. They repeat the whole experiment, changing various aspects of the design to see how similar procedures exemplifying the same behavioral principle can be used. This is called systematic replication, an extremely important tool of science.

The important thing about the material in this book is that it is not based on people's opinions, and the data may conflict with some of our own opinions. But if the data show, with some degree of conclusiveness, that a certain procedure has the effect the teacher wanted to obtain, we must accept (at least provisionally) that the procedure was useful. If we wanted to obtain a similar result, we would do well to use the procedure ourselves, perhaps with a minor variation.

If readers of this book should decide to try one of the procedures the data suggest would be effective, how would they know what variations might likely prove successful? This is where an understanding of the scientific principles of behavior will help. All the procedures used in applied research are related to the principles of behavior that have been formulated as a result of basic laboratory research. The principles are generic: they apply to all people (teachers, students, and everybody else) and many different, even unique, activities (playing piano, making mouth noises, reading, watering plants, writing a book, etc.). The principles always involve relations between actions (including talking, writing, and thinking) and events in the environment (the physical world existing inside and outside our bodies).

The readers of this book will probably be able to participate in behavior technology to better the lives of their students and themselves to the extent that they learn to see behavioral principles as they are exemplified in the daily lives of their students and themselves. We hope that they will use the data generated by applied behavior analysts, and reported in the chapters that follow, to help them to use behavioral procedures in humane and rational ways to make the world a better place. We know of no better way to enhance the lives of those we love than to ensure that their environment provides the events that enable them to behave in ways of which they approve.

For our part, we owe our own understanding of the importance of behavioral principles in achieving humane goals to our friend and teacher Donald L. Whaley, to whom the book is dedicated. As provider of a challenging and exciting intellectual environment and as a model of rational caring, he used behavioral procedures with consummate skill and loving intentions. He survives in the behavior of his students.

There are many people to thank and we hope that most of them will know who they are and will anonymously accept those thanks. We would be woefully remiss if we failed to single out Sharon Ninness, who has aided in the preparation of this book in innumerable ways. Dr. Janet Ellis provided important editorial assistance, and Dr. Donald Pumroy was an ideal reader provided by Greenwood Press. They both made many specific suggestions that resulted in improvements. We thank Greg Madden for taking responsibility for organizing the index. Without the additional help of Leslie Burkett, Irene Grote, and Greg Madden—outstanding students and colleagues—this book would have taken even longer to complete!

APPLIED BEHAVIOR ANALYSIS and SCHOOL PSYCHOLOGY

1

Teacher "Burnout"

In recent years a poster appeared, with telling regularity, on the walls of public school offices and teachers' lounges, and university departments of education. Visitors were often bemused by the depiction of several frazzled women sprawled across desktops, looking dazed and exhausted, books scattered about the floor in a setting that suggested Teachers' Lounge USA. The caption read "Nobody ever said teaching was going to be easy." The not so subtle message may have been designed to assure teachers that their exhaustion and distress are part and parcel of their contracts. Such illustrations may offer a bit of solace in the form of comic relief, but teaching is popularly portrayed and popularly understood as a strenuous and thankless profession.

Most everyone agrees that teachers are overburdened with bureaucratic paperwork, that they are underpaid and sometimes subjected to the tyrannical whims and demands of parents and administrators. But these are not the factors that contribute most strenuously to the teacher's burden. In truth, most teachers could probably survive the bureaucracy and parental complaints if they could be certain that what they were doing was making a real difference, if they felt a sense of accomplishment, if their accomplishments were appreciated—in short, if teachers could walk out of their classrooms every day with the glow that comes from getting returns on their behavioral investment.

Although it seems unlikely that administrators and parents will ever rise up in unanimous acclaim of the teacher's performance, and the chances of reducing the paperwork seem remote, the people who can really make the difference are the students. Who could better find the teacher's work worthy of acclaim? Who is in the best position to show appreciation for the teacher's effort as she struggles to educate the coming generation? A bumper sticker on a passing car reads, "If you can read this sign, thank a teacher." Somebody feels unappreciated.

There are, however, teachers who thrive in the classroom. How is it that some teachers seem rather satisfied and even enjoy the pedagogical process when so many of their colleagues find it discouraging and highly stressful? Much of the answer may lie within the social interaction at the core of the instructional process. When students are a consistent source of positive feedback, teachers have a sense of job satisfaction. When the students are cooperative, teachers are likely to say things are going well. When students bring flowers or the proverbial apple and give hugs, the teacher's heart glows. When students are eager to learn or grasp a new concept or light up with understanding, teachers know they are somebody. When a hardworking student finally shows mastery, and teacher and student share in the satisfaction together, very little that the bureaucracy, or other sources of interference, can do will alter the teacher's commitment to education.

Many teachers, however, seldom have such experiences. Rather, much of their classroom time is spent correcting students' disruptive behavior. Instead of positive social feedback from their students they get smirks or sarcastic, even crude, replies. Some students casually disregard pleas for order. When she screams for silence, the teacher may be rewarded by a lull in the general disorder, but mischief often resumes as her fury fades. The majority of "instructional time" may be spent trying to get students organized or just quiet. Teaching, and therefore learning, is stifled in such environments. All this occurs in most of the better schools, where open violence is not as commonplace as in others.

A number of solutions have been suggested to correct this unhappy situation. Although many people believe that a return to "real" discipline will alleviate the problem, corporal punishment has not disappeared from the educational scene. In many classrooms the proverbial "board of education" is an all too common source of aversive control. This has had some unfortunate side effects, not to mention inconsistent results. More recently devised techniques still tend to focus on controlling misbehavior, as if "discipline" were equivalent to threats and punishment. The focus is often on rules that state a relationship between misbehavior and aversive consequences. Students are told that they have only so many chances to misbehave. On the first such occasion their name will go on the board, the second may result in some more serious corrective action, and subsequent infractions eventually lead the student to the principal's office. The focus on what the students have done wrong, might do wrong, and are doing wrong does little to make children disciples of learning, which is presumably what the discipline is all about. As long as teachers have no systematic techniques for producing academic skills and pro-social conduct in all students, they will be faced with bored and disruptive students whose discipline amounts to subjugation.

More liberal educators have attempted to follow the "progressive" approach, permitting students to involve themselves in whatever activity seems relevant to their natural learning intuitions. This is perhaps another variation on Rousseau's "Noble Savage" theme, but children's innate propensities for learning such culturally devised skills as reading, writing, and arithematic are questionable.

Many teachers who begin teaching with this naive theoretical bias quickly become disenchanted and turn to more aversive systems of providing "classroom control."

But for most teachers the classroom is neither as hostile as depicted above nor as rewarding as they fantasized it while preparing for their profession. Most teachers we know work their way through the school year anticipating various holidays and longing for summer. As with their students, school is a place they must attend; they try to make the best of a difficult and trying situation. Many wish they were more excited about teaching and less involved in baby-sitting; however, as time passes they often come to accept their lot. They become used to unruly children who lack interest in learning, used to maintaining inconsistent control of the classroom by means of threats, penetrating stares, condescending innuendo, and the occasional use of corporal punishment.

Although the foregoing description may seem to overstate the case, and certainly does not apply to all teachers, positive commentary is a relatively infrequent part of most teacher/student exchange. Sprick (1981) found that teachers made about four negative comments for every one positive comment to students during the course of the average classroom day. Our experience has been that in many classrooms, even this ratio would be a substantial improvement. Negative, punitive, and aversive control are all too common throughout the educational structure of most school districts. Teachers and principals often go on using these tactics as their main line of defense because they have one conspicuous effect—a short-term change in students' behavior. That is, subsequent to spanking a student, screaming at the class, or just giving the well-known cold stare, students may stop misbehaving. But for how long and at what cost? Behavioral processes—in effect any time people interact—account for both the students' and the teachers' maladaptive behavior.

The unfortunate truth is that many teachers do not know how to structure a classroom so that students, as well as they themselves, can derive the maximum enjoyment and benefit from the school environment. Managing the instructional environment and the social environment of twenty-five or thirty students five days a week for thirty-six weeks is a complex and rigorous task. Mastering such a task would require a thorough grounding in behavioral principles, along with plenty of practice in applying those principles in the classroom. Rather than devote a significant portion of the curriculum of future teachers to rigorous and systematic training in behavior analysis, most departments provide a blending of old and new, progressive and traditional, innovative and sometimes exotic approaches. Because good technology has evolved only over the past fifteen or twenty years and few people have had the opportunity to benefit from recent advances, most departments necessarily have few faculty with adequate skills in behavior management theory and practice. In addition, few role models exist among experienced teachers. Despite the availability of some extraordinarily successful teachers as models for "practice teaching," the essence of their art cannot easily be transmitted. It is unique to them. Although scientific knowledge about how to teach successfully is available, that knowledge has not made its way into the nation's classrooms.

What is lacking is the transfer of knowledge possible when a technology based on scientific principles is available. In some universities behavioral technology and classroom management are taught in a course or two, but they are often misrepresented in textbooks (Cook, 1984). The teachers of teachers have never, themselves, used behavioral principles systematically and creatively, so they cannot relate those principles to the classroom setting in a way that prepares future teachers to "think behaviorally." And although all teachers receive pre-graduate training and supervision as student teachers, few have an opportunity to work in schools where behavioral technology is a significant feature of the instructional system. Rather, student teachers are assigned to experienced teachers who then provide the student teacher with supervision according to their own prescientific notions of instruction—some quite effective, some not. These are again a blend of old and new, progressive and traditional, functional and antiquated notions of "what makes Johnnie learn."

What is needed is a more thorough understanding of the principles of behavior as they apply to the classroom. What is also needed is a classroom in which to apply these principles so the complex skills involved in behavior management can be acquired. This is a reciprocal process, one in which the principles learned can be applied on a daily basis, and application of this information can provide teachers with feedback as to their usefulness. Under such circumstances learning takes place at two levels: knowledge of scientific principles and skill in technological applications. As in chemistry, the process of change cannot come alive until one can get into the laboratory and experience the transformation. In order to appreciate behavioral technology one needs to see a classroom transformed from an atmosphere of indifference, or even anarchy, to one of enthusiasm and cooperation.

We contend that the majority of behavior problems that occur in the classroom are best treated within the confines of that classroom. In most cases it is not necessary, or advisable, for psychologists to take students out of the classroom in order to apply a "therapeutic technique." Separation-for-treatment models, which require treatment in isolation from the classroom environment, are unlikely to produce new behaviors that generalize back to the classroom. The reason is that children's behavior adjusts to the world in which the behavior occurs. Because the problem occurs in the classroom, the problem may be seen as the result of the kind of interactions that occur or do not occur in the classroom. And the problem will most likely be resolved when different kinds of interactions occur in the classroom. The best place to produce change is where the change is wanted. This is not to say that teachers can never benefit from outside services. It is to say that the teacher is the one who will ultimately apply behavior management strategies if they are to be effectively used.

If the teacher can gain assistance from a behavior analyst who is knowledgeable about classrooms, or a consulting school psychologist who is sophisticated in behavioral technology, the benefits can be substantial. These outsiders, if thoroughly prepared themselves, can provide analytical expertise, can give feedback regarding the ongoing management process in the classroom, can provide modeling of the techniques used in the classroom, can help the teacher design classroom contingencies, or may even design an individualized program or student contract in cooperation with the teacher; but the teacher almost always makes or breaks the overall program.

Perhaps the most critical characteristic of the behaviorally oriented teacher is perseverance. The process of learning can be slow at times. Behavior analysis is not at all like the practice of medicine. One does not give a pill or make an incision, after which the problem goes away with no further effort being expended. Learning is a continuing process, and individual learning often follows an erratic course. Sometimes children who make great strides one day, for reasons that are unapparent, appear to regress on subsequent days. This may be followed by further periods of progress and regression. It is only by looking at the big picture that one can get an indication of change, and the big picture can best be seen through the analysis of data collected over time. Important to note, however, is that many of the strategies described here do not require lengthy intervention. The results are often quick, effective, and durable, particularly when the procedures are used in regular classrooms. Classrooms in which serious problems already exist, such as those with learning disabled or emotionally disturbed children, usually require more consistent effort over longer periods.

The problems of emotionally disturbed or behaviorally disordered students are, though, often best addressed in the regular education classroom, at what is called the prereferral stage of intervention. Prereferral intervention means that the classroom teacher (often with the help of a behavior analyst) introduces a behavior program before special education assessment. Such prereferral intervention can frequently circumvent or preclude the need for special education or psychological services.

PSYCHOLOGICAL SERVICE AND DISSERVICE

Psychological services as they currently exist in many school districts are frequently used only for "mandated services" (i.e., the diagnostic requirements for special education placement). Consistent with Public Law 94–142 and various state-required procedures for classifying handicapping conditions, many school psychologists are primarily involved in labeling. Treatment is supposedly accomplished once the disturbed student is placed in a therapeutic environment (a special education classroom).

Thus, unfortunately, many school psychologists are relegated to a position of exclusively conducting psychological diagnostics. They are essentially and perpetually involved in the preparation of referrals, assessments, diagnoses, and placements. Little, if any, emphasis is placed on direct behavioral service for the diagnosed and disordered students who have been the subject of so much inquiry. Furthermore, there is growing evidence that much of this evaluation and categorization process is all too often sadly lacking in accuracy and reliability. Because of this the school psychologists' professional maladies have been held up to ridicule by colleagues and members of their own profession.

> The school psychologist is not a well man. His malady, while not particularly acute, is nonetheless a chronic one, endemic to his profession. The patient often presents such symptoms as distension of the referral . . . rupture of the arteries of communication . . . atrophied recommendations . . . and accumulation of jargon deposits in the report. . . . The syndrome might best be described as a "paralysis of the analysis." (Forness, 1970, p. 96)

The above diagnosis is at least as accurate as the diagnostic descriptions provided by many psychologists who attempt to classify behavior disordered and/or emotionally disturbed students. The use of labeling and diagnostic systems to classify misbehaving children has been misconceived and overwhelmingly abused. According to prevalence figures reported by the U.S. Department of Education (1985), the proportion of handicapped children described as behavior disordered (essentially the same as emotionally disturbed) is 28.9 in Utah and 2.5 in California. Forness (1987) pointed out that such figures are difficult to interpret but suggested that when one state serves twelve times as many handicapped students in a single category as a neighboring state, "the capriciousness of our identification and diagnostic systems in this area" is apparent."

The capriciousness of the diagnostic system is exacerbated by the recent trend of using psychiatric classifications to corroborate educational classifications. But behavior problems within the school system are not usually like disease entities described in medical textbooks. The categorizing of inappropriate classroom behaviors into clinical syndromes of a medical multiaxial classification system is not only inappropriate; it is often stigmatizing and damaging to the individuals so diagnosed. The use of the *DSM-III: Diagnostic and Statistical Manual of Mental Disorders* (American Psychiatric Association, 1980, 3rd ed.) and the revised *DSM-III-R* edition (American Psychiatric Association, 1987) to identify children as emotionally disturbed has led to confusion and mismanagement. The lack of correlation between psychiatric classification and classroom needs is supported by a study reported by Forness (1987). He provides a summary of 120 children admitted to the UCLA Neuropsychiatric Hospital for behavior disorders who were treated and eventually cycled back into their home schools. He points out that

> subjects in each diagnostic group range across nearly every level of regular and special education classroom placement, indicating little or no pattern of relationship between a child's psychiatric diagnosis and his/her need for special education. These findings have essentially been replicated with another sample of 350 outpatient children in the same hospital, using even more refined diagnostic groups (Sinclair, Forness & Alexson, 1985). Even more damaging was the finding that in a subsample of 12 "psychotic" children in

this second study, not one returned to an SED (seriously emotionally disturbed) classroom. (Forness, 1987, pp. 7–8)

Forness tells us that "this 'calibration fantasy,' i.e., that critical intellectual or behavioral characteristics can be measured in a way that determines treatment, has negatively affected almost every subspecialty of education of the handicapped" (Forness, 1987).

Forness argues that special educators frequently place less value on intervention strategies than on diagnostics. He attributes this unfortunate disposition to special education's early roots in psychology, where the use of differential diagnosis has always been a sacred cow, even when no differential treatment was available or yet devised. However, among those approaches used in special education, behavior modification clearly stands out as one of the few with significant positive effects. Doing what is termed a *meta-analysis* (Kavale, 1983), a multitude of diverse research findings can be analyzed so that a common descriptor called an *effect size* can be used to describe the extent of positive or negative treatment outcomes. The following table provides overall mean effect sizes for various treatment approaches used in special education. Although standard deviations indicate large variations among outcomes, it is still overwhelmingly apparent that behavioral procedures are among the few interventions that demonstrate sizable positive effects.

SUMMARY OF META-ANALYSIS IN SPECIAL EDUCATION RESEARCH

Intervention Deviation	Number of Studies	Effect Size	Standard
Reduction of class size	77	.31	.70
Special class placement	50	−.12	.65
Behavior modification	41	.93	1.16
Psycholinguistic training	34	.39	.54
Perceptual motor training	180	.08	.27
Modality instruction	39	.15	.28
Stimulant drugs	135	.58	.61
Psychotropic drugs	70	.30	.75
Diet intervention	23	.12	.42

Source: Adapted from Forness (1987), which was in turn adapted from Kavale and Forness (1985), with two exceptions: the modality instruction data, which were reported in Kavale and Forness (1987), and the behavior modification data, which were reported in Skiba and Casey (1985).

THE BEHAVIORAL ALTERNATIVE

Some people claim that behavioral management strategies can have only temporary effects, that problem behaviors corrected by such techniques are likely to resurface in some new form because an underlying sickness is still present. This doctrine rests on the assumption that behavior is the superficial manifestation of a more important reality somewhere inside the person. Changes in the symptom of the underlying pathology, that is, changes in behavior, presumably leave the underlying reality untouched. Follow-up research from the earliest applied research to the present has failed to confirm this antiquated notion (e.g., Wolpe, 1964). Further, recent research (Ninness, Graben, Miller, & Whaley, 1985) demonstrates that even general behavioral characteristics called "personality factors," which are typically thought to indicate deeply rooted pathology in emotionally disturbed children, are affected by behavioral management strategies as applied in the classroom.

The main message for this chapter, and indeed for the whole text, is that effective behavior management is possible within the classroom. Further, teacher burnout can be and is being prevented by those teachers who understand behavioral principles well enough to identify and manage relevant classroom contingencies. Teachers, whether or not proficient in behavior analysis, cannot control all the variables that affect the lives of students, especially those that occur outside the school. But they can, to a large degree, control what goes on in their own classrooms. Positive instructional and social contingencies in the classroom will go a long way toward helping students to overcome handicaps resulting from chaotic environments outside their classrooms.

This book is a compendium of strategies and tactics, of methods and theories, of tools and skills, that will come alive only when the reader has the opportunity to apply them in a real classroom setting. Much of what follows requires some analytical understanding of principles of behavior. The basic principles are not easy to understand as they apply to the complex world of schools. But they are critical to improving management skills. Therefore, the next chapter will briefly review basic behavioral concepts as they relate to school settings. The book will then proceed to various methods of application that have been documented in the behavioral literature. The research described in later chapters is a review of scientific findings in the field of applied behavior analysis. The primary sources are the *Journal of Applied Behavior Analysis* and other related journals as they report findings that relate to behavior analysis in school psychology.

REFERENCES

American Psychiatric Association. (1980). *DSM-III: Diagnostic and statistical manual of mental disorders* (3rd ed.). Washington, D.C.: American Psychiatric Association.

American Psychiatric Association. (1987). *DSM-III-R: Diagnostic and statistical manual of mental disorders* (rev. 3rd ed.). Washington, D.C.: American Psychiatric Association.

Cook, N. L. (1984). Misrepresenting of the behavioral model in preservice teacher education textbooks. In W. L. Heward, T. E. Heron, D. S. Hill, & J. Trap-Porter (Eds.), *Focus on behavior analysis in education* (pp. 197–217). Columbus, OH: Merrill.

Forness, S. (1970). Educational prescription for the school psychologist. *Journal of School Psychology, 8*, 96–98.

Forness, S. (1987). Interdisciplinary confessions of a school psychologist: Is there life after special education? Paper presented at the Ninth Annual Conference on Behavior Disorder, Austin, TX.

Forness, S., & Kavale, K. (1987). Holistic inquiry and the scientific challenge in special education: A reply to Iano. *Remedial and Special Education, 8*, 47–51.

Kavale, K. (1983). Fragile findings, complex conclusions, and meta-analysis in special education. *Exceptional Education Quarterly, 4*, 97–106.

Kavale, K., & Forness, S. (1985). *The science of learning disabilities*. San Diego: College-Hill Press.

Kolvin, I. (1967). Aversive imagery treatment in adolescents. *Behavior Research and Therapy, 5*, 245–248.

Ninness, H. A. C., Graben, L., Miller, B., & Whaley, D. L. (1985). The effect of contingency management strategies on the Bender Gestalt diagnostic indicators of emotionally disturbed children. *Child Study Journal, 15* (1), 13–28.

Sinclair, E., Forness, S., & Alexson, J. (1985). Psychiatric diagnosis: A study of its relationship to school needs. *Journal of Special Education, 19*, 333–344.

Skiba, R., & Casey, A. (1985). Interventions for behavior disordered students: A quantitative review and methodological critique. *Behavioral Disorders, 10*, 239–252.

Sprick, R. A. (1981). *The solution book: A guide to classroom management*. Chicago, IL: Science Research Associates.

U.S. Department of Education (1985). *Seventh annual report to Congress on implementation of Public Law 94–142: The Education for All Handicapped Children Act*. Washington, DC: U.S. Government Printing Office.

Wolpe, J. (1964). Behaviour therapy in complex neurotic states. *The British Journal of Psychiatry, 110*, 28–34.

2

Behavioral Principles in a School Setting

A DIFFERENT APPROACH TO BEHAVIORAL BASICS

Most books do not seem, to us, to explain behavioral principles in ways that make contact with the experience of teachers and other school personnel. Yet, to make innovative and effective use of the principles of behavior in their classrooms, teachers need to be so familiar with them that they can recognize behavioral processes occurring before their very eyes. Because behavioral processes unfold in time, to see them occurring is something like seeing a car being built, a flower blooming, or bread rising.

It's even harder to see behavior change than bread rise, however, because the "loaf" is solid and continuous, whereas a behavioral unit is made up of repeated instances of activity that are here one moment and gone the next. Although Johnny's raising his hand may be the unit in which a teacher is interested, she is not simply interested in one hand-raise; she wants consistent, repeatable, predictable hand-raises under specified conditions—perhaps when Johnny wants to be recognized as a speaker, to take a turn at the board, etc. Hand-raises may be seen as the unit of behavior something is to be done about; but in order to do something, all Johnny's hand-raises, as they occur throughout the year, must be recognized as members of a behavioral unit called "raising his hand."

Any question about behavioral change is a question about what's happening to the unit across time, just as the question about bread rising is one about what's happening to the unit across time. In the case of hand-raising the instances may be getting more frequent or less frequent, more consistently related to the "right" time and place or more sporadically related. Perhaps it is apparent that one instance of hand-raising (or failure to raise a hand) cannot tell the teacher whether or not Johnny is improving.

The ability to "see" behavior across time must be learned, and such learning is not particularly easy. This is one reason behavior analysts recommend that teachers make a graph that shows what's happening to the behavior the teacher is observing across time. Behavioral graphs help behavior analysts and teachers alike to see the bigger picture, so they don't give too much import to any one instance of behavior. After a while teachers who invest some of their own behavior in this process find that they are often able to see behavior across time and manage it effectively without counting and graphing behavioral instances. They will then count and graph only if their informal management procedures fail to work.

This chapter is about behavioral processes, procedures, and principles. Behavioral units emerge and stabilize as people interact with the world. The emergence and stabilization of behavior occurs whether or not we want it, intend it, or arrange for it to do so. Behavioral processes are part of nature.

Current knowledge about behavioral processes is the result of scientists' use of experimental procedures to find out how behavior works. In doing so certain procedures are devised to investigate relations between the subject matter of the science (in this case behavior) and other events in the world. The most powerful procedures are experimental—they involve the systematic changing of some events to find out the effects of those changes on other events. Through such techniques, scientists gradually learn about the processes that occur in nature. Experimental procedures are a way of finding out about processes.

Similar procedures also may be a way of entering into ongoing processes and changing their course in the everyday world. Such everyday interference is called technology—a "technical method of achieving a practical purpose." Behavioral technology uses procedures similar to those used by scientists. The human purpose is what is different. Scientists want to discover how nature works; technologists want to change the course of natural events.

Nature is blind, and cannot be counted on to accidentally provide the conditions that will allow children to learn to read, to raise their hands at appropriate times, to use the toilet instead of the floor, to speak kindly to their friends, or to seek an alternative to fighting for possession of the ball. Such being the case, teachers would do well to have a highly developed repertoire of behavioral procedures that will allow them to arrange the environment so children will learn these things. Behavioral technology uses natural (behavioral) processes to serve the human purpose, just as computer technology uses natural (electronic and mechanical) processes to serve the human purpose.

Behavioral principles are simply statements about the relationships that exist in nature between behavior and the world (the environment) in which behavior occurs. The rest of this chapter will be about a few behavioral principles—those we believe critical to the development of basic technical skills for teachers. In stating those principles we will describe a few basic behavioral processes and some of the procedures that applied behavior analysts have used to change the course of ongoing behavior from destructive (to both the child involved and the people around him) to constructive. The reader will have knowledge of behavioral principles when he or she understands behavioral processes and procedures.

BEHAVIORAL PROCESSES

Behavioral processes are the changes in behavior that take place over time as a result of relations that occur between behavior and the environment. Most of the behavior in which teachers are interested belongs to the type called "operant" behavior—behavior that produces changes in the world for the behaver. What people do or say is operant behavior: watering the plants, spelling "cat," reading directions, ducking a spitwad, throwing a spitwad, sharpening a pencil, getting in line, opening a book.

One of the most profoundly important differences between humans and other species is that humans have so many ways to change their environment—they have so much operant behavior. The vast repertoires of operant behavior characteristic of humans are due to several anatomical characteristics (thumbs, bipedal locomotion, large neocortex, complex visual and auditory receptors) and to the fact that the products of one generation are passed on to the next so each generation can benefit from the learning of previous generations. Operant behavior is nature's way of allowing each generation to develop a repertoire of behavior uniquely suited to its own environment; if the environment rapidly changes from one generation to the next, then the next generation's operant behavior will adapt to the new environment.

Reinforcement

Behavioral adaptability is made possible by a selection process called reinforcement—the strengthening of behavioral units by the consequences they produce. Some consequences of behavior are selectors. They increase the likelihood that the behavior will occur again in the future. Consequences may work as selectors (reinforcers) for either of two reasons: they have been programmed as selectors by the evolutionary history of the species to which the behaver belongs; or they have been programmed as selectors through their association with biological selectors in the individual behaver's history. Food, water, much tactile contact (including sexual), warmth, and reduction of painful stimulation are biologically programmed behavioral selectors. They are called primary reinforcers by behavior analysts.

Those reinforcers that are not biologically programmed as selectors are learned or conditional reinforcers. Practically any event can come to work as a learned reinforcer, and different individual histories lead to great differences in what works as a learned reinforcer for different people. However, many people have similar enough histories so that in most cases (not all) we can count on such things as praise, approval, eye contact, and certain feedback (e.g., "right") to work as reinforcers. When these do not work as reinforcers, one of the most important jobs of a teacher is to arrange things so that they do. Without these as reinforcers the teacher is handicapped in teaching a child. What is even more critical is that the child is severely handicapped in his potential for learning, since the social environment responsible for teaching cannot usually provide primary reinforcers in selecting relevant operant behavior.

A fortunate characteristic of reinforcement is that once behavior occurs in strength, it will continue to occur at relevant times so long as reinforcing consequences occur even occasionally. This characteristic, together with the fact that many consequences become learned reinforcers, allows behavior to be maintained indefinitely once it stabilizes.

The behavioral process of reinforcement is nature's way of selecting whatever behavior best suits a given environment. Human beings, over the past 10,000 years or so, have gradually and bumblingly evolved ways of making use of nature's process of behavioral selection. Only in the past fifty years have we used the methods of science to hasten our understanding of that process. We have made more frequent use of another behavioral process in our practical affairs—one that involves the suppression of behavior: punishment.

Punishment

Punishment is the suppression of behavior by the consequences the behavior produces. Because we humans have had, at best, a dim understanding of reinforcement, we are not usually careful about what behavior gets selected. We accidentally and unknowingly reinforce a lot of behavior that is detrimental, in the long run, to both the behaver and those around him. Then we try to lock the barn door. When behavior that is destructive to an individual's future (or that is aversive to those nearby) occurs, we are inclined to strike out at the behaver. We spank, we threaten, we take away privileges, we criticize, we imprison, and we disapprove. If we do these things immediately after the behavior, the behavior may be suppressed (i.e., appear less frequently).

Punishment, as a process, is the suppression of behavior that occurs over time when instances of that behavior have produced certain kinds of consequences. The consequences that have this effect are called punishers. Like reinforcers, punishers may be biologically programmed (like painful stimulation), or they may be conditioned as punishers during people's lifetimes. As in the case of reinforcers, learned punishers may vary from person to person, although many of the same consequences work to punish the behavior of people who grew up in the same culture. Typically, we may punish the behavior of American children by criticizing, frowning, taking away points, or scolding.

Punishment, as a process, does not involve the elimination of behavior from a child's available repertoire. It suppresses the occurrence of the behavior under conditions similar to those in which the behavior has produced the punisher. If severe enough, the suppressive effect may generalize to other situations.

Extinction

Extinction is the disappearance, from a person's repertoire, of behavior that consistently fails to produce reinforcing consequences. Extinction occurs when behavior produces no relevant changes in the world of the behaver. Any behavior that occurs repeatedly and never produces anything is energy wasted. Extinction is nature's way of dropping out useless behavior—a kind of unlearning process. The value of extinction is that it allows the behavioral repertoire to remain current. Old, useless behavior that no longer works fades away. Unless behavior produces some consequences, at least occasionally, it is generally of little value to the behaving person.

Discrimination

Discrimination is the process by which operant behavior comes to occur in one situation but not in others. Subtle dimensions of the world operate kind of like traffic signals for specific behavioral units. Discrimination is occurring when a child learns to raise his hand in Ms. Jones's room and to speak out in Ms. Smith's room; when he learns to whisper in church and to shout on the playground; when he learns to say "cat" when c-a-t is on the board and "dog" when d-o-g is on the board; when he learns to say he has a stomachache when it's time to do math and to say he feels fine ten minutes later when it's time to color.

Discrimination can get much more complex than the examples given above. But whether subtle and complex dimensions of the world cue a particular behavior, or simple and obvious dimensions of the world cue that behavior, the world gains discriminative control over our behavior in the same way. Discrimination occurs when behavior in the presence of certain situations produces reinforcers and that same behavior fails to produce the reinforcers in other situations. If a child says "dog" when c-a-t is on the board and the teacher always says "right," or allows the child to proceed to the next word, or lets the child sit down without making the appropriate "cat" response, then c-a-t spells "dog." At least it does for that child.

If Ms. Jones calls on a child when he raises his hand but Ms. Smith ignores him when he raises his hand, he will raise his hand in Ms. Jones's room (when being called on is reinforcing) and stop doing so or never learn to do so in Ms. Smith's room. He will learn to call out in Ms. Smith's room if Ms. Smith acknowledges the child's response (says "right," stares at him, writes what he says on the board, etc.), and he is likely to do so again *even if Ms. Smith also tells him to raise his hand the next time*. If he should call out in Ms. Jones's room, though, she asks the question again without acknowledging his answer and calls on someone else to answer it (perhaps someone who seldom can answer questions, giving that child the opportunity to benefit from the prompt.) The teachers are using discrimination training, and the child learns to behave one way in Ms. Jones's room and another way in Ms. Smith's.

Discrimination is the process by which subtle properties of the world come to evoke highly specific behavior with a high degree of reliability.

Generalization

In a way, generalization, as a process, is the opposite of discrimination. Behavior is said to generalize when it spreads to new situations because of similarities between the new situation and old situations in which the behavior was previously reinforced. The child who learns to pet the family cat, to pet her stuffed kitten, and to pet the cat next door may reach her hand toward the tiger at the zoo. The child has learned to say ''bigger'' to the thicker slice of cake, to the bulkier sweater, and to the plate with the greatest diameter might say ''bigger'' to the oversized pencil and even to the louder voice.

Although discrimination always occurs through learning, generalization may occur automatically because of the unlearned tendency for behavior to spread to situations similar to others in which behavior has been reinforced. Generalization may also occur through learning, however, which brings us to the notion that the behavioral processes that have been discussed can be brought about by using certain procedures.

Before we turn to behavioral procedures, it is important to note that there are other behavioral processes that have not been discussed. We have found that those that have been discussed must be understood before behavioral principles can be put to effective use in classrooms. We have also found that teachers can do some amazing things by using what they know about these five processes to intervene in the behavior stream of children whose behavior is not progressing satisfactorily. Also, most of the applied-behavior analysis literature deals with these processes, and understanding them will allow school personnel to make use of most of the literature currently available.

BEHAVIORAL PROCEDURES

To say one ''understands'' something may mean many different things. People often distinguish between ''book knowledge''—understanding that involves talking about concepts, using them correctly in one's speech or writing—and ''practical knowledge''—understanding that involves doing something effective to bring about a change. When someone can answer questions about how a carburetor works after reading a book about combustion engines, we say she has book knowledge. She may or may not be able to remove or repair a carburetor, determine if one is defective, or even locate the carburetor in a car. On the other hand, someone may be able to do all of the above things and not be able to explain exactly what a carburetor is, or pass a multiple-choice test about the function of a carburetor in combustion engines. She learned what she knows by messing around with carburetors. Given the choice of which kind of knowledge we would prefer our mechanic to have, if only one were possible, we'd all probably make the same choice. Even so, a mechanic who understood the scientific concepts underlying the workings of the combustion engine would be better able to make use of the skills acquired in dealing with the real thing. Such a mechanic would have a special advantage if she ran into a carburetor problem she had never seen before, and thus had never been able to learn about it through direct experience. Most of us would agree that thorough understanding would involve both kinds of knowledge.

Some school personnel intuitively know how to deal with children; but most of us have not been fortunate enough to learn what is necessary, by simply interacting with people, to be able to effectively handle the more difficult problems. A great deal of trial and error can be saved if people take the time to acquire the basic scientific concepts that allow them to deal with a new problem with some understanding. In fact, many problems will never be solved—many never have been solved—until we have a conceptual understanding of the nature of the problem. On the other hand, many seemingly intransigent problems have been found to have solutions once people learned to be guided in their search for solutions by the relevant scientific concepts.

This book summarizes a good deal of literature that describes scientifically validated solutions to problems that plague teachers and other school personnel throughout the country. Its purpose is to familiarize students and professionals with the range of solutions found and to provide a ready reference for future use.

All the solutions described in this book have two things in common. They are presented as solutions only if they have been tested by the scientific method and found repeatable; and they were derived through an understanding of the basic principles of the science of behavior. In short, the studies reported in this book were done by people who had some of both kinds of understanding.

We believe that teachers, school psychologists, and college students often have had many experiences that might make more sense if they were understood in terms of behavioral principles. We also believe that such understanding would enable them to solve problems heretofore unsolvable. For these reasons we will try to deal with the literature review in a way that helps our readers to see how the behavioral principles involved relate to what's going on in their everyday world.

The sine qua non of behavioral procedures is the reinforcement procedure. Reinforcement procedures are used to increase the likelihood that a particular behavioral unit will occur in the future. A reinforcement procedure is *never* used to get rid of behavior—to stop somebody from doing something or reduce the frequency of some behavior. To reinforce means to strengthen; reinforcement is the strengthening of behavior over time; and a reinforcement procedure is an intervention designed to increase the frequency of behavior.

Using a reinforcement procedure requires several steps. First, the behavior to be reinforced must be identified so that it can be reliably observed. In other words, what is going to count as an instance of the behavior? Second, some event must be specified as a potential reinforcer, or behavioral consequence. Third, the student's environment must be arranged so that the consequence reliably and immediately follows the behavior and does not occur more or less randomly at other times.

If the procedure results in an increase in the frequency of the behavior, the consequence may justifiably be called a reinforcer. Its potential was realized; the guess about its potency was a good one. If the procedure does not result in an increase in the frequency of the behavior, there may be several reasons the reinforcement procedure was not effective. The consequence may be insufficient as a reinforcer—not the right thing, too little of it. Another possibility is that the consequence may not have been properly related to the behavior; too much time may have elapsed between the behavior and the consequence; or the consequence may have occurred at so many other times that the behavior just wasn't "relevant" to producing it.

Sometimes the consequences that have the most potential to reinforce behavior are hard to make occur immediately after the behavior. If going to recess has great potential as a reinforcer, the teacher can't make it immediately follow a behavior that occurs an hour before time for recess. Besides, one can't afford to squander a great reinforcer like recess by making it contingent on one behavior! The only way to beat this dilemma is to use recess as a backup reinforcer.

Here is how backup reinforcers work. When the consequence that has reinforcing potential cannot be delivered immediately after the desired behavior occurs, some other consequence (that has no inherent value as a reinforcer) may be delivered immediately after the behavior. That consequence becomes valuable if it is correlated at another time with a consequence that does have reinforcer value. Points, which don't have any value in and of themselves, may be delivered right after the behavior, and the points may be accumulated for time at recess. Points can also be made valuable by giving them along with smiles, praise, or approval—social events that already have value to most people. It is important to remember that the points do not have any value until they have been traded in for the backup reinforcer.

The reinforcement procedure is incredibly powerful and is seldom used effectively. Although the reinforcement process is occurring hundreds of times a day in the lives of each of us, we are fortunate indeed if the behavior being reinforced is that which we would like in ourselves or others. Because so few people understand the process, we accidentally make consequences with reinforcing potential contingent on all sorts of irrelevant, undesirable, even maladaptive behavior. We unwittingly engage the reinforcement *process* even though we have no intention of implementing a reinforcement *procedure*.

Using a reinforcement procedure is hard at first because the user must pay close attention to what he or she is doing and how it relates to the behavior of someone else. There is little reinforcement for the behavior of using a reinforcement procedure because there is no immediate consequence for that behavior. If Ms. Jones gives points all morning, nothing changes in her world immediately after she gives a point. The payoff for Ms. Jones is desirable behavior from a child. The child is doing something desirable before Ms. Jones gives the point, and Ms. Jones does not produce anything better (for herself) by giving points, except in the long run and over time.

If Ms. Jones is consistent at making point consequences follow desirable behavior from her class, they will behave very well most of the time. Even though her reinforcement procedures are the cause of the good behavior, the good behavior is too unrelated in time to Ms. Jones's point-giving to work as reinforcement. For this reason people do not use the reinforcement procedure effectively: their behavior of doing so is not reinforced. The backup reinforcer (the kids' good behavior) isn't correlated with any immediate consequence for the teacher. The only solution we know for this problem is to relate the kids' good behavior to the data collected by the teacher as she gives points. That way there will be an immediate consequence for giving points. The data and that consequence will be related to a valuable backup reinforcer: the students' good behavior. Reinforcement—procedures and process—works in the same way for all people.

Extinction Procedure

If people can be observed to do or say something more than once or twice, what they are doing or saying is likely to be producing a consequence. To be sure, the consequence does not have to occur after each and every instance of the behavior. It may occur almost every time the behavior occurs, or every now and then, or only on rare occasions. A good guess would be that a consequence is reinforcing the behavior.

Sometimes behavior that produces reinforcing consequences is detrimental to the people around the behaver: sometimes it is detrimental, in the long run, even to the behaver. The child who mutters, "You can't make me," or the one who whines about the work assigned is setting a bad example for other children, and angers and frustrates the teacher. The behavior is even more detrimental to the child, however, because such behavior will eventually result in the child's being categorized in undesirable ways and treated accordingly. Even though such behavior is ultimately detrimental, the behavior continues occurring because the immediate consequences reinforce it. Usually the reinforcing consequence is some response from an adult. (*Note*: Some of the most powerful reinforcers, in many classroom settings, are signs of anger and frustration in the teacher. Any individualized attention from a busy teacher who generally must deal with children as a group is likely to be a reinforcer. If individualized attention seldom takes the form of praise, approval, pat on the shoulder, etc., cold stares and angry threats will do. And, to put it in everyday terms, people do work to upset, frustrate, or anger others who have been the agent of aversive control in their lives. Thus a child who produces such responses from a teacher gets two payoffs for the price of one behavior—individual attention and revenge.)

The best, but not the easiest, way to get rid of the behavior is to use an extinction procedure. An extinction procedure involves arranging the world so that the consequence that appears to have been reinforcing the behavior does not occur any more when the behavior occurs. In the example given above, the teacher would be using an extinction procedure if she completely ignored the "you can't make me" (or the whine). That is, if the teacher did not look at the child, show any facial expression, or say anything to the child, but proceeded as if the behavior had not occurred, she would be using an extinction procedure.

The effects of an extinction procedure, like the effects of a reinforcement procedure, can only be seen over time. Extinction and reinforcement involve changes in the frequency of behavioral units. An extinction procedure, properly designed and carried out, will result in decreased occurrences of the target behavior, and usually it will disappear altogether. Before the behavior begins to decrease in frequency sometimes there is a short period when it occurs *more* frequently—called an extinction burst.

A serious disadvantage of extinction procedures is that they are difficult to carry out. Most people find it hard to keep doing something that has no clear-cut immediate consequence. So, after using an extinction procedure for a while, people tend to go back to what comes naturally—responding to what they don't like—and they thereby reinforce the behavior. Any behavior that is reinforced only some of the times it occurs is being intermittently reinforced. This kind of reinforcement procedure is known to make the behavior resistant to extinction; so when people go back to the extinction procedure, it is that much harder to keep using the procedure until the behavior disappears.

As hard as the extinction procedure is to carry out, it is still an important technique in behavior management. By following two rules school personnel can increase their chances of carrying out an effective extinction procedure. First, use extinction early on, when the behavior first appears—before it is repeatedly reinforced. Teachers can afford to ignore minor misbehavior a few times. By trying to get control of the problem right away, the teacher often inadvertently reinforces the misbehavior.

The second rule involves using a reinforcement procedure along with the extinction procedure. The simultaneous use of reinforcement for desired behavior in a situation and extinction for undesired behavior in the same situation is called differential reinforcement.

Differential Reinforcement

During the same time period that the teacher completely ignores "you can't make me"-type responses, she needs to work just as hard strengthening the cooperative behavior of the same child. That is, when the child does respond as instructed, the teacher will use a reinforcement procedure to strengthen that behavior. For example, the teacher may pat the child's hand, smile at him, wink at him, whisper "right on," or give him brief individual attention immediately after he has done what was asked.

Extinction is hard to make happen when an extinction procedure is used by itself. Imagine a child who produces the teacher's undivided attention only when he is goofing off. Rarely does he get any special attention when he is doing his lessons. If he starts fiddling around with his baseball cards, however, he suddenly achieves that which a day's worth of work couldn't achieve: personalized treatment. Imagine next that the teacher reads a book about behavioral principles and decides to use an extinction procedure. So she ignores his fiddling with his baseball cards. Now the child doesn't get personalized attention for anything; so he can fiddle with his baseball cards and fantasize a career in the major leagues, or he can do his math problems, slowly producing answers that may or may not be right (and he won't find out until tomorrow). The extinction procedure probably won't work; that is, it won't result in extinction because the undesired behavior produces more reinforcers than the desired behavior. Although neither action produces teacher attention, looking at the baseball cards leads to pleasant visions for little effort, and doing math leads to uncertainty for a lot of effort.

In using differential reinforcement the teacher adds her attention to doing math problems while ignoring fiddling with baseball cards. It's as if a weight is not only taken off one side of a scale, but also added to the other. Not only does the undesirable behavior fail to get the social reinforcers, but also the desirable behavior does get them.

The combining of the two procedures of extinction and reinforcement—differential reinforcement—is a powerful behavioral change technique. The extinction component of differential reinforcement is especially effective for undesired behavior that is of the nuisance variety. No great threat is posed by ignoring a muttered "you can't make me" or a few minutes with baseball cards.

Some misbehavior cannot safely be ignored, however; behavior that is dangerous or antisocial requires action. Off-task behavior consistent enough to pose a serious risk to a student's likelihood of learning critical material may also require action. When undesirable behavior (by its nature or its frequency) poses danger for the behaver or others, the slow, but certain, extinction procedure may not be a viable solution. A punishment procedure may be necessary to suppress the behavior as quickly as possible.

Punishment Procedure

When some people speak of discipline they mean punishment. Punishment probably produces less disciplined behavior than any other behavior management technique. That's because punishment doesn't produce behavior; it decreases the frequency of behavior that was produced by other means. If teachers use reinforcement procedures effectively, there will be little need for punishment procedures because so many desirable behaviors will be occurring at high rates that there will be little time for undesirable behavior. Also, with all the reinforcement available, there will be little motivation for engaging in undesirable behavior.

Sometimes students come into a classroom with a repertoire of undesirable behavior learned in other classrooms, at home, or on the playground. Such behavior disrupts the learning environment, pulls other students off-task, diverts the teacher's attention from the lesson, and, of course, focuses the teacher's attention on the misbehaving student. Everybody loses in the long run, and everybody but the misbehaver loses in the short run. In game-talk, the situation appears to be "I win–you lose" for the misbehaver, but it's really lose–lose, which is why such a situation saddens the sensitive observer. The only way to deal effectively with such a situation is to turn it into a win–win one. This is hard to do because teachers, being human, tend to focus on reversing the "I win–you lose" to "you lose–I win." In other words, they focus only on getting control of the misbehavior. True, the best interests of the class as a whole are served if disruptive misbehavior is reduced in frequency. The treatment is often as bad as the problem, though, in terms of its disruptiveness.

The solution is simple to prescribe but not so easy to understand and even harder to carry out. Teachers, school psychologists, and other school personnel need to arrange things so that misbehavior is reduced in frequency and, at the same time, make sure that everybody, including the misbehaver, wins. Because most readers will bristle at the suggestion that the misbehaver be among the "winners," an explanation is due.

In the short-run view "winning" comes down to "receiving reinforcers." In the long-run view "winning" comes down to "receiving reinforcers contingent on behavior that will maximize possibilities for future reinforcement." The problem of misbehavior in classrooms is a lot like the problem of smoking: they both produce short-term payoffs/long-term losses for the behaver. The consequences that strengthen behavior are likely to result in future losses.

All people behave as they do because of the consequences that have been produced by that behavior in the past. If several behaviors can occur in the same situation, the one that occurs will be the most likely to achieve certain consequences. The misbehaving child misbehaves because misbehavior is more likely to produce such things as teacher attention than is schoolwork, etc. The child is going to "win" (produce reinforcers) if there is a way to do it; and if everybody else loses in the process, too bad.

The typical solution is to make the consequences as "bad" as possible for the student in the hopes of suppressing the behavior (or truth to say, sometimes in the hopes of getting revenge for the pain caused to the teacher and other children). The important thing to understand is that most of the consequences designed to punish misbehavior do not suppress the behavior. Thus revenge may be obtained but behavior is not changed, and the dreary cycle repeats itself.

To use a punishment procedure effectively—that is, to suppress behavior—in a classroom, things have to be arranged so that the child loses for misbehavior *and wins* for other (pro-social, academic) behavior. In practical terms this means that better consequences and more of them must be delivered contingent on desirable behavior than are delivered contingent on misbehavior. A stale, moldly crumb (angry attention) is better than nothing when one hasn't eaten (hasn't received attention for anything). However, if one can produce apples and cheese by engaging in some behaviors and a stale crumb for engaging in others, one is likely to forego the crumb.

Most punishment procedures will be effective only in the context of an environment in which desirable behavior can occur and is amply reinforced when it does. In such an environment the teacher's disapproval has a chance to work as a punisher. Even so, more powerful punishers are likely to be needed for most serious cases of misbehavior. Too often disapproval has become conditioned as a reinforcer for students who are highly likely to misbehave.

Provided a teacher finds frequent opportunity to reinforce instances of desirable behavior of a student prone to misbehavior, that teacher may be able to successfully use a punishment procedure for the misbehavior. In a punishment procedure the teacher arranges the environment so that some "worsening" of the environment occurs immediately after the undesirable behavior. The teacher may take away something the child has—points, the opportunity to earn reinforcers, or the baseball cards. Then the teacher can give back what was taken away contingent on some appropriate behavior (completing the lesson, sitting quietly, etc.). If the student fails on that day to earn what was taken away, the teacher can give it back the next day *contingent on and immediately after* desired behavior occurs.

If the procedure is to work, the teacher must not confound the contingency between the misbehavior and the loss of "good things." If the teacher moralizes, explains, criticizes, or otherwise talks to the student as she removes the points (or whatever), then *two* consequences have been produced by the misbehavior: loss of something and gain of something (teacher attention). Also, if the teacher looks upset, angry, vengeful, distressed, or otherwise discommoded, the student has the satisfaction of gigging the teacher, which may be worth the loss of the item. One thing and one thing only must happen contingent on undesirable behavior: loss of something the student has some use for. Sending the student to the office is only a loss if there is something to be gained by staying in the classroom. Taking away points is a loss only if the points are good for something valuable to the student.

In the everyday world of the classroom there is almost no way to use a punishment procedure effectively if the teacher does not extensively reinforce desirable behavior of the same student. In almost all cases no amount of discussing, counseling, preaching, or questioning will suppress the undesirable behavior when it occurs. And almost no consequences available to the teacher will work to suppress behavior in an environment in which there are few reinforcers for the desirable behavior.

In the face of the overwhelming amount of misbehavior of some students, teachers and other school personnel sometimes feel at a loss as to what to reinforce. The misbehaving student does so few things right, so few things that might be expected of a person his age, so few things that he is asked, that finding something to reinforce seems impossible. The procedure of shaping offers a solution.

Shaping

Behavioral shaping takes many forms, but something is common to all of them: they are designed to bring about a final behavioral product by reinforcing better and better approximations to the final product. When the procedure of shaping is used, the teacher may have to do a lot of work before ever seeing one instance of the target behavior. Not doing the work makes it likely that the teacher will never see the target behavior. Although most people intuitively use something like a shaping procedure when teaching something new, the procedure is usually not used very effectively because they do not understand the behavioral principles underlying the technique.

The term shaping was first used to name a procedure used to produce a fairly simple (compared with what's taught in a classroom) behavioral unit—a lever press. To us, a lever press looks simple and straightforward, but that is only because the unit is so well learned in our repertoires. Imagine a five-month-old child learning to press a lever. First, the baby must look at the bar, then move its arm so that its hand rests on the bar, then put weight on the bar (press), and then remove its hand or release the pressure. The chances are that if you put a lever in the baby's playpen and left the baby with it, the baby would eventually do something that moved the lever. But if pressing the lever were a prerequisite for eating, or clean diapers, or the opportunity to explore the living room, the baby would probably be much obliged if you would use your best teaching technology rather than let it learn to lever press as an accidental outcome, or side effect, of its other activities.

To shape the simple behavioral unit called a lever press, a teacher would use differential reinforcement and add one thing: what she reinforced would keep changing. In the procedure of differential reinforcement a particular behavioral unit produces a consequence; and other behavioral units, that might occur instead, do not produce the consequence. If the procedure is effective, the behavior that produced the consequence is strengthened and the other behavior extinguished. In the procedure of shaping, the behavior that produces the consequence keeps changing because the consequence is delivered only if later behavior more closely approximates the target.

In the case of the baby's learning to lever press, the teacher might use a tinkling bell as a consequence. When the baby looked toward the lever, the teacher would sound the bell. (Because humans orient visually to a sound source, the learning process can be shortened by having the sound occur near the lever, let's say from a hidden tape recorder.) The baby would probably stop moving and stare in the direction of the sound (and the lever). After a bit the baby would probably move. If he approached the lever, the teacher would sound the bell. If he moved away, the teacher would do nothing, waiting for the child to look at the lever before sounding the bell. The teacher would sound the bell next if, and only if, some behavior occurred that was getting the baby closer to the target behavior. At each step the criterion for reinforcement would change so that the next consequence was contingent on a closer approximation to the target.

When people first start shaping behavior, they often make many errors, and the process takes a long time. The procedure will be completely ineffective if misused, just as the procedure used to build a computer will not result in a working computer if the builder connects the wrong parts to one another. Once people have developed the skill necessary to shape behavior, behavior can be shaped very quickly.

In a school setting most basic movement patterns have already been learned by the students. Rarely is shaping, in its original sense, used in a classroom. But the notion of reinforcing approximations of a target behavior is a critical one, and the term shaping is often used to label any procedure that develops complex behavior by successive approximations. Often the differential reinforcement of successive approximations is used together with other procedures.

The section on punishment ended with the suggestion that shaping might come to the rescue in a situation in which a student seldom emitted any behavior that a teacher would consider age- and grade-appropriate. By considering the appropriate behavior the target behavior, the teacher could view any behavior that was an approximation of the target behavior as worth trying to strengthen. Instead of stubbornly insisting that the student "do what he is supposed to" before using a reinforcement procedure, the teacher would use a reinforcement procedure to strengthen anything that even approximated the target. For example, if the misbehaving student occasionally did part of an assignment, that would be an approximation of doing a complete assignment. His teacher would do well to provide some praise, encouraging words, or a smile at the time he is working on the assignment. She might also go by his desk and find something he had done right and compliment it: "That's an interesting point you made about the Civil War."

Sometimes teachers respond to such recommendations by indicating their concern that they will "send a message" that the student can rest on his laurels, that he doesn't need to improve, etc. The need for improvement can be stressed at another time, particularly by helping the student set a goal for achievement as he begins the next assignment. As long as the goal is just one short step from his current performance, the student will be likely to achieve it, thereby earning the praise, smiles, etc. given by the teacher. By specifying the goal or, better, having the student specify it, the teacher and the student are both clear about what behavior will produce the consequences.

If the student who often misbehaves can produce the teacher's attention, praise, and affection by working just a little bit harder than yesterday, however little that is, he is likely to do so; and he is less likely to misbehave. If the misbehavior is detrimental enough to require punishment, it will be suppressed at the same time the desirable behavior is being strengthened. If the teacher can manage to extinguish the misbehavior, it will disappear from the repertoire as the desirable behavior gets closer and closer to the target.

When used in conjunction with other procedures, such as modeling, instruction, and reinforcement scheduling, shaping becomes an extremely important procedure to have in a teaching repertoire. In fact, sometimes modeling, instruction, and reinforcement scheduling fail because the need for working toward the target by successive approximations is not well understood. We shall return shortly to the combination of shaping and those procedures. In order to understand modeling and instructional training, though, the procedure of discrimination training must be clearly understood.

Discrimination Training

The discrimination process can be seen when a behavioral unit occurs consistently in one or more specific situations and seldom, or never, occurs in other situations. We say discrimination is evident when, for example, a child responds differently to two stimuli. If a child is shown a circle, the child will say "circle," and if shown a square, the child will say "square." Almost all education comes down to the acquisition of discriminated behavior. The first months of formal education involve a child's learning to respond in precise ways to certain symbols, to make certain marks on the page that correspond with certain sounds, and to follow instructions regarding whole rooms full of items that did not exist for some children before beginning their formal education.

A "well-educated" person is one who has a vast repertoire of behavioral units that occur precisely under certain, specified conditions—often very subtle and complex, even esoteric, conditions. As in the case of finances, in which it is said the rich get richer, the behaviorally rich get richer. The larger a behavioral repertoire, the more readily further acquisitions occur. The earliest discriminations seem the hardest; the more discriminated behavior in the repertoire, the easier it seems to teach—and to learn—further discriminations.

Teachers have the difficult job of bringing about the earliest discriminations in student behavior in one "subject matter" after another. Each year new areas (subject matters) are introduced as students progress from first grade to graduation. Each new area takes for granted a well-developed repertoire of discriminated behavior, presumably learned in previous years. If every child learned everything that must be taken for granted to introduce and teach a new subject (let's say American Government), the teacher would still have to start from scratch regarding concepts of government. But the fact is that every child does not learn everything he needs for even the earliest discriminations relevant to a course in American Government.

One of the reasons teachers believe that students are not learning what they need to learn may be that there is so much to learn (and to teach), and the amount keeps increasing as knowledge explodes around the world. Everything simply cannot be taught—or learned—in twelve short years. But other dissatisfactions may be addressed by a better understanding of discrimination training. When learning is viewed as the acquisition of discriminated behavior, the goal becomes clearer. And when teachers learn how to systematically produce discriminated behavior, they are much closer to reaching the goal than before.

Because discriminated behavior is the bedrock on which education rests, several examples will be given to clarify the procedure of discrimination training. Beginning with a simple form and progressing to more complex cases, discrimination training will be examined. In actuality, discrimination training almost always involves instructions as part of the procedure. Because instructional training is a special case of the general procedure of discrimination training, it will be considered next. To make clear the relation of instructional training to the process of discrimination, examples in this section will not include instructions.

In the simplest case, discrimination training may be used to ensure that a specific behavioral unit occurs at a specified time and place and at no other. If Ms. Smith would like her students to approach her freely outside the classroom but to stay in their seats during the class period, she wants discriminated behavior. The way to get it is to teach it. Assuming for a moment that there is some reason Ms. Smith can't tell them what she wants, she can teach them to behave in the desired way by using a discrimination training procedure. When students approach her outside the classroom—in the hallway, office, football stand, parking lot, or lunchroom—Ms. Smith will greet them, smiling, perhaps ask them a friendly question; she will stop and answer any questions they have; she will converse with them on a person-to-person basis, not as an authority figure, etc. On the contrary, when the same students approach her in the classroom, Ms. Smith will continue what she is doing, avoid looking at them or saying anything to them, etc.

This may look like differential reinforcement to the reader, but there is a difference. In the present example, approaching and talking to the teacher produces positive consequences in all places *except* the classroom. In the classroom such behavior produces no consequences. Both an extinction procedure and a reinforcement procedure are used, as in differential reinforcement; but those procedures are used with respect to behavior under specific circumstances, not just with respect to the nature of the response itself. By making the consequence contingent on behavior *in-situation–1* and unavailable for the *same* behavior *in-situation–2*, Ms. Smith produces discriminated behavior. The students' approaching and visiting behavior comes under the stimulus control of hallway, lunchroom, and wherever that behavior produces consequences. It does not get "attached to" the classroom; and if it shows some tendency to occur there at first, it gets "dis-attached" because it fails to produce consequences in that situation.

The technical term for the situation to which the behavior gets attached is "discriminative stimulus" (S^D). The S^D is said to have stimulus control over the behavioral unit because the behavior is likely to occur when the S^D is present. The behavior is likely to occur when the S^D is present because that is when the behavior produces consequences. The S^D functions as a kind of cue for the behavioral unit. The term for situations in which the behavior does not get reinforced is S-delta (S^Δ). S^Δ does not cue the behavior. An important point to remember is that no event can be said to be an S^D or an S^Δ without identifying the behavioral unit that is attached to it. To say "a green light is an S^D" makes no sense. The statement is incomplete unless the behavioral unit under stimulus control of the discriminative stimulus is specified. "A green light is an S^D for accelerating for most drivers" makes sense because it specifies the relation between green lights and accelerating, and the people in whom the relation may be observed (i.e., most drivers). "Ms. Potts's classroom is an S^Δ for students' chatting" is correct if students do not chat in Ms. Potts's classroom and do chat elsewhere.

The example above describes Ms. Smith's use of discrimination training to produce behavior that might be termed "conduct." The discrimination process does not distinguish between "conduct" and "academic behavior," however, and the procedure is just as useful in generating the kind of behavior called "knowing."

A simple example of discrimination training to produce some historical knowledge may help the reader see the similarity in the procedure, whatever the discriminative stimulus or the behavioral unit. During history class, as students work on their lessons, Ms. Mason might ask, "Joe, what was the date of the Battle of Hastings?" If Joe says, "1066," within one second, Ms. Mason smiles and says, "One point," marking it in her gradebook. If Joe answers with any other response or says nothing before the teacher signals the time is up, the teacher may simply say, "Next time," or nothing if the students are used to this procedure. In many classrooms the teacher's smile would be enough and no points would be necessary (making the procedure easier for the teacher to carry out) as long as she did not criticize failures or subtract credit for incorrect answers. It should be pointed out that if this is all Ms. Mason does to "teach dates" (other than assign them to be learned), she is counting on a great deal of self-teaching on the part of the students, who may or may not have the repertoires needed to prepare themselves to respond to her "oral quizzes" in the classroom. (Any student who teaches himself the dates will do so by arranging the instructional materials so that the discrimination process occurs—a kind of informal discrimination training procedure.)

If the reader understands what has been written up to now, he or she will know that Ms. Mason will, if she is wise, give a student a chance to make such an extra point at a moment when the student is behaving appropriately—doing the lesson, preparing quietly to leave if the bell is about to ring, or getting out materials for the class if the students are just arriving. Because the chance to earn something, with no risk of losing anything, will probably work as a reinforcer, Ms. Mason's giving students such a chance will probably work as a reinforcement procedure, strengthening whatever behavior is occurring when the opportunity is given.

Anytime the educational objective is that students be able to identify, specify, enumerate, operate, recite, describe, compare, or contrast, the process by which these behaviors are acquired is discrimination. And discrimination training is the procedure that produces the process. Discrimination training may be used to teach the appropriate time and place for different kinds of "conduct," and it may be used to teach academic skills.

Instructional Training

Most discrimination training in school settings involves instructions. The teacher instructs the students to do their work in the classroom and do their visiting with her outside the classroom; it is not the instruction that ensures that they do as she asked, however. The instruction may have some critical effect on their behavior, but they will continue to "follow the instruction" only if the behavior of doing so produces consequences. The teacher instructs the students to practice at home, saying the dates of various historical events. They may study the dates the first time, but if no opportunity is ever given for the "date-saying" to produce consequences, they are likely to stop following the instruction.

What is even more important is that, in both cases, the students who followed instructions to no avail will eventually stop following instructions given by those teachers. If enough teachers fail to use a reinforcement procedure for following instructions, students will generally fail to follow instructions. They will so behave until they run across a teacher whose instructions actually presage relations between the students' behavior and some consequences. Then they might follow that teacher's instructions while continuing to ignore those of others. The discrimination process has again occurred.

Instructions may be seen as part of the situation in which behavior is likely to produce consequences. The function of an instruction is to specify the rest of the situation in which behavior is likely to produce a certain consequence. The instruction to converse with Ms. Smith only outside the classroom specifies the situations—in classroom and other places—that will not and will produce conversation with Ms. Smith. Once following the instructions has produced the consequences (talking gets responded to outside the classroom and ignored inside), the instruction won't be needed anymore. Discrimination has occurred and the behavior will continue to occur only in the places where it produces consequences. If a student should "forget," or "test the water" and begin conversing with Ms. Smith in the classroom, all the teacher needs to do is nothing. If Ms. Smith should forget herself and respond to the student's classroom chat, she has taken a step toward undoing the discrimination training. The student will, of course, be more likely to do the same thing again. If Ms. Smith again chats, the discrimination is further broken down.

Unfortunately almost nobody understands that instructions mean nothing if following them does not result in something better than not following them. If the sign reads, "Park only between the green lines," and parking between the red lines results in valuable coupons being left on our windows, while parking between the green lines produces nothing, most of us are likely to park between the red lines. Unless we want our youth to grow up to be fools, we should not be unhappy if they figure out which instructions are worth following and which are not. The solution to this problem is to instruct students to behave in ways that are in their best interests in the long run and use reinforcement procedures to ensure that they follow the instructions.

Instructional training is an important procedure in the teacher's repertoire. Instructions, if they actually work as discriminative stimuli, are extremely valuable as short cuts in getting students under discriminative control of other stimuli. By telling the class which situations are okay for talking and which are not, the teacher shortens the discrimination training necessary for students to learn to chat in some situations and not in others. The instruction only works this way, though, if the teacher remembers to align the consequences with the instruction. Giving students an instruction and failing to use reinforcement and extinction procedures in accordance with the instruction will not result in students following the instruction for any length of time. The discrimination process that results from discrimination training can only be seen across time. In almost any classroom, instructional control breaks down as the semester goes on. The reason is that the teacher does not use reinforcement procedures to maintain her instructions as discriminative stimuli for the instructed behavior.

Modeling

Modeling, like instructional training, is a special kind of discrimination training. In modeling the instructor demonstrates the behavior that will produce consequences, rather than describing the behavior that will produce the consequences. A dance instructor will often show a student how to position his legs. An artist may show a child how to apply water to the paper and wipe excessive paint off the brush. A classroom teacher may show a student how to carry in adding a column of figures.

Modeling is most successful when the student immediately does what the model did. If the teacher uses a reinforcement procedure to strengthen good "matches" between the modeled behavior and the imitative behavior, she doesn't take any chances that extinction might occur. Sometimes, however, there are other consequences for imitative behavior, and these may be enough to strengthen the behavior. For example, the dance student may see his legs in the correct position in the mirror; the art student may paint a stroke without smearing; the math student may find that he has added correctly by checking the answer in the back of the book. Usually, however, when a new behavior is being learned, the teacher is far safer to help the behavior gain strength in early stages by using a reinforcement procedure of her own making.

Adult behavior that produces immediate consequences of value to children is the most likely behavior to be learned by imitation. When adults model rocking in the rocking chair, smoking, or eating sweet foods, the child's imitative behavior will automatically be reinforced by rocking, nicotine, or taste. Adults would like children to imitate their more virtuous behavior, which usually produces abstract, esoteric consequences that have not been conditioned as reinforcers for children. The only solution is for adults to provide social consequences for imitative behavior of the more virtuous kinds. This does two things. The reinforcement procedure strengthens the virtuous behavior; and other, more esoteric consequences (such as a look of quiet happiness on the face of a friend) become conditioned as reinforcers because they occurred in association with the already valuable consequence of approval from a significant adult.

As in instructional training, modeling cuts short the process of discrimination training. It allows new behavior in a new situation to be acquired quickly as long as there is some consequence contingent on the imitative behavior.

Reinforcement Scheduling

When a behavioral unit is being formed or discriminated, learning occurs faster when each occurrence of the behavioral unit produces a consequence. Once the unit is formed or discriminated, it can be maintained by consequences that occur less frequently. For example, when "following instructions" seldom occurs, a reinforcement procedure should follow each instance of following an instruction. Once a student follows instructions at a higher frequency, the teacher might occasionally fail to reinforce an instance of following instructions. As the student becomes more and more proficient, the teacher may use the reinforcement procedure less and less often.

One reason this is possible is that the teacher's reinforcement procedure has been associated over time with a variety of other consequences (such as successful manipulation of materials, social responsiveness from other students, and good test grades). When the teacher's reinforcement procedure is missing, those conditioned reinforcers are there to help maintain the behavior. But sometimes they are not there, and the desired behavior produces no relevant consequence for the learner.

It is hoped that the reader recalls that the extinction procedure involves the failure of a reinforcing consequence to occur after a previously reinforced behavioral unit. When the teacher leaves out the reinforcement procedure, why doesn't the behavior extinguish? As a matter of fact, it will if the teacher leaves out the reinforcement procedure too often. As many teachers have learned, a student's behavioral repertoire can never be taken for granted. But as a behavioral unit gains strength resulting from the reinforcement procedure, the occasional absence of reinforcement cannot wipe out the behavior. The more often the behavior occurs, the less frequently the reinforcement procedure must occur to maintain the behavior. This is one reason the behaviorally rich get richer; less is required to maintain their wealth.

The important thing to know about reinforcement scheduling is that once the desired behavioral unit begins occurring more frequently, the frequency of the reinforcement procedure must be gradually reduced. In essence, reinforcement scheduling is using both the extinction procedure and the reinforcement procedure on the same behavior. The reader should note that this is different from differential reinforcement, a procedure in which reinforcement and extinction procedures are used on *different* behavioral units. If the behavioral unit begins to decrease in rate, the reinforcement procedure has been left out too often, and the process of extinction is under way. As with all behavioral procedures, reinforcement scheduling can be used clumsily and without good effect.

Behavior analysts have a saying that reminds them that if their procedures don't work, they are doing something wrong. It is this: "The organism is always right." Behaving people (students and teachers) always do and say what they have learned to do and say. Some may learn from the environment more quickly than others. Some may have anatomical and physiological characteristics that make it difficult to learn certain things and easy to learn others. But all operant behavior is the result of previous interactions of unique individuals with unique combinations of worldly events. The current environment mainly exerts its influence because of those previous interactions. If a behavioral procedure does not work, it is out of line with the way things are and have been in the past. If reinforcement scheduling results in extinction of the target behavior, the reinforcement procedure was used too seldom and the extinction procedure too often when the behavioral unit occurred.

When reinforcement scheduling is adjusted to suit the individual student's behavior, almost all students can learn to engage in more and more behavior between applications of the reinforcement. It is important to remember that in order to enrich the behavioral repertoire of the behaviorally poor, the reinforcement procedure must occur most frequently and the schedule needs to be slowly "thinned" out.

Shaping Complex Units

When the procedure of shaping was described earlier in this chapter, we made the point that this basic procedure is often combined with other procedures in the development of behavioral units. Often complex behavior comes to exist by way of a series of approximations, in which each approximation that is reinforced is closer to the complex unit that is the target. The example of teaching "borrowing" in subtraction will provide an example.

Borrowing involves a behavioral unit that can be broken down into several steps. The target is for the behavior of borrowing to occur so smoothly and so quickly on any occasion when it is relevant that the behavior will not look like a series of steps, but like a single smooth act. Any teacher who has ever taught borrowing knows it is not learned as a single smooth act. Borrowing is taught by "chaining" together a series of discriminate responses.

First, the student learns to identify that he cannot subtract the bottom number from the top one because the bottom number is larger than the top one. The response "I have to borrow" may be taught to occur on the occasions like that just described, as opposed to on occasions when the top number is larger. This is, of course, discrimination training, providing a reinforcement procedure occurs after correct identification and no reinforcement is contingent on incorrect identifications. (Usually a correction procedure occurs, entailing the student's naming of the numbers in the problem and stating whether the bottom or the top is larger. This procedure is often called "feedback," but it is more like a branching program in computer-assisted instruction, where the learner returns to a previous point and practices what he has already learned that is relevant to the current situation.)

After the student reliably identifies when borrowing is necessary, the teacher instructs and demonstrates the crossing out of the number to the left, changing it to a number one less than it was, and adding 10 to the original number that was too small to subtract. Then the student tries this, probably with some prompting from the teacher as he proceeds through his step, and a reinforcement procedure again occurs after a correct response and not after an incorrect response. Gradually the teacher fades the prompts as the child learns to engage in this step from beginning to end without help. The gradual diminishing of a prompt is called a fading procedure. Verbal prompting is often used in teaching a complex act that has several parts that can't easily be broken down because they form a conceptual unit. The student is finally able to subtract the bottom number from the now larger top number, and the operation is complete.

After the student learns to first identify whether borrowing is necessary, then to do the borrowing without prompts, and finally to subtract, the teacher requires the whole complex unit to occur before using a reinforcement procedure. The emergence of the behavioral unit in its entirety occurs through successive approximations. The teacher begins with the first part of the behavioral unit that must occur if the rest is to follow. In shaping lever pressing the first part of the unit was orienting toward the lever; in shaping borrowing the first part of the unit was identifying the need to borrow. Once that occurs the teacher can reinforce the part of the unit that must occur next if the target behavior is ever going to emerge.

There are some differences between the procedure of shaping lever pressing and that of shaping borrowing, but the common element is the changing criterion for reinforcement. First reinforcement is contingent on one response and then on another. When it's all over, reinforcement is henceforth contingent on orient-approach-press for the baby, and identify-subtract 10-add 10-subtract for the student. When the "steps" in a behavioral unit are clear-cut, as in the case of borrowing, the shaping procedure is sometimes said to develop a stimulus-response chain. When the links in the chain become so tightly forged together that it is not clear to the behaver or another observer where one link ends and the other begins, the whole thing begins to function as a single complex behavioral unit.

Once borrowing reliably functions as a single behavioral unit, reinforcement can occur less and less often for the unit. A well carried out procedure of reinforcement scheduling will result in a behavioral unit that occurs repeatedly over long periods of time with the only reinforcement being the usefulness of an "answer" for further behavior. Getting his division problems correct and, later, getting his checkbook balanced will provide the reinforcement for borrowing as the years go by. If the behavioral procedures are not effective enough to produce the behavior and maintain it long enough for it to be useful, borrowing will fail to occur when the student is confronted with a division problem, or a bank statement, and neither the borrowing, nor the dividing, nor the balancing get reinforced.

Another way that teachers can use a kind of shaping procedure to establish complex behavioral units is in making a reinforcement procedure available for longer and longer periods of appropriate behavior. This is called raising the criterion. The kind of student described in the section on punishment will offer an example. The student who spends little time on schoolwork, and a great deal of time disrupting the class, can be shaped to spend longer and longer periods of time doing lessons. In such a case the teacher is not defining the behavioral unit as "correct responding," but as "on-task responding." At first the teacher will need to use a reinforcement procedure almost every time this student spends even a few minutes on task. In the case of an impoverished repertoire, reinforcement must be almost continuous (not constant, but contingent on each instance of a few minutes of studying, and occurring *while* the student is studying and not a few minutes later). Once the reinforcement procedure has had its effect, and the student is studying for longer periods of time, say between five and ten minutes at a time, the teacher may make the reinforcement contingent on ten minutes of studying. As a result the student's studying range will go up to ten to fifteen minutes or so, and the teacher may use the reinforcement procedure each time the student has been studying for fifteen minutes. When the student gets to the point where he often studies for twenty-five minutes, the teacher may be inclined to drop the reinforcement procedure. Considering that the consequences have already been thinned, in that they occur only after twenty-five minutes of studying, and that the teacher needs to use a reinforcement procedure only twice in about an hour to maintain the formerly disruptive student at work, it seems a small price to pay to ensure behavior that is good for the student, good for the rest of the class, and good for the teacher.

In the last example the behavioral unit was loosely defined as on task and changing criterion for reinforcement was length of time the on-task behavior occurred more or less continuously. The behavior of staying on task was shaped by making certain consequences contingent on longer and longer time on task. Perhaps it should be noted that the on-task behavior will be shaped more readily if the definition of on task is stringent—no fiddling, no lapses into reverie, no sleeping, no doodling. It is better to reinforce five minutes of high-quality on-task behavior than thirty minutes of low-quality on-task behavior, even though the latter is easier for the teacher. Low-quality on-task behavior also is much more likely to slide into off-task behavior, which will eventually result in the teacher's using an extinction procedure more often as the off-task behavior becomes more prevalent. At this point the student is likely to lapse back into disruptive behavior as a way of generating teacher attention.

Generalization Training

Generalization training is designed to have the opposite effect of discrimination training. When Ms. Smith uses a reinforcement procedure for calling out answers in her class and Ms. Jones uses that procedure for raising hands to answer, they are teaching (through the procedure of discrimination training) their students to behave differently in the different classes. If Ms. Smith should decide she would prefer her students to raise their hands to be recognized, she can use a generalization training procedure *if* she has the same students Ms. Jones has.

Because the students already have the desired behavior in their repertoires, the behavior will generalize quickly to the new situation if Ms. Smith uses a reinforcement procedure for the occasional hand-raises and an extinction procedure for calling out answers. Even without explaining her policy, students will see that the few hand-raises get reinforced, and are likely to switch immediately to that behavior. After all, hand-raising does have a history of reinforcement in Ms. Jones's class. If enough teachers follow this policy, students will automatically raise their hands in each new class.

The raising of hands in each new class shows the process of generalization that has resulted from the generalization training provided by Ms. Smith and other teachers. In each new class the behavior of raising hands will be maintained as long as the new teacher does not change the contingencies. If the new teacher responds to some calling out, the behavior of calling out will be reinforced and the calling out is a modeling procedure likely to result in calling out by more students. (*Note*: Calling out is less effortful than raising a hand and also less risky if a punishment procedure should be used when wrong answers occur. In calling out, students are not clearly "on the line." A word to the wise: Putting oneself on the line is brave and should not result in a punishing consequence; when bravery occurs along with a correct answer, that is worth the time it takes to deliver a reinforcing consequence.) In this example the teacher unwittingly uses a discrimination procedure. It counteracts the generalization that resulted from the generalization training the other teachers used and from which they benefited.

BEHAVIORAL PRINCIPLES IN THE CLASSROOM

Not all known behavioral procedures have been discussed in this chapter. As in the case of behavioral processes, however, those that have been discussed are those most often used in applied behavior analysis. This chapter has been written to enable the reader to relate behavioral principles to the events that actually occur in classroom settings at all levels. The research reported in the rest of the book will, in the long run, be valuable only if it can be related to the everyday world of the reader. Specifically, the reader must be able to use behavioral procedures and explain to others how to use them if the knowledge gained from this book is to make a difference.

Although every attempt has been made to remain technically correct in describing behavioral processes and procedures, the minimal use of standard definitions may have left the reader unable to define, in a few words, any process or procedure. For this reason a glossary has been provided so that readers may learn the technical vocabulary as well as make use of these principles in the real world.

3

Hyperactivity

DIAGNOSTIC AND STATISTICAL CRITERIA

In the *DSM-III: Diagnostic and Statistical Manual of Mental Disorders* (American Psychiatric Association, 1980, 3rd ed.), hyperactivity is subsumed under the diagnostic category of Attention Deficit Disorder, specifically, "314.01 Attention Deficit Disorder with Hyperactivity." In the revised *DSM-III-R* (American Psychiatric Association, 1987) the same disorder is recategorized under Disruptive Behavior Disorders and renamed "314.01 Attention-deficit Hyperactivity Disorder (ADHD)." Whatever the diagnostic nomenclature, both versions of this text describe essentially the same symptoms. Hyperactive children have difficulty staying on task. They are impulsive, sloppy, disorganized, and often confused regarding structured activities. They do not appear to attend to teacher or parental directions and may even act as though they have not heard what they have been told. Test protocols reveal what is sometimes referred to as "one-shot thinking" (Whimbey & Whimbey, 1975) but is more commonly called impulsivity or carelessness. Ommissions, insertions, reversals, and general oversights are typical. Most noticeably, these children have trouble sitting still. Group situations appear to be particularly taxing for them. Thus classroom activities that require sustained attention present a circumstance in which inappropriate behaviors are highly probable.

According to *DSM-III*, this disorder is primarily diagnosed on the basis of information provided by the child's parents and teachers, rather than information gathered from direct observation or testing performed by the clinician. *DSM-III* notes that these symptoms are "typically variable," and therefore "may not be observed directly by the clinician." Attention Deficit Disorder with Hyperactivity is described in the manual with several "associated features":

1. Soft neurological signs, such as motor-perceptual dysfunctions, are typical. Electroencephalographic abnormalities may also exist, but "diagnosable neurological disorders" can be ascertained only in about 5 percent of the cases.
2. Age of onset is typically around three, but the disorder may not come to the attention of professionals until the child enters school.
3. Although such children seldom require residential placement, their social interaction may be impaired.
4. The disorder is estimated to exist in as many as "3% of prepubertal children" and is "ten times more common in boys than in girls" (p. 42).

DSM-III also directs our attention to some environmental variables that may be associated with hyperactive behavior. It states:

> Children in *inadequate, disorganized, or chaotic environments* may appear to have difficulty in sustaining attention and in goal-directed behavior. In such cases it may be impossible to determine whether the disorganized behavior is simply a function of the chaotic environment or whether it is due to the child's psychopathology (in which case the diagnosis of Attention Deficit Disorder may be warranted). (p. 43)

Later it goes on to say: "Symptoms typically worsen in situations that require self-application, as in the classroom. Signs of the disorder may be absent when the child is in a new or one-to-one situation" (p. 43). Finally, diagnostic criteria specified by *DSM-III* offer a diverse assortment of indicators loosely grouped into six categories. The first three categories include lists of behaviors that have something in common with one another. They are inattention, impulsivity, and hyperactivity.

A. Inattention. At least three of the following:
   (1) often fails to finish things he or she starts
   (2) often doesn't seem to listen
   (3) easily distracted
   (4) has difficulty concentrating on schoolwork or other tasks requiring sustained attention
   (5) has difficulty sticking to a play activity (p. 43)

Although the wording of these characteristics has intuitive appeal, an experimental analysis requires that observable events be identified in order to determine whether or not they occur. For example, what do teachers and parents see (or hear) when they say a child "doesn't listen," or is "easily distracted"?

B. Impulsivity. At least three of the following:
   (1) often acts before thinking
   (2) shifts excessively from one activity to another
   (3) has difficulty organizing work (this not being due to cognitive impairment)
   (4) needs a lot of supervision

(5) frequently calls out in class
(6) has difficulty awaiting turn in games or group situations (p. 44)

Observant readers may have wondered if some of the impulsive behaviors might as easily be considered inattentive. And so they might. It is important to recognize that some properties called "inattention," "impulsivity," and "hyperactivity" are not suggested as causing the behaviors listed. These terms merely summarize in three words a variety of typical behaviors. Because the complete list of behaviors can be so summarized (albeit loosely and with overlap between categories), we might be prone to jump to the conclusion that there is some necessary relation among the behaviors summarized by, for example, "impulsivity."

C. Hyperactivity. At least two of the following:
(1) runs about or climbs excessively
(2) has difficulty sitting still or fidgets excessively
(3) has difficulty staying seated
(4) moves about excessively during sleep
(5) is always "on the go" or acts as if "driven by a motor" (p. 44)

Here again, it is important to note that "hyperactivity" is the label given to this collection of behaviors. Hyperactivity is not suggested as the cause of these behaviors. *DSM-III* is not saying that the cause of hyperactivity (the behaviors listed) is hyperactivity. That would not make sense.

The last three categories are qualifiers. They tell the reader of *DSM-III* not to consider Attention Deficit Disorder with Hyperactivity unless certain other features accompany the behavior.

D. Onset before the age of seven
E. Duration of at least six months
F. Not due to Schizophrenia, Affective Disorder, or Severe or Profound Mental Retardation (p. 44)

DSM-III-R, in much the same vein as *DSM-III*, points to the highly variable nature of this disorder but alludes to the fact that such behaviors may come under stimulus control:

Manifestations of the disorder usually appear in most situations, including at home, in school, at work, and in social situations, but to varying degrees. Some people, however, show signs of the disorder in only one setting, such as at home or at school. Symptoms typically worsen in situations requiring sustained attention, such as listening to a teacher in the classroom, attending meetings, or doing class assignments or chores at home. Signs of the disorder may be minimal or absent when the person is receiving frequent reinforcement or very strict control, or is in a novel setting or a one-to-one situation (e.g., being examined in the clinicians office, or interacting with a videogame). (p. 50)

DSM-III-R requires that a patient demonstrate eight of the following fourteen symptoms for at least six months duration before qualifying for this category:

1. often fidgets with hands or feet or squirms in seat (in adolescents, may be limited to subjective feelings of restlessness)
2. has difficulty remaining seated when required to do so
3. is easily distracted by extraneous stimuli
4. has difficulty awaiting turn in games or group situations
5. often blurts out answers to questions before they have been completed
6. has difficulty following through on instructions from others (not due to oppositional behavior or failure of comprehension), e.g., fails to finish chores
7. has difficulty sustaining attention in tasks or play activities
8. often shifts from one uncompleted activity to another
9. has difficulty playing quietly
10. often talks excessively
11. often interrupts or intrudes on others, e.g., butts into other children's games
12. often does not seem to listen to what is being said to him or her
13. often loses things necessary for tasks or activities at school or at home (e.g., toys, pencils, books, assignments)
14. often engages in physically dangerous activities without considering possible consequences (not for the purpose of thrill-seeking), e.g., runs into street without looking

(*Note*: The above items are listed in descending order of discriminating power based on data from a national field trial of the *DSM-III-R* criteria for Disruptive Behavior Disorders [p. 53]). The severity of an Individual's Attention-deficit Hyperactivity Disorder is ranked as Mild, Moderate, or Severe, depending on the number of the above symptoms and the degree of social and academic impairment. In general we see a trend in *DSM-III-R* toward trying to provide the clinician with a more operationalized description of this problem behavior. The *DSM-III-R* descriptors seem an improvement over previous editions; however, *DSM-III-R* remains an essentially eclectic diagnostic tool and has very limited usefulness for the applied behavior analyst. It is interesting that the American Psychiatric Association has become increasingly descriptive of behavioral events in categorizing disorders. Perhaps this trend will continue with the eventual publication of *DSM-IV*.

MEDICAL BEHAVIORAL INTERPRETATIONS AND INTERVENTIONS

Hyperactivity in the school classroom includes such behaviors as self-stimulation, squirming, fidgeting, excessive manipulation of objects irrelevant to the task at hand, an inability to work continuously at a given task, poor academic performance, and excessive unpredictable movement. To be precise, hyperactivity is characterized by the rate of such activities rather than by their simple existence or the extent of their irrelevance or inappropriateness. Behaviors like these can be observed in almost any child at times; it is only when the rate of such behavior becomes extraordinarily high that the label of hyperactivity is likely to be applied. In fact, the label itself has become a source of considerable contention.

Perhaps nowhere in the field of school psychology is there a greater controversy and source of disagreement than between those who advocate the use of medical (pharmaceutical) interventions and those who advocate behavioral techniques to reduce hyperactive behavior. Active debate continues after at least ten years of research.

The medical model takes behavior to be the outward symptom of physiological or mental processes, and thus equates maladaptive behavior with "disease" (the running amok of physiological processes). Children who exhibit high rates of irrelevant activity in the classroom are described as having a metabolic dysfunction or, sometimes, a "hyperkinetic impulse disorder" that can best be alleviated by pharmaceutical intervention. Popular drugs such as methylphenidate (Ritalin), dextroamphetamine, and, sometimes, chlorpromazine are commonly used in an effort to reduce students' activity levels. Katz, Saraf, and Gittleman-Klein (1976) note that operant programs do produce an improvement in classroom behavior but that such changes require "constant supervision and reinforcement." They go on to say that their "impression so far is that behavior modification supplies a valuable means of re-establishing healthy relationships among parent, teacher, and child. It does not seem to suffice as a sole treatment modality except in marginally severe cases."

Although we would not argue that medication is never beneficial, the following points seem worth making. If the critical problem of reestablishing healthy relationships between hyperactive children and their parents and teachers can be handled with "behavior modification," then other problems involving operant behavior, such as peer relations, classroom learning and conduct, and toy play, would seem to be amenable. Although the notion that operant procedures require "constant supervision and reinforcement" may overstate the case, that supervision and reinforcement are required cannot be denied. Operant procedures do require the teacher to use consistent or intermittent reinforcement; in the early stages of intervention they do require data collection, the shaping of new behavior, and a variety of other procedures unknown to most people who would like to make a difference. However, such requirements do not make behavior analysis insufficient "as a sole treatment modality."

Using behavioral principles effectively is a technological activity for which few people have received adequate training. An important outcome of effective behavioral intervention is that it provides the hyperactive child with an opportunity to learn new appropriate behaviors despite possible metabolic involvement. Medication that suppresses hyperactivity may also affect the child's opportunity to come in contact with the contingencies necessary for learning on-task behavior and appropriate academic skills. As will be seen in the forthcoming literature review, behavioral procedures have the advantage of permitting the hyperactive child to perform at higher achievement levels than children operating under the influence of psychostimulants.

THE EFFECTS OF PSYCHOSTIMULANTS AND APPLIED BEHAVIOR ANALYSIS ON ACTIVITY LEVEL

The primary index of hyperactivity is rate, frequency, or number of irrelevant behaviors emitted by the child. Such behavior is quite noticeable, since it requires adults to monitor, supervise, intervene, and simply put up with more than they must with other children. Because hyperactivity usually appears correlated with lower than normal school achievement, both problems were once attributed to a common disorder (brain dysfunction). Researchers, parents, and teachers often assumed that if hyperactivity were reduced, increased productivity would automatically follow.

The first study reporting the paradoxical effect of amphetamines on hyperactive children was published by Bradley in 1937. He noted that Benzedrine produced the unanticipated effect of reducing the frequency of stereotyped and disruptive behavior in institutionalized children. The idea caught on quickly in different settings, and by the 1960s psychostimulants were commonly prescribed by physicians for treatment of hyperactivity in the classroom. Teachers and parents reported reduced hyperactivity in children medicated with various stimulant drugs, especially methylphenidate.

Most of the current research on hyperactivity has focused on small numbers of selected individuals and has been aimed at reducing the frequency of overt inappropriate classroom behavior. A range of disruptive behaviors, from talking out loud, running around the room, throwing objects to less dramatic activities such as fidgeting, self-stimulation, and ritualistic hand movements, has been targeted for behavior change.

THE EFFECTS OF PSYCHOSTIMULANTS AND OPERANT PROCEDURES ON ACHIEVEMENT

A few early studies investigated the effects of medications on skills related to learning, but these cannot be described as actually addressing academic performance and achievement before, during, and after intervention. Changes in attention span were investigated by Conners, Eisenberg, and Barcai (1967) and Sprague and Toppe (1966). Intelligence variations have been researched by Knights and Hinton (1969), and paired associate skills were analyzed by Conners, Eisenberg, and Sharpe (1964). More recently Sulzbacher (1972) demonstrated fluctuating and highly variable improvement in academic performance and a reduced frequency of disruptive episodes in students taking dextroamphetamine (Dexedrine). However, some children responded equally well to a placebo.

Individual Performance Changes

The separate effects of medication and behavioral intervention on hyperactivity and academic performance were examined in 1975 by Ayllon, Layman, and Kandell, who demonstrated the efficacy of behavioral alternatives to drug therapy by using a reinforcement procedure to increase levels of academic achievement. This study obtained achievement data on three hyperactive, low-performing elementary school children as they were exposed to alternating psychostimulant and behavioral interventions. Observations of hyperactivity were taken at twenty-five-second intervals as these students participated in math and reading classes. During phase 1 all three subjects were observed on medication for seventeen days. Phase 2 consisted of three days with no medication or behavioral intervention. Phase 3 maintained the abstinence from medication but introduced a reinforcement procedure in which the children were given points for correct academic responses to increasingly difficult math problems. Points earned were exchanged daily for backup reinforcers from a menu of school supplies, lunch items, and free time. Phase 4 continued the procedures used during phase 3 but added the reinforcement procedure to reading as well as math.

Terminating medication independent of operant control resulted in a threefold increase in hyperactive behavior. Obviously the medication had been producing the desired effect of reducing the frequency of impulsive, irrelevant, inappropriate behavior, but at what cost? Academic performance occurred at a level of 12 percent correct in reading and math combined. Taking the children off medication and adding a reinforcement procedure for correct responses resulted in a rise in the percentage correct from 12 percent to 85 percent for reading and math combined. Furthermore, hyperactivity was at a level at least as low as it was on the medication, about 20 percent.

The multiple baseline illustrates the specific effects of task-contingent reinforcement. Initially only math scores increased when reinforcement was contingent on math performance only. Subsequently both math and reading scores accelerated as the contingencies were shifted to include reinforcement for performance in both areas. The authors point out that during drug therapy, these children averaged about 12 percent correct in both areas. When contingent reinforcement was introduced, achievement levels were seven times higher.

The data from the study by Ayllon et al. (1975) strongly suggest that a reduction in hyperactivity is not necessarily correlated with improved performance. Although hyperactivity may tend to displace academic performance, the performance will not automatically occur when medication successfully eliminates (or decreases) hyperactivity. The data did, however, indicate a slight increase in percentage of correct answers in two of the three children as soon as the medication was terminated.

The relation of psychostimulant medication was supported by the results of a study by Sprague and Sleator (1977). They found that the higher the doses of Ritalin, the better were teacher ratings of on-task performance and the less was the measured accuracy of the students' "information-processing" accuracy. The medication also had the disquieting effect of increasing heart rate.

As Aylon et al. (1975) stated:

> The present results suggest that continued use of Ritalin and possibly other drugs to control hyperactivity may result in compliant but academically incompetent students. Surely, the goal of school is not to make children into docile robots either by behavioral techniques or by medication. Rather, the goal should be one of providing children with the social and academic tools required to become successful in their social interactions and competent in their academic performance. (p. 144)

Group Performance Changes

More recently some large-group research has further explored the efficacy of reinforcing academic behavior of hyperactive children. Robinson, Newby, and Ganzell (1981) demonstrated the effects of contingency management on a class of hyperactive children. Their subjects consisted of eighteen hyperactive students who had been placed in a part-time special education class. The researchers arranged the classroom contingencies so that students earned tokens for learning new vocabulary words and for assisting their fellow students in learning new words. Tokens were exchanged for time to play pinball or electronic "pong" games. None of the contingencies were directly aimed at reducing the topographies typically associated with hyperactive behavior.

Using BAB reversal design (i.e., a research design in which data are collected first under standard conditions, then while a change is implemented, and then under standard conditions) it was found that the mean number of tasks completed was nine times greater while free time for games was contingent on academic performance. The authors also describe an anecdotal reduction in overt disruptive behavior and off-task behavior while the program was in effect. They emphasize that this program was just as effective as previous programs directed at single subjects or small groups. Finally, they point out that children of varying achievement levels and socioeconomic backgrounds all responded positively.

A Definitive Study

Perhaps the most well designed and definitive study comparing the effects of psychostimulants and contingency management on achievement was conducted by Rapport, Murphy, and Bailey (1982). These researchers used an ABACBC within-subjects design to compare a response cost procedure with three titrated levels of methylphenidate. The dependent variables consisted of measures of on-task behavior by way of direct observation of in-class behavior, and teacher assessments of amount of work completed and accuracy of problems completed.

During baseline (A) two hyperactive boys, ages seven and eight, were on task during less than half of the observed intervals. In both math and reading, rates of assignment completion and accuracy were generally low. In phase (B) the boys were given increasing dosages of methylphenidate each week. Dosages were titrated at 5 mg/day, 10 mg/day, and 15 mg/day for the first subject and increased up to 20 mg/day for the second subject. On-task behavior increased in frequency along with dosage level. However, number of assignments completed and accuracy of those assignments showed great variability within the titrated dosages of each subject. One subject showed little improvement in the percentage of assignments completed when dosages were increased beyond 5 mg/day. The other subject showed slight improvement in reading, up to 15 mg/day, but dropped below baseline levels during 20 mg/day. In math this subject showed highly erratic changes in accuracy and assignment completion up to 15 mg/day but dropped dramatically at 20 mg/day. Note, however, that teacher observations, based on the Abbreviated Conners Teacher Rating Scale (ACTRS), an index of hyperactivity measured by ratings of classroom teachers, indicated improvements, coinciding with each level of increased dosage. This corroborates previous observations (Ayllon et al., 1975) that observed on-task topographies may increase in frequency while students are under the influence of methylphenidate, but that achievement levels may not show any corresponding improvements. The authors note: "It appears that being "on-task" does not guarantee high academic assignment completion rates" (Rapport et al., 1982, p. 211).

The most critical component of the study occurred during the CBC phase of the experimental design. This phase compared response cost to medication and baseline. On returning to baseline conditions (no medication) both subjects immediately dropped to about 50 percent on task. The teacher rating scale indicated the same loss of classroom control. All measures of accuracy and task completion were conspicuously reduced. Viewed independently, this dramatic transition would seem to indicate that drug therapy had been producing a relatively desirable effect.

However, on implementation of a response cost procedure, on-task behavior jumped well above the previous levels attained during the medication phase of the experiment. Both subjects reached their highest and most consistent levels of task completion and on-task behavior when this strategy was in effect. Response cost exceeded all previous levels of appropriate classroom behavior as noted by teacher ratings and direct observation of task completion and accuracy.

Fortunately response cost was an easy program to initiate and maintain. All that was required was a set of numbered cards ranging from 20 to 0 in descending order. One student was told that he could keep up to 20 points, worth twenty minutes of free time, for staying on task and doing good work throughout the day. He was told, however, that each time the teacher observed him off task, she would flip one of her cards back. He was to do the same with his set of cards. This signaled the loss of one of his free-time minutes.

The same strategy was electronically, and perhaps superfluously, improved for the other subject. This student was given an electronic digital counter that displayed points earned as the subject stayed on task. In the event that the teacher observed him performing some off-task response, she immediately deducted one point (minute) from the digital display by means of a hand-held apparatus. Thus this subject earned the lost points throughout the course of the period.

The data for both subjects are consistent. Both show the most significant and improved performance while response cost contingencies were in effect. Using the digital display does not appear to have produced any identifiable improvement over the simple use of numbered cards, but both systems were significantly better than medication in terms of observed on-task behavior, teacher ratings of in-class behavior, and achievement.

A Broad View of Achievement and Psychostimulants

There are those who might, with some reason, argue that the evidence presented in this chapter is biased and heavily weighted in favor of behavioral intervention methodology. Ironically the coup de grace for stimulant drugs as a vehicle for improving academic achievement of hyperactive children comes from medicine's own quarters. In 1978 Barkley and Cunningham published a broad survey of medical and psychological research in the area of hyperactivity in *Clinical Pediatrics*. Regarding the short-term effects of those studies judged to be methodologically adequate, they state:

> Despite the methodological differences among these studies, their results may be combined to yield a single crude estimate of the effects of the stimulants on scholastic performance. Of the 52 dependent measures used in 17 studies, 43 (86% of total) were not significantly improved by stimulants. In the types of achievement skills, those drug effects which were noted were scattered and inconsistent. (p. 88)

They go on to point out that "it is difficult to attribute the substantial number of negative findings to differences in experimental designs or types of measures utilized. The studies finding no drug effects cut across differences in type of drug, dosage levels, titration procedures, and the degree of experimental control" (p. 88).

The long-term studies reviewed by Barkley and Cunningham are of particular interest because of the consistency of their findings. They cite a paper by Minde, Weiss, and Mendelson (1972), who did a five-year follow-up of 91 hyperkinetic children, and a paper by Huessy, Metoyer, and Townsend (1974), who did a follow-up of 84 hyperkinetic children. In addition, Weiss, Minde, Douglas, Werry, and Sykes (1971) did a three- to five-year comparison of 24 hyperactive children treated with methylphenidate and 22 treated with chlorpromazine; Quinn and Rapoport (1975) did a one-year follow-up of 76 hyperactive boys (29 on methylphenidate, 29 on imipramine, and 18 on placebo); and Riddle and Rapoport (1976) treated 72 of this same group for an additional year. Barkley and Cunningham point out that although the studies above contained methodological differences, their outcomes were quite consistent. Psychostimulants generally produced no long-term beneficial effects on either academic achievement or emotional adjustment of hyperactive children.

Among the explanations offered as to why psychostimulants do not produce a beneficial effect on achievement, Barkley and Cunningham note that stimulant drugs may make children "less alert to other people and their surroundings" (1978, p. 90), and the more likely answer, "stimulant medications are simply unable to influence those etiological variables which create or contribute to the hyperactive child's academic difficulties" (1978, p. 90).

CONCURRENT AND INTERACTIVE EFFECTS OF PSYCHOSTIMULANTS AND BEHAVIORAL INTERVENTION

Because it is fairly well established that both psychostimulants and behavioral analytic procedures can be used to decrease the activity level of hyperactive children, it has frequently been suggested that these procedures be used concurrently to produce the "best of both possible worlds." Although this "shot gun" approach may have advantages in certain situations, there are also a number of good reasons such an eclectic strategy may inadvertently reduce the long-range improvement of these children. The literature describes several studies that have investigated simultaneous interventions. The results are provocative, informative, and, in some cases, contradictory.

Beneficial Effects of Multiple Intervention

Pelham, Schnedler, Bologna, and Contreras (1980) investigated the effect of introducing Ritalin in conjunction with behavior therapy. Their data suggest that high dosages (0.75 mg/kg of methylphenidate) concurrent with behavior therapy produce the most beneficial effect on the level of on-task behavior. They also found that this combination produced the greatest improvement on the ACTRS.

No data were submitted to indicate changes in achievement that might be correlated with the use of medication, behavior management, or a combination. It is not surprising to find that psychostimulants, when used in conjunction with behavior management, may produce an increased level of desirable conduct. The effectiveness of each procedure in improving behavior has been well documented. The critical question as to the combined effects of both on achievement was not addressed.

Other Effects of Multiple Intervention

One of the few studies to analyze the interactive effects of methylphenidate and behavior analysis was conducted by Wolraich, Drummond, Solomon, O'Brien, and Sivage (1978). Using a double blind reversal of treatments in two separate classes of hyperactive children, these researchers exposed half of each class to 0.3 mg/kg of Ritalin and half to a placebo on a daily basis. Both groups were observed for off-task activities, including out-of-seat behavior, inappropriate vocalization, nonattending, peer interaction, and fidgeting. Measurements were also taken of academic behavior, consisting of accuracy of copying letters from the board and correct responses during individual work. Data were collected for two weeks of baseline, two weeks with a token economy, and two final weeks of return to baseline. Fidgeting (squirming within the confines of one's seat) was intentionally not targeted for behavior management in order to assess the frequency of an untreated behavior by way of a multiple baseline. This counterbalanced design permits analysis of the effects of behavioral procedures independently and in conjunction with medication. It also allows us to measure the effects of these treatments on diversified criteria for on-task behavior as well as academic achievement.

Unlike the Pelham et al. study (1980), the results of Wolraich et al. gave no indication of interactive effects between the behavioral and drug treatments. A three-factor analysis of variance with repeated measures (drug × behavior × class) and Tukey Pairwise Multiple Comparisons found that both the behavior management system and the methylphenidate were effective but in different settings. In group settings out-of-seat behavior, inappropriate vocalizations, and nonattending were significantly reduced by behavior management. Fidgeting was reduced by medication but not by behavior management. However, it had not been targeted for treatment by the token system. This testifies to the specificity of token systems. Individual on-task behavior was significantly improved by drug intervention with regard to inappropriate vocalization, nonattending, and peer interaction. Consistent with the findings of Ayllon et al. (1975), only behavior management produced any significant effect on measures of academic achievement. The total daily number of correct responses and the number of letters correctly copied from the board were improved over baseline measures whether or not students were under the influence of methylphenidate. Methylphenidate alone produced no beneficial effects on either academic measure. To quote the authors: "If a classroom program for hyperactive children has as its goal the reduction of undesirable behaviors, amphetamine drugs and operant procedures may each be effective. However, if improved scholastic achievement is hoped for, there is growing evidence that behavior management is the treatment of choice" (Wolraich et al., 1978, p. 160).

Questionable Advantage

Other studies have found psychostimulants to be only marginally effective and accompanied by many side effects. One case study illustrates these phenomena in detail. Shafto and Sulzbacher (1977) took advantage of a serendipitous opportunity to investigate the concurrent and alternate effects of methylphenidate and behavioral intervention. During the baseline phase of a behavior management program a 4½-year-old hyperactive "emotionally disturbed" child was inadvertently placed on Ritalin by a physician who was not associated with the program. This gave these investigators an opportunity to explore the effects of Ritalin on behavior previous to behavior management and in conjunction with behavior management, and, finally, the isolated effects of behavior management.

Using an extended reversal-of-treatment design, it was found that Ritalin was effective in reducing activity level only at maximum dosages (15 mg). The use of Ritalin in conjunction with behavior management was no more effective than behavior management alone. Both procedures were found to reduce the child's activity level by about 50 percent. However, the use of medication was correlated with some disconcerting side effects. At 15 mg of Ritalin it was found that this child mumbled indistinctly, showed an increase in echoic verbal behavior, and suffered some insomnia.

Other studies have documented similar physical problems associated with psychostimulants. Werry and Sprague (1974) found that 50 percent of young students receiving dosages of 1 mg/kg of body weight had diversified problems, including loss of appetite, behavioral upsets, stomachaches, and loss of weight. Large dosages have been associated with insomnia, unprovoked crying, retardation of growth, headaches, and acute psychotic episodes (Roche, Lipman, Overall, & Hung, 1980).

Even in studies that establish significantly fewer classroom disturbances while hyperactive children are on Ritalin, other factors associated with ingestion of this drug mitigate against its advantage. Henker, Whalen, and Collins (1979) found that even though hyperactive boys between seven and eleven years of age were equivalent to normals in terms of acting out episodes while on Ritalin, ingestion of this drug was associated with decreases in verbal interaction, decreases in positive mood, and an increase in negative affect.

Changes across Environments

Generally it is assumed by those who advocate the use of psychostimulants that the effects are somewhat generalizable across tasks, situations, and environments. Substantive research regarding global effects was not conducted until Wulbert and Dries (1977) used a multiple-baseline procedure in two different environments. Their subject was a third-grade nine-year-old of average intelligence who had a history of both aggressive and self-stimulating, ritualistic, tic-like behaviors. He had been on Ritalin for the previous three years.

Two separate, concurrent investigations of this child's achievement, as well as his ritualistic and aggressive behaviors, were undertaken. One series was conducted in the clinic, the other in the child's home. Using a double-blind design, they gave their subject either a placebo or Ritalin every other week.

In the clinic a multiple-baseline procedure tested the subject's ability to perform various memory tasks while data were also collected on the frequency of ritualistic and aggressive behaviors. In this setting it was found that whether the child was on Ritalin or a placebo, the token economy was the only variable that decreased the frequency of self-stimulating rituals and increased the accuracy of task performance. No interaction between the medication and reinforcement procedures was evident.

In the home environment, where no behavior management system was used, it was found that the frequency of aggressive episodes increased during those weeks in which the child was off Ritalin. The rate of tic-like ritualistic responses dropped during the drug-free periods. Thus both medication and behavioral procedures produced effects specific to particular situations. Within the clinic the token program reduced the frequency of self-stimulating rituals and improved the performance of tasks that required reasoning ability. Because there was no behavior management program in the home, this program did not affect aggressive or ritualistic behaviors in that environment.

The drug treatment was paradoxical. The authors noted that the child demonstrated no significant improvements in problem behaviors because of drug intervention while in the clinic; yet significant changes were seen in the home, where no contingency management program was in effect. Data taken at home indicated that Ritalin decreased the frequency of aggressive behaviors but seemed to increase the frequency of ritualistic behaviors.

This study seems to reaffirm the increasingly apparent effects of Ritalin on hyperactive behavior. That is, this drug will reduce the activity level of some behaviors, in some children, below that seen in an environment in which behavior is unsystematically addressed. However, where a consistent behavior management procedure exists, Ritalin does not seem to produce any improvements beyond those that are a function of contingency management. Further, there is increasing concern that such medication may deter some learning of academic and social skills that are in progress during a contingency management program.

NEW BEHAVIORAL ALTERNATIVES TO PSYCHOSTIMULANTS

Biofeedback

Biofeedback has become an increasingly popular procedure to control behaviors that are not easily monitored by the subject. Hyperactivity might be classified as such a behavior, since subjects are typically unaware that they are acting in any unusual way.

Schulman, Stevens, Suran, Kupst, and Naughton (1978) provided continuous feedback to a hyperactive child to determine if such feedback could be used to decrease high rates of physical activity. Their device, described as a "biomotometer," consisted of a small, unobtrusive electronic box worn around the subject's waist. The apparatus operated by means of "angular displacement of mercury switches," which occurred when the subject shifted body location. Such displacements were counted by the biomotometer, and when the count exceeded a preset threshold, feedback was produced by a tone delivered through a crystal earphone. This tone functioned as a discriminative stimulus for keeping still because reinforcement was contingent on remaining sedentary enough to keep the tone from sounding more than a specified number of times. Specifically the number of signals allowed was set so that activity was at least 20 percent below baseline. The subject came under control of the audio feedback almost immediately and reduced rates of body movement were conspicuous to all observers. Conversely, to demonstrate the versatility of this device, it was also used by the authors to increase the activity level of a subject described as hypoactive.

This study made no attempt to ascertain any beneficial side effects, such as increased attention span or improved academic performance. It seems reasonable, however, to assume that the reduced activity levels produced by this apparatus might facilitate a concurrent contingency for improved academic performance. Furthermore, such a device is unlikely to produce any of the harmful side effects frequently associated with drug therapy.

Food Additives

Although all of the variables that contribute to hyperactivity are not understood, one increasingly popular theory attributes some of the cause to dietary sensitivity (Feingold, 1975b, 1976). Ingestion of salicylate-like substances, such as apples, berries, tomatoes, apricots, prunes, and cucumbers, as well as artificial flavorings and coloring and the preservation BHT (butylated hydroxytoluene), has been reported to be correlated with an increase in the rate of erratic, impulsive off-task behavior.

Research by Rose (1978) established rather conclusively that some children appear to be allergic or dietarily predisposed toward the behavioral syndrome of hyperkinesis. To investigate the effect of selected food substances on the rate of hyperactive behaviors, Rose observed two children with well-established histories of hyperactivity who were currently on the Feingold diet. This diet emphasizes the avoidance of suspect food additives, colorings, artificial flavorings, and natural salicylate food compounds.

On-task observations were made in class and anecdotal records were kept in the home concerning the children's general level of activity in a double-blind reversal design. During baseline both children were maintained on the Feingold diet and low levels of disruptive, hyperactive behavior were documented. During subsequent days of intentional dietary infractions, in which a yellow artificial food coloring, tartrazine no. 5, was consumed in cookies, significant increases in activity level were recorded. This coincided with parental observations that the children suddenly became less manageable in the home. This same pattern, demonstrating an escalation of high-rate inappropriate behavior during exposure to tartrazine no. 5, was replicated in two subsequent reversals. On each day that these children consumed cookies in which this food coloring was present their activity level was significantly elevated.

Although this study supports the long-standing suspicion that some children are differentially sensitive to specific food additives, it remains to be established what percentage of the school population is so afflicted.

Whatever proportion of the population is sensitive to food substances or additives, it is clear that dietary regimens, such as those suggested by Feingold, are not always practical. There are hyperactive children who come from families who are unwilling or unable to follow the requirements suggested by Feingold. Furthermore, many school districts refuse to accommodate such dietary idiosyncrasies in their cafeterias.

The behavior analyst who wishes to impact hyperactive behavior is well advised to consider dietary factors. In those all too frequent cases in which dietary restrictions are not possible or effective, it is still very likely that a consistent contingency management program may produce the desired result, although perhaps at some increased behavioral cost for the teacher.

Cognitive Self-instruction

One reason a child might behave erratically and impulsively in the classroom may be due simply to the fact that he does not have the prerequisite skills to stay on task. He may not have come under the control of either internal or external cues associated with "good study habits." In the midst of the increasingly complex array of academic requirements, the very attempt to stay on task may become strongly aversive. A self-instructional procedure that addresses the student's internal dialogue (cues) concerning what to do while on task could facilitate his performance.

Bornstein and Quevillon (1976) demonstrated a self-instructional procedure that increased the amount of on-task behavior in three hyperactive preschool children. The technique was very much unlike what is usually described as behavior management, in that control over hyperactivity was established and maintained within just two hours of training.

The authors believed that many children who are hyperactive and off task are so because they do not know what to say to themselves in order to stay on task. In other words, such children say the "wrong words" to themselves when trying to perform. Their strategy consisted of teaching three 4-year-old hyperactive boys covert verbalizations associated with successful attack and execution of assignments. The authors modeled a series of guided overt self-statements for the children to practice. These modeled statements were arranged so the children were eventually able to say these same statements covertly (to themselves) as they performed their classwork.

Bornstein and Quevillon describe the following series of gradual steps as originally given by Meichenbaum and Goodman (1971):

> (1) the experimenter modelled the task while talking aloud to himself, (2) the subject performed the task while the experimenter instructed aloud, (3) the subject then performed the task aloud to himself while the experimenter whispered softly, (4) the subject per-

formed the task whispering softly while the experimenter made lip movements but no sound, (5) the subject performed the task making lip movements without sound while the experimenter self-instructed covertly, and (6) the subject performed the task with covert self-instruction. (p. 181)

The results of this "cognitive" self-instruction package were immediately apparent in terms of percentage of on-task behavior. All three subjects jumped from about 10 percent to 14 percent on task to about 70 percent to 80 percent on task after only two hours of training. These trends continued throughout the duration of the school semester.

Training in self-instruction would appear to be a new and unique approach to the traditional management procedures used in behavior analysis. The results seem especially impressive, considering the short duration of intervention and the age and academic level of the subjects. Unfortunately these results were not replicated in a subsequent study.

Friedling and O'Leary (1979) followed exactly the same procedures documented by Bornstein and Quevillon (1976), using a slightly older population. Their eight subjects ranged in age from six years ten months to eight years ten months, and had histories of classroom disruption and hyperactive behavior. They found that only a few of their subjects did better on easy math assignments. Self-instruction had virtually no effect on any other behaviors, including easy and hard reading and hard math. No effects were found in class behavior in terms of the accuracy in any of the above areas or in the amount of time spent on task.

They politely suggest that perhaps Bornstein and Quevillon's younger population may have been more susceptible to self-instruction training, or that Bornstein and Quevillon's subjects' improvement may have been related to subtle and unintentional teacher reinforcement of student compliance rather than the self-instruction package.

In a second experiment Friedling and O'Leary found that the common expedient of implementing a token program, with contingencies for gradually increasing levels of on-task behavior, created improved results for all subjects.

Bornstein and Quevillon's (1976) study was again replicated by Billings and Wasik (1985). They, too, were unable to produce the same dramatic and immediate beneficial results found in the Bornstein and Quevillon self-instructional training package. Their procedures were an excellent attempt at direct replication, but were entirely unsuccessful at bringing about any positive changes in the percentage of attending behavior on the part of children in a Head Start center. They, like Friedling and O'Leary (1979), speculate that the original positive results found by Bornstein and Quevillon (1976) may have been an artifact of increased teacher attention after the self-instruction program went into effect.

Bornstein (1985) follows Billings and Wasik's (1985) replication, in the same issue of the *Journal of Applied Behavior Analysis*, with a defensive commentary on the state of the art of self-instructional training. He provides an impressive list of studies wherein self-instruction has been proved both effective and ineffective; several such studies may be found in Chapter 5 of this book. However, few research articles have found self-instruction a beneficial procedure when completed in the short period of time suggested in his 1976 study.

The truth is that there are no quick fixes where hyperactivity is concerned. Students who have not learned the prerequisite skills for attending to academic tasks will not learn them in two hours of self-instruction training, nor will they learn such skills under the influence of medication. Any "instructional package" or drug schedule that claims an immediate transition to learned behavior must be carefully scrutinized.

PILLS OR SKILLS REVISITED

O'Leary (1980) provides one of the finest global perspectives on the current status of interventions for hyperactivity in the classroom. He described three recent historical events that have added impetus to the controversy concerning the pervasive and perhaps indiscriminate use of psychostimulants among hyperactive children in the elementary schools.

1. The 1970 "Omaha Incident," in which the media incorrectly reported that 5 percent to 10 percent of all children in that city were currently receiving some form of psychostimulant medication (Maynard, 1970). Public outcry from this "expose" eventually initiated a congressional investigation.
2. The 1975 investigative report entitled the *Myth of the Hyperactive Child* (Schrag & Divoky, 1975) and its following synopsis in the New York Times, *Readin', Writin', (and Druggin')* (Schrag, 1975). O'Leary notes that although this report contains several inaccuracies and polemics, it does point out many of the problems associated with diagnosis and treatment in the area of hyperactivity.
3. The professional journal of the American Federation of Teachers, *American Educator* (Box, 1978), made a resounding and emotional plea to curtail the promiscuous distribution of psychostimulants in the elementary schools. Box criticized the pseudophysiologizing and imposition of "medical solutions" on problems that are, in fact, a function of "moral, legal, and social" artifacts and inequities within our culture.

Although O'Leary was fair enough to detail many of the inaccuracies and exaggerations, he provided some additionally illuminating statistical and critical analyses. He noted that despite documented side effects, such as increased blood pressure, heart rate, and suppression of growth rate (Roche, et al., 1980; Safer, Allen, & Barr, 1972; Weiss, Kluger, Danielson, & Elman, 1975), "approximately 600,000 to 700,000 children receive psychostimulant medication for hyperactivity during the school year" (p. 193). This fact is in no small part related to the current interest in the development and distribution of these drugs. He noted that between January and September 1979, seven of the nine issues of *Pediatrics* had full-page advertisements advocating psychostimulants for the treatment of hyperactivity.

O'Leary also addressed the popular assumption that psychostimulants are particularly effective on a special group of children who are physiologically predisposed toward accelerated levels of activity. Sometimes this predisposition is attributed to minimal brain damage, sometimes to metabolic dysfunction. However, Rapoport et al. (1979) demonstrated that the same reduction in activity level occurs in normal children who are given such medication. Conversely, only about two out of three children diagnosed as hyperactive show improved behavior under the influence of psychostimulants. He questions the validity of the diagnosis of central nervous system dysfunction in hyperactive children based on differential improvement using psychostimulants. O'Leary recommended terms such as responders and nonresponders to differentiate those who are affected by psychostimulants. Such terms avoid the implication that those who respond to medication are exclusively predisposed toward hyperactivity. O'Leary pointed out that accurate determination of hyperactivity can best be achieved by examining behaviors that occur "across time and situation." One must see the restlessness, short attention span, and high rate of irrelevant responses with different teachers and in different environments before an accurate assessment can be made.

Most important, O'Leary questioned the popular rationale that psychostimulants are justified on the basis of improved academic functioning. Documenting several studies (Conrad, Dworkin, Shai, & Tobiessen, 1971; Gittelman-Klein & Klein, 1976; Hoffman et al., 1974) he stated that "no long term achievement gains on the WRAT have been associated with drug treatment" (p. 198). In addition, he pointed to Barkley and Cunningham's (1978) review of the literature on the effect of psychostimulants on academic achievement. As previously noted, they found that, contrary to the improvements perceived by teachers, most of the current research does not support any improvement in achievement. This may be due to a number of factors related to medication, not the least of which is that Ritalin and other psychostimulants have been found to suppress cognitive functioning in some individuals (Ayllon et al., 1975; Sprague & Sleater, 1977; Swanson, Kinsbourne, Roberts, & Zucker 1978). A more likely explanation might simply be that it is unreasonable to expect a drug that reduces activity level will concurrently and spontaneously increase achievement. There is no simple relationship between sitting still and learning. Just because a child is not running around the room does not guarantee that he is engaging in task-related activity.

UNDER EXCEPTIONAL CIRCUMSTANCES

In closing this chapter let us point out that although we have argued against the promiscuous distribution of psychostimulants and documented many studies that dispute the advantage of medical treatments of hyperactivity, many behavioral psychologists, including ourselves, understand that there are situations in which such medication may be the only reasonable solution to a child's excessive level of activity in the classroom. There are families and teachers who are unable to implement behavioral procedures. Some teachers in regular and special education classrooms operate in such crowded conditions that it would be unreasonable to expect them to implement an individual behavior management program to the exclusion of the rest of the class. Under such circumstances medication may be the preferred procedure. One hopes that this would occur only after other, less restrictive alternatives have been exhausted. To quote O'Leary once more: "I would not initially use pharmacological interventions with most hyperactive children because the behaviors that characterize the hyperactive syndrome are so dramatically, although fleetingly, changed by psychostimulants that the parents, teachers, and children may view the medication as a panacea and we know that such is very far from the truth." (p. 201)

REFERENCES

American Psychiatric Association. (1980). *DSM-III: Diagnostic and statistical manual of mental disorders* (3rd ed.). Washington, DC: American Psychiatric Association.

American Psychiatric Association. (1987). *DSM-III-R: Diagnostic and statistical manual of mental disorders* (rev. 3rd ed.). Washington, DC: American Psychiatric Association.

Ayllon, T., Layman, D., & Kandell, H. J. (1975). A behavioral-educational alternative to drug control of hyperactive children. *Journal of Applied Behavior Analysis, 8*, 137–146.

Barkley, R. A., & Cunningham, C. E. (1978). Do stimulant drugs improve the academic performance of hyperactive children? *Clinical Pediatrics, 17*, 85–92.

Billings, D. C., & Wasik, B. H. (1985). Self-instructional training with preschoolers: An attempt to replicate. *Journal of Applied Behavior Analysis, 18*, 61–67.

Bornstein, P. H. (1985). Self-instructional training: A commentary and state-of-the-art. *Journal of Applied Behavior Analysis, 18*, 69–72.

Bornstein, P. H., & Quevillon, R. P. (1976). The effects of a self-instructional package on overactive preschool boys. *Journal of Applied Behavior Analysis, 9*, 179–188.

Box, S. (1978). Hyperactivity: The scandalous silence. *American Educator, 2* (Summer), 22–24.

Bradley, C. (1937). The behavior of children receiving benzedrine. *American Journal of Psychiatry, 94*, 577–585.

Conners, C. K., Eisenberg, L., & Barcai, A. (1967). Effects of dextro-amphetamine in children: Studies on subjects with learning disabilities and school behavior problems. *Archives of General Psychiatry, 17*, 478–485.

Conners, C. K., Eisenberg, L., & Sharpe, L. (1964). Effects of methylphenidate (Ritalin) on paired-associate learning and Porteus Maze performance in emotionally disturbed children. *Journal of Consulting Psychology, 28*, 14–22.

Conrad, W. G., Dworkin, E. S., Shai, A., & Tobiessen, J. E. (1971). Effects of amphetamine therapy and prescriptive tutoring on the behavior and achievement of lower class hyperactive children. *Journal of Learning Disabilities, 4*, 499–501.

Feingold, B. F. (1975). *Why your child is hyperactive*. New York: Random House.

Feingold, B. F. (1976). Hyperkinesis and learning disabilities linked to the ingestion of artificial food colors and flavors. *Journal of Learning Disabilities, 9*, 551–559.

Friedling, C., & O'Leary, S. G. (1979). Effects of self-instructional training on second-

and third-grade hyperactive children: A failure to replicate. *Journal of Applied Behavior Analysis, 12*, 211–219.

Gittelman-Klein, R., & Klein, D. F. (1976). Methylphenidate effects in learning disabilities. *Archives of General Psychiatry, 33*, 655–664.

Henker, B., Whalen, C. K., & Collins, B. E. (1979). Double-blind and triple-blind assessment of medication and placebo responses in hyperactive children. *Journal of Abnormal Child Psychology, 7*, 1–13.

Hoffman, S., Engelhardt, D. M., Margolis, R. A., Poizios, P., Waizer, J., & Rosenfeld, T. (1974). Response to methylphenidate in low socioeconomic hyperactive children. *Archives of General Psychiatry, 30*, 354–359.

Huessy, H., Metoyer, M., & Townsend, M. (1974). 8–10 year follow-up of 84 children treated for behavioral disorders in rural Vermont. *Acta Paedopsychiatrica, 40*, 230–235.

Katz, S., Saraf, K., & Gittelman-Klein, R. (1976). Management of hyperkinetic children. In D. F. Klein & R. Gittelman-Klein (Eds.), *Progress in psychiatric drug treatment* (Vol. 2). New York: Brunner/Mazed Publishers.

Knights, R. M., & Hinton, G. G. (1969). Minimal brain dysfunction: Clinical and psychological test characteristics. *Academic Therapy, 4*, 265–273.

Maynard, R. (1970). Omaha pupils given "behavior" drug. *Washington Post*, June 29.

Meichenbaum, D. H., & Goodman, J. (1971). Training impulsive children to talk to themselves: A means of developing self-control. *Journal of Abnormal Psychology, 77*, 115–126.

Minde, K., Weiss, G., & Mendelson, N. (1972). A 5 year follow-up study of 91 hyperactive school children. *Journal of the American Academy of Child Psychiatry, 11*, 595–610.

O'Leary, D. K. (1980). Pills or skills for hyperactive children. *Journal of Applied Behavior Analysis, 13*, 191–204.

Pelham, N. E., Schnedler, R. W., Bologna, N. C., & Contreras, J. A. (1980). Behavioral and stimulant treatment of hyperactive children: A therapy study with methylphenidate probes in a within-subjects design. *Journal of Applied Behavior Analysis, 13*, 221–236.

Quinn, P. O., & Rapoport, J. L. (1975). One-year follow-up of hyperactive boys treated with imipramine or methylphenidate. *American Journal of Psychiatry, 132*, 241–245.

Rapoport, J. L., Buchsbaum, M. S., Zahn, T. P., Weingartner, H., Ludlow, D., & Mikkelson, E. J. (1979). Dextroamphetamine: Cognitive and behavioral effects in normal prepubertal boys. *Science, 199*, 560–563.

Rapport, M. D., Murphy, H. A., & Bailey, J. S. (1982). Ritalin vs. response cost in the control of hyperactive children: A within-subject comparison. *Journal of Applied Behavior Analysis, 15*, 205–216.

Riddle, D., & Rapoport, J. (1976). A 2-year follow-up of 72 hyperactive boys. *Journal of Nervous and Mental Disorders, 162*, 126.

Robinson, P. W., Newby, T. J., & Ganzell, S. L. (1981). A token system for a class of underachieving hyperactive children. *Journal of Applied Behavior Analysis, 14*, 307–315.

Roche, A., Lipman, R., Overall, J., & Hung, W. (1980). The effects of stimulant medication on the growth of hyperkinetic children. *Pediatrics, 51*, 1126–1132.

Rose, T. L. (1978). The functional relationship between artificial food colors and hyperactivity. *Journal of Applied Behavior Analysis, 11*, 439–446.

Safer, D., Allen, R., & Barr, E. (1972). Depression of growth in hyperactive children on stimulant drugs. *New England Journal of Medicine, 287*, 217–220.

Schrag, P. (1975, October 19). Readin', writin', (and druggin'). *The New York Times*, p. 13.

Schrag, P., & Divoky, D. (1975). *The myth of the hyperactive child*. New York: Pantheon.

Schulman, J. L., Stevens, T. M., Suran, B. G., Kupst, M. J., & Naughton, M. J. (1978). Modification of activity level through biofeedback and operant conditioning. *Journal of Applied Behavior Analysis, 11*, 145–152.

Shafto, F., & Sulzbacher, S. (1977). Comparing treatment tactics with a hyperactive preschool child: Stimulant medication and programmed teacher intervention. *Journal of Applied Behavior Analysis, 10*, 13–20.

Sprague, R. L., & Sleator, E. K. (1977). Methylphenidate in hyperactive children: Differences in dose effects on learning and social behavior. *Science, 198*, 1274–1276.

Sprague, R. L., & Toppe, L. K. (1966). Relationship between activity level and delay of reinforcement in the retarded. *Journal of Experimental Child Psychology, 3*, 390–397.

Sulzbacher, S. (1972). Behavior analysis of drug effects in the classroom. In G. Semb (Ed.), *Behavior analysis and education*. Lawrence: University of Kansas.

Swanson, J., Kinsbourne, M., Roberts, W., & Zucker, K. (1978). Time-response analysis of the effect of stimulant medication on the learning ability of children referred for hyperactivity. *Pediatrics, 61*, 21–29.

Weiss, G., Kluger, E., Danielson, U., & Elman, M. (1975). Effect of long term treatment of hyperactive children with methylphenidate. *Canadian Medical Association Journal, 112*, 159–165.

Weiss, G., Minde, K., Douglas, V., Werry, J., & Sykes, D. (1971). Comparison of the effects of chlorpromazine, dextroamphetamine, and methylphenidate on the behavior and intellectual functioning of hyperactive children. *Canadian Medical Association Journal, 104*, 20–25.

Werry, J. S., & Sprague, R. L. (1974). Methylphenidate in children: Effect of dosage. *Australian and New Zealand Journal of Psychiatry, 8*, 9–19.

Whimbey, A., & Whimbey, L. S. (1975). *Intelligence can be taught*. New York: Bantam Books.

Wolraich, M., Drummond, T., Solomon, M. K., O'Brien, M. L., & Sivage, C. (1978). Effects of methylphenidate alone and in combination with behavior modification procedures on the behavior and academic performance of hyperactive children. *Journal of Abnormal Child Psychology, 6*, 149–161.

Wulbert, M., & Dries, R. (1977). The relative efficacy of methylphenidate (Ritalin) and behavior modification techniques in the treatment of a hyperactive child. *Journal of Applied Behavior Analysis, 10*, 21–31.

4

Behavioral Contracting

THE CONCEPT

Behavioral contracting grew out of the notion, established by Premack (1965), that a high-probability response can be used to reinforce a low-probability response. For instance, in one of his experiments Premack arranged the environmental contingencies such that a water-deprived rat could make the operant response of wheel-running to obtain water. After wheel-running had increased in frequency he reversed the contingencies. Rats were provided with constant access to water but physical movement was restricted. Under these conditions Premack found that drinking increased three to five times over the usual intake if the opportunity to engage in wheel-running was contingent on drinking. These experiments indicated that response and reinforcer are potentially reversible, and that an activity is only reinforcing relative to an organism's current level of deprivation. This concept is known as the Premack Principle.

Homme (1974) has translated this principle into what he calls Grandma's Law. ''First you finish your dinner and then you get your dessert''; or more to our interests, ''First you do three pages of arithmetic and then you get to have five minutes of free time.'' For semisatiated grandchildren and recalcitrant students, respectively, both eating dinner and doing three pages of arithmetic may be low-probability behaviors relative to the current probability of eating dessert and engaging in free-time activities.

As children advance in age and grade level their verbal sophistication generally increases as well, and contracting combines the best features of both the Premack Principle and the student's increasingly complex verbal behavior. In the contracting procedure the student and teacher negotiate a mutually advantageous agreement. The target is improvement in the student's behavior, and the strategy involves making explicit the conditions under which improved behavior will be recognized and reinforced. Contracting, then, is a covenant that makes high-probability behavior contingent on the performance of low-probability behavior. It is a joint venture, and can best be achieved when both parties involved agree to the specified conditions. Typically contracting is not a coercive procedure, and is most effectively drawn up by mutual arbitration and consent.

Contracting is useful in improving any number of behaviors; however, developing a behavioral contract and carrying it out effectively require a great deal of effort and considerable sensitivity to the student under contract. One might contract with students for better social behavior, improved test grades, better eating habits in the cafeteria, or helping other students with their schoolwork. The possibilities are unlimited. There is one critical requirement: the contracted outcome must be objectively verifiable. Both the student and the teacher should be able to verify the behavior specified in the contract. Thus contracting is only appropriate for behaviors that can be observed and recorded.

An Early Contracting Procedure

One of the earliest studies cited in the *Journal of Applied Behavior Analysis* using contracting in a school system was performed by Cantrell, Cantrell, Huddleston, and Woolridge (1969). This study describes contracting procedures and strategies designed to improve achievement motivation, increase attendance, and eliminate hyperaggressivity, stealing, and school phobia. The authors emphasize the necessity of designing clear and complete programs, and of making them simple enough to avoid making the process aversive for the enforcing agents. To achieve these goals, they list four important questions to be answered before initiating a contract:

1. What are the primary problem behaviors and how often do they occur?
2. What are the typical consequences of the problem behavior?
3. What are the strong reinforcers in the child's environment?
4. What might be used as punishers if they are needed?

Answers to these questions were obtained from the students' adult agents and sent to Cantrell et al. for the determination of specific contract contingencies. Completed contracts were then transmitted by phone or written correspondence to parents or school personnel for implementation. A child's behavioral contract allowed for earning points in the school environment and exchanging these points for privileges and preferred activities in the home. The contract was designed to increase target behaviors specified by school personnel, and the privileges that backed up the points were specified by the child's parents. The contract was simply handed to the child as a fait accompli. The child could, of course, comply with the contract or not. If he did, the contracted points were delivered and the backup privileges obtained. Otherwise, points and backup privileges were withheld. Including the child as partner in negotiating the contract had not yet become a prominent component of the contracting process. Despite this somewhat arbitrary method of establishing the contracts, students' behaviors were reported as improving significantly when adult agents were able to (a) determine the contingencies that were responsible for the problem behavior and alter these contingencies, and (b) maintain the new contingencies specified in the contract.

The Introduction of Daily and Weekly Report Card Systems

Subsequent studies have substantiated the usefulness of home-based backup consequences for classroom behavior. Bailey, Wolf, and Phillips (1970) conducted three programs wherein students residing at Achievement Place (a home for predelinquent problem youth) earned home-based privileges contingent on appropriate classroom behavior at school.

In the first experiment five boys, aged eleven to fifteen years, were exposed to a series of treatment conditions in a specially designed class at the University of Kansas. Rules for proper conduct were placed on the board. Observers, covertly stationed behind one-way mirrors, took notes on classroom rule violations and study behavior at ten-second intervals throughout the experiment. During baseline, students were observed as they engaged in their typical classroom behaviors. Baseline was followed by a "yes-only" period during which all students received "yesses" on a daily report card independent of the behavior that actually occurred in class. The report card specified such behaviors as "studied the whole period" and "obeyed classroom rules." These perfect report cards were exchanged for special snacks, TV time, and permission to go outside. During baseline and the "yes-only" condition, students' study behaviors gradually fell to about 25 percent of the observed intervals, whereas time spent violating rules increased to about 50 percent. However, all students now had sampled the benefits derived from obtaining a perfect report card.

The period of noncontingent positive reports was followed by a period during which "yesses" on the card were contingent on rule-following behavior. In this phase, teachers marked "yes" only when the student had performed adequately in the area specified on the report card. If any negatives were given, the student lost access to privileges. During this period, rule violations immediately dropped to almost zero, and study behavior quickly increased to almost 100 percent.

To substantiate that this effect was independent of outside influences (artifacts), a six-day reversal period was implemented. Throughout this period, privileges were again provided irrespective of the students' classroom behavior. Students were still graded by means of the report card, but these grades had no bearing on the availability of privileges. Students' behavior began to deteriorate at an alarming rate. Again, once the reinforcement contingency was reinstituted, on-task behavior resumed. Study behavior again jumped to nearly 100 percent and rule violations fell to about zero.

In their second experiment, Bailey et al. replicated these procedures in a public school environment and obtained the same positive results. In their third experiment they demonstrated that the program could be gradually faded out, until students presented their report cards to their houseparents only two days a week.

As in the work of Cantrell et al., this program was not designed using current behavioral contracting approaches. The subjects in the first study were actually captive participants selected as a result of having been placed in a home for predelinquent boys. This fact did not detract from the power of the treatment effects, but it may have affected the means by which Bailey et al. structured later classroom and home-based contingencies. In the second and third experiments no attempt was made to negotiate the contingencies. It has become increasingly clear over the past decade that involving the contractee in the process of arranging his own contingencies increases the probability of both immediate and sustained improvements in performance.

Following the lead of Bailey et al. (1970), others have devised contractual formats that include daily report cards. In a series of three experiments, Schumaker, Hovell, and Sherman (1977) demonstrated the effect of including the students' natural parents in the contracting arrangement. In experiment 1 a daily report card and home-based backup reinforcement were combined to change the disruptive, noncompliant, underachieving behavior of three adolescent boys. The parents of these children received daily feedback, by means of the report card, regarding classroom behavior and academic performance. The report card specified points earned for high grades and following rules; parents exchanged these points for items the boys selected from a menu of reinforcers. These reinforcers were divided into daily basic privileges, and weekly and monthly special privileges. Predictably, all three students displayed improved classroom behavior and grades.

Experiment 2 tested the effect of parental "praise only" independent of home-based privileges. Two other disruptive, noncompliant adolescent boys were also given daily report cards to be taken home for parental inspection; however, the only positive consequence for obtaining a perfect report card was verbal praise. Parents were carefully trained to deliver praise statements contingent on improved reports. Only one of the two students brought the report card home, and neither student demonstrated any consistent improvement. This outcome seems to indicate that, at least in the initial stages, tangible reinforcers may be an important component of contracting with disruptive and noncompliant students.

In their third experiment Schumaker et al. evaluated the use of a daily report card program instituted by school personnel. Specifically, they tested the ability of school counselors to implement contracts that involved parents and the daily report card. Counselors were trained with a specially written manual and had no direct contact with the researchers in implementing the procedures. Subjects selected for these counselor-initiated contracts made significant improvements in the percentage of rules followed as well as general improvements in academic performance.

These authors also discussed the question of weaning the students from the report card system. Like Bailey et al., they recommended the use of a fading procedure. Initially, they suggest a shortened version of the report card, later the daily report card, and later still the report card can be brought home biweekly, until the report card is finally terminated. This gradual fading of the frequency should sustain the students' improved classroom behavior.

The programs above proved surprisingly successful with a notoriously difficult population, adolescents. The counselors' ability to run the program after simply reading a training manual further testifies to its efficacy and generalizability.

Stitely (1978) designed a similar program wherein parents interfaced with teachers in managing contingencies to increase students' academic performance. As in previous programs using daily report card contracts, teachers listed categories of required classroom behaviors for each student. At the end of each class period the teacher checked those categories of behavior that the student had successfully demonstrated in class. Parents were then notified of the total number of checks their children had earned, and parents provided privileges in accordance with the contingencies in each child's individual contract. As in the Schumaker et al. study, privileges were made available on a daily or weekly basis, depending on the preference of the individual parent/student pairs. Points acquired by the student were traded for such privileges as daily TV time or a weekly baseball game.

This study gave no quantitative indices of results. The author's only comment on the outcome was: "Though we collected no definitive data to assess the merits of the home-school contract system, it seemed to produce more positive than negative effects" (Stitely, 1978, p. 320). She does, however, mention the need for future quantitative investigation.

Contracting with the Help of Tutors

Schwartz (1977) conducted one of the first studies that emphasized the importance of the negotiation phase of behavioral contracting. He trained forty-two college students as reading tutors and contingency managers to implement a remedial reading program for 146 deficient readers in grades seven through nine. The study addressed three target areas: (1) improved individual reading skills, (2) modified negative self-statements regarding reading, and (3) contingency contracting to increase motivation in acquiring new reading skills.

Before treatment, tutors negotiated a behavior contract with each experimental subject. The negotiators were required to work with predetermined point criteria: 100 points would be required to obtain a grade of B, and 200 points would earn an A. Another constraint was the length of time during which the points could be earned, that is, during ten weekly sessions. The tutors negotiated with individual subjects the number of points needed each week to reach the total goal. Tutors and subjects also selected the required reading materials as part of the negotiation process.

An adjunctive program helped to facilitate an improved attitude toward reading. Tutors took data on each subject's positive and negative verbal comments during the tutorial sessions; after baseline they began to differentially reinforce only positive comments. That is, the tutors gave verbal recognition to positive statements and systematically ignored any derogatory comments. Concurrently the amount of time the student spent reading each night was gradually increased through negotiation. The total program included at least ten hours of one-to-one tutoring and thirty hours of independent reading.

Unlike most experimental designs in the *Journal of Applied Behavior Analysis*, the results of this study were described in terms of the average improvement in reading for the group as a whole and with the aid of statistical procedures. Pretesting and posttesting on the Gates-MacGinitie Reading Test, using the analysis of covariance, indicated that the experimental groups improved significantly over those in the control group. The experimental groups improved 2.1 grade levels, an improvement that was three times that shown by the control students. The number of positive and negative verbal comments the subjects made regarding their reading ability also changed. Analysis of data showed significant increases in the number of positive comments and significant declines in the number of negative comments. A six-month follow-up documented continuation of these trends.

Eller and Eller (1977) have also demonstrated that behavioral contracts can be enhanced by using tutors. Their program consisted of using freshmen psychology students as individual tutors for junior high school students who evidenced significant academic deficits. Students whose grades in English, math, or history were D or below were given contracts that specified the use of a point system for completing assignments and improving test grades. The tutors monitored and administered points for homework and assignment completion three times a week: points were exchanged at the end of each week for items selected from a range of privileges. Depending on the number of points earned during the week, students could obtain milkshakes, car rides from school, a McDonald's supper, or an opportunity to attend a baseball game or movie.

Not only was there a significant improvement in all of the subjects' grades, but also there was a general improvement in attendance records. Such outcomes are particularly significant, since previous research has indicated that tutoring without behavioral contracting is not effective (Cloward, 1966; Kreutzer, 1973).

A Classwide Self-management Program for Vocational Training

Kelly and Stokes (1982) point out that negotiated contracts, beginning at an individual's current level of functioning and gradually increasing requirements as skills develop, give the student the opportunity to practice setting and achieving goals while allowing the teacher to maintain control over pedagogical matters. Their program evaluated the effect of contracting on an entire class rather than on selected individuals, as in the Schwartz (1977) study.

During baseline the teacher instructed the vocational training class, using "traditional discipline procedures." This government-subsidized program paid all students a minimum of $2.35 per hour for attending class. During treatment phase, when the contracting procedure was initiated, teacher and students began negotiating the number of items to be completed daily. These contracts individually detailed daily goals and weekly goals. Salaries were increased as students succeeded in meeting successively more difficult academic criteria. Each week the teacher suggested raising productivity levels by about 10 percent. Kelly and Stokes note that there were discrepancies in individual work loads, reflecting each student's ability and willingness to perform the assignments. Using a reversal design in which baseline and treatment were replicated, they established that most students more than doubled their academic performance when money was contingent on task completion. Both the students and teacher reported a preference for the contracting procedure over the baseline "discipline procedure." Students appreciated knowing exactly how much work was required each day and stated that they experienced a sense of accomplishment, task completion.

Contracting with Delinquents

The use of contracting has even been found to be helpful when dealing with juvenile offenders *outside* the school environment. Dallas's Youth Services Program (YSP) instituted the use of behavior contracting and found that young delinquents were much less likely to get back into trouble with the police after they and their families were given training in the use of contracting (Douds, Englesgjard & Collingwood, 1977). YSP developed a three-step program that involved the following:

1. Establishing a "motivational base" (getting the parents to admit that problems existed and that something could be done about them)
2. Specifying the contingencies (having both the parents and youths write lists of possible backup privileges and the appropriate behaviors on which they would be made contingent)
3. Monitoring the program (parents were taught how to specify expected appropriate behaviors and how to keep data on their children's behavior)

This contracting program apparently operated much the same as behaviors contracted in the academic environment. The success rate indicates that it was at least as effective. Douds et al. note that

> follow-up parent evaluations on factors relating to recidivism outcome show that 74% of the youths improved in following rules at home; 72% improved their communication with parents; 63% improved their school attendance; 54% studied more; and 45% increased their involvement in organized activities. In addition only 10% of the youths who have completed the program (N = 1200) have been re-arrested, as compared with 42.7% in a control group. (p. 411)

Even though this contracting format was not developed within the school, its effect is reported to have generalized to that environment. This is not unusual. Behavioral strategies often have positive effects on behaviors that occur outside the original learning conditions.

DEVELOPING A BEHAVIORAL CONTRACT

Because contracting in school systems has only a short history in behavior analysis, a detailed description of procedures for instituting a behavioral contract with students will be given.

Shaping the Contract

A typical contract might be negotiated to increase homework completion with a student who demonstrates the all too pervasive procrastination syndrome. Negotiations begin with a student/teacher conference. Because the contracting situation provides the opportunity to teach a variety of skills, the teacher may begin by asking the student if he is satisfied with his grades in math (or English or whatever) or if he would prefer to perform better. Usually a student not doing well will express dissatisfaction, but the student with little hope of achieving might declare himself satisfied.

However the student responds, the teacher will express confidence that the student can improve his homework grades by getting the homework done. The teacher can then explain that she thinks it is so important that the student learn to do his homework regularly that she is willing to try to work out a deal she believes will help the student learn to do his homework regularly. The child is then asked if he would consider contracting for homework completion as a means toward improving his grades and acquiring new privileges.

If the student agrees, the teacher begins by asking for an assignment that she is confident the student can complete. If the child is capable of solving seven math problems, she might begin by asking what it would be worth for him to complete three problems on the first night. The number of problems requested is low to ensure that the child completes the assignment. Too often contracts fail because the student does not accomplish the initial task, and thus the reinforcement procedure never occurs. Homme (1974) points out that reinforcement should be provided early in the contracting process to immediately increase the probability of infrequent behaviors. Sometimes children will try to increase the requirement, and this gives the teacher a chance to agree to a slight increase while explaining that the student can contract to do more later.

Children are often willing to contract for an opportunity to indulge in some special privilege, such as being hall monitor, leading the class in some new game, or even having a class party. The possibilities are limited only by the negotiators' imaginations.

When both a suitable consequence and the required behavior are agreed on, the teacher emphasizes the special significance of the contract by providing a written document outlining both the behavior expected and the privileges to be earned on completion of that behavior. After agreeing to the terms, both parties sign the contract. If the teacher emphasizes the significance of this negotiation, and indicates what a remarkable achievement its successful completion will be, that generally encourages the student to put forth a special effort. Once the contingencies are operative, they provide the motivation for improved behavior. If this process continues long enough, the task completion itself may become a form of conditioned reinforcement. When that happens, the student is frequently described as having that most noble of all academic virtues, "self-motivation."

The child's learning to recognize his achievements is an important by-product of behavioral contracts. The teacher helps the child by making it clear how valuable his behavior is. She may, for instance, tell the child that it will be "really tremendous" when he succeeds in completing all of the conditions in the contract. Of course, the contract is rigged so that the child is unlikely to fail; he is thus "set up" for success. When he does succeed his reward is both tangible, because he obtains the objects or privileges specified in the contract, and social, because he receives the teacher's public praise and commendations.

Contracting may be the only way to provide some children with an opportunity to experience success. Because the experience of success can be an extremely satisfying and contagious phenomenon, we, as educators, should endeavor to spread it around as thickly as possible.

Paying Off and Fading Out

When a contract is fulfilled a golden opportunity is created. The teacher can now show genuine enthusiasm and generously provide social and tangible reinforcement. The student is told what an outstanding job he has done and that he is now developing important new skills and abilities. He is given the chance to draw up another contract, and again the probabilities of success are "rigged" in his favor, although the requirements for this contract are slightly more rigorous than those for the first one. When he succeeds on this second occasion he may be heartily commended again and permitted to move to a third. As the student moves from one contract to another, the teacher allows the provisions to come more in line with the general expectations for the rest of the class. If this process continues long enough, gradually the child may be weaned from the contracting procedure and permitted to play by the rules of the general classroom format. This does not mean that the teacher terminates all attention for task completion; all students should receive frequent praise and commendation for staying on task and producing good work.

Contract Failure

If the student fails to fulfill the requirements, there are at least three potential sources of the problem:

1. The child's academic skills were over estimated. In that case the contract can be renegotiated to specify a less demanding criterion.
2. The privilege promised was of little value to the child. In that case the contract can be renegotiated in favor of other, more powerful reinforcers.
3. Because of his history, "beating the system" or disappointing adults, or living up to his reputation as incorrigible is more important than more socially desirable consequences.

The counterproductive behavior, sometimes called "countercontrol," must be dealt with as a problem in its own right. Frequently this can be accomplished by prompting completion of the task to provide the child with exposure to success and accompanying consequences. For example, when the student intentionally answers the questions incorrectly the teacher may prompt and coach him through part of the process by giving correct answers and using a reinforcement procedure for his imitative answer. Once the student has been tagged with the reinforcer he is more likely to try again.

SAMPLE CONTRACTS

Behavioral contracts should specify who, what, when, and where (Enright & Rout, 1979). The following contract, used by one of us with a child who consistently resisted doing mathematics homework, specifies the exact behaviors to be performed by the student and the exact consequences to occur contingent on completion of those behaviors. It provides the name of the contractee and the contractor, specifies the exact behaviors to be performed, and describes the type of reinforcer and its duration and location. Who, what, when, and where are all documented, leaving little room for equivocation. It is structured such that success is highly likely. (Only the names have been changed from the original contract.)

ARITHMETIC CONTRACT 1

This contract between Mrs. Jones and Billy Michaels specifies the conditions under which Billy will be permitted to be the hall monitor. Billy has indicated that he will complete five homework problems in math (problems 1, 3, 5, 7, 9 on page 23) in exchange for the privilege of monitoring the halls the next day, April 7, 1983. He will present the completed problems to me on the morning of that day at 8:30 A.M.. When he successfully complies with this contract, he will also be given the opportunity to create a new contract that will give him a chance to earn further rewards and privileges.

____

Mrs. P. K. Jones

____

Billy Michaels

The second contract is only slightly more demanding than the first. It includes an accuracy criterion, which did not appear on the first contract, and it increases the number of problems. It, too, is designed to make a successful outcome highly probable, by specifying a low level of accuracy, making it easy for the student to meet that criterion.

ARITHMETIC CONTRACT 2

This contract between Mrs. Jones and Billy Michaels specifies the conditions under which Billy will be permitted to be the crossing guard on Monday, April 19, 1983. Billy will perform eight math problems on page 29 (numbers 1, 2, 3, 4, 5, 6, 7, 8). He must obtain at least 50 percent accuracy on this assignment and have the work on my desk by 8:30 A.M. of that morning.

____

Mrs. P. K. Jones

____

Billy Michaels

Each time Billy met the requirements of these and later contracts he was given a new contract, and as he became increasingly familiar with the contracting process, the contractual requirements became more demanding. Eventually, after several weeks of successful, increasingly difficult short-term contracts, a contract was negotiated in which he agreed to maintain continued performance for as long as one week and to perform several concurrent behaviors.

ARITHMETIC CONTRACT 14

This contract between Mrs. Jones and Billy Michaels details the conditions under which Billy will keep his post as school guard for the week of May 10, 1983. Billy has agreed to complete, during this week, all homework assignments given to the class and have them turned in on time. If he keeps his agreement, he will be permitted to continue his position as school guard. On any day that he fails to meet this commitment he will lose the privilege for that day only.

____

Mrs. P. K. Jones

____

Billy Michaels

Terminating Contracts

When teacher and student agree that student performance is occurring at a desirable level but needs some form of continued contractual structure to sustain optimum performance, the teacher may design a terminating contract. Such a contract would specify a group of requirements that should be maintained during the daily work schedule for the remainder of that year. If the criteria are not met on a given day, the student's prerogatives would be revoked for that day, but the contingent privileges might be reinstated the next day if the student once again met the specified conditions. Terminating contracts eliminate the need for continual contract writing, but they should be used only after the student has established a history of successful short-term contract completion.

In the event that a particular contract does not result in a favorable outcome, all is not lost. The contract is simply renegotiated for a shorter term, a lower criterion, or different consequences. If the system fails on a given occasion, remember to check the child's interpretation of the contract. Possibly he doesn't understand the contract terms. Frequently the teacher can either adjust contractual requirements or convince a recalcitrant student that working through a contract is to his personal advantage. If he can be maneuvered into succeeding even once, the chances of persuading him to try again are increased.

Contracting in Perspective

From Cantrell et al. (1969) to Kelly and Stokes (1982) the *Journal of Applied Behavior Analysis* displays a slow transition in contracting methodology. Many studies show a trend toward making negotiation an integral part of behavioral contracting. Personal goal setting and teaching students to design their own self-management system have become important components in this process.

Almost everybody wants something, and almost anything can be negotiated. Given these two axioms, a broad new vista of opportunities awaits the innovative designs of the classroom teacher, student, and parent. Contracting permits all parties to work together to develop a system that will work for everyone. If the system doesn't work initially, nothing is lost; the contract is simply renegotiated, and another attempt is made to establish mutual agreement, success, and satisfaction. Eventually the successful contract is faded out and the child's behavior is maintained by the consequences produced in the natural environment.

REFERENCES

Bailey, J. S., Wolf, M. M., & Phillips, E. L. (1970). Home-based reinforcement and the modification of predelinquents' classroom behavior. *Journal of Applied Behavior Analysis, 3*, 223–233.

Cantrell, R. P., Cantrell, M. L., Huddleston, C. M., & Woolridge, R. L. (1969). Contingency contracting with school problems. *Journal of Applied Behavior Analysis, 2*, 215–220.

Cloward, R. D. (1966). *Studies in tutoring*. U.S. Educational Resources Information Center (ERIC Document Reproduction Series No. ED021 903).

Douds, A. F., Engelsgjard, M., & Collingwood, T. R. (1977). Behavior contracting with youthful offenders and their parents. *Child Welfare, 56*, 409–417.

Eller, B. F., & Eller, B. G. (1977). An empirical evaluation of tutorial behavior contracting on the academic grades of low achieving junior high students. *Improving Human Performance Quarterly, 6*, 133–142.

Enright, B. E., & Rout, M. L. (1979). *Contingency contracting: A technique for developing responsibility and self-control*. Educational Resources Information Center (Document Reproduction Service No. ED216 289).

Homme, L. (1974). *How to use contingency contracting in the classroom*. Champaign, IL: Research Press.

Kelly, M. L., & Stokes, T. F. (1982). Contingency contracting with disadvantaged youths: Improving classroom performance. *Journal of Applied Behavior Analysis, 15*, 447–454.

Kreutzer, V. A. (1973). A study of the use of underachieving students as tutors for emotionally disturbed children (Doctoral dissertation, Brigham Young University). *Dissertation Abstracts International, 34*, 3145A. (University Microfilms No. 73–29, 512)

Premack, D. (1965). Reinforcement theory. In D. Levine (Ed.), *Nebraska symposium on motivation*. Lincoln: University of Nebraska Press, 123–180.

Schumaker, J. B., Hovell, M. F., & Sherman, J. A. (1977). An analysis of daily report cards and parent-managed privileges in the improvement of adolescents' classroom performance. *Journal of Applied Behavior Analysis, 10*, 449–464.

Schwartz, G. J. (1977). College students as contingency managers for adolescents in a program to develop reading skills. *Journal of Applied Behavior Analysis, 10*, 645–655.

Stitely, R. P. (1978). Behavior contracts: A home school cooperative effort. *Peabody Journal of Education, 6*, 318–322.

5

Self-management

Because behavior would cease without a world with which to interact, people can never get away from the behavioral effects of the environment. Yet some do learn to behave in ways that maximize the reinforcement potentials of a complex environment over extended periods. They eschew immediate gratification and keep their noses to the grindstone until the long-term payoffs materialize. They turn their backs on tasty fats and sugars, throw away their cigarettes, exercise regularly, invest their money and go without luxuries, refrain from lecturing their children, and patiently reinforce the behavior they have told their children they want. They go to college for ten years to get an opportunity to do the kind of work they anticipate they will enjoy. They are said to have good self-control, and virtually everyone agrees that good self-control is a desirable characteristic in humans, though probably no one has been observed to be so consistent as the above-described paragons.

Although the phrase ''good self-control'' makes sense as a descriptive term, it leads to serious problems when it is accepted as an explanation of behavior. What is actually controlled is the environment in relation to a person. People who have good self-control have learned how to manage the environment so the environment, in turn, will affect their behavior in line with their long-range goals. And if those long-range goals are in line with the notions of people around them as to what is good and valuable, those others approve of their behavior and extoll their self-control.

The behavior involved in self-control might be more easily understood if the term self-management were used. Everyone is familiar with the notion of management as the manipulation of the environment. Even when people are being managed, managers don't actually do something to the behavior of others. They change the environment—perhaps put up a time clock, tell the employees they must punch in, give small bonuses to those who punch in and none to those who don't, etc. These changes, if effectively implemented, result in changes in the behavior managed. If managing the behavior of someone else amounts to arranging the environment to produce certain behavior, then self-management would amount to arranging the environment to produce changes in one's own behavior.

One of the goals of the educational process is that students be self-managers; but paradoxically the educational establishment wants to—indeed to some extent must—specify the behavior to be managed. That is the only way the culture will be passed on to the next generation. Thus it becomes clear that educators must somehow arrange the environment so that students will learn to manage their own behavior, and the behavior managed will be that which the older, more experienced members of the culture designate as desirable—reading, writing, calculating, speaking politely, cooperating to obtain group goals, playing games and musical instruments, etc.

If students have good self-management skills, then educational personnel will only have to maintain those skills, rather than manage all the contingencies themselves. Of course, the job of teaching the self-management skills remains in all cases except those few where students have learned such skill in previous environments.

Self-management, then, is a learned skill. As in the case of any other learned operant behavior, the behavior of self-management emerges from interactions with the environment. Behavior analysts have recently sought to identify the kinds of interactions that produce self-managing behavior. Call it self-management or self-control—if it can be taught, the teacher's task of managing the classroom environment would be reduced in scope and more feasible. If students had self-management skills, teachers would have more time to manage the instructional environment.

In reviewing the literature on self-control, O'Leary and Dubey (1979) state that the goal in this research has been to teach children to manage on-task behavior so that teacher-maintained contingencies are minimized. The challenge has several dimensions. First, the self-management skills must be learned; second, they must be maintained (ultimately by the products—social or material—of the self-managed behavior); third, self-managing needs to generalize to new areas so that it does not need to be taught from scratch for each new behavior to be managed.

Generalization of self-management has been produced by having students learn nonspecific self-instructions that are capable of influencing a variety of subskills. Polkes, Stewart, and Kahana (1968) had students self-instruct by saying to themselves, "Look and think before I answer." Such heuristic rules, usually stated covertly, prepare the student for carefully attending to forthcoming material. It has been suggested, however, that self-instruction procedures will be maintained only if they occur in conjunction with self-assessment and self-reinforcement (Meichenbaum & Goodman, 1971).

O'Leary and Dubey emphasize that children must be taught, not told, to use self-control procedures. Their method involves a hierarchy of teaching strategies designed to develop the skills necessary for self-instruction. Initially students' use of overt self-instruction is systematically reinforced. Only after they have become overtly proficient do they begin the process of covertly instructing their own behavior. Further, the accuracy of this self-instructing must be checked periodically by external testing. In other words, self-control is a behavior that must be shaped much the same as any newly learned overt behavior. The authors point out that although instruction by others has been successfully faded (Wood & Flynn, 1978), such self-control procedures will need to be supported intermittently by external sources. The self-managing of students will need to be monitored, reinforced, and sometimes even reinstructed.

Although the components of self-control training have varied among researchers, most use variations of the following skills, which are based on those enumerated by Glynn and Thomas (1974).

1. Self-assessment. The student observes her own behavior and decides if her responses are meeting some criteria.
2. Self-recording. The student documents the frequency of her responses that meet the specifications of some criteria.
3. Self-determination of reinforcement. The student specifies the type or amount of consequences contingent on her making the requisite responses.
4. Self-administration of reinforcement. The student has direct access to the reinforcers and makes them contingent on her own performance.

SELF-ASSESSMENT

As O'Leary and Dubey (1979) point out, students who learn self-evaluation techniques in a given classroom will not necessarily be disposed to use these strategies in other locations. Generalization of self-evaluation skills does not occur spontaneously. As has been explained by Baer (1981), generalization of academic skills cannot be anticipated as an automatic result of instruction. Rather, such generalization training should be planned and incorporated into a series of procedures that actively teach the transfer of skills from one setting to another.

In one of the best examples of teaching generalized self-management, Rhode, Morgan, and Young (1983) developed a series of steps for the training of self-evaluation procedures and their transfer from a highly structured setting to regular and resource classrooms. Using two procedural phases, their study was conducted with six behaviorally handicapped elementary students who had consistently demonstrated extreme acting-out behavior in their original regular or resource classes.

In a specifically designed training classroom a sequence of six conditions was used to train students to manage the evaluation and reinforcement of their on-task behavior (phase 1). For periods ranging from fifty to sixty days, three hours a week (one hour two days a week, and a half hour twice a week), students were taught a series of skills relevant to on-task behavior and self-evaluation.

After a ten-day of baseline (condition 1), condition 2 of phase 1 provided students with detailed instructions in proper classroom conduct. Instructors modeled and role-played appropriate academic engagement. Continued feedback was provided as the students learned to approximate appropriate classroom conduct, and a point system was backed up by toys, snacks, and other tangible reinforcers. Points were administered contingent on increasing levels of on-task behavior. Instructors rated each student at the end of successive five-minute intervals according to the quality of the student's behavior. Points were based on a scale of 0 to 5, with 5 being excellent and 0 being unacceptable.

After the students became accustomed to the point system, condition 3 was initiated wherein students attempted to match their evaluations of their own on-task behavior with those of the teachers. Students rated their own classroom behavior and academic performance at the end of each fifteen-minute interval. They were given a bonus point for obtaining the same rating as that given by their instructor. If they were within one point, + or −, of their instructor, they kept the number of points given to themselves. If they were more than one point off the instructor's rating, all points were lost for that particular interval. Eventually the students came to adopt the instructor's performance standards.

As the students developed the ability to accurately self-assess, the frequency with which the instructors provided matching standards was slowly faded out. In condition 4 only one-half the students were compared with the instructor's ratings at each interval. Different students were matched at each interval so that no student could predict when his self-evaluation would come under scrutiny. Condition 5 matched 33 percent of the students and extended the interval to twenty minutes. Condition 6 matched 16 percent at twenty-minute intervals, and condition 7 eliminated instructor matching while extending the assessment and reinforcement interval to thirty minutes. The instructor continued to monitor the self-evaluations for data purposes. The process was essentially one of fading instructor control while shaping the students' self-assessing behavior.

Phase 2 contained seven additional conditions (8 through 14). During phase 2 the program was continued in students' regular or resource classrooms by their teachers. In condition 8 students were asked to self-evaluate every thirty minutes, and they were allowed to keep all the points they earned. However, two or three times a week their regular teacher would randomly match her evaluation with that of a student. This periodic "veracity check" provided continuing feedback to the students regarding their accuracy and honesty. In condition 9 self-evaluation occurred only every sixty minutes, and in condition 10 points earned every hour were exchanged for backup reinforcers on an average of every other day. Surprise teacher monitorings were maintained at least once a week. In condition 11 students were asked to self-evaluate, independent of point exchange, for backup reinforcers. However, teachers continued verbal praise for correct self-evaluation, and general appropriate classroom behavior. Condition 12 discontinued self-evaluation in written form and required only a verbal description from the student to the teacher. Condition 13 extended this form of evaluation to two-day interval averaging. Finally, in condition 14, formal self-evaluation was terminated, but students were encouraged by teachers to continue on their own.

The obvious intent of these sequential steps was the gradual transfer of evaluation from teacher to student. In order to assess the adequacy of this planned generalization procedure, all subjects' on- and off-task behavior was compared, during the three hours of weekly training and the remaining school time. The contrast of individual student on-task means during phase 1 is of special importance. During phase 1, subjects 1, 2, and 4 maintained a mean of 92 percent on task, while subject 3 obtained 96 percent; subject 5, 91 percent; and subject 6, 90 percent during the training sessions. However, comparison with their on-task behavior in their other classrooms during this time provides an illuminating contrast: subject 1, 39 percent; subject 2, 31 percent; subject 3, 34 percent; subject 4, 58 percent; subject 5, 28 percent; and subject 6, 39 percent. Apparently the self-evaluation procedure did not spontaneously generalize to the other classrooms.

As the self-evaluation procedures were transferred to their other regular and resource classes during phase 2, on-task percentages for all six students eventually increased in these locations. Subjects 1, 3, 4, and 5 averaged 93 percent on task. Subjects 2 and 6 required booster sessions of training and performed slightly below the other subjects, but they eventually gained high rates of appropriate behavior in regular and resource classes. All subjects demonstrated elevated levels of appropriate behavior throughout phase 2, despite the fading of the rigorous self-evaluation training procedure initiated in phase 1.

Social validation was provided by comparing the experimental subjects' mean on-task behavior after training with that of the subjects' peers in their regular classes. Subsequent to treatment, randomly selected classmates averaged 94 percent on task, while the experimental subjects who had previously been referred for extreme acting out averaged 92 percent in the same classes. This provides strong evidence not only that the self-evaluation was effective, but also that, by the end of phase 2, the subjects' behavior was now comparable to their "normal" peers.

It is important to note that procedures used during phase 1, in the experimental setting, were too intense and demanding to be practical for implementation by the regular classroom teachers. But as stated by the authors, "the ultimate goal of Phase I procedures was to reduce teacher requirements to proportions manageable by a regular classroom teacher while still maintaining high levels of appropriate classroom behavior by the student" (Rhode et al., 1983, p. 186). Thus, by the time the special training ended, the students were proficient enough in self-evaluation that their teachers could maintain and increase that behavior in regular and resource classrooms. Eventually these students became so well self-managed that they were capable of operating effectively without any more supervision than their peers required.

Although this study provides an excellent series of procedures for training self-assessment, it could have been enhanced by acquiring data relevant to academic performance. It is one thing to provide information proving that students are more likely to conduct themselves appropriately in class after learning to self-evaluate; it is quite another to demonstrate improved scholastic performance as a function of this intervention. Fortunately another study conducted that same year implemented similar procedures but measured the effects in terms of academic performance.

SELF-RECORDING

McLaughlin and Truhlicka (1983) also attempted to improve the quality of self-control by means of matching student and teacher assessments; however, the dependent variables were measured in terms of both accuracy of self-recording and academic performance. This study was initiated in a self-contained special education classroom that was already operating on a point reinforcer token system. Points were earned and lost according to typical behavior management procedures in the classroom.

Subjects were twelve "behaviorally disordered" students placed in three experimental groups, four subjects to each group within the class. Each group was exposed to a different set of contingencies during a daily ninety-minute reading period. Depending on whether they were on task or off task during the period, the self-recording group was told to simply place a + or a − on small squares of a dittoed data sheet. No extra points were given for accurate self-recording. The self-recording + matching group used the same format as above; however, they were awarded 20 extra points for matching their total number of on-task squares with the total their teacher recorded. A control group was differentially awarded points on the basis of accuracy of academic performance alone. No self-recording was performed.

The authors specify two dependent variables: accuracy of self-recording and percentage of academic work performed correctly. Accuracy of self-assessment was checked by comparing the students' data sheets with the totals determined by the teacher and the teacher aides who observed throughout the period. However, both the students and the staff documented on task and off task at erratic intervals throughout the period. Unlike the Rhode et al. (1983) study, no attempt was made to match student and teacher observation intervals. When both student and teacher are observing the same phenomena, but the observations are not occurring at the same points in time, reliability is in doubt, even when acceptable coefficients of reliability are presented.

The other dependent variable, percentage of work performed correctly, is a better index of change. Pretests from the daily reading workbook ranged from

50 percent to 54 percent for all three groups. Posttesting revealed no change for controls; however, the self-recording group rose to an average of 65 percent and the self-recording + matching group came up to 92 percent. These improvements were sustained in a six-month follow-up after treatment. The Mann-Whitney *U* tests indicated significant differences between all three groups.

This study does extend the research of Rhode et al. (1983) by providing data on self-assessment as it positively affects student academic performance; however, using inferential statistics to validate an effect is usually not considered the most useful method. A better measure of the power of the procedure would have been observation of individual changes in performance over time by means of single-subject data. This study was concerned with group data, rather than with each individual as such. Finally it is hoped that future research might be aimed at both on-task behavior and accuracy in academic performance as they are commonly affected by the independent variable of self-evaluation.

Other self-control investigations have negated the need for some of the detailed instructional and shaping procedures used in generating externally validated self-assessment. These procedures assume accurate assessment by the student and simply require that the student record the frequency of target responses. This procedure is evidently effective in increasing on-task behavior of students with a history of minimal compliance in the classroom. Broden, Hall, and Mitts (1971) performed two experiments that demonstrated the viability of having students simply record their own behavior without benefit of training in self-assessment.

In experiment 1 an eighth-grade girl with poor study and attending skills, who had expressed an interest in doing better, was given an opportunity to record her own on-task behavior. Using prepared self-recording sheets that segmented a math period into short intervals, the girl was instructed to keep track of her own attending behavior. The instructions were: "At different times during the period (whenever you think of it, but don't fill them all at the same time) put down a '+' if you were studying, '−' if you weren't" (Broden et al., 1971, p. 193). This strategy was alternated with reversal periods in which the student was not given the chance to self-record. It was found that self-recording was correlated with an increase from about 30 percent to 80 percent in her on-task behavior. Under these conditions her teacher felt more "justified" in giving her attention. When self-recording was combined with a phase in which the teacher made a special effort to praise her on-task behavior, her performance increased to 88 percent on task. At this point the experimenters felt that her study behavior had come under the control of improved grades (from D− to C) so that it was no longer necessary for her to maintain the self-recording procedure. Happily, she continued to perform at approximately the same improved rate of study behavior.

A second experiment conducted by these authors investigated the use of self-recording as an intervention technique to decrease talking out behavior. A student who was especially verbose was instructed to record episodes of inappropriate vocalizations in class. Alternating periods of self-recording with baseline periods, a marginal improvement was observed during treatment. However, data maintained by both the student and an independent observer suggested that even this marginal improvement was not sustained when there was no attempt by the teacher to follow through by praising the student's improved performance. Broden et al. suggest "that secondary level teachers were sometimes reluctant to carry out procedures that did not seem to fit their teaching style" (Broden et al., 1971, p. 197).

After Broden et al.'s demonstration of the effectiveness of self-recording, Glynn, Thomas, and Shee (1973) sought to determine if similar tactics might positively affect on-task behavior of lower grade–level children. Their subjects were a random sample of eight second-grade children from a regular education classroom. These students had presented no special problem for their teacher but were not spending as much time on task as might ensure their academic progress. During a series of daily thirty-minute lessons constituting baseline, it was found that these eight children spent only about 58 percent of their time actually engaged in schoolwork. This may be representative of many schoolchildren operating in regular education classrooms.

In order to facilitate self-recording, tape-recorded beeps were programmed for random emission from a tape recorder at one-, two-, three-, four-, or five-minute intervals such that ten beeps were heard at irregular intervals by the class within every thirty-minute period. Children were instructed to place a check on a piece of prepared data sheet if they had been on task at the moment the beep sounded. This schedule is somewhat comparable to a variable-interval schedule of reinforcement except that the subjects, rather than someone else, determined whether the requisite responses actually occurred. Reinforcement consisted of the exchange of one minute of free time for each recording check. During this phase and a subsequent four-week follow-up, group on-task behavior maintained at an average of 93 percent. Reversal caused a drop to 75 percent on-task behavior, and reinstatement of self-control contingencies returned the class to an average of 90 percent on-task behavior. Reliability of "self-assessment" was high, given the ages of the children assessing their own behavior. Independent observers indicated that 76 percent of the self-assessed on-task determinations correlated with those of observers. Students gave themselves too much credit for being on task only 15 percent of the time, and actually underestimated their academic engagement 9 percent of the time. The subjects in this study did not have a history of serious behavior disorders, and thus they were perhaps more amenable to this simplified self-control procedure.

Glynn and Thomas (1974) note that the procedures above have been effective in improving the level of on-task behavior, but that under some circumstances students may become confused as to whether they have fulfilled the criteria for on-task behavior. For example, students who might be in the process of completing one phase of the teacher's assignment when she gives instructions to begin another assignment may rate themselves as being off task. In fact, any time a lesson is in transition, and the student finds himself lagging behind the teacher's instructions, he may assess his behavior as being off task. Under such circumstances the reliability of self-recording suffers, and the reinforcement contingencies are less than fully effective.

Glynn and Thomas (1974) attempted to eliminate this problem by introducing a procedure to be used in conjunction with self-recording. Using the standard ABAB design, they chose nine students described as generally off task, for another experiment.

During a ten-day baseline taken during fifty minutes of oral and written language lessons, the students were observed to be on task an average of 49.6 percent of the period. It was also noted that the teacher made frequent transitions in class assignments. The period usually began with a question-and-answer session; the remainder of the time was spent completing written assignments. In the initial ten-day treatment condition an intermittent audio signal occurred at random intervals, ranging from 1 to 5 minutes. Students were instructed to place a check on a card if they were on task. These checks were totaled and exchanged for free time in an adjacent recreational area at the end of the period.

Data indicated an increase to 69.8 percent on task during the first treatment condition. A reversal to baseline resulted in a gradual drop to an average 50.78 percent on-task behavior. At this stage these procedures did not differ from those used in the previous study. It was not until the second ten-day treatment that the procedures became more sophisticated and, unfortunately, less clearly delineated. These researchers made the methodological error of instituting two concurrent changes in treatment. They simultaneously shortened the cueing interval to one to three minutes and initiated the use of a behavior specification chart. The behavior specification chart clearly stated the two behaviors expected of all students during the fifty-minute lesson. The students were to be either (a) in their seats and attending to the teacher, or (b) working at their places, involved in reading or writing.

Thus students could more easily define their own activity during the period. Although this change in procedure may have simplified self-recording for the subjects, it may have complicated assessment of the research findings. It would be difficult to know which variable, a shortened cueing interval or the behavior specification chart, accounted for the observed improvement. As a matter of fact, the students' on-task behavior jumped to 91.11 percent under these new conditions. The authors speculated that the primary variable affecting the increase was using the behavioral chart. This chart ostensibly reduced the students' confusion as to what counted as on task when the teacher gave new instruction while the students were working on a previously assigned task. This may well have been the case. Unfortunately, since the cueing interval was simultaneously shortened, the methodological error does not permit a clear statement regarding what accounted for the outcome.

It is apparent from the studies above that not all students require exhaustive instruction and shaping of self-assessment skills before monitoring their own classroom behavior. For students who are interested in improving their own academic behavior, as in the Broden et al. (1971) study, or who are only occasionally disruptive, direct use of self-recording alone may be a reasonable and simple intervention. However, interventions with students who have severer behavior disorders may require the type of elaborate procedures described by Rhode et al. (1983).

SELF-RECORDING OF ACADEMIC PERFORMANCE

A study by Knapczyk and Livingston (1973) targeted reading performance of students who recorded their own academic improvement. These authors noted that three primary problems were associated with the successful administration of a classroom token economy: (1) adequate training of supervisory personnel; (2) the extrinsic, rather than inherent, character of reinforcers; and (3) maintenance of accurate data. In order to compensate for these frequently occurring problems, they implemented a series of treatments in a junior high special education classroom. Thirteen seventh-, eighth-, and ninth-grade students served as subjects during their fifty-minute reading period. During this instructional time these students were required to read material from a sequential reading series (SRA Reading Laboratories). After completing their individual assignments they each answered comprehension questions specifically prepared in their respective selections. As previously indicated, the dependent variable in this study was the reading performance. This was assessed in terms of the percentage of correctly answered comprehension questions.

During the nineteen-day baseline recording these subjects obtained 69.47 percent accuracy on their reading selections. In the following twenty-four-day treatment a token system and self-recording procedure were instituted.

> Upon completion of the Baseline I condition, the students were presented with individual work record books in which they were instructed to enter the percent of correct responses on their daily reading assignments. A conversion chart, which could be used to determine percentage values from the number of correct responses, was available for their use. They were also told that they would earn a particular amount of money based upon their recorded reading performance, and that payment would be made on the last day of each week. Space was provided in the work records for the students to keep an up-to-date account of their earnings. (Knapczyk & Livingston, 1973, p. 482)

Subjects exchanged their earnings daily for various school-related activities. These activities were seen by the authors as being both beneficial for students and an intrinsic part of the school environment. They typically consisted of such potentially enriching behaviors as "listening to stories, Milton-Bradley's Phonetic Quizmo, teacher-constructed language games," or the earnings "could be saved for nine-week payoffs, which included buying the materials necessary to make various craft and homemaking products and/or partake in a field trip" (Knapczyk & Livingston, 1973, p. 483).

By using enriching activities as intrinsic reinforcers, the authors had planned that reinforcement would be a consistent part of their academic endeavors. Although it is clear from the following data that these activities did, in fact, serve as reinforcers, it is not clear that they functioned any better than extrinsic reinforcers (toys, food, free time, etc.), or that their use was directly related to special academic improvement. For this to have been accomplished it would have been necessary to have compared extrinsic and intrinsic reinforcers, which was not part of the experimental manipulation. However, the data from this condition do strongly suggest that the students did perform at improved reading comprehension levels when provided tools for self-recording and tokens for reading comprehension performance. Mean reading accuracy for this group increased 13.45 percent over baseline and averaged 82.92 percent.

In the next phase of the experiment, baseline conditions were reinstated for ten days. This resulted in an immediate return to prior lower levels of reading comprehension (approximately 70 percent) seen in the original baseline. After this return to baseline and demonstration of the independent effects of the previous Token and Self-recording procedures, the subjects were returned to the initial treatment condition for eighteen days. During the second Token and Self-recording phase the reading levels averaged about 82 percent.

The students were then exposed to a variation of that treatment for eight days. In this phase a student teacher was placed in charge of organizing the class's token economy and self-recording of reading comprehension levels. Although the student teacher was unfamiliar with the principles of the token system and the special class teacher was removed from the classroom setting, the token system and students' self-recording appeared to work quite well. Mean reading comprehension levels maintained at the high levels seen during the first and second treatment phases (84.37 percent). When the special class teacher resumed her regular duties after four days (Token and Self-recording III), the comprehension levels remained constant.

The researchers next attempted to assess the independent effects of token reinforcement with effects of self-recording removed (Token I). In this four-day period all student record books were removed, but students continued to earn tokens, and payoffs were made at the end of the school week. This change did not significantly influence student reading levels. After this transition a new variation was implemented for four more days. A second inexperienced teacher was placed in charge of the class, but this time self-recording was not utilized. This time there was a visible drop in student performance. For reasons that are not adequately explained by the authors, reading level fell to about 77 percent. This may have been due to the idiosyncratic effects of the new student teacher or some other evasive variable. In any case, the authors make no attempt to explain this small deceleration, and it is left to the reader to speculate as to what variables may have been responsible for this small interruption in high student reading comprehension levels. However, in the next four days, self-recording was returned to the treatment package (Token, Self-recording, and Student

Teacher) under the direction of the student teacher. This is correlated with an increase in student performance to about 84 percent accuracy. Statistical procedures could not rule out chance as accounting for this difference, so self-recording may or may not have been responsible for the 7 percent improvement.

In the final four-day phase of the study the original special classroom teacher resumed her full-time duties. At this time the self-recording procedure was again terminated. Coincident with transition to the exclusive use of a token economy and termination of self-recording, a slight decrease occurred in the mean accuracy of reading comprehension, to about 78 percent. This represented about a 6 percent drop from the previous phase in which self-recording had been utilized. Although this was found not to be statistically significant, a graph of the ongoing data gives the impression that a conspicuous reduction in student performance occurred at the time at which this final phase was introduced. Not surprisingly, a comprehensive statistical analysis of the entire study revealed differences not attributable to chance only between the baseline sessions and the treatment sessions. No significant differences among treatments were found.

The authors do not claim that the self-recording procedure facilitated the students' academic performance. They refrain from doing so probably because their post hoc comparisons between means, using the Scheffe Test, failed to find further differences other than those found between treatments and baseline conditions. According to the authors, "no significant effects were observed between the token, token and self-recording, token and student teacher, and token, self-recording, and student teacher conditions." This does not mean that changes in student performance did not occur. It means that chance (or unknown events) cannot be statistically ruled out as accounting for the observed changes. However, visual inspection of the graph provided in this study suggests that during two separate experimental conditions, the token plus self-recording phases were superior to the token only phases.

In closing, the authors state that the educational reinforcers (school supplies and activities) served as adequate reinforcers. They go on to note that the students appeared perfectly capable of recording their own progress on their individual worksheets. Teacher reliability checks indicated only one instance of a discrepancy between student and teacher data. In addition, it was pointed that even the student teachers, who had essentially no experience in running token programs, were able to demonstrate improved student reading comprehension when the token economies were used.

SELF-MONITORING OF ATTENTION OR PRODUCTIVITY

Many researchers have argued that an active academic response is crucial to learning. Simply increasing time spent on task does not necessarily improve academic performance, these researchers maintain. Self-monitoring frequently has the reactive effect of increasing the rate of the behavior monitored. In this context, self-monitoring contains components of both self-assessment and self-recording. Harris (1986), unable to find any studies that compared self-monitoring of on-task behavior with self-monitoring of an active academic performance variable, investigated the effects of the two self-monitoring procedures on academic performance and on-task behavior among learning disabled elementary school children. She hypothesized that self-monitoring in both cases would increase time on task, but that self-monitoring of academic performance would lead to greater increases in academic performance.

The subjects of the study were four learning disabled students, two male and two female, nine to ten years old. Their achievement scores were two or more years below grade or age level in at least two academic areas. These students were recommended for the study because their teacher considered them to have "significant attentional and productivity problems." IQ scores ranged from 85 to 115 on the Weschler Intelligence Scale of Children–Revised.

This study was conducted in the regular classroom in the morning, during a fifteen-minute spelling session. All students in the class used a six-step study technique to complete a spelling worksheet and study their words: "Look at the word, close eyes and spell the word out loud, study the word again, cover the word, write the word three times, and check spelling" (Graham 1983 [cited in Harris, 1986, p. 418]). All students had demonstrated proficiency in this study technique. None spelled any words incorrectly during the study period.

During baseline the students used this six-step technique to study their spelling words. A counterbalanced multiple-baseline design was used for the study, with the order of the interventions reversed for two subjects. Interventions consisted of two dependent variables, on-task behavior and academic productivity. These were measured as self-monitoring of attention and self-monitoring of productivity.

On-task behavior or attention was defined as eyes focused on book, paper, or self-monitoring card, lips moving with eyes closed, writing words, and checking words. On-task behavior was measured by the teacher during the last ten minutes of the spelling period three or four times a week, using two-second interval time sampling. Students were not told anyone was being watched, and the teacher was not aware of any theoretical rationale for the study. Reliability was assessed by a trained observer during 32 percent of the sessions, resulting in a percentage of agreement reliability coefficient of 90 percent to 98 percent (mean of 94 percent).

Academic productivity was defined as total number of times a student correctly wrote spelling words. Interrater reliability was 100 percent.

The first intervention, self-monitoring of attention, followed a procedure established by Hallahan, Lloyd, Kauffman, and Loper (1983). The student was taught to ask, "Was I paying attention?" each time a tape-recorded tone occurred. The tone sounded on an average of every forty-five seconds. The student then made a check mark under "yes" or "no" on a scorecard on the desk. Again, this follows the same procedure frequently described as self-assessment. The teacher monitored compliance and found no failures to follow the self-monitoring procedure.

The second intervention, self-monitoring of productivity, involved counting the number of spelling words written during the period and recording this on a graph. This self-recording was found to be highly accurate.

For all four students, on-task behavior increased significantly over baseline during both self-monitoring procedures. Baseline on-task measures ranging from 32 percent to 57 percent increased during monitoring on-task measures to between 77 percent to 91 percent; during productivity monitoring on-task measures ranged between 75 percent and 98 percent.

Results were not as clear for academic response rate. Baseline scores ranged from 14 percent to 32 percent, attention monitoring scores ranged from 27 percent to 44 percent, and productivity scores ranged from 47 percent to 78 percent. Subject 1's academic productivity was the same under both conditions; subject 2's was superior during the productivity monitoring. For subjects 3 and 4, mean productivity was higher during productivity monitoring, but decreasing trends appeared over the two conditions, making it difficult to determine whether productivity monitoring was more effective.

At the end of the second self-monitoring phase, subjects were required to choose one of the two procedures with which to continue. Two subjects chose productivity monitoring, one switched from one to the other, and the fourth combined both procedures.

To assess social validity, the author asked the teacher and subjects about perceived effectiveness of the interventions, personal preferences, and recommendations. All recommended self-monitoring of productivity but also thought that monitoring of attention was important. Harris states that "self-monitoring of productivity also appeared to elicit goal setting in that subjects enjoyed meeting or beating previous personal scores (p. 422)." The teacher considered both self-monitoring procedures to be feasible and easy to implement in the classroom setting. Harris concludes by stating that "these results indicate that self-monitoring alone can be a powerful intervention and that self-monitoring of academic performance variables is a promising research direction (p. 423)."

SELF-SPECIFICATION OF REINFORCEMENT

Self-specification of reinforcement is the label given to a procedure in which the student specifies what, how much, or how often consequences are obtained relative to her classroom performance. This procedure is often called "self-determination of reinforcement," but the word *determination* has such a variety of meanings that it will not be used. *Specification* more clearly defines what the student actually does in this self-management procedure.

Controversy exists as to the value and need for self-specified reinforcement. Several studies have indicated that there is little difference in whether the work standards are determined by the pupil or by the teacher (Bandura & Perloff, 1967; Felixbrod & O'Leary, 1973; Switzky & Haywood, 1974). However, other studies have found that pupil-selected reinforcement standards improved academic performance more than teacher-selected standards.

In one of the first studies addressing this issue, Lovitt and Curtiss (1969) analyzed the effect of allowing a twelve-year-old behaviorally disordered student to impose his own academic contingencies. In order to evaluate this procedure it was necessary to compare teacher-imposed and self-imposed contingencies. Further, it was important to know if the child's understanding of the reinforcement contingency was important for the efficacy of this procedure. Thus three stages of treatment needed to be examined: (1) teacher-imposed contingencies independent of an explanation of the reinforcement contingency, (2) teacher-imposed contingencies with an explanation of the reinforcement contingencies, and (3) student-specification of reinforcement contingencies for his own behavior.

During a nine-day baseline the teachers did not specify any responses-per-point relationship, although the student was given points and backup free time for completion of various assignments throughout the school day. In the second twelve days of baseline the contingent relationship between earning of points and completing of each of the assignments was verbally explained and a written description of the points per assignment was given to the student. During both baseline stages student academic response rate was stable, with medians of 1.8 and 1.65 academic responses per minute, respectively. This lack of variability ruled out the possibility that simply understanding the response to reinforcement relationship was a critical factor.

At this point the student was permitted to specify the number of points he could earn for each assignment. After completing each assignment the student was asked to state the number of points he had earned. This procedure resulted in an immediate increase in on-task behavior. During the twenty-two daily sessions the student maintained a median rate of 2.5 academic responses per minute. For the last seven days the teacher again imposed the academic contingencies, and the student response rate dropped to 1.9, a good indication that the self-imposed contingencies were responsible for the boy's improved performance.

Four weeks later the authors performed experiment 2, which replicated the procedure with the same child. The results of the second study buttressed the validity of the procedure by way of intrasubject replication. However, a confounding variable in the study precludes a clear statement regarding why the procedure was effective. That is, when the students specified the number of points earned, they increased the rate of reinforcement. The question remained as to whether the improved performance was a function of the student's opportunity to specify the reinforcement, or the actual amount of reinforcement provided when the reinforcement was self-specified.

In experiment 3, the teacher first arranged the responses-per-point contingency to match the baseline requirements of experiments 1 and 2. Subsequently the teacher changed the requirements so that it matched that which the student himself had imposed in self-specification phases of the earlier experiments. Lastly, the contingencies were again arranged according to the teacher's original specification. Student performance remained consistent throughout. It is important that although the reinforcement amount changed during the experiment, all three conditions involved teacher-imposed contingencies and all three conditions produced a relatively constant effect on the student's academic response-per-minute rate. Thus the data strongly indicate that, at least for this student, self-specified contingencies of reinforcement were associated with increased performance and that the amount of reinforcement was probably not a relevant variable affecting response rate. As suggested in the chapter on contracting, permitting some subjects to have input into the arrangement of their own contingencies facilitates compliance with academic contingencies.

Dickerson and Creedon (1981) replicated this study in an effort to identify the particular conditions that may account for the added effectiveness of self-selected reinforcement. They used thirty regular education students from second and third grades. Ten students were randomly assigned to each of three experimental groups designated as pupil-selected standards group, yoked experimental group, and no-contingency control group. The dependent variables were the number of written words and the number of correctly solved problems during reading and math periods, respectively. All students were exposed to five days of baseline during which they spent ten minutes on a writing assignment and ten minutes on a math assignment. Subjects worked independently in small groups of five and received feedback concerning the accuracy of their work within twenty-five minutes of completion. Baseline performance was similar for the three groups. Number of words correctly written ranged from 26.02 to 28.28, and the number of correct math problems ranged from 5.48 to 7.66.

In the next five days of treatment the timing of assignments remained the same, but the groups were treated according to their respective reinforcement contingencies. The no-contingency control group was told that they might receive some prizes at the end of the program. Students in the experimental group decided individually how many points writing and problem solving were worth (self-specification of reinforcement). The yoked experimental group was told the number of points each correct problem was worth. The number was based on the number of points selected by each subject's match in the self-selected experimental group.

Results clearly showed that both pupil- and teacher-selected standards of reinforcement improved the students' performance over baseline, but the pupil-selected standards group improved the most during the experimental period. The pupil-selected standards group averaged 40.26 correctly written words and 15.52 correct math problems during the experimental phase, whereas the teacher-selected standards group averaged only 31.64 and 9.16, respectively. The no-contingency group did not perform above baseline levels.

The authors attribute the discrepancy between these results and other research that did not find any difference between pupil-selected and teacher-selected standards to the confounding of previous designs by order effects. That is, previous research frequently allowed students exposure to both teacher-selected and self-selected reinforcers at various stages of the experiment. This may have dampened the effect of self-selection. The authors also note that in their study the students were permitted to select from an unlimited range of point values. The novelty of this arrangement may have contributed to the reinforcing value of the point system. Lastly, they note that, unlike the Felixbrod and O'Leary (1973) study, the students were not left unattended during the work period, nor were they permitted to leave the room on their own. The authors speculate that this "social surveillance" may have been a factor that affected both standard setting and work output.

As previously noted, Felixbrod and O'Leary (1973) also investigated the issue of self-specified reinforcement as it affects increased levels of on-task behavior in the classroom. However, one of their primary concerns revolved around the possible "cognitive" side effects of self-determined reinforcements as described in previous research by Bandura and Perloff (1967). In the Bandura and Perloff experiment it was suggested that when permitted to self-determine the amount of their own reinforcement, some children imposed severer performance requirements than those imposed by the teacher. Bandura and Perloff noted that such children may have failed to optimize reinforcement because they judged the quality of their work to be poor, and thus felt hesitant to demand increased amounts of reinforcement even when it was available.

Although it might be suggested that such behavior is inconsistent with operant theory, that is not the case. The behavior of specifying is itself operant behavior. Reasons for a student's specifying smaller amounts of reinforcement when larger amounts could be specified would best be sought in the student's history. A not unreasonable hypothesis is that students have learned to judge what a performance is "worth" as a result of previous social contingencies. It also seems likely that such students could learn to specify consequences more to their immediate advantage if a reinforcement procedure were used to shape their judging behavior.

There are other, methodological points to consider, too, in the Bandura and Perloff study. First, it should be understood that only six of twenty subjects made such a disadvantageous determination for less than optimal reinforcement. Second, and more important, during the one occasion on which subjects were given the opportunity to self-specify the amount of reinforcement, they were not exposed to the backup reinforcers until after the experiment was completed. As pointed out by Felixbrod and O'Leary, all too often researchers using human subjects assume that the promise of something, in this case a token, is equivalent to the actual delivery of the thing. But this is simply not true. Tokens only function as reinforcers after they have been exchanged for backup reinforcers. Until such time as backup reinforcement is provided, tokens can only be accurately described as cues or discriminative stimuli for particular behaviors. Thus Bandura and Perloff may have been somewhat rash in assuming that some of their subjects actually acted so as to decrease the amount of available reinforcement. Because the tokens had not been conditioned as reinforcers, the subjects' behavior never resulted in a reinforcement procedure. These subjects were, in fact, never reinforced during the course of the experiment. They were only "promised" reinforcement.

Felixbrod and O'Leary went on to further investigate the changes in on-task behavior that occur when subjects are given the opportunity to select the amount of reinforcement. using a 3 × 6 factorial design, three groups of eight second-grade children were matched according to sex and arithmetic skill. Subjects were exposed to one of three conditions for six twenty-minute sessions occurring three days a week. The three experimental conditions consisted of the following:

1. A self-specified reinforcement standard, in which the subjects were permitted to choose how many points could be earned for each correct answer. Subjects could earn from 1 to 10 points for each correct answer, depending on their own selection. Points were exchanged daily for backup reinforcers.
2. An externally imposed performance standard in which matched subjects were individually yoked to subjects in the self-specification condition. The members of this group were assigned the same point-reinforcer ratio as was selected by the matched counterparts in the self-specification group.
3. A control group that received no reinforcement, but was given the same sort of arithmetic problems as the other two groups.

The two reinforcement groups performed equally well with regard to the total number of correct problems and time spent on task. Subjects who had specified the number of points to be earned per problem as well as those who had their earning rate specified by someone else both averaged a higher number of correct solutions and spent more time on task than the nonreinforcement group. The rate of correct problem solving increased across the six sessions for both groups. However, the control nonreinforced problem-solving group declined in rate.

Contrary to the outcome described in the research by Bandura and Perloff (1967), Felixbrod and O'Leary found "a consistent trend in the direction of more lenient self-imposed performance standards across the six sessions" (Felixbrod & O'Leary, 1973, p. 248). Initially several students chose a rigorous performance standard; however, by the sixth session all students were operating so as to receive all points possible per problems solved.

All of these data seem to indicate that although children will tend to take advantage of the best reinforcement rate available, they will not necessarily perform less adequately while doing so. For both time on task and total number of correct problems solved, no difference was found between subjects who chose their reinforcement rate and those who had their reinforcement rate imposed. Unlike the previously cited studies (Lovitt & Curtiss, 1969; Dickerson & Creedon, 1981), the critical variable for both on-task behavior and academic performance related to the probability of obtaining reinforcement, not whether the subject or teacher determined the reinforcement contingency.

Glynn (1970) also applied the concept of self-specification of reinforcement to classroom learning. He compared self-specified and experimenter-specified token reinforcers to establish the effects of withdrawal of these procedures after treatment. Subjects in the experiment consisted of 128 ninth-grade girls selected from four intact classes in a Toronto school. The author emphasized that all of these students appeared well motivated and that disruption or other behavior problems were not a concern during the course of the research.

This study combined a reversal design with a group statistical procedure. During baseline observation all subjects were exposed to a two-week testing period during which they were given three-minute reading passages in history and geography. After each reading they were tested for three minutes. Then, during the Token I phase, for ten days, subjects in all four groups worked from 500-word reading sheets and answered twenty five-option multiple-choice questions. The dependent variable was the average number of correct answers in each group. Four separate alphabetically assigned classes of thirty to thirty-four girls were each provided with one of the following treatment procedures:

1. Experimenter-specified rate of reinforcement (one token for four correct answers)
2. Self-specified rate of reinforcement (subjects individually decided how many tokens they earned)
3. Chance-determined rate of reinforcement (subjects were yoked on a daily basis to the number of tokens earned by a subject in the self-specified group)
4. No-token group (this group received no form of programmed reinforcement, token or otherwise, throughout the course of the study)

Analysis of covariance performed on the Token I phase revealed the between-classes effect as statistically significant ($p < .001$). All pairwise adjusted means were tested, using the Neuman-Keuls procedure. Both the self-specified reinforcement group and the experimenter-specified reinforcement group demonstrated significant increases in their daily test scores over the nonreinforced and the chance-reinforced groups. Surprisingly a ten-day reversal to baseline (in which all reinforcement was withdrawn from all groups) maintained the same effects as in Token I phase, although a smaller magnitude of these differences was evident. Apparently the positive effects of reinforcement during the Token I phase had a strong carry-over effect that continued after treatment.

To gauge whether the students whose behavior was originally reinforced according to the experimenter's imposed standards would continue with these same standards when given an opportunity to self-specify reinforcement, a second token phase was implemented. In this phase all students, except the nonreinforcement group, were permitted to specify individually how many tokens they earned at each session. The data obtained in this phase are more difficult to interpret. A statistical test yielded a weak effect overall. But tests on differences among individual means suggested that any differences could be accounted for by chance. The graphed data for the self-reinforcement and experimenter-reinforcement groups show increases in performance across the sessions of this phase, and the chance-reinforcement group performed at a level lower than the non-reinforcement control group throughout this phase. The author (Glynn, 1970) suggested that the inconsistent relationship between student behavior and token reinforcement in the chance-reinforcement group accounted for the absence of performance increments in phase 1, and the effects of that experience carried over into phase 2 when the students specified the reinforcement level.

During a final five-day baseline of token withdrawal and five days of token reinforcement, there was little performance decrement for the groups receiving experimenter- or self-specified reinforcement. During the last five days the reinstated tokens appeared to have little effect on student behavior. Glynn suggested that the effect of the backup reinforcers was beginning to diminish by this time and noted that a wider menu of more interesting and diversified backup reinforcers might have sustained the initial impact of the reinforcement procedure.

Several important points emerge from this study. Of particular interest is that the group that self-specified reinforcement and the experimenter-specified reinforcement group performed similarly throughout all phases of the study. This occurred despite the fact that the reinforcement ratio for the self-specified group was not as favorable as that for the teacher-specified group. In other words, in this study the self-specified reinforcement group produced more correct answers per token than any other group.

GENERALIZATION OF SELF-ASSESSMENT

The extent of treatment generalization has become an increasingly popular topic in the self-assessment portion of the self-management literature. In fact, sixteen categories of generalization have been specified by Drabman, Hammer, and Rosenbaum (1979). In an attempt to illustrate the various generalization parameters associated with self-management, Stevenson and Fantuzzo (1984) applied a comprehensive self-management program to an underachieving fifth-grade regular education student. Intervention consisted of only two two-hour sessions in which the student was given the "opportunity" to become an "employee" of the researcher if he were interested in doing so. Employment consisted of the student (employee) learning math skills. The treatment consisted of the following steps:

1. Goal setting for problem completion
2. Recording the number of correct problems completed
3. Comparison of goals with the number correct
4. Student-delivery of a gold star for reaching his self-specified goal
5. Exchange of stars for items from a menu of reinforcers

In the first two-hour session math skills were taught, specifically those procedures that require modeling, the rehearsal of new behaviors, and matching.

The second two-hour session required simulation of math drill on problems like those occurring in the regular class. The student received feedback from the "employer" regarding the appropriateness of his goal setting and the accuracy of his checklist, as well as praise for correct use of these self-management procedures. A similar system was developed for the student's homework assignment.

When the in-class phase of the program began, the employer met the employee on a weekly basis to review earnings and exchange stars for backup reinforcers. The student had the option of either spending his gold stars each week or saving them for more expensive items at a later time. Interestingly, this study concurrently measured generalization effects of this intervention on the untreated behavior of a second student, who sat adjacent to the subject.

Using an ABAB single-subject design, it was found that both math performance and on-task behavior were positively affected. The experimental student averaged only 28.7 correct problems during eleven days of baseline. The first six-day treatment brought his average up to 54.2. A six-day reversal to baseline caused a reduction to 41.2 and a thirteen-day reinstatement produced a dramatic reacceleration to 96.7 correct problems. At the end of a two-month follow-up the student had maintained most of his academic gains, averaging 78.2 correct problems. Homework performance and observation of on-task behavior followed the same general trends during treatments and reversals. Interestingly, the untreated subject, who sat adjacent to the subject, showed gains and regressions correlated with the subject's improvements and regressions. However, the transitions for this untreated subject were not as large.

The real focus of this study did not relate to direct treatment outcomes. The primary concerns of these researchers revolved around generalization. Using fifteen of the sixteen kinds of generalization originally specified by Drabman et al. (1979) the treatment was found to generalize as follows:

(a) *behavior* generalization (decreases in disruptive behavior in school setting);
(b) *setting* generalization (increases in math performance in the home setting);
(c) *behavior-setting* generalization (decreases in disruptive behavior in the home setting where training did not occur);
(d) *time* generalization (sustained treatment levels of math performance in the school setting during follow-up);
(e) *setting-time* (increases in math performance that were maintained in the home setting during follow-up).

Generalization was not present across the following classes for the treated subject:

(a) *behavior-time* (decreases in disruptive behavior in the school setting during follow-up;
(b) *behavior-setting-time* (decreases in disruptive behavior in the home setting during follow-up).

The effect of the treated student's intervention on the untreated student resulted in the following:

(a) *Subject* generalization (increases in math performance in the home setting)
(b) *Subject-behavior* generalization (decreases in disruptive behavior in the school setting)
(c) *Subject-setting* generalization (increases in math performance in the home setting)
(d) *Subject-behavior-setting* generalization (decreases in disruptive behavior in the home setting)
(e) *Subject-time* generalization (increases in math performance in school setting during follow-up)
(f) *Subject-setting-time* generalization (increases in math performance in the home setting during follow-up)
(g) *Subject-behavior-setting-time* generalization (decreases in disruptive behavior in the home setting during follow-up)

There was no generalization of *subject-behavior-time* class (decreases in disruptive behavior in the school setting during follow-up). (Stevenson & Fantuzzo, 1984, pp. 209–210)

Unlike the Rhode et al. (1983) study, in which generalization was a function of a series of planned procedures, this study simply documented the kinds of spontaneous generalization. The proposition presented by the authors stated that "freedom within form" (defined as the subject's option to actively engage in management of contingencies affecting his behavior) permitted generalization to occur without implementing the type of rigorous programs reminiscent of the Rhode et al. (1983) study.

REPLICATION FOR SOCIAL VALIDITY AND GENERALIZATION

Two years after Stevenson and Fantuzzo (1984) published the results of their competency-based self-management training package, the same authors reported a replication that demonstrated the social validity and generalization effects of that treatment (Sevenson & Fantuzzo, 1986). Using a reversal of treatments design, they obtained data on three pairs of regular education fifth-grade students who were at least one grade level behind in arithmetic skills and of low socio-economic status. One of each pair of subjects served as the direct recipient of the treatment package, while the other yoked subject stayed in proximity to the treated subject and served as a control for generalization effects. Data on all pairs of subjects were collected concurrently, and the treatment was administered in both the classrooms and the homes of the treated subjects.

During baseline and treatment all class members were exposed to two arithmetic drill sessions in class each morning. These were conducted seven minutes before and seven minutes subsequent to a classroom arithmetic lesson. The first drill session contained worksheets with random combinations of basic math problems. Students were given feedback as to the accuracy of their problem solving as soon as the worksheets were turned in and corrected. Subsequently the students were given a classroom arithmetic lesson that was composed of twenty minutes of oral instruction followed by the second seven-minute drill session. The second drill was composed of highly diversified problems, such as obtaining place values with decimals, solving financial problems, and identifying the values of Roman numerals. The problems reflected information from the day's lesson.

Homework activity for the student pairs was similarly structured. A research assistant acted the role of teacher and also transported each experimental and yoked control subject to the home of the treated subject, where the same form of classroom lesson and drill was carried on after school throughout the course of the study. Furthermore, the parents of the treated subject were actively involved in the organization of the homework exercise. This was arranged so as to enhance the probability of naturally occurring contingencies maintaining post-treatment generalization effects.

During eleven days of baseline in the classroom and four days of baseline after school, in the homes of the treated subjects, arithmetic accuracy was monitored. The only consequence subjects received during this time was feedback regarding the number of problems solved correctly in each of the two drill sessions. Data indicate quite clearly that all three pairs of underachieving students consistently performed at or below the class averages while in school. This low level of accuracy was highly correlated with the home arithmetic drill.

The six-day self-management intervention in this study was slightly modified. In order to further enhance generalization effects, a "self-scorecard" was used. The card specified *goal options* (three possibilities as to the number of problems to be completed), a *menu of reinforcers* (six backup reinforcers), and a daily score and rating for completion of the drill session. Subjects were permitted to choose low, medium, or high goal options. However, the treated subjects were invited to attempt more strenuous goal options when they had achieved their respective goals during two previous consecutive drills. Furthermore, the treated subjects, in each pair, were individually trained as to the use of the above-mentioned modifications in environments that approximated the home and school setting. The sequential details of this training are of special interest, and probably account for the success of the treatment package:

> Students were individually trained by a coach of the same sex and race (a) to choose a goal option and a reinforcer from his or her self-scorecard, (b) to count the number of problems completed correctly on the corrected arithmetic sheet and record the number on his or her scorecard and on a card adjacent to his or her desk (displayed in a place that was easily visible to the control student), (c) to compare the number with the predetermined goal to determine whether criterion had been met, and (d) to decide at the end of the week whether to exchange or save the points on the scorecard for the predetermined reinforcers. These skills were modeled and subsequently practiced during

> simulated arithmetic drills until, after two 3-hr training sessions, students achieved a level of competency of at least 90 percent. (Stevenson & Fantuzzo, 1986, p. 271)

After six days of treatment the subjects were returned to baseline conditions for four days. This was followed by ten more days of treatment and, finally, a six-day follow-up conducted over a two- to three-month period after the final treatment phase.

Results demonstrated that instituting the self-management procedures caused improved arithmetic performance in all treated subjects. Specifically, the three treated subjects individually improved 18.4 percent, 16.1 percent, and 35.1 percent from baseline to the treatment phases.

Social validation in this study is given particular attention by way of two measures: by comparing the arithmetic accuracy of the treated and untreated students with the average accuracy of the rest of the class and by having teachers complete a questionnaire concerning the effectiveness and acceptability of the treatment package. The authors point out that during baseline, all three pairs of treated and untreated students performed consistently below their classmates during the arithmetic drill sessions. With the implementation of the treatment package all subjects, with the noted exception of one of the untreated controls, improved to math averages that were at or above the rest of the class. Questionnaires were also indicative of positive social validation. Teachers rated the treatment package as being easy to implement and ''helpful'' or ''very helpful.'' They all indicated that they would be likely to use such a program in the future and that they would recommend the use of such a program to their colleagues. In fact, two of the three teachers involved in the study actually used the program during the next school year.

The generalization ratio was quantified in the same fashion as it was previously (Stevenson & Fantuzzo, 1984). ''This ratio quantifies generalization by dividing the percent change for the desired generalization dimension (the untreated student/setting/behavior/time) by the percent change for the treated students' targeted behavior during treatment in the treatment setting × 100'' (Stevenson & Fantuzzo, 1986, p. 272). The authors provide the particular classes in which generalization occurred for the treated and control students'

> behavior, setting, behavior/setting, time, setting/time, behavior/time, and behavior/setting/time with a mean (range) generalization ratio of 102 (68–152). The effect of intervention with the treated students on the performance of untreated students showed generalization across subject, subject/behavior, subject/setting, subject/behavior/setting, subject/time, subject/setting/time, subject/behavior/time, and subject/behavior/setting/time with a mean (range) generalization ratio of 86 (49–139). (Stevenson & Fantuzzo, 1986, p. 272)

The previous Stevenson and Fantuzzo (1984) study failed to produce generalization effects in classes relating to behavior/time, behavior/setting/time, and subject/behavior/time. This study extended the generalization effects to include all classes specified by Drabman et al. (1979). The authors attribute these improved results to three primary factors: (1) the use of the same sex, race, and socioeconomic status in relation to the treated and untreated subjects; (2) the physical proximity of the untreated student to the treated student during the administration of the reinforcement procedure; and (3) the implementation of a program for the student pairs in the home setting of the treated student. All of these factors apparently maximized the extent to which the generalization phenomenon could occur.

SELF-ADMINISTRATION OF REINFORCEMENT

What frequently is described as vicarious reinforcement, or modeling effects (Bandura, 1971), can be understood as a form of *subject generalization* as described by Drabman et al. (1979). *Subject generalization* can be defined as behavior change in a nontreated subject that is a function of observation of a treated subject. The extent to which specified behavior of nontreated subjects change in conjunction with targeted behaviors of a treated subject can be quantified. By dividing the percentage of response increase or decrease (change) for a nontreated subject by the percentage of change in the treated subject, the correspondence between the subjects' behavior may be calculated. If the resulting percentage is positive, there is improved correspondence of target behaviors, while a negative percentage indicates a decrease in behavioral correspondence.

Fantuzzo and Clement (1981) investigated two forms of subject generalization and response generalization as affected by teacher-administered reinforcers, self-administered reinforcers, and a subject's opportunity to "self-reinforce." Each of these three treatments was conducted as a single-subject experiment with two replications. A confederate student, the ostensible target for intervention, served as a model in individual sessions with nine "nontreated" subjects. All participants were second-grade students described as lower socioeconomic, underachieving, inattentive blacks. Because the teacher was described as a white, teenage, middle-class female from a private school, the fact that the subjects were members of a minority group may have had a particularly important bearing on the outcome of the study.

During twenty-minute "tutoring" sessions each nontreated subject was "tutored" alone with the confederate. The first ten minutes of each session were used for video instruction of math problems, and during the second ten minutes both subject and confederate worked math problems on worksheets. Data were collected only during the second ten minutes of each period. This format was maintained throughout all three experiments.

After two habituation sessions, baseline was conducted for five days. During baseline the confederate was prompted, by way of a bug-in-the-ear apparatus, to maintain on-task behavior for 20 percent of each session and off-task behavior for 80 percent of each session. Both confederate and subject followed the format of listening to the taped math instructions and then working independently. At no time did the confederate initiate or partake in any verbal communication with the subjects. The confederate and the subject each received a small edible treat at the conclusion of each session. Baseline conditions were the same in all three sets of experiments.

Treatment for the first experiment and its two replications involved a *teacher-administered reinforcement* procedure. By way of the bug-in-the-ear, the confederate was prompted to maintain 80 percent on-task and 20 percent off-task behavior throughout the ten-minute independent work sessions. Points were provided to the confederate only when a sixty-second variable-interval tone sounded. These points were provided mechanically by way of the teacher, who pressed a button on a reinforcement box and activated a counter/recorder, which produced a light flash, on the confederate's desk. If the confederate student was on task at that time, the teacher said "Good (name of confederate)" and pressed the button on the reinforcement box, which was on her desk. When the session ended each subject was given a small edible treat as during baseline; and the confederate received additional edible treats based on the number of points he had obtained during the ten-minute treatment session. The nontreated subject was not provided any special explanation as to why he did not receive points or treats for his on-task behavior during the session. The same format was used throughout the next two sets of experiments except for variations in the administration of reinforcement.

In the second experiment and replication the treatment consisted of a *self-administered reinforcement* procedure. The confederate student administered points and praise contingent on his own on-task behavior. As in the experiment previously described, the tone sounded on an average of every sixty seconds. If the confederate was on task at the time the tone sounded, he stated out loud the word "good" and pushed the button on the reinforcement box, which produced a flash and advanced the counter on his desk. At the conclusion of each session both students received their usual small noncontingent treat, and the confederate exchanged his points for additional edible rewards.

In the *opportunity to "self-reinforce"* set of experiments the nontreated subjects were given an opportunity to manipulate the reinforcement box, which had (in the previous study) been used exclusively by the confederate student. The teacher arranged boxes on the desks of both students and stated, "Children, these boxes are not toys. You may use them to help yourself, if you wish" (Fantuzzo & Clement, 1981, p. 438). No further instructions regarding the manipulation of these apparatuses were provided to either student. Only the confederate, however, was provided backup reinforcers based on the number of points he gave himself. The nontreated student had only the "opportunity" to self-reinforce with points, not the "opportunity" to further benefit by the exchange of self-administered points for edible reinforcement.

The three treatments discussed above—teacher-administered reinforcement, self-administered reinforcement, and opportunity to "self-reinforce"—constituted the B condition of the three ABAB reversals. Baseline and treatment were alternated at five-day intervals in each of the three experiments.

Dependent variables were the calculated generalization effects of the treatments. The behaviors observed for generalization included attending (on-task behavior), glancing (observed student looking at adjacent student), and academic achievement (score on math work sheet). The calculations were performed according to the following methods:

> *Subject generalization* was determined by dividing the amount of change in attending for each nontreated student by the change in attending for the confederate during Phases II, III, and IV. . . . *Subject-response* generalization was determined by dividing change in glancing and in academic achievement for each nontreated student by change in attending for the confederate during the last three phases of each study. (Fantuzzo & Clement, 1981, p. 439)

In the *teacher-administered reinforcement* experiment the data on all three subjects failed to suggest subject generalization or subject-response generalization for glancing or academic achievement.

In the *self-administered reinforcement* experiment a pattern of subject generalization emerged. When the confederate used the reinforcement box, ostensibly to reward his own attending behavior, this was accompanied by corresponding increases in the nontreated subject's attending behavior. For example, one nontreated subject, during this phase, showed generalization of on-task percentages of 57 percent, 48 percent, and 61 percent for phases 2, 3, and 4, respectively. However, glancing behavior of the nontreated subjects was seemingly unaffected by the attending behavior of the confederate in this condition. This indicator of subject-response generalization was calculated at very low percentages. For example, one subject obtained −25 percent in phase 2, −6 percent in phase 3, and −12 percent in phase 4. Other nontreated subjects approximated these low levels of behavioral correspondence when their glancing behavior was divided by the concurrent attending behavior of the confederate.

Subject-response generalization data regarding achievement, in the *self-administered reinforcement* experiment, varied among the three nontreated subjects. One subject obtained 137 percent, 0 percent, and 138 percent for on-task behavior in phases 2, 3, and 4, in that order. Other subjects obtained exceedingly low percentages during all these phases. Evidently subject-response generalization, in the self-administered reinforcement condition, is a highly variable phenomenon.

In the *opportunity to "self-reinforce"* experiment, consistent subject generalization was demonstrated. Data from one subject reveals the strong tendency of nontreated subjects to imitate the behaviors of the confederate when the nontreated subjects had access to the "reinforcement box." Generalization percentages for this subject were the highest of all subjects under any of the experimental conditions. He obtained 132 percent, 314 percent, and 66 percent in phases 2, 3, and 4, respectively. The other two subjects obtained generalization percentages of 90 percent, 54 percent, 72 percent, and 93 percent, 66 percent, and 69 percent for the second, third, and fourth phases. It would appear that, for these subjects, subject generalization is most likely to occur when nontreated subjects have the *opportunity* to perform similarly to a model who administers points contingent on his own performance.

Subject-response generalization for glancing did not occur under these conditions. All subjects obtained low or negative percentages throughout all phases of the experiments. However, subject-response generalization for academic achievement (number of math problems solved) was more variable. One subject demonstrated obvious subject-response generalization with percentages of 109 percent, 133 percent, and 51 percent for the three consecutive phases. The other two subjects were partially affected in the last phases of this condition. They obtained −11 percent, 4 percent, and 47 percent, and −10 percent, 16 percent, and 84 percent, respectively, for phases 2, 3, and 4. Thus academic achievement appeared to be partially, but variably, influenced by the self-administering model's increased on-task levels.

It is important to note that the confederate also came under the influence of generalization. Although he received covert cues to demonstrate various levels of on-task behavior throughout the course of the study, no prompts or explicit reinforcers were directed at the confederate's glancing or academic achievement within the tutoring sessions. Thus the confederate's own response generalization is assessable. Data reveal that virtually no response generalization occurred in reference to glancing, but that there was improved academic achievement associated with increased attending behavior. When averaged across all conditions the confederate obtained response generalization scores of 58.2 percent, 19.1 percent, and 88.2 percent for academic achievement, in the three successive phases.

The authors note that, in general, it can be said that when a teacher used a reinforcement procedure for a peer's on-task behavior, there was no evidence of any tendency toward subject or subject-response generalization. The mean subject generalization, collapsed across all phases of teacher reinforcement, was −14 percent. It would appear that these second-grade students were unimpressed by peers who earned the teacher's attention and token reinforcement.

Again, the fact that the teacher and the untreated student subjects were of different race and socioeconomic background may be relevant to the results. Perhaps it is not surprising that these students were not interested in adopting behaviors that the teacher found admirable.

However, generalization indicators were observed. Nontreated students who were exposed to a peer, providing himself with reinforcement, and nontreated students who observed a peer self-reinforcing and also had the opportunity to manipulate an apparatus similar to that of the peer demonstrated high levels of subject generalization. In these conditions nontreated subjects obtained overall averages of 60 percent and 85 percent for the experimental arrangements discussed above.

Subject-response generalization for glancing was generally inconsistent and low for all subjects under all conditions. This simply means that there was not a consistent tendency for the nontreated subjects to glance in the direction of the confederates irrespective of the experimental conditions. This does not mean that the nontreated subjects did not observe the confederates; rather, it indicates that their observational behavior was not differentially correlated with the various reinforcement contingencies. In contrast, overall averages of subject-response generalization in academic achievement, for self-administered reinforcement and the opportunity to self-reinforce, yielded high levels of 60 percent and 85 percent, respectively. It appears that this population is more easily influenced by the self-reinforcing activity of one of their peers than by reinforcers provided by authority figures from the mainstream culture. The authors close with a profound commentary:

> The findings of this study have significant implications for the utilization of behavioral techniques with children in classroom-like settings. Generally, they bespeak the importance of not assuming that all behavioral interventions with children will automatically generalize and have positive effects on neighboring students. Some interventions, such as the teacher-administered reinforcement condition in the present study, may have negligible or inconsistent effects on certain nontreated students. These may require additional techniques and procedures to program needed generalization effects (Stokes & Bear, 1977). More specifically, these findings suggest that exposing ''deprived'' grade school children to successful self-regulation interventions results in improvements in nontreated peers. (Fantuzzo & Clement, 1981, p. 445)

SELF-DIRECTED SPELLING IMPROVEMENT

There has always been considerable speculation about the best way to teach spelling to elementary students. Many believe that simply having students spell new words many times (i.e., increasing the ''opportunity to respond'') is the most advantageous instructional method (Delquandri, Greenwood, Stretton, & Hall, 1983). Another perspective indicates that students benefit from imitating former errors on particular misspelled words (Kauffman, Hallahan, Haas, Brame, & Boren, 1978). Theoretically, having students attend to specific high probability errors allows them to differentiate cues associated with correct versus incorrect letter arrangements. This instructional format requires that both negative and positive examples of spelled words be alternated during practice. In addition, it may be helpful to highlight particular letters in order to draw more attention to the source of previous errors. Another aspect to this procedure relates to whether students benefit most from practicing spelling as a self-directed drill or a teacher-directed drill. In this context, student-directed instruction takes on some of the same components as self-management—self-assessment and self-recording. In fact, the words student-directed and self-managed might be used interchangeably.

In order to try to reach some conclusions regarding method of instruction (cues versus no cues) and method of management (self-directed or teacher-directed), Gettinger (1985) enlisted the cooperation of nine poor spellers (six boys, three girls) ranging in age from eight to thirteen years in grades three through eight. These students were described as being of average intelligence, but performing one year below their current grade level in the area of spelling.

Spelling words were taken from the *New Iowa Spelling Scale* (Greene, 1954). The author notes a special criterion for word selection; training words were spelled correctly by only 35 percent to 55 percent of children at a particular subject's normative grade level, and words were divided between regular and irregular spellings. In four sets of forty-eight words, twenty-four regular and twenty-four irregular words were selected for each subject. Eight separate drill lists, with three regular and three irregular words per list, were used for training. Subsequently each set was assigned to one of four experimental conditions in which either the author or one of three graduate assistants acted as teacher. The instruction was delivered twice weekly, after school, for sixteen weeks. The author specifies that during each week, twelve words were practiced in sets of six words per thirty-five minute practice session.

All subjects were pretested and posttested during an initial no-instruction control phase. After testing subjects received alternated weeks of instruction with and without cues, and alternated biweekly instruction with and without teacher direction. "A total of sixteen 6-word lists (4 lists from each set) were presented during this phase" (Gettinger, 1985, p. 168). In the last phase of the experiment student-directed instruction with cues was maintained for all word sets (four sets, two lists per set).

After baseline, there were four experimental conditions. In the two experimental conditions that were teacher-directed each child was pretested on six words. The students were praised for correctly spelled words. Errors were corrected by imitating the students' errors and having the correct spellings placed adjacent to the students' incorrect spellings. In the *teacher-directed practice without cues condition* the following correction procedure occurred. "For teacher-directed practice, the teacher (a) showed the word on a card and said it, (b) removed the card, (c) instructed the child to write it, and (d) checked the spelling" (Gettinger, 1985, p. 168). This was repeated until the student produced two consecutive correct spellings of the word. In the *teacher-directed practice with cues condition* all of the above occurred, in addition to which

> the teacher provided cues by circling in red the part of the word that was misspelled in both the error imitation and correct model saying, "This is the part of the word you need to remember. Look carefully at this part." Pointing to the circled part in the correct word, she said, "Here is how this part should be spelled," and, pointing to the circled part in the error imitation, she said, "not like this." The child was told to study the difference carefully. During practice, the teacher pointed to the difficult part in each word when she presented it and instructed the child to remember this. (Gettinger, 1985, p. 168)

In the two experimental conditions that were student-directed, pretests were corrected by the students themselves. These practice sessions were also conducted with and without cues.

In the *student-directed practice without cues condition* the subjects corrected their own pretests. After checking all words with a word card, they copied incorrectly spelled words as originally misspelled. They then copied the word with the correct spelling and enunciated the word. "Students carried out the practice on their own by (a) looking at the word on a card and saying it, (b) turning the card over, (c) writing the word, and (d) checking it. This continued until students had written the word correctly two times. Finally, words were posttested" (Gettinger, 1985, p. 169).

In the *student-directed practice with cues condition* all of the above procedures were performed in addition to which

> students circled in red the part of the word that was misspelled in both the error imitation and correct model saying, "This is the part of the word I need to remember." They pointed to the circled part in the imitation and studied the difference. During practice, students pointed to the difficult parts in words and circled them on every practice trial. (Gettinger, 1985, p. 169)

As in all other conditions, these exercises were followed by posttesting.

All of the procedures above were rehearsed previous to being used. None of the experimental procedures were implemented until the students had demonstrated three successful performances of the strategy. Furthermore, during each condition, a printed description of the procedure was posted on the blackboard for review by the subjects. One week after the conclusion of each treatment posttest, all students took a retention test.

Results comparing these four conditions are somewhat surprising. Although all four conditions increased the number of correctly spelled words over baseline posttesting (between 1.00 and 2.50 spelled correctly), it appears that students performed better independently than they did with teacher assistance. Under the student-directed conditions (with and without cues) the average ranged from 4.50 to 6.00. When the teachers provided assistance in the instructional process the averages were lower (between 3.25 and 4.25). Furthermore, when teachers added the facility of visual and verbal cues to their instructional procedure, spelling was not improved; but within the contexts of student-directed practice, cues appeared to facilitate learning. In the final phase, when all students were operating under the condition of *self-directed practice with cues*, the average accuracy ranged from 5.00 to 6.00. The advantage of student-directed practice over teacher-directed practice was even more conspicuous in the results of the retention tests. Under student-directed, an average between 4.25 and 5.50 words was obtained; under the direction of the teacher only 2.25 to 3.75 words were accurately spelled. However, for reasons that are not made clear by this study, the use of visual and verbal cues did not improve accuracy during the retention tests.

The author notes an important detail of this study. The fact that students performed better under their own direction should not be construed as an indictment against teachers. Although students were self-directed, instruction was teacher-determined. Previous to using the self-management program, students were rigorously trained in the details of this highly structured procedure. Teachers reported that students appeared more active and on task while in the midst of the self-directed instruction. Gettinger attributes these seemingly paradoxical results to the increased student involvement when they practice under their own direction and management.

SELF-INSTRUCTION

The term self-instruction is sometimes used to refer to the same type of self-control procedures as those associated with self-management. However, self-instruction is perhaps more accurately described as one component within the broader topic of self-management. Self-instruction is a verbal instruction that, hopefully, changes the probability of some other behavior in the same person. Self-instruction does not necessarily include self-assessment, self-reinforcement, self-determination of reinforcement, or self-administration of reinforcement. Self-instruction merely requires that a student learn a verbal instruction and repeat the instruction as a prompt in the process of completing a task. Assessment, determination, and administration of reinforcement may be left in the hands of teachers or other socializing agents.

Roberts, Nelson, and Olson (1987) analyzed the effects of self-instruction on arithmetic problem solving. Six first-graders and six second-graders who lagged behind their peers in math performance were assigned to four groups in five experimental conditions (one group received two separate treatment conditions). This study utilized a multiple baseline across subjects in each group; that is, the three students in each of the four groups were given a separate duration of four, six, or eight baseline sessions. Students were asked to complete twenty addition and subtraction problems during each baseline and treatment session.

Following baseline, self-instruction procedures were initiated. With the exception of the three students in the comparison group, each student was given extensive training in both the detailed procedures involved in self-instruction and the arithmetic strategies necessary for accurate completion of addition and subtraction problems. The particular method of self-instruction is explained most adequately by the authors:

> First, the experimenter modeled the use of self-instruction to solve the problems. For a problem such as 8 + □ = 15, the modeled self-instruction would be: "First, I have to read the problem. Eight plus some number equals 15. This is an addition problem so I have to circle the sign. I circle the plus. Now I put eight sticks over the 8 and put sticks over the box until I get 15. 1, 2, 3, 4, 5, 6, 7, 8, and 9, 10, 11, 12, 13, 14, 15. Now I count the sticks over the box. 1, 2, 3, 4, 5, 6, 7. There are seven sticks over the box.

Seven is my answer so I write it in the box. Eight plus seven equals 15." The subject was then given a similar problem to solve and was prompted in the use of self-instruction. Verbal praise was used to reinforce the subjects for correct verbalizations and solutions. These prompts and social reinforcers were faded over the course of the training session. By the end of the training session, subjects were able to state all necessary self-instruction without prompting. (Roberts et al., 1987, p. 237)

After completion of the self-instruction training, each group was exposed to a different experimental condition for ten treatment sessions. Students in their respective experimental groups received one of the following conditions in which tokens, in conjunction with verbal praise, were contingent on (1) the overt use of self-instructions, (2) the accuracy of problem solving—independent of overt self-instructions, and (3) the use of self-instructions in conjunction with the accuracy of problem solving. In the third group students were given tokens and praise for the correct completion of each problem only if the student self-instructed overtly during the process of problem solving.

The comparison group did not receive any of the above instructions and received tokens for accuracy only; however, after eight sessions for one student and nine for the other two, this group was provided instructions in math problem-solving strategies without the benefit of the detailed self-instruction training described above. Two of these students were then given three treatment sessions and one student was given only one treatment session in which the problem-solving strategies were utilized. Thus, the students in this comparison group were exposed to two conditions post baseline: one in which only accuracy was reinforced, and a second, short condition in which they had the benefit of problem-solving strategies, in conjunction with reinforcement, to help improve their accuracy.

During baseline all subjects in each of the four groups performed at low levels of accuracy when attempting to solve grade-level arithmetic problems. Most students did an average of 25 percent or less of their twenty assigned problems correctly. All three treatment groups demonstrated approximately the same level of immediate and sustained improvement in arithmetic performance when operating under the influence of self-instruction and rewards. Graphed data indicate that all three groups of students generally improved from arithmetic averages below 25 percent during baseline, to averages above 75 percent during all three of the treatment conditions, although a great deal of variability is apparent both between subjects and sessions. The authors note that the multiple-baseline design establishes that subjects began to demonstrate improvement only at the point in time at which the various intervention strategies were implemented. Thus, other potentially confounding variables, such as history, maturation, testing, instrumentation, and so on, cannot account for the immediate transition to improvement demonstrated at the respective times at which the treatment was initiated across subjects.

Group and individual numerical averages, with the exception of one subject, are not provided. Thus, it is difficult to provide specifics regarding baseline-to-intervention changes. Given this lack of detailed data analysis and the variability between and within subjects, it is not apparent that one method is noticeably superior to the others. It is only apparent, by visual inspection of the graphs, that all three experimental groups performed better after treatment than they did before.

In the comparison group there was clearly some improvement in performance after baseline sessions when these students were simply provided reinforcement for accuracy. Adding instructions as to the correct methods of solving math problems further improved all three subjects' performances. Again, there is great subject variability in this condition, and the general extent of improvement is difficult to ascertain.

The data regarding the general effectiveness of self-instruction as a sole vehicle to improve academic performance appear rather inconclusive:

> The observation of self-instruction use indicated that children whose self-instruction use was reinforced used the procedure, whereas children whose self-instruction use was not reinforced tended not to use it. Only one child in the comparison group was ever observed to use self-instruction. This occurred only during one session of the no-training condition. Moreover, when the degree of association between arithmetic accuracy and over use of self-instruction was assessed by means of a phi coefficient, the resulting phi was .1934. This shows a very weak association between arithmetic accuracy and the use of overt self-instruction. (Roberts et al., 1987, p. 240)

Thus, self-instruction may not be a necessary condition to enhance arithmetic performance above simple direct reinforcement contingencies. Nevertheless, these data suggest that the training in proper use of self-instruction and continued reinforcement of overt self-instruction, independent of accuracy contingencies, may be a sufficient condition to improve accuracy to a level commensurate with simply reinforcing accuracy or accuracy and self-instruction.

THE SKILL OF SELF-MANAGING

Some studies described in this chapter provide evidence that students can be taught self-management skills, and they provide some workable tactics for teaching them. Other studies demonstrate that some students can manage certain environmental events in ways that produce desired academic and on-task performance. Taken together, these studies suggest that contingency management in the classroom can often be implemented by students themselves. However, students must learn the skills involved in managing the contingencies that affect their own behavior. Some may have acquired such self-management skills as a result of fortuitous life circumstances or extraordinarily adept parents, but others will surely require systematic teaching in the school setting. Although the task of developing procedures that teach self-management has just begun, research has at least pointed to the feasibility and desirability of working toward that end.

REFERENCES

Baer, D. M. (1981). *How to plan for generalization*. Lawrence, KS: H & H Enterprises.

Bandura, A. (1971). Vicarious and self-reinforcement processes. In R. Glaser (Ed.), *The nature of reinforcement*. New York: Academic Press.

Bandura, A., & Perloff, B. (1967). Relative efficacy of self-monitored and externally imposed reinforcement systems. *Journal of Personality and Social Psychology, 7*, 111–116.

Broden, M., Hall, R. V., & Mitts, B. (1971). The effects of self-recording on the classroom behavior of two eighth-grade students. *Journal of Applied Behavior Analysis, 3*, 191–199.

Delquadri, J. C., Greenwood, C. R., Stretton, K., & Hall, R. V. (1983). The peer tutoring spelling game: A classroom procedure for increasing opportunity to respond and spelling performance. *Education and Treatment of Children, 6*, 225–239.

Dickerson, E. A., & Creedon, C. F. (1981). Self-selection of reinforcement standards by children: The relative effectiveness of pupil-selected and teacher-selected standards of performance. *Journal of Applied Behavior Analysis, 4*, 425–434.

Drabman, R. S., Hammer, D., & Rosenbaum, M. S. (1979). Assessing generalization in behavior modification with children: The generalization map. *Behavioral Assessment, 1*, 203–219.

Fantuzzo, J. W., & Clement, P. W. (1981). Generalization of the effects of teacher- and self-administered token reinforcers to nontreated students. *Journal of Applied Behavior Analysis, 14*, 435–447.

Felixbrod, J. J., & O'Leary, K. D. (1973). Effects of reinforcement on children's academic behavior as a function of self-determined and externally imposed contingencies. *Journal of Applied Behavior Analysis, 6*, 241–250.

Gettinger, M. (1985). Effects of teacher-directed versus student-directed instruction and cues versus no cues for improving spelling performance. *Journal of Applied Behavior Analysis, 18*, 167–171.

Glynn, E. L. (1970). Classroom applications of self-determined reinforcement. *Journal of Applied Behavior Analysis, 3*, 123–132.

Glynn, E. L., & Thomas, J. D. (1974). Effect of cueing on self-control of classroom behavior. *Journal of Applied Behavior Analysis, 7*, 299–306.

Glynn, E. L., Thomas, J. D., & Shee, S. M. (1973). Behavioral self-control of on-task behavior in an elementary classroom. *Journal of Applied Behavior Analysis, 6*, 105–113.

Graham, S. (1983). Effective spelling instruction. *Elementary School Journal, 83*, 560–568.

Greene, H. A. (1954). *The new Iowa spelling scale*. Iowa City: University of Iowa.

Hallahan, D. P., Lloyd, G. W., Kauffman, J. M., & Loper, A. B. (1983). Academic problems. In R. J. Morris & T. R. Kratochwill (Eds.), *Practice of child therapy: A textbook of methods* (pp. 113–141). New York: Pergamon Press.

Harris, K. R. (1986). Self-monitoring of attentional behavior versus self-monitoring of productivity: Effects on on-task behavior and academic response rate among learning disabled children. *Journal of Applied Behavior Analysis, 19*, 417–423.

Kauffman, J. M., Hallahan, D. P., Haas, K., Brame, T., & Boren, R. (1978). Imitating children's errors to improve their spelling performance. *Journal of Learning Disabilities, 11*, 33–38.

Knapczyk, D. R., & Livingston, G. (1973). Self-recording and student teacher supervision: Variables within a token economy structure. *Journal of Applied Behavior Analysis, 6*, 481–486.

Lovitt, T. C., & Curtiss, K. A. (1969). Academic response rate as a function of teacher- and self-imposed contingencies. *Journal of Applied Behavior Analysis, 2*, 49–53.

McLaughlin, T. F., & Truhlicka, M. (1983). Effects on academic performance of self-recording and self-recording and matching with behaviorally disordered students: A replication. *Behavioral Engineering, 8*, 69–74.

Meichenbaum, D. H., & Goodman, J. (1971). Training impulsive children to talk to themselves: A means of developing self-control. *Journal of Abnormal Psychology, 77*, 115–126.

O'Leary, S. G., & Dubey, D. R. (1979). Applications of self-control procedures by children: A review. *Journal of Applied Behavior Analysis, 12*, 449–465.

Polkes, H., Stewart, M., & Kahana, K. (1968). Porteus Maze performance of hyperactive boys after training in self directed verbal commands. *Child Development, 39*, 817–826.

Rhode, G., Morgan, D. P., & Young, K. R. (1983). Generalization and maintenance of treatment gains of behaviorally handicapped students from resource rooms to regular classrooms using self-evaluation procedures. *Journal of Applied Behavior Analysis, 16*, 171–188.

Roberts., N. R., Nelson, R. O., & Olson, T. W. (1987). Self-instruction: An analysis of the differential effects of instruction and reinforcement. *Journal of Applied Behavior Analysis, 20*, 235–242.

Stevenson, H. C., & Fantuzzo, J. W. (1984). Application of the ''Generalization Map'' to a self-control intervention with school-aged children. *Journal of Applied Behavioral Analysis, 17*, 203–212.

Stevenson, H. C., & Fantuzzo, J. W. (1986). The generality and social validity of a competency-based self-control training intervention for underachieving students. *Journal of Applied Behavior Analysis, 19*, 269–276.

Stokes, T. F., & Bear, D. M. (1977). An implicit technology of generalization. *Journal of Applied Behavior Analysis, 10*, 349–367.

Switzky, H. N., & Haywood, H. C. (1974). Motivational orientation and the relative efficacy of self-monitored and externally imposed reinforcement systems in children. *Journal of Personality and Social Psychology, 30*, 360–366.

Wood, R., & Flynn, J. M. (1978). A self-evaluation token system versus an external evaluation token system alone in a residential setting with predelinquent youths. *Journal of Applied Behavior Analysis, 11*, 503–512.

6

On Task: A Time for Learning

THE PROBLEM

In the past decade the term *on task* has gained increasing popularity as a generic term for student behavior previously categorized as studying, writing, reading, calculating, attending, and so on. These activities describe, with varying degrees of specificity, behavior appropriate to a school environment. These are the behaviors teachers love to see most from their students. They suggest that the students are in the process of learning.

Many students, however, are discouragingly seldom on task, and sometimes those who appear to be busy with schoolwork are covertly daydreaming. That is, their eyes are directed toward the book, but they are seeing themselves hit a homerun, or talking to a friend, rather than seeing the scenes described in the text. In short, some students have learned how to look busy. Under such circumstances the teacher may not be aware that a student has been off task until he fails to perform adequately on periodic exams or standardized tests. Other students never even pretend to be academically engaged. In either case the teacher may eventually form the opinion that the student is not capable of performing grade-level work. Such a student frequently becomes a candidate for referral to special education.

After such a referral the student may be given a battery of intelligence and achievement tests by an educational diagnostician; if a significant discrepancy is found between his "intelligence" and his current level of achievement, he may be assigned the diagnostic label of learning disabled (LD). This will result in eligibility for placement in a special education classroom for all or part of the school day. The determination of placement in a special education program will be accomplished only after consensus of an Admission, Review, Dismissal (ARD) Committee (composed of teachers, parents, administrators, diagnosticians, and, sometimes, psychologists), which reviews all diagnostics on special education referrals and decides on the most suitable placement.

Special education, like much of regular education, has fallen on hard times. Monies to support special programs have been cut, staff has been reduced, and special education classrooms are frequently overcrowded. Some students who are placed in special education for remediation may, in fact, receive less personal attention than might be possible in their regular classrooms. Even when this is not the case, assignment to special education does not provide an automatic solution. Although one of the goals of special education has been to help LD children compensate for their academic deficiencies and return to the "least restrictive environment" of mainstream education, some students who are placed in LD classes tend to fall further behind as time passes. More important, many children who have been labeled as LD, or in some cases "brain damaged," are lacking the relevant academic skills commensurate with their measured intelligence simply because they have not been on task for some time.

Their problem may actually be prolonged extinction of academic behavior. That is, they do not engage in academic behavior because such behavior does not get reinforced. It is usually the case that such children do make fractional attempts to comply with the teacher's requests to get on task, but such attempts typically go unnoticed and unreinforced. The extinction process—the gradual decrease in behavior, resulting from a paucity of reinforcement—is brought about by the unwitting use of extinction procedures.

When academic behavior is on extinction, children are unlikely to simply sit idly by and observe others partake in achievement-oriented tasks. Most often they will find some diversion to occupy their time—a diversion that produces more favorable consequences than does on-task behavior. Sometimes the diversion is reinforced in several ways. First, there is the minor, but consistent, consequence of making something happen that changes the sensory environment. Twirling the string and doodling produce visual patterns, clicking the pen produces a sound pattern. Second, such behavior displaces the academic behavior that is likely to produce criticism and bad marks. So these might be classified as avoidance behaviors. Then, too, the diversion is far more likely, than is on-task behavior, to produce the focused attention of the teacher on the off-task student.

Thus we may see students reading Superman comic books behind their history texts; we may find students doodling on desks during math lessons; and when all else fails such children may be satisfied to simply play with their fingers. Most of these off-task behaviors occur occasionally in all elementary students, but when they occur at high rates relative to the child's academic performance, it is time to consider alternatives. What is needed are techniques that will develop a repertoire of on-task skills early in the school history of every child. This can often be best accomplished while the student is still in the regular classroom.

What follows is a compilation of studies that have attempted to address the problem of motivating students to put forth their best effort on academic tasks.

These studies address a variety of problems regarding on-task behavior and provide a wide assortment of solutions in different settings. Many of these studies were performed within the context of special education; however, this need not hinder implementation of these procedures in regular classes. Most of the strategies are flexible enough to be applied in a variety of learning environments.

EARLY RESEARCH

The first article printed in the *Journal of Applied Behavior Analysis* contains some of the most critical and fundamental components for implementing on-task procedures. Hall, Lund, and Jackson (1968) investigated the on-task rates of inner-city, lower socioeconomic grade-school children. Observations of children who had low study rates and frequent incidents of disruptive or dawdling behavior revealed an all too common phenomenon. Teachers, in an apparent effort to "prompt" such children into initiating study tasks, would periodically reprimand, coax, lecture, or just stare at students who were involved in off-task behaviors. Although such methods sometimes worked to get children started back to work, the effect on the behavior over time was quite different. In reality, teachers were inadvertently using a reinforcement procedure and increasing the frequency of off-task behavior. An equally paradoxical act was that these students were seldom, if ever, noticed during those brief intervals when they were actually on task.

Hall et al. implemented several simple and effective techniques to reverse the contingencies that were inadvertently maintaining the pervasive off-task behavior.

1. They provided teachers with daily graphed results of both student and teacher interactions. These graphs depicted the relationship between teacher attention and student behavior.
2. They initiated weekly conferences to describe improved teaching skills. Teachers were praised for improving student behavior.
3. Teacher cueing was implemented. This consisted of having observers signal teachers on appropriate occasions to reinforce their students' on-task performance. Observers simply held up a small colored piece of paper as a signal. Subsequently teachers attended to the specified child by moving closer and making some positive verbal comment regarding the student's improved behavior.

In most cases these simple steps were sufficient to bring about an almost immediate transition in the students' classroom behavior. Studying as well as academic performance dramatically increased during the treatment phase. Reversal periods, during which attending to students' on-task behavior was temporarily terminated, brought about the return of dawdling and disrupting. Reinstatement of task-contingent attention was correlated with a return of academic performance. The results were irrefutable, and during these early days of behavior modification perhaps somewhat startling. This was one of the first studies that demonstrated the effectiveness and reliability of contingency management in a regular education classroom. Using two of the teacher's most powerful resources, attention and approval, experimenters demonstrated that simple rearrangements of classroom contingencies could bring about immediate and sustained improvements in some of the most recalcitrant students.

There will always be cases of children with such exceptional histories of noncompliance that, at least in the initial stages of intervention, special, "more restrictive" arrangements are necessary. Walker and Buckley (1968) found that typical classroom contingency management strategies were ineffective in reducing one nine-year-old underachieving subject's disruptive and distractive behavior. In this circumstance special individual arrangements were made to supplement the classroom management procedures.

To compensate for lack of classroom control, Walker and Buckley designed an isolated study area in which all extraneous and distracting stimuli were virtually eliminated. In this cloistered environment the subject was given maximum opportunity to concentrate on areas of academic deficiency, and a reinforcement procedure was used to strengthen such behavior. Study blocks were divided into three ten-minute periods and a single ten-minute period later in the day. The student was told that he would receive points, exchangeable for backup reinforcers, such as toys, when he managed to stay at work during these study blocks.

Administering these points was a particularly important component of this intervention. Initially a click sounded at the end of each thirty-second interval during which the student had remained on task. This indicated successful completion of that time segment and the earning of a point. Fading in longer intervals of on-task behavior was accomplished by gradually increasing the required duration of on-task behavior between the clicks. After the subject was able to perform successfully for twenty thirty-second intervals (ten minutes), interval length was doubled. The subject had to remain on task for sixty seconds before the click, now worth 2 points, sounded. After maintaining ten sixty-second intervals, interval length and the number of points earned per interval were again doubled. This gradual increase of interval length continued until the subject worked on task for an entire 600-second block before receiving feedback from the click. The subject had averaged 42 percent on-task behavior during baseline. During the contingent reinforcement condition that average jumped to about 93 percent.

To substantiate the independent effects of this treatment a reversal was implemented. Attending behavior immediately decreased to baseline levels of about 44 percent. Subsequently the subject was reintroduced to his original classroom setting. His teacher was instructed in the use of a variable-interval reinforcement system wherein the subject received points and praise for intervals averaging thirty minutes of on-task behavior. The subject's on-task behavior immediately jumped to the high levels seen in the previous individualized treatment setting.

It is important to note that such a transition to near-perfect attending behavior was possible only after the subject had undergone extensive individualized training that involved shaping the complex behavior of remaining on task for longer and longer periods.

The effect of this type of program on academic performance might have been even greater had the contingencies in the preceding experiment addressed performance outcomes. When on-task behavior is defined, targeted, and reinforced under conditions of having subjects assume the physical topography associated with attending to task, it can be anticipated that the student will, eventually, look like one who is working. But this does not guarantee improved academic performance. Such contingencies only set the stage for improved achievement by allowing performance-oriented contingencies to become more easily programmed. Subsequent research has found that targeting achievement, rather than just the appearance of on-task behavior, is a more expedient procedure for improving both classroom conduct and academic performance.

FEEDBACK

Many teachers find the process of administering tokens, or even points, to students to be incompatible with their teaching styles. They think that students should perform at their very best independent of incentive programs. Furthermore, for many students, the acquisition of tokens and points, as well as their respective backup reinforcers, is not nearly so important as the recognition they indirectly receive in such systems. In other words, many students do not need to be given special favors or privileges to improve their productivity; concrete evidence of correct responding and the peer recognition obtained from improving their performance can function as powerful conditioned reinforcers. What is needed, in such cases, is a simple feedback system that will provide students with direct information regarding the accuracy of their recently completed performance. Emphasis here is on "recently completed performance." One of the most critical features regarding any type of feedback is that it be given as soon as possible after the relevant behavior has occurred.

Group Feedback

Van Houten, Morrison, Jarvis, and McDonald (1974) investigated the effect of setting a time limit for a writing assignment, and posting information regarding the number of words each student wrote. Data were collected on length and quality of comparisons. The target behavior (number of words) never received systematic praise or any consequence other than public posting of the data. Van Houten et al. arranged the experiment so that a group of twenty-one second-grade students was evaluated using the standard ABAB reversal-of-treatment design. Another group composed of two classes of seventeen fifth-grade students was evaluated by way of a multiple-baseline design. The treatment was the same for both groups. It consisted only of timing the students for ten-minute intervals and then posting each student's total number of written words so that the whole class could observe group and individual progress. Both groups improved in the absolute number of words written as well as in mechanical aspects of writing. Using an index developed originally by Brigham, Graubard, and Stans (1972), Van Houten et al. also established that the quality of compositions doubled as a function of the timing and posting intervention. Vocabulary, number of ideas expressed, development of ideas, and internal consistency were all judged as significantly improved.

The second-grade students more than doubled their mean written words per minute during this treatment. Similar rate improvements were seen in two fifth-grade classes. In the second-grade class, in which a reversal of treatments was used, baseline rates were never recovered during the reversal period. This may have happened because the students persisted in counting the number of words composed during the reversal, despite being told that it was no longer necessary.

The results of this simple intervention process are intriguing and significant. There remains, however, a question as to which independent variable was responsible for these remarkable effects. Because the intervention consisted of simultaneously introducing the timing and posting, it is not clear whether or not either of these two procedures, used independently, could have had similar effects.

Van Houten, apparently recognizing the limitations inherent in the 1974 study, published, in 1975, a replication with improved design. Using two classes of fourth-grade students and a reversal design, Van Houten, Hill, and Parsons (1975) performed two more experiments. In their first experiment they measured writing rate, percentage of time on task, and the performance comments students made before, during, and after the composition period. Students in class A were given twenty minutes, and students in class B, who found writing more difficult, wrote for only ten minutes.

During five days of baseline, group A composed 4.5 words per minute, while group B, the less adequate readers, wrote only 1.8 words per minute. In the next five days students in both classes were explicitly timed and given feedback on the number of words composed. Feedback was accomplished by simply having each student count the number of words written, and having that number placed on the top of the composition. Scores were not posted for public display. This contingency, which provided no form of tangible reinforcement or public posting, resulted in improved writing rates for both groups. Group A averaged 8.3 words per minute and group B averaged 3.5 words per minute. On-task behavior improved for both groups. It was also noted that the number of comments that students made to one another concerning their writing performance jumped from almost none during baseline to an average of about 13 for class A and about 8 for class B. It appears that timing with feedback, independent of posting, is sufficient to improve academic performance to some degree.

At this stage of the experiment Van Houten et al. (1975) had approximated the results of the 1974 study. However, posting of each student's daily word total had not yet occurred, as it had in that original study. So during the next five-day period all students had their total number of words posted on the board. A check was placed beside the name of any child who exceeded his previous high score. Students in class A jumped to an average of 10.8 words per minute and class B, to 5.4 words per minute. This corresponded with similar improvements in on-task behavior. Posting of individual word totals also had the concomitant effect of making writing performance a more likely topic of conversation. Students in classes A and B averaged around 19.8 and 23 performance comments per day, respectively. Terminating the posting procedure for five days produced an immediate drop in performance and student commentary concerning writing. Written words per minute fell to 7.9 and 3.4 for A and B. However, reinstatement of the posting procedure produced an immediate return to the previous high rates in both composition and student comments regarding composition performance.

The results suggest that timing with feedback can improve academic performance but that posting of outcomes of student performance can increase the extent to which students both discuss and produce the written word.

Another important variable, when coupled with all of the procedures above, may be teacher praise. When teachers added their own verbal reinforcement for improved performance, class A produced 13 words per minute and class B, 5.3 words per minute. On-task behavior during the writing period maintained at near 100 percent, and students were heard discussing written word totals even more frequently. Removing teacher praise for five days resulted in a slight drop in most dependent variables. Words per minute fell to 10 for class A but did not significantly affect class B.

As a result of the later study, it is now clear that timing with feedback regarding the total number of daily written words can operate independently to increase the speed and quality of students' compositions. These dependent variables are even further positively affected when public posting and teacher praise are added to the treatment conditons. The study also suggests that the procedures produced some rather interesting social ramifications. The number of comments students made to one another regarding class compositions corresponds with the number of treatment variables applied concurrently. Adding teacher praise to timing with feedback and posting apparently accelerated the rate of student comments and the number of words written per minute. Teacher praise was one of the stronger treatment variables in generating enthusiasm for writing behavior.

In the first study there had been considerable discussion regarding the effect such treatment had on the improved quality of student writing. The latter study merely indicated that one judge found the quality improved, but that the other judge failed to detect any change in the students' writing quality under the various experimental conditions. The authors' note that this poor reliability with regard to quality control may have been related to the students' poor spelling and reading skills. This is a curious and somewhat disconcerting commentary, and it leaves the whole issue of how these procedures affect the mechanics and style of composition unresolved.

Replication

Van Houten et al.'s 1975 publication included two experiments. The one just described (experiment 1) essentially replicated the 1974 study in a direct way but sorted out the effects of several independent variables. It also added the extra treatment of praise during one phase of the experiment. The replication added to our understanding of what variables motivate students to produce higher rates of writing.

Having obtained results that supported the use of timing, feedback, public posting, and praise as a treatment package that cumulatively affected performance, Van Houten performed a second experiment to test this treatment package on two more dependent variables, comprehension and word meaning. If it could be established that this treatment package could also improve student performance in these two areas, generalizability of this procedure would be further established.

Thus in experiment 2 Van Houten et al. (1975) performed a multiple baseline across behaviors that might be dubbed "reading comprehension" and "vocabulary." During a seven-day baseline nineteen fifth-grade students were given twenty-five minutes to answer ten questions on various reading selections (comprehension). Concurrently, these students were exposed to a second baseline that tested their skills regarding matching words to their correct definitions (vocabulary). The treatment package was introduced at separate times for the two behaviors of the same students. On the eighth day these students were explicitly timed and allowed to score their own comprehension answers only. Their comprehension scores were posted and improvements in comprehension scores were praised. This had the immediate observable effect of doubling the comprehension scores over baseline but, predictably, produced no noticeable change in performance on the vocabulary task. These academic behaviors, answering comprehension questions and matching words with definitions, were established as being independent of each other. Five days later, when the treatment package was introduced in the vocabulary task, the students' scores increased by almost 50 percent. On day 35, students were returned to baseline conditions for all schoolwork and simultaneously scores on both vocabulary and comprehension tasks dropped to baseline levels.

The second experiment established the effects of timing with feedback, public posting, and praise not only for composition, but also for reading comprehension and word definition exercises. The authors point out the possibility that this treatment package may work equally well in a variety of other academic areas.

Still unresolved, however, was the effect of explicit timing separate from feedback. Perhaps Van Houten was questioned by students and colleagues regarding this problem because in 1976 Van Houten and Thomas published yet another study that investigated the effects of explicit timing, independent of any components previously seen in the treatment package. This time the independent variables were examined in terms of their effect on math performance. Subjects consisted of twenty second-grade, underachieving students. In the first phase of an ABAB design, students were covertly timed during five thirty-minute baseline sessions in which they solved addition and subtraction problems. The group performance rate averaged around 3.5 correct problems per minute. During eight subsequent days of treatment, timing of on-task behavior was made explicit in two ways.

1. The teacher specifically stated that work on the math problems was being timed for a total of thirty minutes.
2. Students were also informed that the thirty minutes would be divided into one-minute intervals. At the end of each interval students were to draw a line indicating the number of problems completed during that minute.

Because this second process of continually starting and stopping at one-minute intervals necessarily consumed more time than simply timing thirty consecutive minutes, two rates of problem solving were calculated during the treatment phase. Overall rate was determined by counting the number of correctly completed problems over the entire thirty minutes. The local rate was derived from the number of problems completed only within each one-minute time frame. During treatment, local rate averaged 10.5 correct problems per minute; overall rate jumped to an average of 6.8. A reversal to baseline contingencies for five days resulted in a drop to 5.5 correct problems per minute, and a reinstatement of the timing contingencies produced an increase in mean local and overall rates of correct problem solving to 11.5 and 8.1, respectively. Accuracy of problem solving maintained at approximately 95 percent throughout all phases of the experiment.

Van Houten and Thomas note that reversal to baseline contingencies did not result in a complete reversal in student performance. They postulate that failure to recover baseline performance may have been a function of some children continuing to "act like" they were still being explicitly timed. This study finally substantiates the independent effects of timing students' academic performance and extends the dependent variables to include solving math problems. It appears that this procedure is powerful enough to improve behavior independent of posting or teacher praise, and that it is capable of affecting diversified academic areas. It is also clear from Van Houten et al.'s earlier studies that posting and praise can even further facilitate academic performance.

Questions

It has often been suggested that students who ask questions of the teacher are in a better position to progress academically than those who do not. Knapczyk and Livingston (1974) pointed out that the process of asking questions is a form of reciprocal feedback for teacher and student. The teacher obtains feedback on how quickly the student is learning specific concepts and what areas of deficiency exist in the student's developing repertoire. The teacher can, thus, make necessary adjustments in her presentations. The teacher's answers reduce confusion, and questions that result in reduced confusion enhance the learning process.

Knapczyk and Livingston (1974) experimentally investigated the behavior of asking questions with two special education students. These two students were typically off task, demonstrated inaccurate performance on reading tests, and asked no questions in class.

The experimental design was arranged so that one subject received the standard ABAB reversal-of-treatments design and the other subject was run on an extended baseline until the last phase of the first subject treatment. During treatment these two students were specifically told to ask questions if there were any words or directions they did not understand.

This amazingly simple treatment had the same decisive effect on both subjects. When instructed to ask questions both subjects demonstrated an increase in question-asking and on-task behavior and an improvement in reading accuracy. A reversal of treatments for subject 1 produced an immediate reduction in gains, but reinstatement of instructions to ask questions was correlated with improved performance on all measured variables.

Obviously the asking of questions had to result in the answer from the teacher for the instructions to continue being effective as prompts. In addition, the answer presumably was given in a positive manner. Thus the instructions set the stage for students to attend to the material so they could ask a question that the teacher would respond to with both confusion-reducing information and positive attention. This kind of academic interaction decreases the probability of students' academic behavior succumbing to the all too common fate of academic extinction.

Perhaps worth noting is the similarity in this type of student-teacher interchange and the type of interaction often programmed between student and computer, by means of computer-assisted instruction. In both situations quick positive feedback occurs for accuracy and corrections, and further instruction is immediate when errors are made. The computer has the obvious advantage of infinite patience and, in some schools, infinite availability. The teacher, on the other hand, can help a child formulate a useful question when the one he asks would not be adequate to meet the preprogrammed responses of the computer.

Biofeedback

Providing feedback for reading behavior can be accomplished in a number of ways. In recent years the procedure generally referred to as "biofeedback" has become increasingly popular. Although usually used for clinical purposes, Ninness (1980) established that biofeedback could be used to increase reading speed while maintaining a constant level of comprehension. Using an electromyograph (EMG) to measure subvocalization in five college-level subjects, the author took baseline reading rates, comprehension levels, and subvocalization rates for twenty baseline sessions. During baseline all subjects demonstrated significant levels of subvocalization while reading difficult material but showed varying degrees of reading speed and comprehension. Reading speeds, before treatment, ranged from a low of about 120 words per minute for one subject to a high of about 260 words for another.

During treatment audio feedback on subvocal reading behavior was provided to these subjects as they read through various reading selections. Each time the electromyograph detected the subject producing a laryngeal movement while reading, a tone sounded. The reading selections were predetermined by means of the Close Test (Bormuth, 1969) to be at a high level of difficulty for all subjects. When audio feedback was introduced all subjects demonstrated an immediate drop in subvocal behavior, and by the twelfth treatment session subvocalization was eliminated. Concurrent with the elimination of subvocalization was a temporary drop in comprehension for all subjects. However, by the tenth treatment session subjects regained baseline comprehension. Data indicated a delayed treatment effect regarding reading speed for four of the five subjects, but by the fifteenth treatment session reading speed for all five subjects had increased by fifty to eighty words per minute above baseline. After twenty sessions subjects were returned to baseline conditions in that feedback during reading was no longer provided. By this time, however, subjects were no longer demonstrating any subvocal behavior while reading, and thus were not receiving audio feedback concerning subvocalization. As a result, returning to baseline conditions represented no change in feedback from immediately preceding conditions. Comprehension was sustained at the same levels seen during baseline and reading speed continued to stay well above baseline levels. These increases were maintained throughout the course of the posttreatment phase and during the follow-up testing without feedback that occurred one month after the termination of the posttreatment phase.

Generally these results failed to confirm any simple relationship between subvocalization, comprehension, and reading speed. Those subjects who performed at particularly slow reading rates during baseline did not improve to baseline reading rates of the faster-reading subjects. One subject was capable of reading approximately 220 words per minute during baseline while still subvocalizing. This was faster than posttreatment reading rates achieved by some subjects who had their subvocal behavior eliminated as a function of biofeedback treatment. Thus, although it is true that all subjects did significantly increase their reading speed over baseline, it is evident that subvocalization is not the only variable that interferes with reading efficiency.

As Tinker and McCullough (1962) pointed out, rapid recognition and understanding occur only when the text contains words that have been encountered frequently in previous readings. Unfamiliar words are recognized less quickly, and only after a slight delay. The number of unfamiliar words and the existing subvocal tendencies may combine in determining a person's reading rate. It would, therefore, seem inadvisable to promote reading methods that increase reading speed at the expense of allowing adequate time for word recognition.

Ninness (1982) performed a follow-up on three of the five subjects, those who were still available after 2.5 years, to determine what effect the passage of time had had on this biofeedback treatment. During this follow-up the author provided no form of feedback, but took measures on reading speed, comprehension, and subvocalization as in the original baseline conditions.

After eight sessions it was apparent that no significant changes had taken place in these subjects' ability to read difficult material without subvocalizing. Comprehension levels and the improved reading speed were seen 2.5 years after intervention. Time-series analysis, performed on comprehension, reading rate, and subvocalization for these subjects, revealed no trend changes in the data from the one-month follow-up conducted 2.5 years before the data obtained in the final follow-up.

The fact that these subjects displayed no subvocal behavior during laboratory observation should not be construed as indicating that these subjects had forever abandoned subvocalization. On the contrary, personal discussion with these subjects revealed that all three were occasionally aware of some subvocalizing during their private reading. But they also indicated that they were able to detect the behavior when it occurred and to successfully instruct themselves to cease subvocalizing.

Implementation of feedback associated with EMG-measured movement enables a person to monitor his laryngeal movements. He may, thereafter, be capable of relaxing his larynx, and thereby increase his reading rate. The amount of time elapsing after treatment does not seem to influence the ability of the subjects to sustain this skill.

SCHEDULES OF REINFORCEMENT

The immediate change in the environment produced by behavior is critical to the future likelihood of that behavioral unit. The pattern of consequences in relation to instances of behavior is also important. The term *schedules of reinforcement* refers to such patterns. Sometimes the consequence occurs after every instance of the behavioral unit—a pattern known as continuous reinforcement (CRF). Sometimes the consequence occurs after a certain number of instances of the behavioral unit have occurred. Such *ratio* schedules may be fixed (the number of responses is the same between each two consequences) or variable (the number varies). Sometimes the consequences occur after the first instance of the behavioral unit after a given period of time. Such *interval* schedules may be fixed (the length of time that must pass before some behavior will produce a consequence remains constant) or variable (the length of time varies from one interval to the next).

Schedules of reinforcement, as they impact human behavior in natural environments, have typically been given little attention in the literature; yet it is apparent that such schedules are continually operating in all academic environments. Of particular importance in the classroom setting is the function of intermittent schedules. Both ratio and interval schedules are subsumed under this category.

Multiple-Ratio Schedules

Early laboratory research revealed that organisms respond at higher rates of performance on intermittent schedules of reinforcement than they do on continuous reinforcement schedules (Skinner, 1938), and it has been speculated that this same function applies to human behavior whether it occurs in a laboratory experiment or in the everyday world. Skinner points out that "if we only occasionally reinforce a child for good behavior, the behavior survives after we discontinue reinforcement much longer than if we had reinforced every instance up to the same total number of reinforcements" (Skinner, 1953, p. 70). This is exactly the type of function that has not received adequate attention in the literature. Only a few studies have provided information regarding this critical issue in any academic context. One such investigation was conducted by Lovitt and Esveldt (1970).

In a series of experiments Lovitt and Esveldt (1970) used multiple-ratio schedules of reinforcement to increase academic performance in a child with a low rate of such behavior. During the first phase of the initial experiment a twelve-year-old behaviorally disordered boy gained access to free time on a fixed ratio (20:1) reinforcement schedule. That is, for every twenty math problems he finished during a one-hour period, he gained access to one minute of free time in a "high-interest" room. Rules for earning points for access to this area were explained to the subject each day. During the first phase the subject demonstrated a median response rate of 0.8 responses per minute. When the reinforcement contingencies were changed so that a multiple-ratio schedule of reinforcement came into effect, the subject's rate of academic behavior increased. During this phase, reinforcement was available only for solving math problems at a rate higher than one correct behavioral unit (problem solved) per minute. Lovitt and Esveldt provided the following four multiple-ratio bands of reinforcement during this phase:

1. No points if fewer than 60 problems per hour were solved correctly
2. Three points for 60 to 89 correct solutions
3. Nine points for 90 to 119 correct solutions
4. Fifteen points for more than 120 correct solutions (adapted from Lovitt & Esveldt, 1970, p. 262)

Notice that the density of reinforcement became "richer" as the subject moved from one reinforcement ratio bandwidth to another; however, the reinforcement simultaneously became "leaner" as the subject came closer to completing the number of problems required in the next bandwidth. This multiple-ratio schedule resulted in a median response rate of 1.7 correct problems per minute.

On return to a simple fixed ratio (20:1) schedule, performance decreased to a median of 0.6 correct problems per minute. Thus it was demonstrated that the multiple-ratio schedule positively affected the rate of solving math problems. The authors note, however, that this increase was erratic and sometimes only slightly higher than performance under the single fixed-ratio schedule. They note that this may have been partially due to the variable nature of problem difficulty in the subject's workbook. They also mention that this first experiment did not account for error rates; therefore, the quality of the subject's performance could not be adequately ascertained.

To assess the subject's response to the multiple-ratio contingencies independent of the relative level of various math skills, the second experiment used a standard problem format that included only problems of the type 49 + 23 =____, in which no answer exceeded 198. Experiments measured both the number of correct answers and the number of errors. Because, by this time, the subject was well acquainted with the question format, the baseline fixed ratio of 20:1 produced a median correct answer rate of 3.1 per minute. During the second phase another series of multiple-ratio bandwidths, with richer reinforcement densities, produced an immediate change in the subject's correct answer rate. These four ratio bands included the following:

1. No points for 0 to 44 correct solutions in one hour
2. Three points for 45 to 59 correct solutions
3. Six points for 60 to 74 correct solutions
4. Fifteen points for more than 75 correct solutions (adapted from Lovitt & Esveldt, 1970, p. 264)

The respective reinforcement ratio equivalents for each bandwidth were 15:1 to 20:1 for number 2, 10:1 to 13:1 for number 3, and 5:1 to 8:1 for number 4. The authors point out that the same leaning of reinforcement density occurred, as in the first experiment, when the subject's performance improved within a given bandwidth. However, moving to the next bandwidth exposed the subject to a richer schedule of reinforcement. This variation in the reinforcement pattern is reminiscent of a typical variable-ratio schedule of reinforcement, but the fact that this multiple-ratio schedule included an increase in points at increasing response rates complicates the analysis. Although the subject vacillated at correct rate medians of 5.35 during the multiple ratio, 3.9 during the return to single ratio, and 6.4 during a return to multiple ratio, the increases could be accounted for by both the use of multiple-ratio bandwidths and the increasing reinforcement density at each bandwidth.

To isolate the effects of reinforcement density separate from the independent variable of multiple ratios, a third experiment was conducted. This experiment simply alternated the baseline ratio of one reinforcement for twenty completed problems (20:1) with a richer single fixed-ratio reinforcement schedule that required only five completed problems per reinforcement and then returned to the 20:1 ratio. Thus reinforcement density was manipulated while the variable-ratio aspect of the previous experiments was held constant. During all three phases of the experiment the subject's response rate remained relatively stable, fluctuating just slightly around medians of 5.65, 5.9, and 5.5 for the three respective phases. This stable performance is in direct contrast to that seen in experiment 2, in which multiple-ratio schedules were operating, and during which time the subject's rate of math problem solving accelerated as the number of points increased with the richness of the multiple-ratio reinforcement bandwidths. The authors noted, however, the possibility of another artifact during experiment 2. Various problems had been marked in order to notify the subject that he was moving from one bandwidth to the next. This signaled increasing reinforcement density and may have acted as a source of incentive. In order to investigate this possible artifact the researchers conducted a fourth experiment on the same subject.

In experiment 4 the number of required problems to be answered in order to move to the next bandwidth were marked inaccurately throughout all phases of the experiment. Surprisingly, the irrelevant cue marks had little influence in the subject's rate of problem solving. All of these outcomes seem to indicate that the subject's improved academic functioning was primarily related to the multiple-ratio schedule of reinforcement. The authors indicate that the subject performed according to the underlying contingencies of reinforcement and not according to the various inaccurate cue marks.

The authors state: "To be precise, the purpose of this investigation was to compare performance rate when one reinforcement rate was scheduled and when several reinforcement schedules were simultaneously available" (Lovitt & Esveldt, 1970, p. 261). This is an interesting point, for although different schedules of reinforcement were simultaneously available, the subject was apparently not notified of the number of points he had earned until the close of the session. In what sense can the notification of the number of points earned at the close of a session be described as a schedule of reinforcement? Further investigation is needed to explain how and why the subject's behavior changed concurrent with changes in earnings that were apparently not associated with any events that occurred as the problem-solving behavior occurred.

Another study by Saudargas, Madsen, and Scott (1977) investigated fixed- and variable-time feedback schedules on academic production rates. In this study, details regarding each elementary student's work load were given at the beginning of each week. A fixed-time schedule was approximated by informing all students that at the end of the week they would be taking home a production report card that detailed their academic performance. In this condition, the announcement was made one week in advance of the date that parents would be notified of students' school progress. During these conditions students completed an average of 83.1 percent of their assignments. When exposed to a variable-time schedule, in which reports might be sent home on any given day during the week, the assignment completion rate jumped to an average 92.8 percent for the first week and 110.9 percent during the next week. Percentages in excess of 100 indicated that students were even doing extra work.

A one-week reversal to a fixed-time schedule resulted in a regression to 73.9 percent assignment completion, but return to a variable-time schedule for the last week resulted in an overwhelming 154.2 percent completion rate. The variable-time schedule apparently acted to increase the rate of assignment completion. As the authors of this study noted, however, there is a discrepancy between fixed- and variable-time schedules used in this classroom context, and schedules of reinforcement typically used in the laboratory. For one thing, it is not clear that receiving a report card necessarily constitutes a reinforcer. Second, the report cards were given out independent of performance. Lastly, the data derived in this study were presented by way of group averages. As the authors note: "The individual results, while an indication of an increase in production during variable-time conditions, fail to demonstrate any consistent patterns analogous for animal literature (e.g., Ferster and Skinner, 1957)" (Saudargas et al., 1977, p. 677). Yet, for applied purposes, this extrapolation from the laboratory offers a useful tool to enhance on-task behavior.

Adjusting Schedules

The question arises as to whether it is more expedient to make consequences contingent on behavior of specified topographies that appear to be consistent with academic engagement, or to make the consequence contingent on the tangible academic outcomes of on-task behavior. In the former case the student receives points (tokens, etc.) at times when he looks as though he is working; in the latter case the consequence is delivered according to the products of his labor. The answer is not simple and may depend somewhat on the history of the particular student in question. Students who seldom, if ever, evidence even low levels of academic behavior are probably poor candidates for contingencies that specify problem solving or question answering to obtain reinforcement. If, on the other hand, the student has some minimal problem-solving skills in his repertoire but does not currently engage in this behavior, then a program that emphasizes academic output might be a good choice.

Kirby and Shields (1972) produced a study that demonstrated this effect. Their subject was a thirteen-year-old seventh-grade boy who apparently was "unwilling" to perform his math assignment in class. If prompted by the teacher, however, and given her exclusive attention, he would work for short periods of time. Thus it was determined that this student had some minimal repertoire of arithmetic skills but was simply not emitting much arithmetic behavior.

The subject's behavior was sampled for twenty minutes a day during four phases of the following experiment. In five days of baseline it was observed that this student spent only 51 percent of his time attending to task and that during this time his mean correct answer rate was .47 per minute. Subsequently, during treatment 1, his math problem-solving behavior was placed on an adjusting fixed-ratio schedule of reinforcement. On days 6 and 7 praise was given at the completion of every second problem. On days 8 and 9, as he began to demonstrate higher rates of problem solving, the fixed ratio was adjusted upward to reinforce completion of every fourth problem. Then, on days 10 and 11, the number of solutions per instance of praise was increased to eight, and finally, during the final two days of treatment 1, sixteen problems were required to obtain praise. During this adjusting fixed-ratio schedule the student's problem-solving rate significantly improved over baseline. He averaged 1.36 correct answers per minute and was observed to demonstrate attending behavior 97 percent of the time. A reversal resulted in an eventual decline in these behaviors, but reinstatement of the adjusting fixed-ratio contingency brought a return to 97 percent attending behavior and 1.44 correct answers per minute.

It is interesting to note that the reversal of contingencies did not result in an immediate return to baseline levels of performance and attending. This is probably accounted for by the intermittent nature of the adjusting fixed-ratio schedule. This is one of the great advantages to programs that adjust schedules of reinforcement by requiring gradual increments in work loads and reinforce on an intermittent basis. The subject appears to become accustomed to irregular and increasing work requirements. The same strategy may be used to wean students from the formal program; but occasional praise is still important.

RESPONSE DEPRIVATION

Premack has given considerable attention to influencing the frequency of behavior by manipulating the probabilities of various schedules of reinforcement. The Premack principle was previously described in Chapter 4, on behavioral contracting. The princple, sometimes referred to as the probability differential hypothesis, predicts that any response that occurs at a high probability (frequency) can be used to reinforce any response that occurs at a lower probability. Thus if a student spends more time drawing than doing math assignments, the opportunity to draw (contingent response) may be used as a reinforcer for the math performance (instrumental response).

Laboratory research by Timberlake and Allison (1974) advocates a response deprivation hypothesis that subsumes the Premack principle. The response deprivation hypothesis states that any response, irrespective of its probability relative to any other response, may be used as a reinforcer, provided the frequency of the contingent response is suppressed relative to its baseline or operant level. In other words, if a student is given reduced access to any behavior, whether it be drawing or math, relative to the naturally occurring level in the classroom, then the opportunity to engage in that behavior has become a potential source of reinforcement. Therefore, the opportunity to engage in any regularly occurring behavior can be used as reinforcement so long as the behaving person has been deprived of the opportunity to engage in that behavior. (Mathematically, the ratio of instrumental to contingent responses [I/C] must be greater, when the contingency between them is in effect, than the operant ratio during baseline [Oi/Oc], when either response may occur at any time.) Thus, paradoxically, math may be used to reinforce drawing (the instrumental response) if the naturally occurring level of math behavior is restricted below its baseline level (I/C > Oi/Oc). This may seem intuitively inconsistent; however, Konarksi, Johnson, Crowell, and Whitman (1980) provided two excellent demonstrations of this effect with four average first-grade students.

The first experiment demonstrated that a low-probability behavior (math tasks) could function as a reinforcer for a high probability behavior (coloring tasks) when the frequency of the low probability behavior (math) was suppressed through response deprivation. In the six-day baseline period two students were told that they could either perform math or coloring, but that they must remain seated at the tables where the materials were available. During each twenty-minute session the amount of time spent coloring and doing math were individually assessed and their respective probability ratios were calculated from the duration of time spent in each task. Math was found to occur at a much lower rate in both children. Thus it would serve as the contingent response (reinforcer) for coloring. In a series of counterbalanced reversals the following conditions were arranged:

1. In the response deprivation condition the contingent response (math) was available only after the instrumental response (coloring) was met, and the duration of the instrumental response relative to the contingent response was kept greater than the baseline ratio (I/O > Oi/Oc).
2. In the no-response deprivation condition the same contingency was in effect, but the ratio of instrumental to contingent response was smaller than during baseline conditions (I/O < Oi/O/c).
3. In a matched control condition the contingent response (math) was randomly presented during the session, independent of the child's responding. These conditions were presented in different orders for the two children to control for sequence effects.

In the response deprivation condition coloring time for both students increased. As the authors point out, "this suggests that math acted as a reinforcer for coloring when the conditions of response deprivation were presented even though it was clearly shown in the baseline period to be a lower-probability response" (Konarski et al., 1980, p. 600). Coloring time did not increase in the no-response deprivation condition, but the matched control condition was equivocal. One child showed the expected decrement in instrumental responding owing to lack of contingency, the other did not. This suggests that deprivation of the contingent response alone may suffice to increase instrumental responding. In any case, the outcome is clearly inconsistent with requirements specified by the Premack principle, which indicate that a higher-probability response is required to act as a reinforcer for a lower-probability response.

Experiment 2 was conducted in an attempt to determine if the Premack principle (probability differential hypothesis) would be an accurate predictor of behavior only when it was consistent with the response deprivation hypothesis. Two different children from the same first-grade classroom were observed during a five-day baseline to assess the naturally occurring frequency of reading and math problems. Using the same design as experiment 1, a series of counterbalanced reversal of treatments (which included response deprivation, no-response deprivation, and a matched control condition) was arranged to test the assumption that a higher-probability contingent response (in this case math) would increase the instrumental performance (reading) only under response deprivation conditions. For both students the opportunity to do math (higher-probability response) was made contingent on reading (the instrumental response). If the Premack principle were a necessary and sufficient condition for reinforcement to occur, then math should have been able to act as a reinforcer whether or not a condition of response deprivation existed. Predictably both children demonstrated significant increases in the instrumental response, reading, when under the response deprivation condition. However, neither child showed any increase in reading when response deprivation did not exist. That is, unless these students were deprived of the opportunity to perform math problems, performing math problems did not act as a reinforcer. To quote the authors, "in sum, the increases in instrumental responding of both children can be better interpreted by the presence/absence of response deprivation in the schedules than from the existence of a probability differential between responses" (Konarski et al., 1980, p. 604). They go on to clarify that the Premack principle is perhaps best understood as a special case of the response deprivation effect amplified by the contingent application of high-probability responses as reinforcers.

PEER TUTORING

Behavioral research has recently emphasized the value of having students assist one another in the learning process. How this can best be accomplished has been the source of considerable investigation. The use of peer tutors has proved beneficial to those tutored as well as to those who provide instruction.

Collateral Behaviors

Collateral behaviors are those that occur in conjunction with a primary set of learned behaviors. In general it can be said that any treatment that produces multiple changes in behavior is producing "collateral" effects. For example, when a reinforcement procedure is used, one person provides reinforcement for the behavior of another and sometimes the behavior of both is affected. That is, the teacher or tutor who provides reinforcement to one who is on task may be collaterally affected by the presentation of the reward.

In an experiment conducted by Greer and Polinstok (1982) the extent to which tutors were collaterally affected by their distribution of verbal and token reinforcement to tutees was documented. In their first experiment three students from an urban junior high school, all of whom had a history of poor academic behaviors, were provided with an opportunity to act as tutors for groups of five equally poor eighth-grade students in a remedial reading class. Using an ABCBC design in conjunction with a multiple baseline across groups, tutors were initially asked to help their five tutees follow classroom rules but were given no instructions as to how to accomplish this feat. During this baseline period a number of important observations were made concerning the tutors' and tutees' academic performance. The reading scores for both tutors and tutees were depressed. The three groups of tutees averaged 8.96, 5.91, and 6.1 correct answers out of twenty comprehension questions. The tutors averaged .22, 0, and 3.52 for the same type of reading materials, which was presented to them in a nonexperimental setting. On-task behavior for both groups was very low. Data were also accumulated on the number of approval statements made by the tutors to the tutees during this baseline period. These were practically nonexistent.

Tutors were then given five training sessions during which they were instructed in the procedure of token and verbal reinforcement of on-task behavior. In addition, they were given directions on how to ignore their tutees' off-task behaviors.

During the intervention phase, tutors were given tokens for providing contingent verbal and token reinforcement according to their instructional package. Not only did this treatment immediately affect the performance of the tutees, but the tutors themselves at once demonstrated the collateral effect of increased academic performance *in a nonexperimental class*. Reading scores more than tripled. These results occurred despite the fact that no formal reinforcement procedure was implemented in the nonexperimental class for the tutors' own academic behavior.

In a series of reversals that followed, the tutors were instructed to first terminate and then reinstate both verbal and token reinforcement procedures. Both the tutees and tutors demonstrated correlated decrease and subsequent increase in performance. After sixty-eight sessions, however, the effect of such training maintained independent of any explicit contingencies. In a follow-up check in which tutors were not given instructions to provide tutees with tokens or verbal reinforcement, their approving comments continued at a high rate. Likewise, the tutees continued to benefit from this verbal reinforcement by demonstrating continued performance gains.

Most remarkable was the collateral effect this training had on tutors. Noting again that no explicit consequences were contingent on the tutors' behavior, it is rather remarkable that by the end of the postcheck, seventy-four sessions later, tutors' correct reading comprehension responses had risen to an average of 11.8,

9, and 13.6 for tutors A, B, and C, respectively. Moreover, on-task behavior maintained at a very high rate for all three tutors.

In a second experiment, one year later, Greer and Polinstok replicated their original study while measuring additional dependent variables. Using three eighth-grade boys as tutors and fifteen seventh-graders from a remedial reading program as tutees, all of the previously measured variables were assessed. In addition, data were collected concerning the tutees' responses to their respective tutors' reinforcing comments and token dispensing. The Scholastic Aptitude Test (SAT) was given at the beginning of the school year, at midterm just before administering the experimental procedures, and as a posttest at the end of the year. The results of experiment 2 were essentially the same as for the first experiment, but provided further verification that collateral effects were a function of tutor reinforcement of tutee on-task behavior.

It was found that the tutees systematically reciprocated the verbal reinforcement provided by the tutors. As the tutors increased their contingent approval for on-task behavior, tutees in turn made attention responses indicative of appreciation.

Furthermore, whereas no improvements were seen during the first semester of regular instruction, by the end of the second semester of tutoring both tutors and tutees showed significant gains in SAT scores. This provides further verification for the collateral improvements previously indicated by improved on-task behavior and daily test scores. The authors note that demonstrating collateral gains by such procedures does not provide evidence concerning the mechanisms or underlying principle of such a phenomenon. However, these procedures do lay the foundation for further investigation into an apparently powerful and valuable technique.

Opportunity to Respond

Much of what goes on in public school classrooms has little to do with generating academic skills (Skinner, 1984). Teachers and administrators often assume that children learn by passively absorbing information that is presented to them via a lecture format. In more progressive classrooms, experiential exercises may supplement or replace didactic instruction; but such exercises rarely include the critical elements of immediate error checking, feedback, and differential reinforcement. In both traditional and experiential classrooms, teachers of young children present elaborate descriptions of abstract concepts while providing no structured opportunities for the students to respond.

Systematic observation of classroom activity has provided disconcerting data on the amount of time students actually spend on academic responding. Fox (1974) noted that first-graders averaged about twenty seconds per day in overt reading behavior. Time spent in computations involving basic math facts was documented as occurring less than five seconds per day (Ritschl, Grinstead, Whitson, et al., 1980). The majority of time in which the students are supposedly involved in school lessons is most often spent passively listening to teacher presentations, copying from the board, attending to overhead projectors, and participating in other auxiliary, tangential activities. However, none of these auxiliary behaviors are correlated with academic achievement. Only active academic responding is correlated with academic achievement.

Delquadri, Greenwood, Stretton, and Hall (1983) investigated the effects of increasing students' "opportunity to respond" in order to determine what effect high and low rates of overt responding would have on spelling performance. Using an ABAB design in an intact third-grade classroom, they compared the effects of dramatically increasing and decreasing the rates of overt spelling among both poor and average students.

During eighteen weeks of baseline the teacher continued her usual system of spelling instruction. In a lecture discussion format she had children illustrate word meanings, and directed their attention to various regular and irregular verb forms. Children worked independently from spelling workbooks as she moved throughout the classroom helping them look up definitions of words and perform sentence completion tasks, crossword puzzles, and matching and vocabulary exercises. Every Friday the whole class was given a quiz over the words studied that week. The reader may note that, again, none of these tasks required students to spell targeted words accurately and frequently.

During the treatment phase, students were randomly divided into two teams (red and blue). Each team member spent five minutes playing the role of tutor and then five minutes playing the role of tutee. Tutors simply asked tutees to spell words tutors read from lists of targeted words. For each correctly spelled word the tutee earned 2 points for his team. If a word was incorrectly spelled, the tutee was given the correct spelling and asked to write three consecutive correct spellings for the earning of just 1 point. As the game progressed the teacher moved throughout the class, verbally praising student performance and giving bonus points. The team that accumulated the most daily and weekly points won the daily and weekly competitions. The team with the most points was applauded by the losing team.

Every Friday, as during baseline measurement, all students were required to take a test over the words they had practiced during the preceding week. This simple program proved to be immensely successful for both the poor and the average spellers. Slow students, who previously averaged 9 errors during the weekly quiz, decreased their error rate to only 2.5. Average students dropped from an average error rate of 3 during baseline to .5 during treatment. A reversal of baseline and treatment replicated these results.

The program was carried out using standard classroom materials. It involved the whole class of students simultaneously, required no backup reinforcers, and was later found to be an effective procedure in a number of academic areas.

Teacher versus Peer Instruction

A study designed to analyze the effects of several instructional variables in classwide peer tutoring as compared with the effects of those variables in teacher-controlled procedures was conducted by Greenwood et al. (1984). The authors examined how various characteristics of the two instructional procedures and various characteristics of student behavior related to student achievement.

Three experiments were conducted with 128 student participants, half male and half female, and five female teachers. Student participants (83 percent of whom were black, 15 percent white, and 2 percent oriental) were, as a group, five months below grade level on standardized achievement tests. The four lowest-performing students from each class were selected for frequent observation and for measurement of weekly test performance. Another group from each class was assessed by weekly tests but not observed.

In experiment 1 three classes were exposed to peer tutoring and to a teacher-developed instructional procedure. In their twenty-minute spelling session class 1 first participated in classwide peer tutoring, then the teacher's procedure, and then peer tutoring again. The procedures were applied in reverse order in the spelling session in class 2. Students in class 3 followed the first order in their twenty-minute vocabulary session. Students' scores on weekly spelling (or vocabulary) tests were the dependent variable. Scores on standardized tests were used to assess the validity of the weekly tests as measures of learning.

Direct observation was used to measure the independent variables, which were events that occurred in the classroom, five involving instructional context and three involving student behavior. Observers noted the activity, task, and structure during an initial ten-second interval. Then they recorded student behavior, as well as teacher position and behavior relative to the student during the next six ten-second intervals. Observations continued at ten-second intervals throughout the twenty-minute sessions, Monday through Thursday. Each of the four low-achieving students was observed once a week for five weeks, and student behavior was categorized as either academically engaged, managing the environment as a prerequisite to academic behavior, or inappropriate. On Fridays the teacher gave fifteen-minute tests in vocabulary, spelling, and math.

During the *teacher-mediated procedures* phase in each class the teacher's tasks were to engage the class in discussion, paper/pencil tasks, worksheets, and books to teach the vocabulary (one class) or spelling (two classes) lessons. The teacher set a timer for twenty minutes and focused only on the target content area during that session, while avoiding teaching that content at other times during the day.

During the *classwide peer tutoring* phase, students were randomly paired each week. This procedure closely approximates the format previously described in Delquadri et al. (1983). For ten minutes the tutor dictated instructional items one at a time, and the tutee responded in writing. The tutor gave 2 points after each correct response or provided the correct answer contingent on errors. After the tutor modeled the correct response the tutee could earn 1 point for writing the correct response three times. During the second ten minutes the tutor and tutee roles were reversed. After the instructional period total points turned in by students were summed and a winning team announced in each class.

Classwide tutoring resulted in higher scores on weekly tests than did teacher-mediated procedures, irrespective of the order in which the strategies were implemented. Differences were especially great for the low students (class 1 peer tutoring resulted in 81 percent and 74 percent correct for low students on weekly tests versus 46 percent correct during teacher-mediated procedures). Class 3 scores for low students were 94 percent and 91 percent versus 30 percent. In class 2, in which procedures were used in reverse order, teacher-mediated procedures resulted in 45 percent and 54 percent correct versus 92 percent correct for peer tutoring procedures for low students. The other students showed the same effect, but the differences were smaller, ranging from a difference of 3 percent in the smaller case to 27 percent in the largest case.

Experiment 2 involved twenty-three students in a multiple-baseline design across math, spelling, and vocabulary. During baseline, tests were given on four consecutive Fridays over material not taught during the week. At the beginning of the fifth week teacher-mediated procedures were implemented to teach the material in all three subjects during the first four days of succeeding weeks. Peer tutoring replaced teacher procedures in spelling at the eighth week, in math at the fourteenth week, and in vocabulary at the ninth week. Direct observation was carried out as in the first experiment, and tests were given on Fridays.

As in experiment 1, classwide peer tutoring resulted in increased responding in students on paper/pencil and worksheet tasks, while there was less discussion than during the teacher-mediated procedures. The four students who performed at the lowest levels during baseline improved most, and the highest scores were obtained during peer tutoring sessions. These students' scores went from 54 percent (baseline) to 73 percent (teacher procedures) to 94 percent (peer tutoring) in spelling, from 44 percent to 73 percent to 77 percent in math, and from 38 percent to 79 percent to 96 percent in vocabulary. The other students' test scores followed the same pattern, but the differences were smaller (for example, gaining 8 percent, 4 percent, and 9 percent from teacher-mediated to peer procedures in spelling, math, and vocabulary, respectively). Standardized tests showed gains of five months in spelling and math. Vocabulary scores showed a drop in performance, perhaps related to the short period during which peer tutoring was in effect (three weeks).

Experiment 3 was undertaken, to replicate experiment 2, with a class of seventeen students. The replication was not fully carried out, however, because the teacher deviated from the peer tutoring procedures after session 15 in spelling and used less teacher-student discussions and more of other tasks (paper/pencil, worksheets, media) during teacher procedures. Students' weekly test scores were again highest when peer tutoring was in effect, but dropped off in spelling after week 15, when the peer tutoring procedure drifted. The spelling response drifted from students writing the words they were learning to their saying the words. The experimenters suggested that this change was associated with two problems: the learning involved different responses (saying) from those required on tests (writing), and tutors probably gave less feedback because their training involved giving feedback on written answers.

Taken together, the three experiments reported by Greenwood et al. (1984) provide good evidence that inner-city students properly trained to tutor their classmates can provide an instructional environment that is superior to that which the teacher can provide when the teaching procedures focus on teacher-student discussion. Further, the lowest-performing students benefit most dramatically. The superiority of peer tutoring may have been related to the "greater variety of academic responding (i.e., writing, reading aloud, reading silent, and academic talk)" that occurred during peer tutoring (p. 536).

Classwide Field Replication

Greenwood et al. (1987) performed a large-group, statistically analyzed replication of the peer tutoring spelling game as described by Delquadri et al. (1983); Greenwood et al. (1984); and Greenwood, Delquadri, and Hall (1984). This study, like its predecessors, emphasized the value of increasing the students' "opportunity to respond" as the variable that most critically influences acquisition of improved spelling behavior, as well as other subjects. However, previous studies in this area used relatively few subjects and were of short duration. As stated by the authors, "The purpose of this study was to examine the effects of a large-scale and long-term implementation of classwide peer tutoring procedures on spelling achievement and participant satisfaction" (Greenwood et al., 1987). Specifically, they attempted to ascertain whether spelling performances were improved most by teacher or peer tutoring procedures. They also compared peer methods used during two consecutive years and the contributions of low pretest versus high pretest spelling scores. Last, they collected information regarding teacher and student appreciation of the program. Greenwood and colleagues point out that there have been few large-group investigations in this area for a number of reasons: effective educational procedures have not been adequately outlined, there has been a lack of administrative support, and there exists the common belief that peer tutoring is essentially a short-term strategy.

In order to substantiate the broad-range and long-term (two years) effects of increasing student opportunity to respond via peer tutoring, Greenwood et al. again enlisted the cooperation of the public school system. This time subjects consisted of 211 inner-city first- and second-grade students. Many of the same students served as subjects during consecutive years.

This truly was a large-scale investigation. In all, four separate schools were involved. This encompassed sixteen teachers: eight during the first year with the first-grade students and eight in the second year with the second-grade students. Furthermore, six consultants helped train the teachers in the details of the program and were available throughout the course of the study to ensure correct implementation of teacher strategies.

The authors indicate that students' spelling was assessed in their regular classes on a weekly basis. Each Friday tests over the week's spelling words were given. Results were posted on a classroom chart. In order to obtain measures for posttest gains, pretests were also given (on alternate Mondays) in the second year of the study. No posting or contingencies were associated with these pretests; they merely served as a running index of word difficulty. For statistical purposes students were assigned to high or low pretest groups, depending on their average weekly spelling scores obtained during the second year of the study. Students who scored at or above an average of 50 percent were assigned to the high group; the remaining students were assigned to the low group.

During the implementation of the experiment different procedures were used on the same subjects during selected phases of the study. The authors describe these experimental arrangements:

> The specific designs used in each class and across individual students over the 2 years varied. For example, the number of baseline-reversal phases received by individual students ranged from one to four. Since the emphasis of the study was the long-term implementation of the classwide peer tutoring procedures, baseline and reversal probes were kept to a minimum duration, ranging from 1 to 3 weeks per phase. (Greenwood et al., 1987, p. 154)

In the traditional teaching phases of the experiment, the classroom teachers simply continued their standard spelling curriculum. No form of the peer tutoring spelling game was used, nor was there any effort to increase the usual rate of student responding. The authors specify common elements used across teachers in this phase as: standard word lists and spelling exercises from textbooks, use of the overhead or chalkboard for illustrating and discussing rules concerning new words, homework, independent study, spelling out loud with teacher feedback for correction. These methods probably constitute the standard spelling procedures used by classroom teachers in most school districts.

During the classwide peer tutoring phases of the study, students engaged in actual spelling behavior more frequently. As previously described in Delquadri et al. (1983) and Greenwood et al. (1984), Greenwood et al. (1987) arranged the peer tutoring spelling game contingencies to increase the students' ''opportunity to respond'' to appropriate academic stimuli. Each class was divided into competing teams that approximated contingencies in athletic competition. Team members were randomly assigned into pairs (tutors and tutees). These pairs of students called words to each other from prepared lists (ten words per list during the first year and twenty words per list during the second year). Tutors and tutees exchanged roles every ten minutes. As each word was called by one member of the student pair (tutor), the other student (tutee) wrote the word on a piece of paper. The word was immediately checked for accuracy by the tutor. If correct, the student earned 2 points for her team (as in basketball); if it were incorrect, the tutor spelled the word aloud and the tutee wrote it correctly three times and earned only 1 point. This provided immediate error checking and feedback, which are critical elements in gaining academic skills. Since all student teams were randomly reassigned on a weekly basis, every student had an equally high probability of winning. This system generated high rates of student responding, which were maintained by the controlled competition between teams.

The teacher's job primarily consisted of making sure the rules of the game were consistently and correctly followed. Teachers occasionally gave bonus points and praise to student pairs who demonstrated correct game procedures. At the end of each day's thirty-minute session, the team with the largest number of points applauded the losing team. Scores were publicly posted for both teams and individual players. While this reinforcement system is obviously simple and inexpensive, it was found to be amazingly effective.

Statistical analysis of this study was accomplished by comparing group averages of test scores under each condition. Means were obtained for the following procedures: teacher procedures implemented during the first year (Tpro1), classwide peer tutoring during the first year (Cwpt1), pretests given during the second year (Pre2), teacher procedures used in the second year (Tpro2), and classwide peer tutoring in the second year (Cwpt2). The authors compared the group outcomes via the analysis of variance (ANOVA):

> For the 99 students with complete data, the mean percentage of correct responses under each procedure was 74.9% (Tpro1 and 2), 85.0% (Cwpt1), and 89.0% (Cwpt2). The ANOVA yielded a significant main effect for *Instructional Procedures*, F (2, 194) = 37.1, $p < .001$. Pairwise post-hoc comparisons of the *Instructional Procedures* means indicated that during tutoring, students in both years made statistically significant gains ($p < .01$) in spelling performance relative to the teacher procedures. There was no difference between tutoring in Years 1 and 2 as students maintained high levels of performance in both years. (Greenwood et al., 1987, p. 156)

It is thus apparent that classwide peer tutoring had a more pronounced effect on spelling performance than all or any of the standard procedures used by teachers in the regular classroom.

With regard to low versus high pretest performance it was found that

> the main effect for *Groups* produced means of 75% for the low pretest group versus 90% for the high pretest group, $F(1, 97) = 31.9$, $p < .001$. Thus, the initial difference of 40% between groups at Pre2, 30% versus 70%, $F(1, 95) = 200.4$, $p < .001$, was substantially reduced but not entirely removed as a result of both teacher and tutoring procedures. (Greenwood et al., 1987, p. 156)

This study also investigated the extent of teacher and student satisfaction with the implementation of the peer tutoring system. Again, according to the authors: "The teacher rating means over six general satisfaction items ranged from 3.9 to 4.6 in Year 1 and from 3.3 to 4.3 in Year 2 on a 5-point scale. These results reflected generally positive evaluations of the peer tutoring program" (Greenwood et al., 1987, p. 156). Student satisfaction, as measured on a 3-point scale, also indicated extremely high levels of enthusiasm for the program.

While behavior analysts traditionally seek to understand relations between environmental events and the behavior of individuals, in this case they were interested in classwide improvement of spelling performance; therefore, a group-comparison design was appropriate. Thus far, there have been at least sixteen separate studies that have verified the effect of increasing student's "opportunity to respond." Three of these have been described in this chapter. Whether or not colorful teacher presentations and bulletin boards turn out to be critical to the acquisition of academic skills, behavior analysts have amply demonstrated that such acquisition is improved when contingencies are arranged to maximize students' "opportunity to respond" and to provide reinforcement for doing so.

Mutual Coaching

Other studies have been less explicit about defining the roles of the tutor and tutee. A study by Harris and Sherman (1973) determined that even unstructured peer tutoring improved the math performance of both fourth- and fifth-grade students. During twenty-minute morning and afternoon math assignments it was found that when the math sessions were preceded by fifteen minutes in which the teacher had all students arrange themselves into small groups of two or three for mutual coaching, the mean percentage of correctly solved math problems rose by 8 to 10 percent. Further, the mean rate of problems performed nearly doubled when peer tutoring was used.

When a reinforcement contingency (which specified that those children who had completed all problems at 90 percent accuracy would be given immediate access to free time) was added, accuracy was further increased. Thus an accuracy criterion used in conjunction with tutoring appears to be a powerful combination for improving both rate and accuracy. Unfortunately, the unstructured tutoring program used in this design did not specify differential effects for those students who were most actively involved in providing assistance and those who were given help. Irrespective of this methodological problem, all of the outcomes provide strong evidence that peer tutoring can supplement the standard instructional format in elementary classrooms and benefit the tutors as well as the tutees.

HOMEWORK

Several studies have attempted to evaluate the potential benefits of assigning homework to students (Goldstein, 1960; Maertens, 1968). As Harris and Sherman (1974) point out, the value of homework in improving student performance is clouded by the fact that most studies simply compared a circumstance in which homework was assigned with one in which it was not. The critical components of the assignments, completion and accuracy, were usually not addressed. In an attempt to ascertain the critical variables relating to improved student performance by way of homework assignments, Harris and Sherman (1974) ran two experiments. In their first study two sixth-grade classes composed of twenty-five and twenty-seven students served as subjects. Assignments consisted of completion of sentences derived from reading various segments of a social studies text. During social studies period the teachers divided the class into two teams, who answered fifteen questions based on the previous day's assignments. Answers were graded after each question, and the team with the most correct answers was given the opportunity to place either an X or an O on the board in a game of tic-tac-toe.

Subsequently various successive conditions were compared in both groups:

1. just assigning homework with no external contingencies beyond the tic-tac-toe game;
2. homework assignments plus the opportunity to leave school ten minutes early if 80 percent of the sentences were correctly completed;
3. the opportunity to leave fifteen minutes early if 80 percent of the assignment was done correctly; and
4. same as condition 3 but students who did not achieve the 80 percent criterion were denied access to recess. During recess they made up their assignments and, on completion, were permitted to go to the remainder of recess.

Before the procedures above, when homework had not been assigned, only 5 percent to 15 percent of the class questions had been correctly answered. However, each of the conditions above led to a mean increase in the percentage of students who completed homework and an increase in the mean percentage of correct answers during the classroom game in classroom A. The best performance was seen in the consequences included both being able to leave school early if questions were completed with 80 percent correct and being made to complete the work during recess when that criterion was not met. Under these conditions 67 percent of the students completed their homework, and answers in class had an average accuracy of 74 percent. In classroom B the various consequence systems produced less noticeable differences; however, all conditions produced greater improvements in percentage of homework completion (73 percent), percentage of homework performed correctly (67 percent), and percentage of accuracy in class (66 percent). Note that when no consequences were in effect, only 13 percent accuracy had been obtained.

It might be tempting to conclude that the game of tic-tac-toe was responsible for the dramatic improvements in the accuracy and completion rates. However, comparing conditions in which the game was played, independent of contingencies for homework completion (21 percent correct), with conditions in which consequences were provided (69 percent) shows the effect of assigning consequences for homework completion.

In an attempt to further clarify the impact of homework on performance, Harris and Sherman (1974) conducted a second experiment in which a series of increasingly demanding conditions was used for math assignments. Twenty-five sixth-grade students who were performing below grade level in mathematics were exposed to two separate thirty-minute math sessions in a series of counterbalanced reversal-of-treatment designs.

When no consequences for homework completion were provided, only 16 percent of the students completed their assignments. When they were given the opportunity to go to lunch ten minutes early for completing the previous day's homework, 62 percent of the students finished their homework. Better still, when students were allowed both an early lunch and the privilege of going home ten minutes early for successful completion, 85 percent finished their assignments.

This first series of contingencies provided no consequences for accuracy, and not surprisingly, where consequences were not provided, behavior was not affected. Accuracy in solving math problems in class rose only 2 percent. In the next phase consequences for accurate completion of homework were assessed. Only students who completed all homework assignments at 60 percent accuracy or above were permitted early lunch and early dismissal. Overall, in-class accuracy improved from 36 percent to 57 percent when the accuracy contingency on homework was in effect. Note, however, that up to this point no direct consequences had been provided for improving in-class math performance.

In the next phase of the experiment consequences for accurate completion of homework were combined with consequences for accurate classroom performance. Throughout this phase both early lunch and early dismissal for accuracy at or above 60 percent in homework were maintained. In addition, a second contingency gave immediate recess to students who completed their in-class math assignments with 90 percent accuracy. Under these conditions 72 percent of the class reached the 90 percent criterion. Under altered conditions, consequences for 90 percent classroom accuracy were provided, but no concurrent consequences for accuracy of homework were included; only 58 percent of the students met the 90 percent criterion. It thus appears that the homework accuracy contingency contributed to the students' level of in-class performance.

Both of these experiments demonstrated that simply assigning homework to students is unlikely to affect classroom performance. But contingencies with positive consequences for accurate completion of homework relevant to the next day's assignment do have an extremely powerful effect. As the authors point out, this is as might be expected; but unfortunately this is not necessarily the fashion in which homework is normally assigned or in which consequences are provided.

VOCAL BEHAVIOR

Although increased writing productivity and performance has been a frequent objective for behavior analysts, the rate of appropriate vocal behavior has seldom been addressed. Yet demonstration of the operant nature of speech was accomplished in the laboratory as early as 1955 (Greenspoon, 1955).

Further, the process of manipulating the variables that control vocal behavior need not be complex. In two experiments Broden, Copeland, Beasley, and Hall (1977) demonstrated that teachers can modify students' rate and style of on-task vocal responding by simply altering the types of questions asked, specifying particular instructions for grammatical usage, and ignoring students who failed to comply with these instructions.

In their first experiment seven lower-socioeconomic, special education junior high boys were observed every morning for eight days for a two-hour period. Although these students were observed to be well behaved and were seldom involved in any form of disruptive behavior, their production of vocal responses in answering teacher questions averaged only 2.0 words per question. After baseline the teacher changed her questioning format by increasing the number of questions that required multiple-word answers. Questions beginning with the word *why*, for example, required more words to answer. The teacher also presented more new questions, that is, those that inquired into subject matter not discussed in their text or in previous class presentations. The researchers arranged this procedure so that other factors, such as teacher attention, could not systematically influence the rate of student vocal responding. During this nine-day treatment the average length of student responses to teacher questions doubled. A four-day return to baseline and subsequent seven-day reinstatement of this procedure replicated the outcome. Student responding dropped back to baseline and, on reintroduction of the same treatment, doubled again.

In a second experiment the authors used the same design to determine the effects of instructions on the use of complete sentences when responding to teacher interrogatives. At the beginning of every class the teacher announced that complete sentences would be required when answering. During class, students who responded in sentence fragments were given five seconds to correct their commentary. If they failed to make a response in complete sentence form, another student was called on. Thus the responses of students who failed to comply with correct grammatical usage were put on extinction with regard to teacher attention. Results were similar to those for the first experiment. Baseline use of sentences was practically nonexistent. Only 4 percent of all student responses were judged as fulfilling the requirement of a complete sentence. On the introduction of instructions for use of complete sentences and the systematic ignoring of responses not in compliance with these instructions, complete sentence usage jumped to about 90 percent for all students. A replication by way of a reversal and reinstatement of treatment contingencies produced almost the same results. The authors point out that an analysis of the types of questions used at various times during the experiment suggested that they did not differ significantly and thus could not account for this dramatic change in rate of complete sentences. It was further verified that neither praise nor the biased calling on particularly garrulous students could account for this effect.

The results of this study are encouraging for behavior analysts. As the authors note, ''it may be that complex speech patterns can be developed more easily than has been assumed previously'' (Broden et al., 1977, p. 486). Their research and conjecture are supported by Hart and Risley (1968), who demonstrated that lower-socioeconomic, inner-city black preschool children had all of the basic language structures required for middle-class language in their verbal repertoires.

However, such children use complex speech patterns less frequently than do children from middle-class environments. Such information may at least partially account for the immediate transition in speech complexity seen in the study above.

Proper Phrasing

Another aspect of classroom vocal behavior is the manner in which students phrase questions before giving an answer. Lovitt and Curtiss (1968) analyzed the effect of proper phrasing of mathematics problems before answering. Their subject, an eleven-year-old boy who was attending a special class for children with behavior disorders, displayed a highly erratic rate of correct answers to mathematics problems. Increasingly complex problems were used in three experiments. Each experiment consisted of three conditions. First, the student simply solved the problems. Second, the student was required to vocalize the problems aloud before answering. Third, the requirement for vocalization was removed. Each time a new experiment began, an increasingly complex set of problems was used. In all three experiments the subject displayed erratic, generally poor problem-solving behavior, when no external vocalization of the problem was required. On having to vocalize each problem, his error rate dropped to near zero. In the third phase the subject maintained the same high level of accuracy, although he no longer overtly vocalized the problems. Apparently the child began to covertly verbalize the problem before answering. An important point to note is that each time a new experiment began, with more complex problems, the subject had a high error rate. This was in spite of the demonstrated improvement obtained in previous experiments by using external vocalization before answering. Only after the subject was reinstructed in the technique of reciting each new type of problem aloud did accuracy increase. The authors point out that although this child demonstrated an ability to generalize from overt to covert verbalization within each new set of operations in a given experiment, the vocalization did not generalize to problems for which complexity of operations increased. This suggests, once again, that generalization should be planned rather than assumed.

Presentation Rate

Another variable in the classroom is the rate at which the teacher presents academic material. There has been considerable conjecture as to whether students benefit most from a fast-rate or slow-rate presentation. Carnine (1976) investigated the effect of two different rates of teacher presentation as they influenced two underachieving first-grade students' off-task behavior, correct answering, and participation during a small-group direct instruction program.

Using an ABABAB design, Carnine provided DISTAR reading phases in which both slow- and fast-rate presentations were made by the teacher. During the slow-rate presentation the teacher was instructed to silently count to 5 after each response from the students. During the fast-rate presentation the teacher immediately responded with the next step in the DISTAR presentation. In order to preclude the possibility of confounding the dependent variables by the teacher's inadvertent social reinforcement of students at particular times, this experiment was arranged so that a preprogrammed tone, delivered by way of earphone, signaled the teacher to praise students in a variety of ways at ninety-second intervals throughout all phases of the experiment. Thus differences in reinforcement procedures could not account for any differences in performance of children given fast-rate and slow-rate presentations.

The results of this intervention are incontrovertible. Off-task means during the slow-rate presentations for subject 1 were 52.6 percent, 81.3 percent, and 75.3 percent. These phases were alternated with fast-rate presentations, in which the means for off-task behavior were 3.9 percent, 8.7 percent, and 4.5 percent. Similar proof was obtained regarding the means for correct answering. Means for slow-rate presentations were 25.8 percent, 38.8 percent, and 29.1 percent. The fast-rate presentation phases averaged 75.4 percent, 76.4 percent, and 79.3 percent. Means for subject 2 followed the same pattern. Although this experiment provides data from only two subjects, the phenomenon is no doubt indicative of a broader population when using DISTAR materials. However, it is important to emphasize that this experiment was conducted using the DISTAR curriculum only. The components of this direct instruction program are highly sequential and well structured. Pacing of DISTAR formats is a critical component of implementing this reading program. Whether one could generalize the extreme results of this experiment to reading programs less carefully structured is not established by the study. However, the experiment leaves no doubt as to the timing requirements necessary to provide optimal DISTAR presentations.

Another issue concerns the amount of time spent with individuals during a given presentation. Even when the pacing of academic materials occurs at an optimum rate, extended verbal interaction with individuals, to the exclusion of the rest of the class or group, may produce paradoxical effects. Most teachers want to address the majority of their time and energy to the teaching of students, and spend as little time as possible managing problem (off-task) behaviors. Ironically, as teachers tend to direct their attention exclusively to a given student's academic endeavors, the probability of surrounding students simultaneously going off task increases. Scott and Bushell (1974) researched this problem, specifically examining the length of teacher contacts with individual students and the concurrent off-task behavior of other surrounding students in a small-group setting.

Subjects consisted of four boys and two girls who were frequently off task in a third-grade public school classroom. These students were variously placed in four small mathematics groups for twenty minutes every day. During nine days of what was termed the free contact phase the teacher was asked to maintain her usual pattern of individual contact and instruction of students within the group.

The average verbal contact duration for individuals within the small-group lesson lasted for 37.7 seconds. Excluding hand-raising, the mean off-task behavior for all individuals within the group during this phase was 34.2 percent. Next the teacher was asked to follow her same routine, but to maintain her individual discussions for at least fifty seconds per child. An observer cued the teacher when fifty seconds had elapsed, at which point the teacher could sustain contact for as much more time as she deemed necessary to provide the student with the information needed. The average duration of teacher verbal contact rose to 82.6 seconds, 30 seconds over criterion. Interestingly, the mean level of group off-task behavior averaged 55 percent during this twelve-day phase. In order to further investigate the functional relationship between teacher contact of individuals and the effect the duration of such contact had on the groups' off-task behavior, a reversal was implemented. During a final seven-day limited-contact phase the teacher was asked to hold her contacts with individuals to twenty seconds and to attempt to terminate her instruction of individuals as quickly as possible thereafter. The mean contact duration fell to 42.4 seconds and group off-task behavior fell to 27.4 percent. Thus we see an all too obvious relationship between the amount of time a teacher spends with individual students in a group and the probability of other members of the group concurrently drifting off-task. The authors point out that under such circumstances of extended time with individual students, the teacher is less able to render aid to members of the group who have either finished their assignments or are frustrated with a particular problem. Anticipating the obvious rebuttal that some students require extended individualized coaching from the teacher, the authors took data on students' math problem-solving progress throughout all phases of the experiment. During free contact students were off task 34.2 percent, during extended individualized contact average student off-task behavior increased to 55.7 percent, and finally, during abbreviated individualized contact, the off-task rate dropped to 27.4 percent. It appears that group on-task behavior may be reduced and individualized progress improved through the simple expedient of limited verbal contact with students during small-group lessons.

Vocal Praise

Criticisms of operant procedures have often centered around allegations that behaviorists bribe students, that highly structured and reinforcing environments are not consistent with experience in the everyday world, and that token programs produce token results. Although it is true that tangible reinforcers are helpful in initiating academic motivation, it is also true that they can and should be phased out as the students are concurrently exposed to verbal reinforcement. In fact, once the teacher has established herself as a provider of social reinforcement, she may even decrease the frequency of contingent praise statements and still sustain a high level of performance from her students. This point is empirically verified by a study conducted by Chadwick and Day (1971). They studied the effects of both tangible and verbal reinforcement on total work time, academic efficiency, and accuracy.

Using a population of twenty-five underachieving minority children, averaging ten years of age, they arranged a highly structured summer school program. The experimental conditions were studied in three phases. During three weeks of baseline the children received instructions characteristic of a normal classroom. Children also obtained lunch, candy, toys, and other items noncontingently (i.e., not related to behavior in any systematic way). In the next six weeks of treatment 1 a reinforcement procedure was introduced. A point system was introduced for improved academic work and on-task behavior (independent work, staying in their seats, not talking, etc.). Inappropriate behaviors typically resulted in verbal warnings or redirection to on-task behavior. Fighting or serious disruption resulted in response cost (loss of earned points) or time out. Points were exchanged daily for backup reinforcers (lunch, items purchased from a school store, and weekly field trips). It is important to emphasize that the giving of points was consistently paired with teacher praise and approval. Approval statements jumped from 13 per hour, given during baseline, to 47 per hour, given during treatment 1. Disapproval statements dropped from 27 per hour to 7 per hour during the same time.

The experimenters, aware that programs using such reinforcement of appropriate behavior seldom exist in public schools, introduced a second treatment in order to extend the long-term effects of treatment 1. In treatment 2 only verbal reinforcement was contingent on the same appropriate classroom behaviors.

A series of dramatic and important changes in group behavior took place during the various phases of the experiment. The percentage of total available time spent working moved from a group average of 39 percent during baseline to 57 percent during treatment 1, to 42 percent during treatment 2. More important, academic performance, as measured by total problems completed divided by time spent at work, revealed improvements ranging from 83 percent in math to 410 percent in reading exercises. This high level of academic performance was sustained throughout treatment 2, despite the exclusive use of verbal reinforcement procedures. Accuracy, as measured by the percentage of correct problems, jumped from a baseline average of 50 percent to 70 percent during treatment 1, and up to 73 percent during treatment 2. The authors note one further indicator of overall improvement during this eleven-week summer program; the pre-experimental average grade placement on the California Achievement Test was 3.60. Subsequent to the summer school program the average grade placement was 4.02. This provides an excellent source of external validity. Thus we see significant improvements in all areas of academic endeavor and that, with regard to accuracy of work, verbal reinforcement proved slightly more powerful than tangible reinforcement. However, it is most likely that this kind of improvement, using only praise statements, could only have been accomplished after a suitable history of pairing verbal and tangible rewards.

This study illustrates quite clearly what behaviorists have been claiming for years—that once academic behaviors come under operant control using tangible reinforcers combined with verbal praise, they often can be sustained with the use of verbal reinforcers alone. In fact, in this study, even the use of contingent praise was reduced. In treatment 2 the actual number of approval statements eventually dropped from 47 per hour to 27 per hour. This may be one of the most critical outcomes of using behavioral procedures in the schools. Once student behavior comes under adequate control of the teachers' social reinforcement procedures, it is no longer necessary to maintain the initial high rate of such procedures. Students can be quite well "motivated" with a moderate level of contingent verbal reinforcement. Referencing the type of criticism directed against behavioral technology described at the beginning of this section, perhaps this is the best approximation of the real world that can be accomplished in a classroom. Certainly the results obtained are not token.

CURRICULUM-BASED ASSESSMENT

One of the most important articles addressing on-task behaviors in the classroom comes from Gickling and Thompson (1985). These authors contend that a primary variable in the failure of many students to maintain adequate on-task performance, comprehension, and task completion is the excessive level of curriculum difficulty for low-achieving individuals. These authors put forth the proposition that as a direct result of improperly gauged academic materials, many students are constantly subjected to a "frustration level" that precludes their acquiring basic skills. They point out that there is a consistent and growing mismatch between the grade-level curriculum offered in public schools and the assessment of students' grade-level functioning by norm references testing. According to the authors, "test scores are usually inflated while the reading difficulty level of materials is underestimated" (Gickling & Thompson, 1985, p. 210). Thus many students are subjected to a curriculum that does not match their entry-level abilities. They do not possess the minimal skills needed for comprehension and task completion. Frustrated by an inadequate and inaccurate assessment system, they are, in growing numbers, drifting off task and into special education. The authors cite Gerber (1984) in pointing out that learning disabilities now constitute 40 percent, and in some states more than 50 percent, of the special education population. States are now forced into the unpopular but necessary position of finding new ways to "enforce strict eligibility requirements."

Gickling and Thompson describe a method of evaluating and remediating student performance. Curriculum-based Assessment (CBA), which can be used not only as an evaluation tool, but also, more critically, as a way in which to adjust the students' level of curriculum so as to optimize academic performance, is a *pre–special education referral intervention*. CBA is "a procedure for determining the instructional needs of students based on the student's ongoing performance in existing course content" (Gickling & Thompson, 1985, p. 206). This determination is made by gauging two types of learning activities: reading and drill. Reading is simply the decoding (saying the words in a test), but drill is meant to include all other types of academic practice activities that prepare a student for reading. These activities may include writing, spelling, phonics, answering questions, word attack, and any other related sets of subskill acquisition. The correct instructional level for each child is a proper ratio of known to unknown (or hesitant) items in the reading text and drill material. The authors define a known item as one that the student responds to immediately and correctly. They distinguish between unknown and hesitant by pointing out that some responses are consistently found to be incorrect (unknown), whereas others are missed with variability and take on a delayed pattern of responding. In either case such items are scored as belonging to the same category, called *challenge* items. These are subtracted from the known items to obtain a ratio of known to challenge items.

This leads to a further analysis of curriculum levels by calculating instructional, independent, or frustration ratios. An instructional ratio that is one that will permit the student to make consistent academic gains, requires a curriculum with between 93 percent and 97 percent known items and a challenge rate of only 3 percent to 7 percent. Comprehension must concurrently be at least 75 percent. Drill does not require as high a ratio of known items. Known items need constitute only 70 percent to 85 percent of the curriculum and challenge items, between 15 percent and 30 percent for drill on phonics, spelling, word attack, writing, and other related activities that support reading. At a totally independent level of student functioning, it is suggested that assignments contain at least 90 percent known material and that reading material contain at least 97 percent known items. Gickling and Thompson indicate that frustration is likely to be inadvertently induced any time a student's drill curriculum contains fewer than 70 percent known items and reading is permitted to contain items with less than 90 percent correct recognition.

The authors state their primary thesis quite clearly:

> Experience has shown that students profit most when materials or learning tasks are on an instructional level—meaning that the items of each tasks are sufficiently familiar yet provide the right measure of challenge to ensure an optimum learning situation. It has also shown that some performance on an independent level is desirable; but under independent conditions, neither assignments nor teacher assistance are used to full advantage. Of course, assignments that produce frustrational learning are to be avoided. (Gickling & Thompson, 1985, p. 211)

In order to use the information above to full advantage, students should be provided a highly individualized curriculum to match their entry skill levels for specific academic subjects. For many students this may require an ongoing analysis of the student's ability to function within the instructional-level ratios.

When it is suspected that a student is operating at levels below his instructional ratio, CBAs should be conducted. This may be accomplished in a very direct way. In the case of reading, all that is required is that a short photocopy (two or three pages) of the student's text be made for the teacher's inspection. The teacher then simply listens to the student read aloud from the same pages in the original text as she follows along on the photocopy. As the student misses given words, the words are marked on the photocopy by the teacher and then totaled. The ratio of known items to challenge items is then calculated. A short comprehension quiz is also given, and an accuracy percentage is determined. Ratios for drill items can be determined in like manner. Subsequently it is sometimes necessary to design, and individually modify, curriculum materials to match the student's current skill level. This may be accomplished by either selecting texts that conveniently coincide with the student's current instructional level, or, when necessary, changing textual materials by rewriting materials. This means that, in some cases, the teacher must develop textual passages that are similar to the primary text but have a reduced frequency of challenge items. Rewriting or paraphrasing primary text curriculum is referred to as writing "transitional stories." Although this process may sound strenuous, it has been found that such transitional stories can be used, and reused, by a large number of students who share common entry-level skills. The use of such materials may present an initial inconvenience, but in the long run they may save the teacher and the student years of "frustration" and provide a format by which academic progress may be initiated and maintained. The authors provide several other techniques and rules that further facilitate the use of CBA. Four of the more critical are the following:

Items of Undetermined Status Are Treated as Unknowns. The probability of jeopardizing an appropriate instructional ratio is increased if there are items of undetermined status within the task.

Prepare Content Before Drill. Too many times, teachers drill students on items which are unrelated to the next instructional task. By examining planned content and then designing drill work to conform to the content, the two tasks become coordinated, enhancing the learning situation.

Present Drill Before Content. Drill activites are presented to the student in order to prepare him for the task. If drill goes well, and drill and content have been coordinated, then the student should be able to perform on an instructional or independent level when the next task is presented.

All Tasks Are Carried to Their Logical Conclusion. No task should be left at a subskill level. The goal should be to take every task to a mastery level, which requires both independent performance and comprehension on the part of the student. Naturally, there is a concerted effort to make every task as contextual as possible. (Gickling & Havertape, 1981, p. R6)

Two Studies on CBA

Gickling and Armstrong (1978) provide an excellent description of the results of full utilization of these procedures. Their study provides an analysis of three manipulations of instructional ratios that produced frustrational, instructional, and independent levels of academic functioning. Their subjects consisted of first- and second-graders with poor academic histories. Students were observed every Monday, Wednesday, and Friday over 21 one-hour sessions. Baseline was collected during the first six sessions, and frustration level ratios were intentionally imposed during the next five sessions. These frustration ratios were individually set at challenge ratios of 50 percent. The data clearly indicate that these poorly performing students were operating during baseline in much the same way as they were when frustration levels were intentionally invoked. During six sessions of baseline, task comprehension averaged around 10 percent to 15 percent; during the subsequent five sessions of the frustration level condition, task comprehension moved up just slightly to about 20 percent. On-task behavior fluctuated between 40 percent and 50 percent during both of these conditions; but task completions bounced between 55 percent and 75 percent during baseline and fell to 40 percent and 50 percent during the frustration level phase. The authors indicate that these data demonstrate that many low-achieving students are routinely subjected to frustration levels of task difficulty in their normally assigned grade-level tasks.

When an instructional ratio of known items to challenge items was established for five sessions, an impressive change occurred. At an instructional reading level of 93 percent to 97 percent known items, task comprehension and task completions rose to an average of about 90 percent. On-task behavior jumped to between 80 percent and 90 percent. When, in the final five sessions, an independent level ratio of known to challenge items was provided to these same students, another transition occurred. While task completion and comprehension behavior remained at about the same high levels, on-task behaviors dropped to between 40 percent and 55 percent.

The authors state the obvious conclusion:

> When assignments were too difficult, the percentages of the three behaviors were relatively low. When assignments were at an independent level, comprehension and task completion came easily, leaving large percentages of off-tasks behaviors representing unused time. However, when assignments were within the appropriate ratios, enabling students to function on an instructional level, the percentages of task completion, comprehension, and on-task behaviors were consistently high. (Gickling & Thompson, 1985, p. 215)

Gickling and Thompson (1985) describe one other study that used CBA to its full advantage. However, this time the effects of both controlled instruction and medication were analyzed. Eighteen students in six separate elementary classrooms were observed during an eight-week period. The eighteen students were selected as representative of three categories: low-achieving, attention deficit disorders with hyperactivity, and average-achieving. The six hyperactive students in the study were scheduled for appropriately titrated levels of methylphenidate (Ritalin) previous to the implementation of CBA. Concurrent with the hyperactive students' exposure to the above-mentioned conditions they were observed both on and off their normally prescribed medication dosages. On those days during which the hyperactive students were off medication they were provided a placebo. As a double-blind study, hyperactive students were observed while under either the regular instruction or the controlled instruction conditions. Other students in the low-achieving and average-achieving conditions were simply observed under the influence of regular and controlled instruction with no medication influence. Performances under these conditions were evaluated with respect to three criteria: on-task behavior, task completion, and task comprehension.

The results are unequivocal. While under the influence of their standard instructional program, both the low-achieving students and the hyperactive students consistently performed more poorly than their average-achieving peers on all target behaviors, with one outstanding exception. In the regular instructional condition the hyperactive students demonstrated high rates of on-task behaviors when operating under the influence of Ritalin. Specifically, these students were recorded at about 75 percent on task while on this medication but only at about 50 percent on task when off medication. But, paradoxically and more important, their rates of task completion and task comprehension were comparatively low both on and off medication (about 60 percent to 70 percent) during the regular instructional condition. When exposed to the controlled instruction condition, in which the advantages of using CBA could be demonstrated, these hyperactive students were capable of demonstrating high levels of on-task behavior (approximately 75 percent) both on and off medication. Likewise, the low-achieving students demonstrated equally high levels of on-task behaviors when exposed to controlled instruction. Furthermore, and most critically, both of these groups demonstrated dramatic improvements in task completion and comprehension levels during the controlled instruction condition. Whereas the low-achieving students and the hyperactive students (on and off medication) had previously performed at around 60 percent to 70 percent task completion in the regular instruction format, these students uniformly improved to about 80 percent during controlled instruction. In task comprehension low-achieving students improved from around 75 percent to 85 percent when given controlled instruction. The hyperactive students were even more impressive under these conditions. When given controlled instruction, task comprehension improved from just below 70 percent to just above 85 percent; and this occurred whether or not these students were medicated.

What is generally seen, when analyzing these data, is that both groups are beneficially affected by the use of CBA with regard to on-task behavior, task completion, and task comprehension. The hyperactive subjects show a particularly critical pattern, however. Even when the curriculum is too difficult for them to achieve, these students look on task when on medication. They stay in their assigned seats and assume the topography of normally achieving students even while they are failing. Off medication, a regular curriculum will not sustain their appropriate behavior. They become agitated, noisy, disruptive, and generally off task. They perform at about the same task completion and comprehension levels as they do on medication (i.e., they are failing). When provided a curriculum that allows them to perform at an optimal success and challenge rate, not only does their behavior improve, but comprehension and task completion show significant improvements. The authors point out that it is important to understand that although these students may not be functioning on the same academic levels as their normally achieving peers, they are, at least, making academic gains and showing a general improvement trend. Gickling and Thompson summarize the results:

> The results of this study, along with the former study, help support the concept that it is the curriculum, the day-to-day instructional match between the child and the actual learning task at hand, that is most conducive to high rates of performance within the classroom. Whether or not in conjunction with medication, ADD (Attention Deficit Disorder with Hyperactivity) and LA (Low Achieving) students achieved higher task-related scores across three observational variables when the curriculum match was consistently controlled. (Gickling & Thompson, 1985, p. 217, [parentheses added]).

All-Positive Approach

Ever since the 1950s researchers have been looking for alternatives to the traditionally predominant use of punishment and negative feedback in classroom management. Behavior analysts doing such research were inspired by Skinner's experimental findings and theoretical discussions regarding the importance of positive environments for individuals as well as for the culture (Skinner, 1973/1978). Subsequent research, though, demonstrated that performance and conduct levels deteriorated with the use of praise alone as positive consequence (Rosen, O'Leary, Joyce, Conway, & Pfiffner, 1984).

In the current experiment, however, Pfiffner, Rosen, and O'Leary (1985) managed to maintain high levels of on-task behavior and academic productivity by adding to praise powerful incentive systems with individualized and daily varied rewards. The study was conducted in a special education class at Woods Lab School, where high academic and conduct levels had been established with the use of positive and negative reinforcement combined. Eight second- and third-grade children (five boys and three girls) had been referred by their teachers for inattention and for conduct, but otherwise they had functioned successfully for the five months they had attended class. Their background was that of middle-class suburban families and their intelligence was at least average.

From behind two-way mirrors, and blind to the experimental hypothesis, observers recorded on-task behavior at ten-second intervals daily between 10:00 and 11:00 A.M.. Teachers' interactions with children were recorded as either (a) positive physical and verbal behavior showing approval, (b) negative physical and verbal behavior showing disapproval, or (c) neutral, nonevaluative instructional interactions. In addition to on-task behavior, from the thirteenth day on, academic productivity was measured.

In order to measure the effects of particular consequences contingent on behavior or academic performance, or both, data were collected during forty-six days, divided into seven experimental phases as follows:

Phase 1—Condition A—Five Days: Regular positive and negative consequences were combined, including praise, bonus work, posting test results, verbal reprimands, time out, and withdrawal of privileges.

Phase 2—Condition B—Four Days: Regular positive consequences only were used; negative consequences were withheld; inappropriate behaviors were ignored.

Phase 3—Condition C—Ten Days: Enhanced positive consequences were used alone. The regular positive consequences were increased, and new rewards were added and varied daily, including music, novel recess events, display of classwork on "superstar" board, access to comic books and musical instruments, as well as creative activities such as writing stories and artwork.

Phase 4—Condition B—Four Days: Regular positive consequences alone were contingently administered at the same frequency as during the first A and B phases.

Phase 5—Condition B—Four Days: Regular positive and negative consequences were used at the same rates as established during the first A phase.

Phase 6—Condition C—Ten Days + Five Days: During the first ten days enhanced positive consequences of the same types used during the first C phase were increased in frequency. Because of variations in behavior, daily varied menus were added (e.g., positive note home, board games, helping teacher with chores, special lunch privileges) during the last five days of this phase. During this five-day condition deserving students themselves selected one privilege from the daily reward menu as opposed to the teacher's selecting rewards as in previous days of condition C.

Phase 7—Condition A—Final Four Days: Regular positive and negative consequences were contingently administered. Rate levels were equivalent to those of the previous two A phases.

During all phases and conditions the rate of teachers' neutral interaction time per child was maintained at the same level as that of the first phase (six minutes on the average per child per hour).

The recorded data from all phases were compared to determine whether the enhanced incentive program would allow for an all-positive classroom environment as a realistic alternative to environments providing negative and positive consequences combined or providing consequences in the form of praise only. The results showed that, for all eight children, regular positive consequences only were not effective enough to maintain on-task behavior. Enhanced positive consequences (C conditions) were more effective than regular positive consequences (A conditions) for six of the eight children. The level of functioning during C conditions (especially when the reward menu was used) closely approached that of A conditions in which verbal positive and negative consequences alone were used.

The results for academic productivity were similar for five of the eight children.

Productivity deteriorated when the regular positive consequences were used alone and improved during the remaining phases of the experiment. During all phases mean accuracy rates remained stable. For three children no systematic differences in performance were apparent.

From this experiment the authors conclude that individualized incentive programs and positive verbal consequences in the absence of any punishment or negative feedback are a viable solution for conduct problems of some children. Thus Rosen et al.'s (1984) demonstration that an all-positive environment is not advisable holds true only when praise is the exclusive form of positive feedback.

To generate such an all-positive environment, teachers need to maintain high rates of praise and individualized reward programs. They also need to carefully balance the selection of rewards, either by the teacher or by the students themselves. The instatement and maintenance of an all-positive environment may also require a baseline of high-rate on-task behavior previously established by a combination of positive-negative consequences. The children in this study had a repertoire of classroom rule–following conduct, acquired during the five months before the experiment during which teachers used a combination of positive and negative consequences. High levels of teachers' time and effort also turned out to be an important variable to instate and maintain an all-positive classroom environment.

All-Positive Continued

Behavior analysts agree with a variety of other specialists that children cannot be properly socialized in the absence of positive environmental events, particularly the positive reactions of other people. In addition, behavior analysts have repeatedly demonstrated that the *relation* of positive events to children's behavior (as contingent consequences) is a critical factor in the emergence of productive and pro-social behavior of children. On the contrary, the necessity of negative consequences contingent on counterproductive and antisocial behavior of children is less clear. Pfiffner et al. (1985) found that children engaged in a high rate of desirable and a low rate of undesirable behavior whether a "powerful, individualized incentive system" (p. 265) or "a combination of primarily verbal positive and negative consequences" (p. 265) was used. However, the appropriate behavior was originally established in an environment where positive and negative consequences were contingent, respectively, on desirable and undesirable behavior.

In order to ascertain whether a history of negative consequences contingent on undesirable behavior was necessary before an all-positive environment, by itself, would result in outcomes similar to those of the earlier study, Pfiffner and O'Leary (1987) conducted a study during a five-week summer program in reading and mathematics. The child participants were four fourth-grade, two second-grade, and two third-grade children whose regular teachers reported that they performed below grade level in reading and/or math, and that six of the eight had "behavioral problems" as measured by the Conners Teacher Rating Scale (Conners, 1969). The teacher who participated in the study was experienced in behavior technology.

Beginning on the second day of the summer program, the teacher was instructed to avoid negative consequences and to use "regular" positive consequences contingent on academic work and on appropriate behavior. Data collected on the teacher's behavior during this three-day phase showed that the teacher was successful in following the instructions (as was also the case in all other phases of the study). The children as a group began by behaving on task 77 percent of the time, but during this phase their on-task behavior decreased to a mean of 41 percent. Data on individual children showed that each child's on-task behavior decreased during this phase.

The experimenters then arranged for the teacher to increase the frequency and variety of positive consequences. Children earned stars, on an individual basis, for good behavior and schoolwork, which were exchanged for time to do puzzles, color, read comic books, and play sports. Also, stars could be traded for stickers, extra recess, good notes to take home, and the chance to run errands for the teacher, among other things. Praise from the teacher occurred at a rate of six times per hour per child during the four days of this phase. The results were that the enhanced positive consequences successfully reversed the trend of decreasing on-task behavior and raised on task to an average of 56 percent. Five children's behavior remained steady (as well as somewhat improved from the end of the previous phase), and three children showed variability from day to day but overall improvement.

During the third phase of the experiment, the contingencies with enhanced positives remained in effect, and the teacher was requested to administer negative consequences to whatever extent necessary to "maximize on-task behavior and work productivity with a minimum of one per child per hour." On-task rates increased immediately to an average of 80 percent and on-task behavior increased for every child. During this six-day phase the teacher shaped the children's behavior to more stringent criteria, and the increased on-task behavior remained high. Also in this phase the children's accuracy in academic work improved from about 55 percent to about 80 percent.

The experimenters then asked the teacher to cease delivering all negative consequences and to continue delivering the positive consequences contingent on appropriate conduct and academic work. On-task performance dropped for six of the eight children during this two-day phase.

During the last phase the teacher followed the experimenters' instructions to return to using the combination of negative and enhanced positive consequences and to gradually reduce the rate of reprimands during the last six days of the summer program. Children's on-task rate and accuracy remained high throughout the last phase as the negative consequences were faded out.

The results of Pfiffner and O'Leary's 1987 study suggest that a combination of social- and activity-positive consequences (contingent on appropriate behavior and academic performance) and negative consequences (teacher reprimands) are likely to be needed to establish a high rate of desirable classroom performance. Once established, the teacher can reduce, and possibly eliminate for the most part, the negative consequences if she fades them out over time.

SUMMARY

A multitude of studies have described methods to improve students' on-task behavior. In most cases the procedures used are relatively simple in a technical sense; however, most do require that the teacher or other intervention agent use the procedure for an extended period. If on-task procedures are terminated or phased out without adequate attention to generalization techniques, students typically regress to former dawdling, disruption, and low level of achievement. Behavioral programs are only as good as the behavior of the people who implement them, and usually only last as long as the intervention or generalization procedure is sustained. The message is clear. To make permanent changes in the behavior of human beings, sustained changes must be made in the contingencies supporting that behavior. We ignore the nature of behavioral processes at our own peril.

REFERENCES

Bormuth, J. R. (1969). Factor validity of cloze tests as measures of reading comprehension ability. *Reading Research Quarterly, 4*, 358–365.

Brigham, T. A., Graubard, P. S., & Stans, A. (1972). Analysis of the effects of sequential reinforcement contingencies on aspects of composition. *Journal of Applied Behavior Analysis, 5*, 421–429.

Broden, M., Copeland, G., Beasley, A., & Hall, R. V. (1977). Altering student responses through changes in teacher verbal behavior. *Journal of Applied Behavior Analysis, 1*, 479–487.

Carnine, D. W. (1976). Effects of two teacher-presentation rates on off-task behavior, answering correctly, and participation. *Journal of Applied Behavior Analysis, 9*, 199–206.

Chadwick, B. A., & Day, R. C. (1971). Systematic reinforcement: Academic performance of underachieving students. *Journal of Applied Behavior Analysis, 4*, 311–319.

Conners, C. K. (1969). A teacher rating scale for use in drug studies with children. *American Journal of Comparative and Physiological Psychology, 126*, 884–888.

Delquadri, J. C., Greenwood, C. R., Stretton, K., & Hall, R. V. (1983). The peer tutoring spelling game: A classroom procedure for increasing opportunity to respond and spelling performance. *Education and Treatment of Children, 6*, 225–239.

Ferster, C. B., & Skinner, B. F. (1957). *Schedules of reinforcement*. New York: Appleton-Century-Crofts.

Fox, R. G. (1974). The effects of peer tutoring on oral reading behavior of underachieving fourth grade pupils. Unpublished doctoral dissertation, University of Kansas, Lawrence.

Gerber, M. M. (1984). The Department of Education's sixth annual report to Congress on P. L. 94–142: Is Congress getting the full story? *Exceptional Children*, 51 (3), 209–224.

Gickling, E. E., & Armstrong, D. L. (1978). Levels of instructional difficulty as related to on-task behavior, task completion, and comprehension. *Journal of Learning Disabilities, 11*, 559–566.

Gickling, E. E., & Havertape, J. F. (1981). Curriculum based assessment. In J. A. Tucker (Ed.), *Non-test base assessment*. Minneapolis: National School Psychology Inservice Network, University of Minnesota.

Gickling, E. E., & Thompson, V. P. (1985). A personal view of Curriculum-Based Assessment. *Exceptional Children, 52*, 205–218.

Goldstein, A. (1960). Does homework help? A review of research. *Elementary School Journal, 60*, 212–224.

Greenspoon, J. (1955). The reinforcing effect of two spoken sounds on the frequency of two responses. *American Journal of Psychology, 68*, 409–416.

Greenwood, C. R., Delquadri, J. C., & Hall, R. V. (1984). Opportunity to respond and student academic performance in school. In W. Heward, T. Heron, D. Hill, & J. Trap-Porter (Eds.), *Behavior analysis in education* (pp. 58–88). Columbus, OH: Charles E. Merrill Publishing Co.

Greenwood, C. R., Dinwiddie, G., Terry, B., Wade, L., Stanley, G. O., Thibadeau, S., & Delquadri, J. C. (1984). Teacher versus peer-mediated instruction: An ecobehavioral analysis of achievement outcome. *Journal of Applied Behavior Analysis, 17*, 521–538.

Greenwood, C. R., Dinwiddie, G., Bailey, V., Carta, J. J., Dorsey, D., Kohler, F. W., Nelson, C., Rotholz, D., & Schulte, D. (1987). Field replication of classwide peer tutoring. *Journal of Applied Behavior Analysis, 20*, 151–160.

Greer, D. R., & Polinstok, R. (1982). Collateral gains and short-term maintenance in reading and on-task responses by inner-city adolescents as a function of their use of social reinforcement while tutoring. *Journal of Applied Behavior Analysis, 15*, 123–139.

Hall, R. V., Lund, D., & Jackson, D. (1968). Effects of teacher attention on study behavior. *Journal of Applied Behavior Analysis, 1*, 1–12.

Harris, V. W., & Sherman, J. A. (1973). Effects of peer tutoring and consequences on the math performance of elementary classroom students. *Journal of Applied Behavior Analysis, 6*, 587–597.

Harris, V. W., & Sherman, J. A. (1974). Homework assignments, consequences, and classroom performance in social studies and mathematics. *Journal of Applied Behavior Analysis, 7*, 505–519.

Hart, B., & Risley, T. R. (1968). Establishing use of descriptive adjectives in the spontaneous speech of disadvantaged preschool children. *Journal of Applied Behavior Analysis, 1*, 109–120.

Kirby, F. D., & Shields, F. (1972). Modification of arithmetic response rate and attending behavior in a seventh grade student. *Journal of Applied Behavior Analysis, 5*, 79–84.

Knapczyk, D. R., & Livingston, G. (1974). The effects of prompting question-asking upon on-task behavior and reading comprehension. *Journal of Applied Behavior Analysis, 7*, 115–121.

Konarski, E. A., Johnson, M. R., Crowell, C. R., & Whitman, T. L. (1980). Response deprivation and reinforcement in applied settings: A preliminary analysis. *Journal of Applied Behavior Analysis, 13*, 595–609.

Lovitt, T. C., & Curtiss, K. A. (1968). Effects of manipulating an antecedent event on mathematics response rate. *Journal of Applied Behavior Analysis, 1*, 329–333.

Lovitt, T. C., & Esveldt, K. A. (1970). The relative effects on math performance of single- versus multiple-ratio schedules: A case study. *Journal of Applied Behavior Analysis, 3*, 261–270.

Maertens, N. (1968). Effects of arithmetic homework upon the attitudes of third grade pupils toward certain school-related structures. *School Science and Mathematics, 68*, 657–662.

Ninness, H. A. C. (1980). The effects of elimination of subvocalization with electromyographic feedback. *Behavioral Engineering, 6*, 77–90.

Ninness, H. A. C. (1982). Two and one-half year follow-up on the effects of elimination of subvocalization with electromyographic feedback. *Behavioral Engineering, 8*, 5–10.

Pfiffner, L. J., & O'Leary, S. G. (1987). The efficacy of all-positive management as a function of the prior use of negative consequences. *Journal of Applied Behavior Analysis, 20*, 265–271.

Pfiffner, L. J., Rosen, L. A., & O'Leary, S. G. (1985). The efficacy of an all-positive approach to classroom management. *Journal of Applied Behavior Analysis, 18*, 257–261.

Ritschl, E. R., Grinstead, J., Whitson, D., et al., (1980). Effects on verbal and written math reponses through increased verbal opportunities: Preliminary findings. (Juniper Gardens Children's Project. Working Paper) Unpublished manuscript, University of Kansas, Lawrence.

Rosen, L. A., O'Leary, S. G., Joyce, S. A., Conway, G., & Pfiffner, L. J. (1984). The importance of prudent negative consequences for maintaining the appropriate behavior of hyperactive students. *Journal of Abnormal Child Psychology, 12*, 581–604.

Saudergas, R. W., Madsen, C. H., & Scott, J. W. (1977). Differential effects of fixed- and variable-time feedback on production rates of elementary school children. *Journal of Applied Behavior Analysis, 10*, 673–678.

Scott, J. W., & Bushell, D., Jr. (1974). The length of teacher contacts and students' off-task behavior. *Journal of Applied Behavior Analysis, 7*, 39–44.

Skinner, B. F. (1938). *The behavior of organisms*. New York: Appleton-Century-Crofts.

Skinner, B. F. (1953). *Science and human behavior*. New York: Macmillan.

Skinner, B. F. (1973). The free and happy student. *New York University Education Quarterly, 4*, (Winter), 2–6. Reprinted in *Reflections of Behaviorism on Society* (1978). New York: Prentice-Hall.

Skinner, B. F. (1984). The shame of American education. *American Psychologist, 39*, 947–954.

Timberlake, W., & Allison, J. (1974). Response deprivation: An empirical approach to instrumental performance. *Psychological Review, 81*, 146–164.

Tinker, M. A., & McCullough, C. M. (1962). *Teaching elementary reading* (2nd ed.). New York: Appleton-Century-Crofts.

Van Houten, R., Hill, S., & Parsons, M. (1975). An analysis of a performance feedback system: The effects of timing and feedback, public posting, and praise upon academic performance and peer interaction. *Journal of Applied Behavior Analysis, 8*, 449–457.

Van Houten, R., Morrison, E., Jarvis, R., & McDonald, M. (1974). The effects of explicit timing and feedback on compositional response rate in elementary school children. *Journal of Applied Behavior Analysis, 7*, 547–555.

Van Houten, R., & Thomas, C. (1976). The effects of explicit timing on math performance. *Journal of Applied Behavior Analysis, 9*, 227–230.

Walker, H. M., & Buckley, N. K. (1968). The use of positive reinforcement in conditioning attending behavior. *Journal of Applied Behavior Analysis, 1*, 245–250.

7

Withdrawal, Depression, and Suicide

OUR PRESENT CONDITION

Data gathered by the National Center for Health Statistics (1980) indicate that youth suicide for all races has more than quadrupled since the 1960s and that currently more than 6,000 adolescents and young adults kill themselves each year. In 1960, 1,239 cases of suicide for young adults between fifteen and twenty-four years of age were reported in the United States. By 1970 the number had reached 3,128. The 1980 vital statistics show that 5,239 youths and young adults had taken their own lives. Although the senior suicide rate has decreased by almost 50 percent since the 1950s, the rate of teenage suicide continues to accelerate. Thus, although suicide is only the ninth leading cause of death among all people, it is the third leading cause of death of people aged fifteen to twenty-four.

Although the incidence of suicide in children under ten years of age is very low (Aleksandrowicz, 1975), suicides by children between the ages of ten and fourteen years of age are definitely on the rise. The National Office of Vital Statistics documented elevations in the suicide rate in this segment of the population rising from 0.4 per 100,000 in 1955 to 1.2 per 100,000 in 1975 (Pfeffer, Conte, Plutchik, & Jerritt, 1980). Although this is still a relatively low rate, the circumstances that give rise to suicidal tendencies in adolescence often occur in early and late childhood.

PREVENTING SUICIDAL TENDENCIES

Jacobs (1971, p. 27) has suggested that "a long standing history of problems (from early childhood to early adolescence) is a primary factor in the development of suicidal tendencies." Bornstein, Bellack, and Hersen (1977, p. 184) point out that "poor competency as a child may set the stage for inappropriate interpersonal functioning as an adult, accentuating the potential for psychiatric disorder." Suicidal people are typically loners in early childhood and have conspicuous introverted tendencies (Johnson, 1985). Such people frequently lack the social skills to successfully interact with their peers, and are more likely to withdraw further from others in times of crisis. Long-standing interpersonal problems in childhood and histories of social withdrawal are frequently described as indicators of potential risk by suicide prevention agencies as well as by researchers.

One way of precluding the circumstances that give rise to suicide might be to teach socially inept young children new and appropriate social skills. The following series of research studies describe procedures that have taught children and young adults social interaction skills and self-assertion. Among other beneficial effects, these procedures help to build the social repertoires necessary to combat isolation, withdrawal, depression, and loneliness. Such procedures may affect the adolescents' later ability to deal effectively with events typically relating to depression and suicidal risk. Several studies describe procedures that can be applied to children who suffer from deficits in social skills.

Assertiveness Training—Modeling

An early study by O'Conner (1969) illustrates a parsimonious procedure for enhancing social behavior in preschool isolates. O'Conner tested modeling theory, as described by Bandura (1969), that suggests that children can develop elaborate and sophisticated interpersonal repertoires by observing others. O'Conner compared the behavior of a group of nursery school children who were exposed to a film that depicted assertive social interactions with that of another group of children who had watched a film that displayed no social interactions.

Six early childhood subjects were chosen because they exhibited extreme withdrawal behavior (as judged by their nursery school teachers) and displayed isolate behavior (as judged by observers unaware of the purpose of their ratings). Pretreatment observations and ratings were also made regarding a control group of seven children with similar behavior and a group of twenty-six nonisolate children used for comparison purposes. Objective pretreatment observations revealed that the nonisolate comparison subjects displayed a mean of 9.10 social interactions over thirty-two fifteen-second intervals. The pretreatment social interaction means for isolate children in the control and experimental groups were only 1.50 and 1.75, respectively.

During treatment the experimental subjects were individually exposed to a twenty-three-minute film that portrayed eleven sequences of nursery school children joining in increasingly vigorous social interactions. In each sequence the models portrayed assertive behavior that was always socially reinforced. In order to accentuate relevant cues and reinforcers associated with social behavior, a narrative sound track described the events in the film. Control subjects individually observed a twenty-minute nondidactic film on acrobatic dolphins. The nonisolate children were not exposed to treatment of any form.

After observing these films the children resumed normal activities in their classroom and were again observed for thirty-two sequential fifteen-second intervals. A posttreatment T-test between groups revealed that the experimental subjects improved their number of social interaction episodes significantly over control subjects (T = 2.70; P = .01). In fact, the experimenters point out that posttest interaction scores of children who were exposed to the sequential modeling film were higher than those of the comparison nonisolate children. This study provided no observational follow-up data; but teachers who remained naive regarding experimental and control group assignment were asked to identify the five most isolate children at the end of the school year. Only one of the experimental subjects was rated among the five showing isolate behavior, whereas four of the seven control subjects were again rated as extremely withdrawn.

Amazingly, this study demonstrates that experimental subjects were able to acquire new socially assertive responses after one training session, and that they were able to accomplish this without systematic practice of assertive behaviors. However, as the authors point out, "the application of systematic reinforcement of appropriate social responses would ensure the maintenance of the induced behavioral changes" (O'Conner, 1969, p. 19). Presumably children in the classroom responded favorably to isolates whose social behavior increased after seeing assertiveness modeled and the new repertoire was "trapped" by the social environment.

Classroom Managers Help Themselves

Sainato, Maheady and Shook (1986) developed an easy to implement and relatively fast acting method of enhancing social behaviors in withdrawn kindergarten students.

Three four-year-old regular kindergarten students identified as socially withdrawn were selected on the basis of direct observation, teacher ranking, and peer sociometric assessment. During daily twenty-minute free play time four categories of social behavior were measured: positive vocal verbalizations (friendly vocal interactions), positive gestures (holding hands, hugging, etc.), negative vocal verbalizations (tattling, yelling, etc.), and negative gestures (hitting, pushing, etc.). Also recorded was whether the observed students initiated or responded to these forms of social interaction.

Before the initiation of treatment, sociometric data were collected. The sixteen children in the kindergarten class performed peer ratings by pointing to one of four variations of "smiling faces" (smiling, straight line, frowning, or question mark) (Agard, Veldman, Kaufman, & Semmel, 1978) after hearing the name of each of their classmates. Each student was also asked to point out his or her best friend. Students were then asked to identify various types of toys, games, or activities they enjoyed during free time. These were later used by the subjects when they assumed the role of classroom manager.

The experimenters used a multiple-baseline design with reversal of treatments for thirty-five consecutive school days. Subjects 1, 2, and 3 had baseline observations of five, fifteen, and twenty-five successive days, respectively. During this time the children played spontaneously during their twenty-minute free time and the teacher did not attempt to prompt any pro-social interactions. Data from this period revealed that all three subjects had exceptionally low rates of social interaction.

With implementation of treatment each target child had an opportunity to assume the role of "classroom manager" during the free-time period. Students were called to the front of the class and awarded a special "manager" button to wear for the two weeks that they occupied that position. Their specific responsibilities in this role were

> leading and/or directing the class in previously-rated, highly-preferred activities, which included directing the feeding of the class guinea pig, collecting milk money and taking lunch count, ringing the bell for clean-up time, and handing out the "keys" to the barber shop and shoe store. Prior to beginning school each day, the teacher reviewed the manager's duties with the target child and the rest of the class. In addition, a picture board depicting the manager's major tasks was displayed in front of the classroom to prompt the target child not to forget an assignment. (Sainato et al., 1986, p. 190)

With the implementation of this ten-day treatment all three subjects demonstrated an immediate and sustained increased frequency of positive social interactions commensurate with the levels demonstrated by classroom peers. Targeted subjects' interactions escalated from baselines averaging around five to ten to between fifteen and thirty positive social contacts per period. Sainato et al. indicate that the first subject tripled the number of positive interactions and received about seven times as many such interactions from peers. The other two subjects performed similarly during their terms as managers. Parents and teachers were quick to note that these students suddenly appeared more interested in school activities and became enthusiastically involved in a wide range of social behaviors. Negative interactions that were low during the baseline period of all subjects remained low during treatment.

The two subjects who were returned to baseline conditions, after their terms as managers, demonstrated reductions in the frequency of social contacts. However, recordings of these students' interactions showed a partial maintenance of improved social behavior even after they resumed their former roles as ordinary students. Generally their rate of positive social interactions during the second baseline averaged midway between the original baseline period and the treatment conditions.

The multiple-baseline procedure demonstrated quite clearly that the targeted subjects' improvement was solely the function of treatment. Before the subjects' exposure to the treatment contingencies they maintained low levels of social interaction. This was true until they became "classroom manager." Other subjects, still on baseline, were not affected until their term in treatment commenced.

Sociometric ratings corresponded with improved social interactions during the treatment period of each subject. Both best-friend nominations and smiley-face ratings improved as each subject took his turn as "classroom manager." More important, these improved ratings and peer nominations were sustained even after the targeted subjects completed their terms.

Four weeks after the conclusion of the experiment these three students were again observed in this setting under baseline conditions. Sociometric information was also gathered once more. Data reveal quite clearly that all subjects still demonstrated continued peer acceptance and higher levels of positive social contacts than those observed during the original baseline conditions.

Thus it appears that an easy to operate environmental support system was able to quickly affect the frequency of withdrawn students' social interactions. One might speculate that simply raising the rate of socializations is not necessarily indicative of having improved a child's social repertoire. However, when one also considers the other assessment strategies that were used in conjunction, which also established improved peer acceptance, the results are quite impressive. Such techniques seem to offer another important method whereby shy, withdrawn, and potentially depressed children might, at least, initiate improved social behavior.

Modeling, Behavior Rehearsal, and Feedback

An earlier study conducted by Bornstein et al. (1977) provided systematic reinforcement in the form of feedback with modeling. The format by which the modeled behavior was communicated differed drastically from that of the O'Conner (1969) study. In this study a social skills training package consisting of didactic instructions, feedback, behavior rehearsal, and modeling was brought together in a multiple-baseline analysis of these treatment variables, which were applied sequentially.

Four elementary school students, ranging in age from eight to eleven years, were selected on the basis of demonstrating excessive social withdrawal and unassertiveness. All four of these subjects were identified as being deficient in at least three target behaviors: poor eye contact, low speech volume, and an inability to make reasonable requests of others. These students were also classified as being weak in overall assertiveness.

In order to assess the students' behavior in a reasonable facsimile of everyday circumstances that require assertiveness, responses were measured using videotaped sequences of training situations that involved interpersonal encounters. This was an adaptation of the Behavioral Assertiveness Test (Eisler, Hersen, & Miller, 1973), subsequently referred to as the Behavioral Assertiveness Test for Children. The test required subjects to role-play scenes narrated by the experimenter and videotaped for data collection purposes. After establishing the scene an adult delivered a prompt in which the subject had an opportunity to respond assertively. An example is provided here for the reader.

9. Narrator: Imagine you're standing in line for lunch. Jon comes over and cuts in front of you. Prompt: "Let me cut in front of you."

Nine baseline scenes were videotaped. The subject's responses were then rated by naive observers for level of assertiveness demonstrated. Ratings for both verbal and nonverbal behavior included eye contact, loudness of speech, number of new requests, and a general rating of overall assertiveness. Subsequent to baseline recordings, the experimenters invoked a treatment designed to increase one of the assertive behaviors. The authors list the training sequence as follows:

(a) The therapist presented one of the scenes from the Behavioral Assertiveness Test for Children, the model delivered a prompt, and the subject responded. (b) The therapist provided the subject with feedback on his/her performance, with reference to the specific target behavior. (c) The therapist then discussed the feedback with the subject to ensure that he/she understood. (d) The role models then modeled responses, with specific attention to the target behavior. (e) Specific instructions were then given by the therapist concerning the target behavior, followed by the subject responding a second time. (f) Rehearsal continued for a scene until the therapist felt that the criterion for that target behavior had been reached. (g) Training then advanced to a new interpersonal situation, proceeding in similar fashion through all training scenes. (Bornstein et al., 1977, p. 189)

After completion of training on all target behaviors, follow-up data were taken at two- and four-week intervals.

Data acquired during the three baseline sessions, twelve social skills training sessions, and two follow-up sessions were analyzed by means of a multiple-baseline design. Treatment was initiated with intervention directed at the ratio of eye contact to speech duration. Subsequently this treatment incorporated intervention on loudness of speech; and finally treatment included the student's initiation of requests for new responses.

All four subjects showed changes in the target behavior correlated with treatment of each behavior. The authors note that each targeted area improved independent of other targets as training advanced along the multiple baseline. Improvements were seen only when training was directed at specific behavioral targets. First eye contact ratings jumped from an average rating of 0 to about 1.0; then, with the introduction of training on improved speech volume, this target moved from an average baseline rating of 1 and 2 to about 4. Finally, with the treatment of increased number of requests for new behavior, that target moved from an average rating of 0 to about 6. Interestingly, it was not until the last treatment regarding the instruction of requests for new behavior that the rating on overall assertiveness showed a substantial improvement, advancing from a baseline rating of 1 to a treatment rating of around 5 for all subjects.

Most important, follow-up data taken at two- and four-week intervals demonstrated that all four subjects were able to sustain the recently learned assertiveness skills. All subjects were rated on follow-up at or above the level of performance demonstrated during their three-week social skills training program.

The authors point to two major implications that may be drawn from this study:

1. These results demonstrate that it is possible to identify specific verbal and nonverbal components of what is generally termed shy, withdrawn, and unassertive behavior. Eye contact, speech volume, and the number of verbal requests all contributed to a global description of self-assertion.
2. Results also indicate that the treatment package, composed of instructions, feedback, behavioral rehearsal, and modeling, is an effective means of bringing about favorable changes in self-assertion.

The extent of generalization produced by these procedures remains unknown. Although these children did demonstrate an ability to perform self-assertive behaviors with adults in situations that were different from those used in the original training setting, no measures were taken on improved interaction with other children in a more natural environment. This would seem to be a particularly critical index of the overall degree of effect. The authors note that subsequent studies in this area might give this factor particular attention.

Social Skills and Problem Solving for Shy Adolescents

A more recent study did look for posttreatment changes in behavior in the natural environment. Christoff et al. (1985) provided six shy adolescents with both social skill training and social problem-solving training. The authors identified several elements of conversational skill (i.e., verbal behavior occurring in a social situation, such as self-disclosures, positive opinions, statements of fact, open-ended questions) and measured the skills directly by counting the number of times such behavior occurred in audiotaped five-minute conversations.

Social problem solving was verbal behavior describing ways of dealing with problems in social situations, such as planning ways to meet others, describing ways to increase contacts, and identifying potential contacts and opportunities for initiating conversations. Social problem solving was measured by Christoff et al. by rating the responses that students made when asked to "tell what happens between" the beginning of a story (where a problem situation is described) and the end of the story (where the problem is solved). Global rating scales were also used to assess self-esteem and self-reported social interaction in general. Conversation diaries were kept by student subjects and general social ratings were obtained from parents and teachers as a validation measure.

The effect of training on social behavior in the natural environment was measured by direct observation of students' conversational behavior in the school cafeteria. Reliability of measurement was assessed for all measures.

A multiple-baseline design was used to assess the effects of social skills training and of problem-solving training. All interventions occurred during eight forty-minute sessions in which all six subjects participated. Before training sessions, data were collected during four baseline sessions on conversational skills and problem-solving skills. Training of problem solving commenced in the fifth session (first training session) and training of conversational skills, in the ninth session (fifth training session).

During intervention two clinical psychology interns conducted group sessions in which all subjects participated. Problem-solving skills training consisted of the following procedures:

1. Offering students a rationale for learning problem solving and outlining what such skill involved
2. Arranging for students to practice problem solving during each training session
3. Providing stories similar to assessment stories for students to practice writing what happened between beginning and end

Students practiced recognizing and defining problems, generating solutions, evaluating possible consequences of each solution, choosing the best solution, and planning implementation of the solution. Problem solving was practiced with respect to joining a group conversation, initiating conversation, and making requests of adults and peers.

Conversational skills training consisted of modeling by the therapists of such social skills as listening, making requests, starting conversations, and self-disclosing. Students then rehearsed the modeled skills and received feedback from peers and therapists.

On introduction of problem-solving training, both global measures and frequency of problem-solving responses in the stories improved. In addition, the continued baseline measures of conversational skills showed improvement in the seventh and eighth sessions, even though the training had only occurred for problem solving. When training commenced for conversational skills, some further improvement occurred in both problem-solving and conversational skills. All improvements were maintained at follow-up, five months after training ended.

The subjects reported increased frequency of interaction with peers in their conversation diaries; self-evaluations were more positive after training, as were positive reports of social skills from others on social validation ratings. Interestingly, observations of students in the school cafeteria showed no change in the subjects' conversational behavior in that setting. The authors suggest a possible confounding variable in that students spent less time in the cafeteria as the study continued and spring weather ensued. Thus generalization of skills, which would best have been demonstrated in the students' interactions, was not observed.

Direct Reinforcement of Social Interaction

The acquisition of social skills by way of modeling is obviously an effective and expedient procedure. However, for children who demonstrate weak intellectual functioning, imitative skills have also been found to be poor. Thus, for children who demonstrate concurrent isolate behavior and weak intellectual functioning, more direct procedures may be required.

An early study by Verplank (1955) exemplifies a theoretical base for a social skills training procedure that operates independent of modeling. This system demonstrates the impact of social reinforcement on the frequency of conversational behavior. In an experiment designed to study the rate of human verbal behavior under various conditions of verbal reinforcement, verbal punishment, and extinction, Verplank arranged for an undergraduate confederate to sit with a subject in a waiting room while both ostensibly waited for a psychology experiment to begin. During three consecutive ten-minute intervals the confederate first ignored all comments made by the subject, then expressed agreement or paraphrased the subject's opinion statements, and finally disagreed or remained silent after the subject's commentary. It was found that the subject's opinion and information statements dramatically increased during the time in which these comments were systematically reinforced, and that such comments virtually terminated during periods of extinction and punishment. This type of social psychology experiment has clear implications for research in applied behavior analysis as it pertains to the training of socialization skills in isolate children having intellectual and imitative deficits.

A study by Strain, Shores, and Timm (1977) used direct systematic prompting and reinforcement of social interaction to increase social responses and initiations. They investigated the effect of placing a confederate, who emitted positive social behaviors, in the midst of a triad of isolate, low-intelligence, behaviorally handicapped boys.

Two confederate children were given extensive training in initiating social contact with isolate children. Two groups of three behaviorally handicapped subjects, ranging from thirty-nine to fifty-three months of age, were observed in a free-play situation. During eight consecutive twenty-minute baseline sessions the trained confederate initiated no social play activities. During this time both groups of subjects demonstrated a low level of social contact. Then, during intervention 1, the confederate child in each group was instructed to attempt to get the other three withdrawn children to play with them. The confederate child in each group increased his social initiations among all three of the isolate children for nine treatment sessions. During this treatment the confederate children both initiated new verbal responses for play activities and also responded favorably to any minimal social gestures on the part of the subjects. Even when the confederates were ignored, they persisted in initiating social contact.

With the implementation of the confederates' social initiations both groups of behaviorally handicapped subjects showed an increased frequency of social responses as well as higher frequencies of initiating verbal and gestural social contacts. However, the subjects' behavior differed in some ways. Some subjects demonstrated social contact only when directly approached by the confederates. Other subjects began to initiate their own verbal or gestural contacts. During reversal to baseline conditions the confederates terminated their initiations of social interactions. Concurrently, social initiations on the part of the isolates dropped back to original baseline levels. On reinstating the social initiations of the confederates, in treatment 2, the social isolates once again demonstrated higher levels of both social initiations and responses to social initiations. This provides reasonably conclusive evidence that the improvement in subjects' social behavior was a function of the confederates' social behavior toward them.

The authors point out that even though the procedures above were overwhelmingly successful, "the mere integration of children with divergent social repertoires would probably not result in positive social development. Rather, careful instruction and programming of peers seem to be required" (Strain et al., 1977, p. 296).

The strategies described above were designed to prevent depressed and isolate children from becoming depressed and isolate adolescents. Such individuals have been documented at high risk for suicide (Johnson, 1985). Anything that can be done to provide these children with the social skills to overcome such problems is likely to improve their chances of survival by reducing suicidal tendencies. The procedures above provide some techniques for teaching social skills to children at an early age. However, once an individual has developed the pattern of isolation and avoidance of social interaction, certain events appear to predispose suicidal behavior. Dealing successfully with such events may also be important in prevention.

Predisposing Feelings and Events

Husain and Vandiver (1984), authors of *Suicide in Children and Adolescents*, propose an array of factors that increase the likelihood of an adolescent's taking his own life. Under the rubric of "constitutional factors," they propose that adolescents who demonstrate high levels of *suggestibility* and *hypersensitivity* are suicide risks. They point out that adolescents who are intellectually below average, or even those with motoric difficulties and learning disabilities, are likely to be suggestible and hypersensitive.

Other factors that seem to predispose adolescents toward suicide include *poor impulse control* and *magical thinking*. Husain and Vandiver suggest that poor impulse control is often observed in those who have "minimal brain dysfunction" and "episodic violent behavior syndromes." They are reportedly less capable of resisting temporary impulses to do harm to themselves. *Magical thinking* is also associated with suicide risk. Some individuals believe themselves to be invincible and appear impervious to the threat of death. Others suffer from delusions that their demise will alter the course of history. Although such notions may appear ludicrous to adults, such magical thinking sometimes is associated with self-destructive behavior. *Loneliness* and *hopelessness* are also seen in presuicidal adolescents. Sometimes loss of a loved one results in extreme grief and a sense of being alone in the world. In moments of desperate grieving the absence of the loved one may lead to feelings of hopelessness. When current circumstances provide little hope for the future, one may see little reason for continued existence. At such a point in time recurring thoughts of self-destruction may occur.

Husain and Vandiver also indicate that *low self-esteem* is associated with teenage suicide. In a culture that predicts personal, professional, and financial success based on scholastic achievement, and often equates an adolescent's personal worth with his or her academic or even athletic prowess, the possibility of academic and athletic failure can prove emotionally devastating.

Sometimes the events that lead to feelings of loneliness, hopelessness, and low self-esteem increase the likelihood of suicide—the ultimate in escape/avoidance behavior. It is unlikely, however, that any given incident or factor is sufficient to initiate a self-destructive episode. When individuals with a history of unresolved personal conflict experience such difficulties, the effects may accumulate to increase the probability of a suicide attempt. Jacobs (1971) theorizes that no single behavioral or emotional factor is a necessary or sufficient condition to provoke suicide. Rather, it is the nature, number, and order of these conditions that ultimately combine and lead to the suicide attempt. He describes a series of stages in which the adolescent gradually develops the progressive social isolation that results in an attempt at self-destruction. These conditions include the following:

1. A long history of problems (from childhood to early adolescence).
2. The escalation of problems (since the onset of adolescence) above and beyond those usually associated with adolescence.
3. The progressive failure of available adaptive techniques for coping with the old and new increasing problems, leading to the adolescent's progressive isolation from meaningful social relationships.
4. A chain reaction dissolution of any remaining social relationships in the days and weeks preceding the attempt which leads to the adolescent's feeling that he has reached "the end of hope."
5. The process by which he justifies suicide to himself, and thus manages to bridge the gap between thought and action. (Jacobs, 1971, pp. 27–28)

CRISIS INTERVENTION

When the propensity to actually engage in suicidal behavior has developed, direct intervention is required. Although behavioral procedures that teach children to overcome shy, withdrawn, isolate, and depressed behaviors have been well documented, little research has been conducted in the use of behavioral models that directly apply to crisis intervention in the case of adolescent suicide attempts. Journal articles that report behavioral studies on suicide intervention are unknown to us. Because behavioral research usually requires some manipulation of independent variables relating to a particular type of overt behavior, it would seem that experimental investigation of this subject matter is precluded. Obviously the possibility of exposing subjects to experimentally controlled conditions that even temporarily increase the risk of their inflicting harm to themselves cannot be considered. However, retroactive analyses of both attempted and completed suicides have been undertaken (Jacobs, 1971). Furthermore, several eclectic journal articles provide models for crisis intervention regarding attempted or threatened suicides. The following description of such a model was derived from a journal that is not behaviorally oriented. Because a behavior analytic approach attempts to deal with relations among empirical events, we have taken the liberty of interpreting some of the metaphorical descriptors into descriptions of empirical events likely to have given rise to the metaphorical behavior of the journal authors.

One of the more popular conceptions of suicidal ideation is that the suicidal adolescent's problems are intertwined with those of the family. Interventions are, therefore, directed at the adolescent as part of a constellation of disturbed family functioning. An article by Walker and Mehr (1983) provides an example of a popular tactic used in crisis intervention. These authors propose that the adolescent suicide attempt is a "cry for help," owing primarily to the chaotic contingencies existing in the home. The self-destructive adolescent in this circumstance has become the "expressor of family conflict." These individuals have run out of behavioral options, so to speak, and having failed to resolve the problems with which they are faced, they attempt something desperate in an effort to "communicate their suffering." It becomes the job of the therapist to help these individuals recognize and overtly state their feelings so that family members may "share them," that is, learn to feel as if they, too, were affected by the events experienced by the sharing member. If the family members are able to experience the shared feelings, it is hoped that they will consider alternative behavior patterns, and that the suicidal child will be motivated to consider alternatives to self-destruction. The suffering adolescent thus may gain "emotional equilibrium."

From a behavior analytic perspective, intervention is aimed at providing the adolescent with a verbal community that differentially reinforces accurate labeling of events and the feelings associated with those events. The family's acceptance of the adolescent's report and their participation in responding to the situation as if they were in the adolescent's place provide the condition that makes examination of alternative behavior possible. When family members gain the skills necessary to provide ongoing and contingent social reinforcement for alternative behavior from the adolescent, the probability of self-destructive behavior is reduced.

Walker and Mehr emphasize that intervention be initiated as quickly as possible after the initial suicide attempt. All members of the family are expected to be present during the subsequent series of sessions. They go on to suggest that in the initial session the therapist's primary goals are "to assess strengths and weaknesses of the family" and "to provide assurance, concern and support." In return the goals of the family should be to learn "to trust the adolescent" and "to continue to support change within the family." The role of the therapist is to encourage the family members to collectively express their feelings of anger or guilt. This is accomplished by an effort to find out why the adolescent has resorted to such drastic measures. Expressions of guilt are also encouraged to "test the reality of these beliefs" (i.e., to allow others to confirm or disconfirm them). After these initial goals are met the family is encouraged to provide "emotional support" for the suicidal adolescent in the initial session. Most important, it is critical that each member of the family commit to not leaving the adolescent alone during the immediate weeks after the suicide attempt. This is a period during which it is thought that the adolescent is still at high risk.

The next intervention phase involves biweekly sessions for a four- to six-week period. The therapist's primary goals are "to begin problem-solving" and "to support new behaviors." The family in turn must learn "to understand family dysfunction" and learn "to begin to solve family problems." The authors note that during the immediate weeks and months that follow there is a distinct tendency for family members to try to seal over the trauma of the suicide attempt by denying the further existence of the problem. According to Walker and Mehr, the therapist must exert a special effort to prevent family members from making a "rapid recovery from near-tragedy."

By this, presumably, it is intended that the family should not be permitted to quickly describe themselves as having gained all the social skills necessary to provide the adolescent with a differentially reinforcing environment. Further behavioral interpretation of this intervention period suggests that family members are encouraged to work together to find new ways to solve interpersonal problems. Illogical beliefs are replaced with more rational and appropriate statements of expectations. The therapist reinforces approximations of increasing positve social initiations and encourages family members to participate in group activities that are mutually reinforcing. During this process the family members learn to act as a unit and to accept responsibility for their role in one another's actions.

In the termination period, which may last anywhere from two to four sessions, the therapist's goals are primarily "to withdraw from the family" and "to provide direction for the family for the future." The family goals are "to trust the adolescent" and "to continue to support change within the family." The authors point out that the family now has an opportunity "to re-nourish the adolescent." It is, however, recommended that the adolescent continue individual "psychological care to ensure a healthy developmental growth process." The authors close by stating that "the family therapist, by guiding and supporting the adolescent and the family through this crisis, may help to turn a potentially fatal act into a positive and constructive growth experience'' (Walker & Mehr, 1983, p. 292).

More empirically stated, the authors appear to suggest that, subsequent to the therapeutic intervention, the family relies more and more on one another and less on the therapist for cues that occasion positive social discourse. They also become more and more likely to provide positive consequences for desirable behavior in one another. Having learned this social repertoire, the family will now allow and encourage the adolescent to make decisions based on his or her own experience rather than on the parents' instruction. The therapist gradually withdraws weekly sessions but remains available for intermittent consultation at increasingly longer intervals.

A Multimodal Behavioral Treatment of Depression

Lazarus (1974) provides an interesting description of a highly diversified behavioral treatment procedure he believes to be effective with both depressed and potentially suicidal clients. Although depression and suicidal tendencies may not be the same in children as in adults, there are probably enough common etiological factors to make his multimodal behavioral treatment applicable to both populations.

Lazarus uses seven interactive modalities in the broad-spectrum intervention program he recommends. This system monitors and attempts to intervene continuously along the dimensions of behavior (overt), affective processes, sensory reactions, imagery (emotive), cognitive components, interpersonal relationships, and a form of drug therapy. The initial letters of each modality ironically produce the acronym BASIC ID. Lazarus does not suggest any theoretical implication for this acronym; it is simply a mnemonic device.

Lazarus contends that depression is primarily a function of deprivation of reinforcement. The resulting extinction process brings about an impoverished repertoire, decreasing the probability of the individual engaging in *behavior* that might produce reinforcement. Thus the individual is caught in a behavioral trap. Lack of activity results in decreased opportunity for reinforcement, and decreased opportunity for reinforcement further lowers the activity level. The inevitable result is a decreased rate of behavior and loss of stimulus control by social stimuli. The individual tells himself that he is unworthy, and he resists prompts from others to engage in reinforceable behaviors. He may lie in bed all day and avoid interpersonal contacts that the therapist attempts to arrange or to get him to arrange. In many cases it is necessary for the therapist to become directly involved in prompting such individuals into action. Lazarus indicates that the therapist may have to go to the homes of depressed and suicidal patients in order to get them out of bed and provoke them into activity. He has had such patients follow him around all day, through his daily regimen, to provide them with increased opportunities for social interactions and increased activity levels.

Lazarus further recommends the use of an activity chart for such persons. After three days of baseline data on the patient's daily activities, a menu of highly active and, hopefully, highly reinforcing activities is produced. This is referred to as a "pleasant events schedule." This could include playing tennis, cards, or music. It may also include everything from making love to visiting a friend. The attempt is to prompt the patient to perform these social behaviors so that the verbal community can provide social reinforcement. Anything that is enjoyable and nondestructive is potentially useful in helping the patient escape the behavioral trap.

There are additional components to the therapeutic intervention. Lazarus suggests that the subtler dimensions of behavior be directly dealt with by the therapist. The depressed individual's *affect* is addressed by way of standard forms of assertiveness training. His *sensory* modality is enhanced by using "bioenergetics," an attempt to improve muscle tone and physical vigor with robust movements (pushing, pounding, etc.). *Imagery* is brought into play either by using desensitization procedures or in an attempt to simply have the patient visualize forthcoming reinforcers. The *cognitive* modality involves the elimination of self-deprecating comments by the patient. This is accomplished with the training of positive "self-talk," and "thought-stopping" to terminate negative ruminations. At the *interpersonal* level the emphasis is on teaching new social skills through role playing and behavioral rehearsal. Lastly, *drug* therapy is considered on a temporary basis as a means of elevating and stabilizing the patient's mood so that he or she is more likely to respond to other forms of intervention.

Unfortunately Lazarus does not provide us with any data to substantiate the utility of this highly diversified set of procedures. However, Lazarus's suggestion that behavior of all kinds be included in the treatment is consistent with the theory that underlies applied behavior analysis. The relations among covert and overt, verbal and nonverbal, emotional and motor, respondent and operant behavior have not yet been systematically studied. Professionals must deal with problems as they are presented and can't always wait for laboratory research to lead the way.

REFERENCES

Agard, J. A., Veldman, D. J., Kaufman, M. J., & Semmel, M. I. (1978). *How I feel toward others: An instrument of the PRIME Instrument Battery*. Bloomington, IN: Project PRIME Technical Report.

Aleksandrowicz, M. K. (1975). The biological strangers: An attempted suicide of a seven-and-a-half-year-old girl. *Menninger Clinic Bulletin*, *39*, 163–176.

Bandura, A. (1969). *Principles of behavior modification*. New York: Holt, Rhinehart & Winston.

Bornstein, M. R., Bellack, A. S., & Hersen, M. (1977). Social-skills training for unassertive children: A multiple baseline-analysis. *Journal of Applied Behavior Analysis*, *10*, 183–195.

Christoff, K. A., Scott, W., Owen, N., Kelly, M. L., Schlundt, D., Baer, G., & Kelly, J. A. (1985). Social skills and problem-solving training for shy young adolescents. *Behavior Therapy*, *16*, 468–477.

Eisler, R. M., Hersen, M., & Miller, P. M. (1973). Effects of modeling on components of assertiveness behavior. *Journal of Behavior Therapy and Experimental Psychiatry*, *4*, 1–6.

Husain, S. A., & Vandiver, T. (1984). *Suicide in children and adolescents*. New York: Spectrum Publications.

Jacobs, J. (1971). *Adolescent Suicide*. New York: John Wiley.

Johnson, B. (1985, February 18). These teenagers feel that they have no options. *People*, pp. 84–89.

Lazarus, A. A. (1974). Multimodal behavioral treatment of depression. *Behavior Therapy*, *5*, 549–554.

National Center for Health Statistics, Division of Vital Statistics, (1980). 3700 E. W. Highway, Hyattsville, MD.

O'Conner, R. D. (1969). Modification of social withdrawal through symbolic modeling. *Journal of Applied Behavior Analysis*, *2*, 15–22.

Pfeffer, C. R., Conte, H. R., Plutchik, R., & Jerritt, I. (1980). Suicidal behavior in latency-age children: An outpatient population. *Journal of the American Academy of Child Psychiatry*, *19*, 703–710.

Sainato, D. M., Maheady, L., & Shook, G. L. (1986). The effects of a classroom manager role on the social interaction patterns and social status of withdrawn kindergarten students. *Journal of Applied Behavior Analysis*, *19*, 187–195.

Strain, P. S., Shores, R. E., & Timm, M. A. (1977). Effects of peer social initiations on the behavior of withdrawn preschool children. *Journal of Applied Behavior Analysis*, *10*, 289–298.

Verplank, W. S. (1955). The control of the content of conversation: Reinforcement of statements of opinion. *Journal of Abnormal and Social Psychology*, *51*, 668–676.

Walker, B. A., & Mehr, M. (1983). Adolescent suicide—a family crisis: A model for effective intervention by family therapists. *Adolescence*, *18*, 285–292.

8

On Aggression

AGGRESSIVE TENDENCIES

In the past fifty years there has been considerable discussion regarding the nature and origin of aggressive behavior. Various authorities have argued that aggression is an innate, instinctual behavior in both humans and animals. For example, Konrad Lorenz, a Nobel Prize–winning ethologist, has published a controversial book entitled *On Aggression* (1966). The controversial aspect of this book concerns Lorenz's contention that aggressive predispositions may occur among the more highly evolved organisms, including humans. Lorenz postulates that such instinctive aggressive behavior served an adaptive function in the evolution of homo sapiens, ensuring the dispersion of human populations over a wide geographic area. This once adaptive predisposition has, according to Lorenz, outlived its usefulness and currently threatens the survival of civilization.

A similar point was made long before Lorenz came on the scene. Much of Freud's early work described what he called man's destructive Id impulses, which ostensibly evolved from primeval, unconscious, innate drives toward death and destruction (thanatos). In *Civilization and Its Discontents* Freud describes his conception of man's aggressive character:

> Men are not gentle, friendly creatures wishing for love, who simply defend themselves if they are attacked, but . . . a powerful measure of desire for aggressiveness has to be reckoned as part of their instinctual endowment. The result is that their neighbor is to them not only a possible helper or sexual object, but also a temptation to them to gratify their aggressiveness . . . to seize his possessions, to humiliate him, to cause him pain, to torture and to kill him. (Freud, 1930, pp. 85–86)

Conversely, it has been proposed that man is innately endowed with a peaceful disposition and that he is only corrupted to do violence by society's influence.

Carl Rogers (1961) points out that man is essentially good when fully himself. He tells us that "We do not need to ask who will control his aggressive impulses, for as he becomes more open to all of his impulses, his need to be liked by others and his tendency to give affection will be as strong as his impulses to strike out or seize for himself" (Rogers, 1961, p. 194).

Still others have suggested that humans are infinitely malleable in regard to aggressive or peaceful inclinations. The Arapesh, a primitive tribe living in the mountains of New Guinea, were described by Margaret Mead as a peaceful people. Their entire culture was based on the premise that "all human beings . . . are naturally unaggressive, self-denying . . . concerned with growing food to feed growing children" (Mead, 1939, p. xix). Mead points out that a neighboring tribe, Mundungumor, were generally hostile, cruel, and warlike.

Although it is unclear whether humans are predisposed toward either violent or peaceful behavior, it is quite clear that other animals are likely to react aggressively, in certain clearly delineated circumstances. Several conditions described in the animal learning literature increase the probability of aggressive behaviors. A classic example was demonstrated by Azrin, Hutchinson, and Hake (1966). In their experiment a hungry bird was trained to peck at a disk within the confines of an experimental space. A target bird was immobilized and placed on a set of switches such that any abrupt movement of that bird would be recorded on a cumulative record. Each time an extinction procedure was imposed, the experimental bird attacked the confined target bird. Attacks were vicious and aggressive and lasted for up to ten minutes. However, these attacks did not simply occur when food was unavailable, but when food had been available on a schedule of reinforcement, and was then discontinued during extinction. Thus we find that aggression is one class of adjunctive behaviors that occurs spontaneously during extinction.

Extinction is not the only experimental condition that provokes aggressive behaviors. Dove, Rashotte, and Katz (1974) trained pigeons on variable interval (VI) schedules of reinforcement while a stuffed target bird was available. Attacks on the stuffed bird were initiated and increased in frequency as the length of intervals increased. These attacks were most probable during the postreinforcement period, a time at which reinforcement had never occurred. Important to note is that these conditions provided no external stimulus associated with nonreinforcement. Subjects simply learned to discriminate certain nonreinforcement periods in the schedule. These conditions reliably elicited aggression.

Environmental conditions such as those described above are called "frustrating," and it has long been recognized that many types of organisms, including man, are much more prone to hostility when frustrated. This long understood fact about aggression was elevated to the status of a theoretical statement in the frustration-aggression hypothesis (Dollard, Doob, Miller, Mowrer, & Sears, 1939). This theory states that every instance of aggression must necessarily be preceded by a state of frustration. Frustration was defined as a state produced by the blocking of an ongoing goal-directed activity; and aggression was defined as behavior aimed at inflicting injury. The frustration-aggression hypothesis is consistent with Freud's conception that any act of aggression releases energy. That is, the release of such "cathartic" energy was said to reduce the strength of other aggressive impulses. As noted above, however, these positions are somewhat inconsistent with the finding that at least one other condition, aversive stimulation, reliably evokes an aggressive response.

In the case of humans, an innate, species-specific propensity toward aggression is particularly open to question. Research conducted by Bandura (1965) suggests that what passes for children's natural inclination toward aggression is, in fact, frequently a function of modeled behavior. Bandura found that children who observed an adult role model pummeling an inflated Bobo doll were inclined to behave similarly if they observed that the model's attacking behavior was not punished. In situations where the attack was conspicuously reprimanded, the children were less likely to behave violently. Also, research by Liebert and Baron (1972) demonstrates that children who had an opportunity to observe violent episodes on TV, such as *The Untouchables*, were subsequently much more likely to aggress than a control group that observed a nonviolent program. The role of the environment in shaping and maintaining aggressive behavior is clearly worth investigating.

RESEARCH ON AGGRESSION

Psychologists have had difficulty devising a commonly accepted definition of aggressive behavior. As Horton (1970) points out, "the labeling of a response as aggressive frequently involves social judgments concerning intentionality (e.g., Dollard et al., 1939) and intensity (e.g., Walters & Brown, 1963) of responses." Many behavioral theorists agree that behavior produced in an obvious attempt to induce "pain" or "harm" can be defined as "aggressive" (McGinnis, 1984). In a more scientific vein B. F. Skinner defines aggression as behavior that is reinforced by evidence of damage to others (Skinner, 1953).

Many of the research articles on child aggression appear in journals that favor "cognitive" interpretations. Although these journals may not be entirely consistent with the behavioral definitions of aggression given above, some of them contain a great deal of useful data. Sometimes cognitive researchers deal with variables that have not been given much attention by behavior analysts. Such variables include characteristics or life experiences of children most likely to aggress, what maintains and terminates their violent behavior once it is initiated, covert self-statements regarding the consequences of violent actions, and the conditions that seem to foster violent behavior. Because the independent and dependent variables are, in most cases, not as well controlled or precisely measured as they usually are in applied behavior analysts' studies, cognitive psychologists tend to describe their results in terms of large-group statistics. This approach apparently assumes that idiosyncracies and discrepancies in individual responses average out and that general trends may be adequately described in terms that allow acceptance or rejection of research hypotheses. Although behavior analysts generally prefer other methodology, such research may be useful as a precursor to a more rigorous experimental analysis.

Perry and Perry (1974) provide an excellent example of research using a group statistical design. Following Sears's (1958) suggestion that a successful aggressive act, one that elicits indicators of suffering from the victim, gains secondary reinforcing value, Perry and Perry proceeded to demonstrate this phenomenon in aggressive boys. In their study Perry and Perry demonstrated that highly aggressive boys seek out overt pain cues from individuals they assault. They point out, however, that once an aggressive attack is initiated, signs of a victim's suffering may terminate the assault. This may occur either through what they refer to as "empathic arousal" of aversive emotional states and/or by providing information to the attacker that the assault has proved adequately damaging. They also note that the anticipation of causing serious damage to the victim and the ensuing retribution by socializing agents may be a further deterrent.

The research goal was to determine the effects of victims' overt declarations of pain on the aggressor's tendency to continue aggressing. They used a $2 \times 2 \times 2$ factorial design. The design included two levels of aggression (high and low) as determined by a peer nomination inventory, two levels of the victim's pain cues (high and low), and two levels of prior anger arousal (nonangry and angry).

In this design the male subjects and confederates were paired and sent to a room where the experimenter described a block assembly game to them. It was explained that both boys could earn money for successfully arranging the blocks in various designs. Once the boys began their task, the confederates either constantly interfered with the subject's progress in block arrangement or, in the "nonangry" group, assisted the subjects in attempts to complete the block designs. Subsequently, all subjects were taken to an adjoining room where it was explained that the confederate would be working on some math problems and that the subject could "help" the confederate learn by providing consequences to the confederate when he made mistakes. These consequences were to be administered by means of an "aggression machine." This apparatus supposedly told the subject if the confederates' responses to various problems were right or wrong by flashing a blue or red light, respectively. It was the subject's job to let the confederate know of his error by depressing one of ten possible feedback buttons that produced aversive noise. The first button produced an extremely mild noise and the tenth, an extremely loud noise. All others ranged, in successive intensity, toward highly aversive loudness at number 10. In response to the noise the confederate would signal to the subject how much pain the noise caused. A "pain indicator" was located on the aggressive machine panel. The pain indicator ranged from 1 to 5. The number 1 meant that very little pain was felt, but each succeeding number was a graduated index of pain. The confederate looked extremely anguished on 5. In order to signal math errors or correct answers, a prearranged sequence of either blue or red lights occurred at fifteen-second intervals on the subject's aggression panel. During twenty-four trials there were twelve unpredictable errors. After each of the subject's administrations of aversive noise, the subject pushed one of the five buttons to indicate a level of pain feedback that was ostensibly felt by the confederate. In the experimental condition designed to suggest to the subjects that the noise produced low levels of pain, lights 1, 2, and 3 were lit corresponding to noise buttons 1 to 3, 4 to 6, 7 to 10, respectively. In the experimental condition that suggested high levels of pain, lights 3, 4, and 5 were associated with buttons 1 to 3, 4 to 6, and 7 to 10 in the same sequence.

The results of this study supported the hypothesis that the denial of felt pain by the victim produced an increased tendency for the high-aggressive subjects to escalate their level of pain administration. There was a significant pain × aggression interaction such that low-pain feedback produced increasingly intensified levels of pain administration by high-aggressive subjects. To quote the authors:

> It would seem that the aggressive child is particularly sensitive to the cues with which his victim provides him as to the successfulness of his aggression. When the aggressive child is denied the satisfaction of knowing he has successfully injured his victim, he may in fact become extraordinarily hostile. That this may be the case was dramatically illustrated by the behavior of the high-aggressive boys in the low-pain-cues condition. Over the course of the test for aggression, as their victims continued to deny the experience of pain, many of these boys tried to evoke a response by simultaneously depressing noise buttons 8, 9, and 10 in an obvious attempt to maximize the noise level. One high-aggressive boy in the angry, low-pain-cues condition held down button 10 for a period of 115 seconds on a single trial. No such behavior was witnessed in the low-aggressive boys, and it was observed in high-aggressive boys only in the low-pain feedback-group. (Perry & Perry, 1974, p. 61)

The findings that highly aggressive children respond differently to a suffering victim than low-aggressive subjects was also supported by Perry and Bussey (1977). In their study twenty-four fifth-grade boys who had all been identified by their peers, by way of the Peer Nomination Inventory, as demonstrating aggressive and unnecessarily rough behaviors were compared with an equal number of boys for whom the same instrument designated low aggression. These authors surreptitiously arranged a condition in which all subjects were purposefully aggravated by a confederate student. This was intended to raise the probability that subjects would attempt to aggress. Again, however, the opportunity of actually harming the confederate never existed.

Subsequently the subject and confederate were sent to perform a card-sorting task during which the subject was given a toy for his participation. In the course of the card sorting the confederate expressed annoyance because he had not been given a similar toy. The confederate then smashed the subject's toy. Subsequent to this attempt to aggravate the subject, the students were placed in a situation in which the subject's apparent task was to let the confederate know when he made a mistake on an arithmetic problem (on which he was working in an adjoining room). To accomplish this the previously described "aggression machine" was again used.

After the "teaching session" terminated, subjects were instructed to reward themselves. They were told that they could select as many tokens as they believed they deserved for negatively consequating the other boys' arithmetic errors. These tokens were exchangeable for toys. It was at this juncture of the experiment that the low-aggression boys were differentiated from the high-aggression group. The low-aggressives were apparently reluctant to take very many tokens when under the impression that they might have hurt the confederate. The high-aggressives demonstrated no hesitancy in this regard. The authors note that they seemed unaffected by whatever suffering they might have inflicted on their victim and took large quantities of tokens. Perry and Bussey concluded that highly aggressive boys do not experience the negative self-reactions after their aggressive behavior that are experienced by boys who generally express less aggression. They indicate that although their study does not permit the conclusion that low-aggressive children behave as such because they experience negative self-reactions after aggression, their data suggest that such might be the case.

Such cognitively oriented studies add to our understanding of the dynamic characteristics of aggressive behavior. They do not, however, tell us what to do about students who act aggressively in the school setting. To change aggressive behavior we must manipulate the variables of which aggressive behavior is a function. Therefore, it is to a functional analysis of behavior that we now turn.

A Functional Analysis of Aggression

In order to produce permanent changes in aggressive behavior it is most advantageous to use procedures aimed at weakening aggressive responses or strengthening socially desirable responses that are incompatible with aggression, or both. To this end, a review of procedures described in behavioral journals provides several fruitful systems of intervention.

It has long been recognized that treating aggressive behavior of delinquents is particularly difficult. This group appears less susceptible to therapeutic intervention primarily because peer groups provide more powerful (and incompatible) contingencies than therapists often have at their disposal (Cohen, 1955). However, one study (Horton, 1970) used adolescent peer group influence to scientific advantage to investigate the generalization effects of learned aggression. His subjects consisted of six adolescent male residents of a home for delinquent, emotionally disturbed children.

In this study, reversals of reinforcement contingencies occurred over four experimental periods. Reinforcement procedures were used alternately for aggressive and nonaggressive responses in two experimental settings. During seven twenty-minute baseline sessions subjects were first permitted to engage in a competitive card game called War. The winner of each trial had an opportunity to either confiscate one of his opponent's tokens (nonaggressive response) or slap his hand (aggressive response). Subsequent to baseline a differential reinforcement procedure was initiated for aggressive responding. The experimenter placed a small cardboard box on the table of each pair of players and informed them that he would, during the course of the games, occasionally drop a bean in their box. Players were told that these beans could later be exchanged for backup reinforcers at a ratio of 5:3 (for every five beans, three cents were earned). Experimental contingencies were arranged so that the reinforcement procedure was used in the first trial in which an aggressive (hand-slapping) response occurred. No rationale was given to the subjects for this apparently random distribution of beans.

At the conclusion of each game of War, subjects joined in another game that permitted (but did not necessitate) an opportunity to indulge in physical aggression. A game called Steal the Bacon was organized as a generalization measure of aggression. In this game pairs of opposing team members had their respective numbers called; pairs of subjects attempted to remove a towel from the center of a circle without allowing the opponent to remove a handkerchief from their rear pockets. As in the game of War, instances involving physical violence were documented. In this generalization measure no financial reward was provided. Subjects were only told which teams had earned the most points.

During the seven baseline sessions there were relatively few aggressive responses during the game of War. In fact, during the fifth, sixth, and seventh sessions no aggressive responses were recorded. However, during the generalization situation, Steal the Bacon, aggressive responding was demonstrated by all players. The author documents the violence as consisting of punching, kicking, pushing, and pulling. He notes that "hitting another subject with an object was also counted as an aggressive response" (Horton, 1970, p. 207). The average number of aggressive responses during this time was twenty-nine per session.

Initiating a reinforcement procedure for aggressive behavior produced an immediate increase in the frequency of violence during the game of War. During the four subsequent experimental sessions subjects averaged more than one act of aggression per trial. That is, some subjects engaged in spontaneous retaliation when given authorized slaps during the game. The average number of aggressive responses jumped to eighty-one per session. Concurrently, aggressive responding also generalized to the game of Steal the Bacon. The mean number of aggressive responses was forty-eight per session.

When reinforcement contingencies were reversed, for nine sessions, and nonaggressive behavior was reinforced during the game of War, aggressive behaviors ceased during that game. However, this reversal contingency did not affect the frequency of aggressive episodes during the game of Steal the Bacon. In fact, the mean number of aggressive responses in this generalization situation continued to fluctuate at a high level, despite the fact that there existed no direct reinforcement for such behavior during that game or the preceding game of War. The total number of aggressive responses were about equal to those counted during the previous experimental period.

When reinforcement for aggressive responding was reinstituted during the next four sessions, reacquisition of aggression in the game of War was rapid and intense. The author notes that the mean number of aggressive responses soared to eighty-five. At this point side effects were observed.

> For example, during the third session, a player and a bystander became involved in a fist fight, with one subject jumping from a table to attack the other, and it was necessary in our opinion to restrain them. Furthermore, by the fourth session, aggressive behavior in the form of slapping, punching, and verbal aggression, directed at the experimenter was frequently observed. (Horton, 1970, p. 209)

However, for the purpose of data acquisition, only hand-slaps were tabulated.

During this period the game of Steal the Bacon became almost unmanageable. The author indicates that almost every call of a number resulted in some serious physical altercation. The average number of aggressive responses increased to eighty-one, the highest level attained during any generalization period. However, during a final reversal phase of reinforcement of nonaggression, aggressive behaviors dropped out almost immediately in the game of War. Aggressive responses dropped to an average of forty-five during the generalization period of Steal the Bacon.

The critical feature of this research pertains to the escalating scale of violence seen in the generalization situation. During the second experimental period, when aggressive responding was reinforced in the game of War, there was a 68 percent increase in aggressive responses in the generalization situation. Even though subsequent reversals to nonaggressive contingencies in the game of War produced corresponding decrements of aggression in the generalization situation, baseline rates on nonaggression were never recovered. It seems apparent that reinforced aggression has an exceedingly high probability of generalizing to other situations and environments. It, therefore, appears that intervention procedures aimed at eliminating aggression will be most effective if they are directed at specific methods of teaching generalization. Many of the following studies, particularly those described by McGinnis (1984), attempt to produce such effects.

Aggression on the Playground

A common problem in many elementary schools is the rough and aggressive play that frequently occurs on playgrounds during the early-morning preschool time. Students who arrive early may find themselves in an unstructured setting. Some of these students become involved in various forms of unorganized "contact games," fights, and rule violations on the school property. Some schools may have as many as 200 or 300 students variously engaged in such rowdy behavior before school opens each morning. This circumstance presents a dangerous physical climate for the students and may place the school in legal jeopardy. Because the problem is often so overwhelming, most schools have either chosen to ignore it or make arrangements to keep students off its property until school hours officially begin. Neither of these alternatives is entirely satisfactory.

In order to deal satisfactorily with the problem, it is necessary to pose it in a manner in which a solution can be devised. Murphy, Hutchinson, and Bailey (1983) set out to answer this question: how can individual or group contingencies be managed to allow a large and diversified group of children to occupy a small area of land for about twenty minutes? They devised a program for a group of about 344 kindergarten and first- and second-grade students, to address just such a problem. Using a reversal (ABAB) design, these authors organized specially designed sports and games to structure early-morning playground activities, and thus preclude most violent behavior on the school grounds. Specifically, these authors directed their attention to reducing the number of physically aggressive episodes, instances of property abuse, and playground rule violations occurring during morning preschool time. By manipulating precurrent conditions on the playground these acts of aggression were largely precluded.

After twelve days of baseline it was determined that an average of 212 aggressive incidents per twenty-minute period occurred each morning. During intervention, foot races and rope jumping were organized. Race lanes were constructed by tethering ropes to plastic pipes planted in the earth. Races were organized by having participants line up in single file in the lanes between the ropes. Similar lanes were created for the organized game of jump-rope. Students who refused to cooperate in maintaining organized lines or who otherwise became unruly were sent to a time-out area for two minutes and denied the privilege of returning to the game. The authors provided a clear statement of rules and procedures for the adults who would monitor organized activities. Specifically, a two-page handout described the inappropriate behaviors and their consequences, gave instructions as to how to patrol and scan the playground, explained methods of delivering unemotional discipline, and described appropriate social reinforcement procedures for acceptable behaviors: This information was read by all monitoring adults.

Using the above-described procedures for seven days reduced the average number of incidents from 212 to 91. A reintroduction of baseline contingencies for a four-day period resulted in an increase to 191 aggressive episodes. Reinvoking the intervention system for six days brought the average back to 97.

The authors point out that time out was an infrequently used adjunctive procedure. Of the total thirteen experimental days the time-out procedure was used only on ten days, with an average of 2.5 time outs per day. However, other mild disciplinary tactics were used quite often. Children who purposefully ran into others on their way back from the finish line were required to walk slowly back to the finish line and then return slowly to the waiting area before they were permitted to resume the activities. This could be construed as a form of response cost. In the same fashion, those who caused problems in the jump-rope area were required to go to the end of the line before being permitted to resume participation in that activity.

The authors point to a serendipitous outcome regarding "fan control." Students who preferred to watch the game and cheer for the participants rather than play also became more manageable during the intervention periods. When the spectators became disruptive the games were temporarily halted, which resulted in immediate crowd compliance. When spectators stood too close to the racing lanes games were stopped. Not only did most fans move back away from the racing lanes, but they also admonished more resistant students to do the same.

Peer Monitors on the Playground

The behavioral literature is replete with studies that have used able classmates to work with their peers who exhibit social and academic deficits (e.g., Strain, 1981). Other investigators have noted that benefits also accrue to the children who serve as interveners (e.g., Dineen, Clark, & Risley, 1977; Dougherty, Fowler, & Paine, 1985). Fowler, Dougherty, Kirby, and Kohler (1986), however, have moved one step further and implemented a behavioral program that focuses on changing the behaviors of the *change agents* themselves. These authors designed a study to examine whether or not being appointed as an intervention agent will promote behavior changes in children with problem behaviors and if these changes are likely to maintain or generalize to untreated sessions or settings.

Three seven-year-old boys who engaged in disruptive behaviors during recess periods were selected as peer monitors to observe and consequate the playground behaviors of their nineteen classmates. Screening, baseline, and intervention observations occurred on the playground during morning and afternoon recess (ranging from fifteen to twenty minutes each) and noon recess (twenty-five to thirty-five minutes). Data were collected five days per week during noon recess and approximately three days per week during morning and afternoon recesses. One adult observer was assigned to each child monitor during the entire recess.

Although the primary dependent variable was occurrences per minute of monitor's negative interactions with peers, eight other categories of child behavior (as defined by Dougherty et al., 1985) were observed and recorded. These included positive interactions with peers, rule infractions, and negative behaviors from peers toward the observed child. Recorded adult and monitor behaviors included prompts to improve behavior and praise (whether delivered by a monitor to his classmate or by an adult to the monitor), monitor's delivery of point awards and point fines, and adult use of time out. A reversal design (A-B-A-B) was used during noon recess; effects were subsequently replicated with two subjects in a multiple-baseline design across morning and noon recesses.

Generalization was assessed through an extended baseline in the morning and afternoon recesses. Four experimental conditions were implemented:

1. *Baseline*, during which teachers supervised recesses and sent children to time out if they repeatedly broke rules (e.g., stealing equipment, leaving the playground, fighting, etc.).

2. *Peer-monitoring condition*, during which the three subjects received thirty-minute individual training sessions on identifying appropriate and inappropriate playground behaviors, opportunities for awards and reasons for fines. The subjects also rehearsed how to award these points and fines. The entire class received thirty minutes of social skills training before appointing peer monitors. Each subject monitored a different classmate each day during the noon recess.

   Before each recess an adult reviewed the monitoring rules and reminded the monitors to model appropriate behavior and to check with their "point buddy" at five-minute intervals. The adult remained on the playground, occasionally prompting monitors to check their point buddies. The prerecess prompting session was gradually faded out and, for two of the subjects, eliminated.

   Four bonus points could be added by the peer monitor. The assigned point buddy started recess with 2 points that the monitor could take away for negative behavior. The three peer monitors recorded points and fines using two strands of movable beads (for bonus and regular points, respectively) and single points were added or subtracted from totals contingent on each occurrence of positive or negative behavior. Daily outcomes were posted in the classroom—point buddies praised for earning points and for not being fined—and the three subjects also received weekly feedback on their monitoring and play behaviors.

   Recess points were accumulated for a weekly class reward (e.g., popcorn, a film), which was continued throughout the study.

3. *Adult-monitoring condition* (for two subjects), wherein the adult consequated the monitors' negative behaviors—4 points were available for fines and 2 bonus points for appropriate interactions. When the two subjects met the criteria, points were added to the class total.

4. *Monitored-by-peer condition* (for one subject), instituted to further decrease this child's negative interactions. Six classmates monitored this subject's behavior, and the procedures used during condition 2 prevailed in this experimental phase.

The results of this study support the finding of Dougherty et al. (1985) that children with severe behavioral problems can reduce these behaviors when they are assigned to monitor classmates for better behaviors. Appointment as a peer monitor produced an immediate decrease in rate of negative interactions by the three subjects. When their appointments were discontinued, rates of inappropriate interactions increased to pretreatment levels; however, reintroducing peer monitor appointments produced concomitant decreases for two subjects. These two boys increased their rates of positive interactions by almost 50 percent during their first appointment condition and maintained these increases throughout subsequent reversals and interventions. No change occurred in one subject's consistently high rate of positive interactions throughout the study.

Treatment gains were limited to sessions and settings wherein the boys were appointed to be peer monitors (or in which they received monitoring from adults or peers). There was limited generalization and maintenance. To discover why generalization and maintenance did not occur, the authors suggested more research in this area of "reversing the traditional treatment roles from treated to treater" (Fowler et al., 1986, p. 444).

Time Out Contingent on Aggression

The use of a time-out procedure has been found to be a simple and effective method for terminating children's aggressive behaviors. When a student behaves aggressively in the classroom, other students are keenly aware of the teacher's reaction. Sometimes verbal reprimands are effective; frequently they are not. In fact, some behavior seems to thrive on the teacher's negative attention and other students' reactions. One can stop reinforcing aggressive behavior with negative attention, but such an extinction procedure is difficult to carry out and may allow too much damage to occur before the extinction process is complete. The most efficient method for use in the classroom is the time-out procedure.

Ninness, Graben, Miller, and Whaley (1985) describe the implementation and advantages of the time-out procedure. Time out means *time out from reinforcement*. The "from reinforcement" component of this term is critical. It clarifies the point that a time-out procedure is designed to remove the opportunity for the child to engage in behavior that produces consequences that are reinforcing. The implementation of this procedure is designed so that disruptive or inappropriate behavior results in loss of opportunity to engage in reinforceable behavior. During time out all usually available activities that produce consequences are temporarily suspended and unavailable. This can most often be accomplished by simply having the student place his head down on the desk, in folded arms, for a period of about two minutes. This procedure is simple and can be used repeatedly throughout the school day. Such short time outs immediately contingent on all behavior serious enough to require intervention are preferable to fewer but longer isolations sporadically implemented. In fact, long-term isolation should be invoked only in the event that the student refuses to comply with the short-term time-out procedural requirements of being still with head down for two minutes.

It is essential that the teacher not wait until a full-blown aggressive episode erupts to use the time-out procedure. At the first sign of hostility the offending child should be directed to take a time out. He should be told succinctly and firmly that he has violated a class rule regarding arguing or hitting and that he must stay in time out for two minutes. Elaboration on his misbehavior, moralizing, predictions of future consequences, cajoling, and asking for explanations should not occur at this time. If necessary, they should occur in a later conversation. Arrangements regarding the circumstances under which time out is used and its duration should be explained to the class well in advance of any actual implementation of the procedure. Teachers may find that they must, at first, use the time-out procedure as often as ten to twenty times a day for some children.

So be it. It takes some behaviors a long time to diminish in strength, and aggression is often one of them.

In a case where a particularly belligerent student refuses to go to time out, he should be informed that he is earning more time out while he delays. If further refusals ensue, then the student should be required to compensate for this time during recess or after school. In most cases even relatively belligerent students comply with time-out requirements once these are systematically implemented and procedurally confounding reprimands and other attention fail to occur contingent on either noncompliance or the aggressive behaviors. Stronger penalties for noncompliance are usually required only in the initial stages of the students' exposure to the time-out procedure.

It is important to emphasize that time out constitutes the total intervention. When a child goes into time out no form of lecture or scolding should accompany its administration. When the child is released from time out no subsequent form of threat or disapproval is necessary, and in fact such commentary only compromises the effectiveness of time out. It is also important to note that no praise or special attention should be given to the student within the first minute or so after dismissal from time out. Sometimes such comments initiate a cycle in which the child may seek the attention of the teacher by first earning time out.

Time out, when used in the preceding manner, has been found to be an especially effective strategy for eliminating aggressive behavior in children; however, it is more effective when the teacher uses the procedure before students become involved in overt aggression. Most aggressive episodes are prefaced by a period of conspicuous antagonism. It is during this prelude to the actual aggression that time out can be used most strategically.

Time-Out Duration and Delayed Time Out

A matter of some contention has been the question of exactly how long an offending student should be kept in a time-out area. A study by White, Nielson, and Johnson (1972) attempted to shed some light on this issue. The authors designed a study to examine the relative effectiveness of one-minute, fifteen-minute, and thirty-minute time-out durations as they affect the frequency of deviant behaviors. The specific target behaviors in this study included overt physical aggression, self-destruction, tantrums, and running away. The subjects were twenty moderately to severely retarded inpatients ranging from seven to twenty-one years of age. This population included subjects with both high and low social maturity. Subjects were randomly divided into three counterbalanced groups. The within subjects design consisted of three experimental phases—one-minute, fifteen-minute, and thirty-minute treatments—received in different orders by the three groups. Subjects were placed in time out for the specified amount of time when the target inappropriate behaviors occurred. An analysis of variance for repeated measures showed that time out had a significant overall effect in reducing these deviant behaviors ($p < .001$). In terms of group results, the fifteen-minute condition reduced the occurrence of target behaviors 37.16

percent; the thirty-minute condition reduced it 34.20 percent, and the 1-minute condition reduced it 12.09 percent. The authors concluded that the thirty-minute condition was no more effective than the 15-minute condition in terms of group effects. The authors note that the 1-minute time out was primarily effective when preceded by one of the other, longer time-out conditions. Social maturity did not appear to affect treatment effectiveness. It is important to note, however, that this experiment did not use a short-term (two-minute) time out that was followed by longer time out for noncompliance. Had this been used, it is possible that the authors might have found that even the shortest time-out durations were immediately effective.

Surprisingly, it has even been reported that time out may be effective when it is delayed and used as a backup consequence. Ramp, Ulrich, and Dulaney (1971) arranged a simple experiment in which a disruptive third-grader, previously found unsusceptible to psychostimulant medication, was placed in time out only during the time he would have spent in gym or recess. Observations were conducted, during baseline and treatment, at continuous ten-second intervals. This subject had a small red light placed on the top of his desk during class time. On any occasion during which the child behaved disruptively in class (e.g., aggressive, vocal, out-of-set behaviors) the light was turned on for one to three seconds. Each light signal was backed up by five minutes of time out to be served during the child's normally scheduled recess or gym time.

During baseline the subject averaged 23.7 out-of-seat intervals and 17.1 talking out intervals per fifteen-minute session. Frequency of these behaviors was not reduced when the subject was given only verbal instructions regarding the particulars of the forthcoming time-out procedure. However, with the actual implementation of the program, the student's out-of-seat and talking out behavior dropped and stayed at near zero. On the first day of the delayed time-out procedure the subject left his seat on two occasions and talked out on one occasion. This resulted in fifteen minutes of time out from recess. This effectively terminated all inappropriate behavior during the twenty-three-day experimental phase of the experiment. However, with a reversal to baseline contingencies, the subject's inappropriate conduct resumed at even higher rates.

Intervention in the Preschool

Although it is commonly understood that much childhood aggression is maintained by attention, extinction of aggressive behaviors has not often been the treatment of choice. Ignoring a physical assault creates the possibility of real harm to the victim of the assault. Most alternative interventions include some form of punishment, verbal or physical, directed to the assailant. However, the punishment procedure is often poorly implemented because it usually follows the reinforcing attention. Thus the aggression is first reinforced and then punished, with the reinforcement procedure occurring temporally closest to the behavior. Furthermore, in punishment, the socializing agent often provides a model of aggressive behaviors and the concurrent possibility exists of providing a form of negative attention that inadvertently reinforces the assailant's behavior. Even the time-out procedures, as previously described, may contain elements of negative attention for some aggressive behaviors.

Alternatively, extinction of aggression might be a tenable procedure if a means of protecting the victim from physical harm were established. Most often, owing to the size and physical capabilities of elementary and high school students, such physical protection of a potential victim is not a real and consistent possibility. However, at the preschool, kindergarten, and perhaps up through the first and second grades such physical protection can be accomplished without exposing the potential victim to any real risk of physical harm. Most often children at these ages are not large enough to overpower a teacher or aide who might simply block the assailant's path of assault. Under such conditions extinction of overt aggression becomes tenable.

Pinkston, Reese, LeBlanc, and Baer (1973) described just such an intervention. The experiment was carried out in an experimental classroom containing four teachers and sixteen preschoolers, ranging in age from three to five years. The subject was an active 3½-year-old boy who exhibited a high frequency of aggressive behavior and inappropriate peer-interacting skills.

A multiple-baseline design was used to study the effects of intervention on two classes of behavior, aggression and peer interaction. Two reversals of contingencies occurred during the experiment. The first target behavior, aggression, was analyzed during a seven-day baseline during which teachers provided their usual means of discipline after any form of verbal or physical aggression. They verbally reprimanded the subject or physically restrained him from attacking others. During the next nine days the subject's physical and verbal assaults were placed on extinction. Teachers did not attend to his aggressive behavior, and they precluded his hurting other children by physically coming between him and the likely victim. The teachers also made a conspicuous attempt to console and attend to the comfort of the target of the subject's aggression. The baseline condition and extinction procedure were alternated during two subsequent experimental reversals. The second target behavior, peer interaction, was observed throughout the course of the first two reversals of treatment for aggression. During the final extinction phase for aggressive behavior a reinforcement procedure for the subject's appropriate peer interaction was instituted.

Results reveal a clear and consistent reduction in aggressive behavior when the subject was ignored while attention was given to the victim. The multiple-baseline design allowed the experimenters to demonstrate that the reduction of aggressive behavior facilitated peer interaction. The reversal design applied to the class of aggressive behavior enabled the experimenters to demonstrate experimental control. By reversing the extinction procedure with the reinforcement procedures the original baseline frequency of aggressive behaviors was successively recovered and extinguished. During baseline the subject spent an average of 28 percent of his peer interaction time involved in some form of overt aggression. At the time of follow-up the subject spent less than 3 percent of his peer interaction time in any form of aggressive behavior. It was also demonstrated that teacher attention contingent on peer interaction significantly improved the subject's interaction with peers. Peer interaction, which ranged during baseline from 1 percent to 25 percent, increased during follow-up to about 43 percent of the time observed.

Cognitive Training and Response Cost

In recent years researchers billing themselves as "cognitive behavior therapists" have devised a variety of treatments that have primarily focused on what people say to themselves or what they imagine. Most behavior analysts would simply consider covert verbalizations and imaginings as operant behavior and deal with them as such. Because most cognitive behavior therapy techniques focus on "cognitions" (e.g., covert verbal behavior) as the dependent variable (i.e., what is to be changed by manipulating the environment), much research they do proves useful and is reported in journals of behavioral orientation.

One such study by Forman (1980) sought to compare the relative effectiveness of a "cognitive restructuring program" with a traditional response-cost program as both influenced aggressive tendencies of elementary school children. Subjects were eighteen inner-city children who were referred to the school psychologist because of their aggressive tendencies. These students were randomly assigned to the above-mentioned treatment approaches and a control group. The dependent variables were of the type not normally emphasized in behavior analysis; that is, they were in large part composed of rating scales, schedules, and anecdotal records rather than directly observable aggressive behaviors. Specifically, these measures consisted of subscales from the Devereaux Elementary School Behavior Rating Scale (Classroom Disturbance and Disrespect-Defiance), teacher records of aggressive behavior, and two measures from the Schedule of Classroom Activity Norm (Inappropriate Behaviors and Inappropriate Interactions). Pretreatment and posttreatment measures were used for all variables.

The cognitive restructuring group met twice weekly for thirty minutes over six weeks, with two graduate students conducting the group. Group members described situations in which they had become angry. They first developed "scripts," things they would say to themselves to avoid getting angry, and then imagined saying these things to themselves in new situations while in a state of relaxation. Finally, they were encouraged to practice these procedures at home.

The response-cost system consisted of subtracting two minutes per aggressive act from time spent with two graduate students who were available twice weekly for thirty minutes over six weeks. Classroom teachers were responsible for recording minutes deducted. A control group noncontingently met with two graduate students twice weekly for thirty minutes over six weeks for reading tutoring.

Both treatment groups showed reduced aggressive behavior over the control group and there were no significant differences between cognitive restructuring and the response-cost procedure in reducing aggression when averaged across dependent variables. The treatments did differ in which measures contributed most to the overall difference in pretreatment and posttreatment assessments. In the cognitive restructuring group the dependent measure that showed the most change was the rating scale. In the response-cost group, teacher reports of aggressive incidents and teacher ratings contributed most to overall change.

A number of problems arise from methodology of this type. The fact that the primary sources of data were secondary accounts of the subjects' behavior opens the possibility of contamination by response bias and retrospective inference. The response-cost findings may well have been influenced by the involvement of classroom teachers in the treatment and measurement of data. The fact that the number of subjects was small for a statistical design (seven in treatment and only four in control) and that these subjects' behaviors were averaged across dependent variables further limits the usefulness of these findings.

Contingent Exercise

A number of aggressive children are seemingly unaffected, or at least not adequately affected, by time out, response cost, cognitive restructuring, or differential reinforcement of other behavior (DRO). For some students a direct and aversive form of stimulation may be the most suitable means of controlling aggressive behavior. Both teachers and school administrators know that some children will respond to corporal punishment, at least on a temporary basis. However, a number of undesirable side effects are associated with the use of corporal punishment, and it is difficult to use it in a punishment procedure because of the delay in its administration required by legal formalities. Furthermore, spankings produce "feelings of alienation," guilt, and contempt between the parties involved. Many teachers inadvertently wait until the student's behavior is absolutely intolerable before using corporal punishment. Consequently applied behavior analysts have been investigating the effectiveness of more functional procedures to reduce inappropriate or undesirable behaviors in the classroom.

As one alternative to corporal punishment, Luce, Delquadri, and Hall (1980) investigated the effects of contingent exercise on verbal and nonverbal aggressive responses. The authors conducted two single-subject experiments. Experiment 1 was a reversal design (ABAB) and attempted to determine the effects of contingent exercise alone on nonverbal aggressive behavior. The subject in experiment 1, Ben, was a seven-year-old male, diagnosed as "developmentally delayed," who was enrolled in a public school program for severely disturbed children. The aggressive behavior targeted for treatment was hitting; this was defined by the authors as any hit with open hand or closed fist instigated by Ben throughout the school day. During baseline (days 1 through 17) no systematic contingencies for aggressive behavior occurred. Fighting that appeared to be dangerous was handled by physically restraining and separating the children.

The first treatment phase (days 18 through 27) implemented exercise (consisting of standing up and sitting on the floor ten times) contingent on hitting. The contingent exercise had to be prompted at first but was eventually evoked by the verbal command, "Ben, no hitting. Stand up and sit down ten times." A return to baseline conditions (days 28 through 35) followed by reinstatement of treatment conditions (days 36 through 43) concluded the first experiment. Results indicated a rapid decrease in the number of hitting responses with the introduction of contingent exercise. More important, the authors demonstrated that hitting behavior could be suppressed independent of DRO.

In the second experiment the subject, Peter, was a ten-year-old male enrolled in the same class as Ben. Records indicated that Peter had been nonverbal at age four and was legally blind, although he wore glasses to enhance his residual vision. An expert rated Peter as more verbal than any children with whom contingent exercise had been used. He had been diagnosed as "borderline trainable retarded" but was deemed too disruptive for the special class for retarded children. In addition to self-stimulatory behaviors, Peter had a history of aggressively acting out.

Experiment 2 was a combination reversal and multiple-baseline design. The authors' intent was to determine the relative effectiveness of DRO and contingent exercise in controlling aggressive actions and comments. Contingent exercise was initially introduced to determine if the reduction of aggressive actions had any effect on aggressive comments. The dependent variables were operationalized as actions that included hitting, kicking, choking, and punching, and threats said in an angry tone of voice, such as "I'm going to kill you" or "I'm going to step on your face."

Using an ABABACAB design, the frequency of these behaviors were counted over the entire school day. The baseline period A (days 1 through 7) included no systematic consequences for hits, kicks, chokes, or pushes. As in experiment 1, dangerous aggressive incidents were handled by separating the children. During condition B (days 8 through 11) aggressive actions were immediately consequated with contingent exercise (defined as standing up and sitting down ten times). This was followed by a reversal to baseline for days 12 and 13, a reinstatement of condition B for days 14 through 19, and return to baseline on days 20 and 21. DRO was then implemented during condition C (days 22 through 25), and Peter received points for "not fighting" that could be exchanged for privileges or edibles. Also, verbal praise accompanied fight-free intervals (approximately fifteen minutes) throughout the day. Finally, on days 27 through 33, the contingent exercise in condition B was reintroduced as a punishment procedure.

Concurrently, an ACACAB design was implemented to clarify the roles of DRO (C) and contingent exercise (B) in regard to aggressive comments. A baseline period (A) prevailed from day 1 to day 16 during which aggressive comments were ignored. During the DRO phases (C, days 17 through 20 and 22 through 25) "talking nicely" was reinforced in the same manner described above for "not fighting." A return to baseline (A) on day 21 and again on day

26 consisted of once again ignoring aggressive comments, and in addition, reinforcement for "talking nicely" was removed. DRO was again implemented on days 22 through 25, and the experiment ended by introducing contingent exercise on days 27 through 32 that paralleled its implementation to consequate aggressive actions (days 27 through 33).

Results reflect the differential effects of the two treatments. The mean number of aggressive actions recorded under the three contingent exercise phases was substantially lower than the number observed during the DRO phase (8.3, 2.7, 2.3 versus 38.5). Similar results occurred with the mean frequency of aggressive comments during the two DRO and contingent exercise phases (14, 48.5 versus 8.5). The authors conclude that not only can contingent exercise alone be used to reduce or completely eliminate undesirable behaviors such as aggressive actions and verbalizations, but also it appears to be a more effective technique than DRO (at least for Peter's aggressive behavior).

Because a reversal to the contingent exercise condition did not occur with aggressive comments, conclusions are not as strongly supported as they were in the case of aggressive actions. The methodology involved in this research is commendable. Independence of the two target behaviors (aggressive comments and aggressive actions) was established by a multiple-baseline strategy, and the effects of the two treatments were compared. The results of experiment 1, which established the effectiveness of contingent exercise as a sole treatment modality, suggest important considerations for researchers as well as educators. The findings remind us that when two techniques are successfully used together, the resulting change in behavior does not necessarily require both. One might be sufficient.

Behavioral Rehearsal

It has often been postulated that aggressive behavior is associated with an emotional response to frustrating circumstances (Dollard et al., 1939). However, a specific aggressive act may be a learned adaptive operant behavior. As such, having an aggressive student practice behaviors that produce positive consequences but are incompatible with aggression, in the presence of conditioned stimuli that evoke autonomic arousal, might be a reasonable technique. Such a procedure, which attempts to address both respondent and operant features of aggression, was developed by Gittleman (1965). This procedure, referred to as behavior rehearsal, contains many of the characteristics found in classic desensitization (Wolpe, 1958) and modeling (Bandura, Ross, and Ross, 1963), as well as techniques normally associated with psychodrama (Moreno, 1959).

The technique involves a form of role-playing whereby various instigative situations are played out by the student members of a group. These situations are ones that have been described by the subject as having previously provoked him or her to violence. As in desensitization, a hierarchy of provocative situations is developed and the student is instructed to respond "innovatively" in a peaceful manner. The child is rated by other participant observers in the group as to the adequacy of his or her peaceful and appropriate responses. Points are awarded by the group as an index of the subject's performance. Gittelman used a 5-point scale, ranging from −2 (overt retaliation and a poor performance) to +2 (an innovative nonaggressive response that mollifies the provocateur). As each pacifistic plateau is reached, the student is challenged with an even more difficult circumstance to address peacefully. Sessions are provided weekly for one-hour intervals until improvement is seen both inside and outside the instructional environment.

Gittelman described two case histories in which this procedure was used successfully. However, the primary data are apparently anecdotal. Accounts derived from subjects, parents, teachers, and counselors are used to substantiate the effectiveness of this procedure. Although this technique appears to hold promise as a means of decreasing frequency of violent behavior in schoolchildren, quantitative evidence remains to be gathered. Furthermore, the implicit expectation that disturbed children are capable of spontaneously ''innovating'' unique appropriate responses under stressful conditions may not be warranted. In addition, this procedure makes no explicit provisions for transfer of training to other environments.

Social Skills through Behavior Rehearsal

McGinnis (1984) describes a *structured learning approach* for teaching social skills that is designed to remediate a variety of social deficits, including dealing with stress, listening, asking for help, sharing, dealing with fear, expressing affection, conversation skills, and verbal and physical aggression. This section describes only those portions of McGinnis's work that are most germane to aggressive behavior. Although McGinnis does not provide research data to substantiate the effectiveness of the following procedures, the tactics are so well designed that they deserve special consideration.

Many students, particularly those classified as behaviorally disordered or emotionally disturbed, have not shown general improvement in social and interpersonal functioning even when their academic performance improves in the classroom. Furthermore, the previously described study by Horton (1970) documents the extent to which aggressive behaviors do quickly generalize. Therefore, if behaviorally disordered students are to learn pro-social skills, instruction in these skills will have to be as systematic as academic instruction. However, learning in this context does not simply mean that the students can verbally describe appropriate social conduct in a classroom setting. The student must be willing and able to perform these behaviors when the occasion demands it.

McGinnis (1984) describes a student, Tricia, who was adequate at describing the appropriate pro-social response to peer antagonism. This student could state quite clearly that she was to ignore such provocation. However, in the actual circumstances, she typically reacted with physical or verbal retaliation. McGinnis points out that we are often inclined to believe that if a student can describe the appropriate response, he or she can perform it. "Knowing that" is, however, different from "knowing how" (Hineline, 1983). The conditions under which Tricia described pro-social behavior were very different from the stressful conditions present in aversive situations. McGinnis's *structured learning approach* (1984) uses modeling, role-playing, feedback, and planned generalization to maximize the impact of instruction and the extent of generalization. The particular tactics involved in implementing these procedures are developed through a series of group exercises described below.

Modeling

According to Bandura (1977), pro-social modeling, in and of itself, is insufficient to bring about lasting, positive change in behavior. Learning observed behavior is most likely when the subject must attend to the model's actions, verbalize what has occurred, and reproduce the modeled behavior. Reinforcement procedures must be implemented for these behaviors.

In the case of aggression, subjects should be provided with a model who demonstrates difficulty in demonstrating pro-social behavior when antagonized by a peer. It has been noted that subjects "identify" with a model (view a model as being similar to themselves) when the model demonstrates coping rather than mastery of a newly acquired skill (Bandura, 1977). For example, a model who overcomes the temptation to physically retaliate when provoked by a peer might be more likely imitated if he or she walks away with clenched fists and is demonstrably irritated, rather than if the model simply walks away with a smile. To further dramatize the model's "self-control," he or she may be heard to say something like "It's hard to walk away."

Role-playing

This is accomplished in much the same manner as the previously described behavioral rehearsal by Gittleman. However, McGinnis uses specific tactics designed to facilitate transfer of training. After observing a modeling of appropriate pro-social behavior the student tries to replicate these behaviors while some other students are chosen to play the role of active antagonists, attempting to perform their roles in much the same way as would naturally occur in the school environment. As an example, students might role-play teasing the primary student during lunch period. The scene could be rehearsed in the cafeteria in order to enhance generalization effects. Other students in the group may simply act as observers and provide constructive feedback at the end of each vignette. The instructor directs the scenario.

During rehearsal the primary student will overtly verbalize the pro-social behaviors he or she has learned. Such overt "thinking" will generally consist of two important phases. In the first phase the student calms himself or herself by overtly vocalizing words that are designed to have an effect on autonomic arousal that is opposite to the arousing effect of the difficult situation. McGinnis recommends such self-statements as "I believe I am being teased because they are looking at me and laughing. I don't like to be teased, but I won't let them know that! I'm angry, so first I have to cool down. I need to count to five. 1 . . . 2 . . . 3 . . . 4 . . . 5. Okay, now I think of my choices" (McGinnis, 1984, p. 101). The student, by engaging in operant behavior inconsistent with aggressive behavior, has allowed the first rush of emotion to subside and has checked the immediate impulse to react in an aggressive manner. At this point the second phase of the technique comes into play. The student reviews the reasonable noncombative options that exist at this time. He or she may say: "I might raise my hand and tell the teacher what is going on here. I could simply ignore them. OK, I think I'll just ignore these people. That will show them how little I care about their silly behavior" etc. The student then follows her own instruction, ignoring other students who continue to tease for a short period of time.

This form of rehearsed vocalization assists with retention and teaches the child to restrain his or her retaliatory behavior. With practice the child should gradually become less overtly vocal during succeeding rehearsals. That is, he or she will continue rehearsal, in this same format, while saying these same words silently (covertly). Rehearsal will thus come closer and closer to resembling the scenario as it might occur in the everyday world. This type of practice will be most effective and generalize furthest if it occurs many times in many types of situations.

McGinnis indicates that elementary school students can benefit from about twenty to thirty minutes, whereas secondary school students need about thirty to forty-five minutes three times a week. Adequate learning is demonstrated only when students engage in these new behaviors in a spontaneous way outside of the instructional setting. It is also important to review previously acquired prosocial skills throughout the course of instruction.

Ideally the instructor should provide social reinforcement throughout the course of instruction. Students vary in their preference for various types of reinforcement; however, reinforcement menus may be altered in order to best accommodate individual tastes. Furthermore, it is always important to provide contingent praise independently or in conjunction with tangible reinforcers.

Feedback

Another critical component of this process is providing consistent, immediate, and accurate feedback from the other participants and instructors, as well as the subject's own self-evaluation at the end of each vignette. Such feedback may be based on many dimensions but should always be predicated on the extent to which the subject's performance approximated that of the model. Numbers between 1 and 5 could be used to convey degree of proficiency; perhaps more familiar is the use of a letter grade, A through F. In conjunction with a grade given by each member of the group, constructive criticism can also be provided by way of verbal descriptions of the subject's performance. Such descriptions should first emphasize the positive aspects of the performance and then point to changes in various dimensions of behavior that might enhance the effect. This type of feedback not only provides the subject with valuable information as to what could be done differently, but also teaches the subject how to accept constructive criticism. Thus it remains essential that the instructor not allow others in the group to focus too heavily on the negative features of any subject's performance. This can be partially accomplished by the instructor's modeling the way in which feedback is to be delivered.

Transfer of Training and Planned Generalization

Among others (e.g., Walker, 1979), McGinnis (1984) points out that social skills training is a two-stage process. She states that:

> stage one consists of strategies to change the behavior (i.e., social skills instruction). Stage two consists of a second set of strategies to ensure that the learned behavior is applied over time, under a variety of conditions and in other environments. Our teaching must not overlook this second, critical aspect of social skills instruction. Teaching is only effective if the students actually use these skills. (McGinnis, 1984, p. 108)

In order to obtain maximum transfer of training it is essential that students practice their newly acquired social skills in many situations. This necessitates the use of an old but frequently reliable system, homework. McGinnis (1984) points out that homework in social skill training is divided into specific techniques at three stages of sequential development.

1. Students, in conjunction with the instructor, determine situations in which to practice their new behaviors. Together they plan ways in which to implement pro-social skills in their everyday environment.
2. After the student has had a chance to practice these behaviors in real social interactions, students are told that they will be "set-up" in various social contexts such that confederates may intentionally antagonize them. After the premeditated provocation is over the teacher will call "red flag," indicating that a test had been in progress. At this time the instructor and the student evaluate the extent to which the situation was addressed by the subject in a rational, nonretaliatory, pro-social manner.
3. As the student gains in social agility he or she will practice these skills on a daily basis and self-record the extent to which they were successful in daily nonaggressive interactions.

As students evaluate their behavior homework using the system described above, assignment outcomes are shared with the social skills instructional group. Sharing of outcomes provides a natural opportunity for the group to socially reinforce not only the completion of the assignments, but also the following of pro-social steps in overcoming aggression and violent behavior. It is more important to reinforce following correct procedures than it is to pay off social success. Sometimes the use of these new skills will not be successful; nevertheless, students must learn a consistent system of carefully orchestrated responses to stressful and provocative circumstances in order to maintain their skills. Initially these students must be provided with an environment that reinforces even unsuccessful attempts at pro-social, nonaggressive behavior. This is the purpose of group feedback. It is also possible to arrange the contingencies in the school environment so that students who are attempting to use these new social tools are more likely to meet with success in the early stages. Environmental support can be provided by instructing parents, peers, and school personnel to make special attempts to show their appreciation to subjects as they demonstrate new social behaviors. "Instructing the student to use the skill when a situation suggests its use (instructed generalization) facilitates continued performance and transfer of the skill" (McGinnis, 1984, p. 107).

A Closing Note

It has been frequently observed that even very young students (first- and second-graders) are beginning to operate according to their misguided conceptions of self-defense, as defined by their peers, parents, and the media. However, most elementary school students are also very much influenced by what their teachers say. Teachers are, or can become, one of the most significant influences in a child's life. This sets the stage for an opportunity that is not always taken. The teacher may, by storytelling, game playing, or straightforward didactic advice, provide adaptive rules that successfully compete with the less adaptive rules regarding aggression that so much of our culture unwittingly promulgates. The teacher has access to the child for about six hours a day. The teacher may know and understand these children better, in some ways, than do their own parents. She may deliberately provide stories and programs that both cater to the child's intellect and advocate peaceful and humane coexistence with one's neighbors. In parochial schools this is usually attempted during religion class; sometimes it is promoted under the name of civics in public schools. Whatever the name, the message might be the same. Rules that pertain to mutual respect and sharing are effectively taught in the form of simply stated codes of conduct: "Sharing makes everyone feel good." Rules that describe cooperation during playtime and recess can be instilled by telling stories with simple didactic morals. All the rules that govern civilized conduct can be described and appropriately modeled by teachers. The trick, however, is not just in the promulgation of rules; in addition, the teacher must provide reinforcement procedures for classroom behavior that is consistent with the rules important to cooperative living. When an individual in the class demonstrates sharing or does not retaliate when provoked by another student, there is a golden opportunity to commend that child's mature behavior.

As a further vehicle for establishing the importance of altruistic behavior, each day a citizen-of-the-day can be selected. This honor goes to a child who has demonstrated some act of kindness or has acted as an arbitrator, or performed any behavior indicative of civilized, caring conduct. This program may sound exceedingly simple, but in fact it can be quite effective. It is especially valuable when the teacher targets those students who normally are not good candidates for such honors. Students who are most often inclined toward combative behavior need most to be "caught being good." Such generalized preventive tactics will be most effective when aggressive behavior is not already a well-established pattern in the student's repertoire. Although differentially reinforcing behavior incompatable with aggression may not be effective when a combat situation is already in progress, such tactics may be used as a deterrent.

REFERENCES

Azrin, N. H., Hutchinson, R. R., & Hake, D. F. (1966). Extinction-induced aggression. *Journal of the Experimental Analysis of Behavior*, *9*, 191–204.

Bandura, A. (1965). Influence of model's reinforcement contingencies on the acquisition of imitative responses. *Journal of Personality and Social Psychology*, 1, 589–595.

Bandura, A. (1977). *Social learning theory*. Englewood Cliffs, NJ: Prentice-Hall.

Bandura, A., Ross, D., & Ross, S. A. (1963). Vicarious reinforcement and imitative learning. *Journal of Abnormal Social Psychology*, *67*, 601–607.

Cohen, A. K. (1955). *Delinquent boys: The culture of the gang*. Glencoe, IL: The Free Press.

Dineen, J. P., Clark, H. B., & Risley, T. R. (1977). Peer-tutoring among elementary students: Educational benefits to the tutor. *Journal of Applied Behavior Analysis*, *10*, 231–238.

Dollard, J., Doob, L. W., Miller, N. E., Mowrer, O. H., & Sears, R. R. (1939). *Frustration and aggression*. New Haven, CT: Yale University Press.

Dougherty, B. S., Fowler, S. A., & Paine, S. C. (1985). The use of peer monitors to reduce negative interactions during recess. *Journal of Applied Behavior Analysis*, *18*, 141–153.

Dove, L. D., Rashotte, M. E., & Katz, H. N. (1974). Development and maintenance of attack in pigeons during variable-interval reinforcement of key pecking. *Journal of the Experimental Analysis of Behavior*, *21*, 563–570.

Forman, S. G. (1980). A comparison of cognitive training and response cost procedures in modifying aggressive behavior of elementary school children. *Behavior Therapy*, *11*, 594–600.

Fowler, S. A., Dougherty, B. S., Kirby, K. C., & Kohler, F. W. (1986). Role reversals: An analysis of therapeutic effects achieved with disruptive boys during their appointments as peer monitors. *Journal of Applied Behavior Analysis*, *19*, 437–444.

Freud, S. (1930). *Civilization and its discontents*. London: Hogarth (Republished: Westport, CT: Associated Booksellers, 1955.)

Gittleman, M. (1965). Behavior rehearsal as a technique in child treatment. *Journal of Child Psychology and Psychiatry and Applied Disciplines*, *6*, 251–255.

Hineline, P. N. (1983). When we speak of knowing. *The Behavior Analyst*, *6*, 183–186.

Horton, L. E. (1970). Generalization of aggressive behavior in adolescent delinquent boys. *Journal of Applied Behavior Analysis, 3*, 205–211.

Liebert, R. M., & Baron, R. M. (1972). Short-term effects of television aggression on children's aggressive behavior. In P. P. Murray, E. A. Rubinstein, & G. A. Comstock (Eds.), *Television and social learning*. Washington, DC: U.S. Government Printing Office.

Lorenz, K. (1966). *On aggression*. London: Methuen.

Luce, S. C., Delquadri, J., & Hall, R. V. (1980). Contingent exercise: A mild but powerful procedure for suppressing inappropriate verbal and aggressive behavior. *Journal of Applied Behavior Analysis, 13*, 583–594.

McGinnis, E. (1984). Teaching social skills to behaviorally disordered youth. In *Social/Affective Interventions in Behavioral Disordered Youth*, 87–120.

Mead, M. (1939). *From the south seas: Studies of adolescence and sex in primitive societies*. New York: Morrow.

Moreno, J. L. (1959). Psychodrama. In *American Handbook of Psychiatry* (ch. 68). Edited by S. Arieti. New York: Basic Books.

Murphy, H. A., Hutchinson, J. M., & Bailey, J. S. (1983). Behavioral school psychology goes outdoors: The effect of organized games on playground aggression. *Journal of Applied Behavior Analysis, 16*, 29–35.

Ninness, H. A. C., Graben, L., Miller, B., & Whaley, D. (1985). The effect of contingency management strategies on the Bender Gestalt diagnostic indicators of emotionally disturbed children. *Child Study Journal, 15*, 13–28.

Perry, D. G., & Bussey, K. (1977). Self-reinforcement in high- and low-aggressive boys following acts of aggression. *Child Development, 48*, 653–657.

Perry, D. G., & Perry, L. C. (1974). Denial of suffering in the victim as a stimulus to violence in aggressive boys. *Child Development, 45*, 55–62.

Pinkston, E. M., Reese, N. M., LeBlanc, J. M., & Baer, D. M. (1973). Independent control of a preschool child's aggression and peer interaction by contingent teacher attention. *Journal of Applied Behavior Analysis, 6*, 115–124.

Ramp, E., Ulrich, R., & Dulaney, S. (1971). Delayed timeout as a procedure for reducing disruptive classroom behavior: A case study. *Journal of Applied Behavior Analysis, 4*, 235–239.

Rogers, C. R. (1961). *On becoming a person: A therapist's view of psychotherapy*. Boston: Houghton Mifflin.

Sears, R. R. (1958). Personality development in the family. In J. M. Seidman (Ed.), *The child*. New York: Rinehart.

Skinner, B. F. (1953). *Science and human behavior*. New York: The Free Press.

Strain, P. S. (Ed.) (1981). *The utilization of classroom peers as behavior change agents*. New York: Plenum Press.

Walker, H. M. (1979). *The acting-out child: Coping with classroom disruption*. Boston: Allyn & Bacon.

Walters, R. H., & Brown, M. (1963). Studies of reinforcement of aggression: 3. Transfer of responses to an interpersonal situation. *Child Development, 34*, 563–571.

White, G. D., Nielson, G., & Johnson, S. M. (1972). Timeout duration and the suppression of deviant behavior in children. *Journal of Applied Behavior Analysis, 5*, 111–120.

Wolpe, J. (1958). *Psychotherapy of reciprocal inhibition*. Stanford, CA: Stanford University Press.

9

Token Economies

TOKEN REINFORCEMENT PROCEDURES

In a classroom where conditions are optimum for learning, hundreds of different behavioral units are desirable. Included among desirable behaviors are such general categories as academic behavior; pro-social, ''citizenship'' behavior; constructive, caring, interpersonal behavior between students and teachers as well as among students; and generalized skills such as on task, task completion, and careful, thorough work behaviors. We hope that it is obvious by now that reinforcement procedures must supplement the natural contingencies that prevail for some behavior of some students.

Many events or objects that would function to reinforce desirable behavior cannot be made immediately contingent on that behavior. Furthermore, many more behavioral instances require a reinforcement procedure than there are items to use as reinforcers. In addition, frequent, small reinforcers are much more effective than infrequent large ones. All of these facts suggest that conditioned reinforcers must be found and made contingent on many instances of desirable behavior. But how many events are readily available to use as conditioned reinforcers? If a conditioned reinforcer had to be found and correlated with each backup reinforcer, the problem would remain the same as before.

The way out of this dilemma is to establish a generalized conditioned reinforcer (an object or event that is backed up by many reinforcing events). Money is an example of a generalized conditioned reinforcer that maintains a great deal of behavior in most people. Money has no value other than the value of the things and the opportunities to behave that money can buy. In a money economy money is a powerful generalized reinforcer that can be traded for virtually all other reinforcers.

A classroom might be seen as a miniature economy in which there are many objects or events that would reinforce desirable classroom behavior. Unfortunately there is often no contingent relation between desirable behavior and those potential reinforcers. But if some inherently useless item or event were made contingent on desirable behavior, and if that item could be traded for a variety of inherently valuable items or opportunities, the useless item would become a powerful generalized reinforcer. It would function in the small classroom economy as money functions in the larger economy outside the classroom.

The tokens in a token economy can be poker chips (the equivalent of coins), slips of paper (paper bills), points (credit slips), or numbers on a counter (bank balance). As in the larger economy, the less concrete the token, the more sophisticated the behavior must be in understanding the economy.

The use of a token economy in a classroom can teach children some extremely important concepts as well as provide behavioral procedures that effectively increase the rate of productive and personally satisfying behavior and decrease the rate of destructive and inherently unproductive behavior. A well-managed token economy can teach children that they, like all other living creatures, live in a world where behavior is required for sustaining the world in which they live, that few things are magically available merely for the asking, that interpersonal relations must be carefully nurtured, and that people who need more help than others can still be productive and their contributions worthwhile.

Token economies are not simple to implement or maintain, but they can be very effective. These programs tend to be most effective when the procedural details are kept simple. It is also important to run the token program with an eye toward eventually fading out the entire system. Token programs are initiated in order to get certain problem behaviors under control; they are not meant to maintain student behavior as a way of life. All token systems should be developed with fade-out procedures as an integral part of the token process.

In this chapter the use of tokens is examined with regard to a wide range of research questions. Research has been selected to answer at least some of the questions that teachers and school personnel often have regarding the use of tokens in the classroom.

A Token Reinforcement Program in a Regular Second-grade Class

In classrooms with token reinforcement programs tokens are usually earned contingent on some form of on-task behavior. Such programs have become increasingly popular in recent years as a means of both improving student performance and controlling classroom disruptions. However, it has been suggested that the positive outcomes associated with token reinforcement systems are primarily related to the imposition of more conspicuous rules and educational structure that frequently accompany a token economy. It has been suggested that these variables, rather than differential reinforcement of appropriate behavior, are primarily responsible for the improvements seen in classroom behavior and achievement when token systems are used in schools.

In order to gauge the independent effects of such potentially confounding variables, O'Leary, Becker, Evans, and Saudargas (1969) developed a step-wise analysis of classroom rules, educational structure, and teacher praise and a token reinforcement program. Their study also sought to investigate the generalization effects of afternoon token reinforcement programming on morning classroom behavior.

Twenty-one students in an average second-grade class were simultaneously exposed to a progressive series of behavioral contingencies. However, only seven students were continually observed and their behavior recorded for data purposes. The dependent variables were motor behaviors (walking about the classroom without permission), aggressive behavior (hitting, kicking, etc.), disturbing another's property, disruptive noise (clapping, stamping feet), turning around (not facing the teacher), verbalization (talking without permission), and inappropriate tasks (performing math during spelling).

The step-wise series of contingencies occurred over a twenty-nine-week period. During a six-week baseline period students were instructed and disciplined using the same format that had existed before observation. During this period the graphs indicate that the average percentage of disruptive behavior vacillated between 45 percent and 65 percent. According to the authors, "stars and various forms of peer pressure were sporadically used as classroom control techniques, but they usually had little effect and were discontinued until experimentally reintroduced during the Follow-up Phase" (O'Leary et al., 1969, p. 5). Teachers and parents often believe, as did the teacher in this study, that they have tried various token systems, but that these programs don't improve behavior. But consistently and correctly implemented, such systems do produce improved behavior. In fact, the next two phases of this experiment demonstrate that the promulgation of classroom rules and imposition of an educational structure must be accompanied by consistent contingencies of reinforcement to positively influence student behavior.

For three weeks, during phase two, the following rules were placed on the blackboard and reviewed by the teacher and class each morning and afternoon: "We sit in our seats; we raise our hands to talk; we do not talk out of turn; we keep our desks clear; we face the front of the room; we will work very hard; we do not talk in the hall; we do not run; and, we do not disturb reading groups" (O'Leary et al., 1969, p. 5). Other than the review of these rules, the teacher carried on her daily activities according to her own design. The authors point out that most classroom activities revolved around reading groups and independent seat work. Data from this phase of the experiment is consistent with baseline percentages. No changes in the frequencies of disruptive behaviors occurred.

In the next two-week period a highly structured educational organization was added. The classroom rules remained, and the teacher reorganized the class into well-defined educational segments: "Mrs. A. was asked to reorganize her program into four 30-minute sessions in the afternoon in which the whole class participated, e.g., spelling, reading, arithmetic, and science. Thus, the purpose of the Educational Structure Phase was to assess the importance of structure *per se*" (O'Leary et al., 1969, p. 6). Once again, the data indicate that no reduction in inappropriate behavior occurred. The average percentage of disruptive behavior remained between 45 percent and 60 percent of the observed intervals. This would seem to argue rather strongly against the notion that educational structure, even in conjunction with the presentation of classroom rules, is a sufficient condition to improve classroom behavior.

If the promulgation of rules together with a conspicuous educational structure had no effect on reducing classroom disruption, then perhaps the addition of praising appropriate behavior and the ignoring of disruptive behavior would have some significant beneficial influence on these second-grade students. During the next two-week praise and ignore phase Mrs. A. bravely attempted to ignore most disruptive episodes and tried to be especially reinforcing of appropriate behavior. Not only did this intervention fail to reduce classroom disruptions, but the average percentage of disruptive behavior slightly increased. Although several students initially seemed to respond to this treatment, others continued their violations. When it became obvious that these students could violate classroom rules with impunity, misbehavior of others accelerated. This phase had to be terminated early, as the teacher found the conditions quickly becoming intolerable.

When the token system was finally instated all of the previous interventions remained concurrently in effect. Even though they may have been inadequate when used independently or in conjunction with one another, rules, educational structure, and praise and ignoring were used as part of the first complete token reinforcement intervention (token 1). During the first five-week implementation of the token 1 program the children could earn from 1 to 10 points for following the rules on the blackboard as well as for appropriate class participation and improved performance in math and spelling. Students who were even partially disruptive could not earn more than 5 points at a given evaluation. Appropriate classroom behavior and small daily improvements in performance could earn 5 to 7 points at each rating. Large improvements provided 8 to 10 points per rating. In order to provide some measure of consistency and accuracy to this subjective system, initially one of the experimenters covertly assisted in the evaluation of students' performance. The distribution of points occurred four times each afternoon by placing the number of earned points in each student's personal booklet. These were kept in each student's desk. Although morning activities were monitored, they were not part of the afternoon program and in no way related to the acquisition of points in the afternoon.

Backup reinforcers from a menu of toy vehicles, various candies, comics, and other low-cost but diverse items were exchanged daily. For the first ten days points were exchanged for backup reinforcers immediately after the fourth rating, near the end of the school day. An important tactical procedure used by these researchers involved "priming the interest" in the items on the reinforcement menu. All the prizes were put on display for student inspection in the first part of each afternoon. Each student was asked to choose, in advance, the particular item for which he or she would try to earn points. Two levels of prizes were available. The following graduated progression of exchange was instituted:

1. For ten days points were cumulated over the afternoon and exchanged at the end of each day. For a two- to five-cent prize (level 1) 25 points were required. A ten-cent prize required 35 points (level 2).
2. For the next six days points were then cumulated over two afternoons and exchanged at the end of the second day. A ten-cent prize (level 1) required 55 points; a twenty-cent prize (level 2) required 70 points.
3. For six days points were cumulated over three afternoons and exchanged at the end of the third day. A twenty-cent prize required 85 points and a thirty-cent prize required 105 points.

Students continued to be rated by the teacher four times a day to earn these points. When backup reinforcers were exchanged, students had to spend all their points so that none were carried over to the next day.

With the implementation of these program changes there was an immediate decrease in the frequency of disruptive behaviors. The average percentage of disruptive behavior dropped from a range of 50 percent to 70 percent to a range of about 25 percent to 35 percent. This represents the only significant improvement in student behavior up to this point in the study.

To assess the independent effects of the token program, this reinforcement system was withdrawn for five weeks. However, rules, educational structure, and praise and ignoring were continued. Graphs indicate that the percentage of disruptive behaviors immediately escalated to a range of about 42 percent to 48 percent. It is important to note, however, that this is well below the level of disruption that existed before the token 1 program. Evidently some carry-over effects from token 1 were still evident during this phase of the program. Reinstating the reinforcement contingency in the subsequent two-week token 2 phase of the experiment resulted in the reduction of disruptions to an all-time low ranging between 20 percent and 27 percent of the observed intervals. Analysis of variance for repeated measures showed that differences among the various experimental conditions were not due to chance ($F=7.3$; $df=7, 42$; p .0001). Thus both statistical analysis and visual inspection of graphed data substantiated the positive and independent effects of the token economy. They provide ample evidence that token reinforcement was primarily responsible for the extraordinary reduction in classroom disruptions.

Furthermore, carry-over effects from this system appeared to transfer to the follow-up phase of the study. During the last four-week period the program intentionally reverted to a variation used by the teacher before the experiment. It may be recalled that the teacher had been using, rather ineffectively, a system of giving stars to good students. In the follow-up phase of the experiment stars and a form of peer pressure were reinstated. From one to three stars were given on two occasions in the morning and once in the afternoon. Stars were also available at other times during the day when appropriate behavior was especially important. To create peer pressure, stars were also given to whole rows of students who exhibited particularly good behavior. At the end of the day gold stars were given to individual students who had obtained at least ten stars. These were placed on a highly visible wall chart; seven to nine stars earned the student a green star to be placed on the same chart. Peer pressure was again brought to bear in the process of backing up these stars. At the end of the week group members with the greatest number of gold and green stars were each given a piece of candy. Individuals who had maintained gold stars throughout the week also received candy. Data from the follow-up phase show that students maintained a low level of disruption almost comparable to that of the token 2 phase. Average disruptions occurred at around 35 percent to 40 percent of the observed intervals. Positive transfer effects occurred in this instance because the follow-up program was very much a natural extension of the token 2 phase of the experiment.

However, the authors point to important procedural differences between this program and the token programs. Most important, the expense and frequency of the backup reinforcement was substantially reduced in the follow-up star system. Although it cannot be established with this particular experimental design, it is likely that the follow-up program would not have proved as successful had the class not been exposed to the more rigorous and systematic token 1 and token 2 programs.

Another aspect of this study relates to the extent to which the effects of the morning token 1 and token 2 programs might spontaneously transfer to the afternoon sessions. Analysis of variance showed no significant differences in disruption across treatments during the morning hours. This is not surprising, since no procedural bridge was built between the afternoon intervention and morning activities. As mentioned in Chapter 8, in the discussion of social skills training, spontaneous generalization cannot be taken for granted. Transfer of training is a phenomenon that occurs most often when generalization of the desired behavior is specifically programmed in alternative environments.

Yet there were related gains in this study. Prescores and postscores on the California Achievement Test are indicative of some generalized improvement. Four of the seven students under observation gained an average of 1.5 years from October to June. Although this study provided no control group to substantiate this effect, such advances are well beyond those that usually occur in such a period (Tiegs & Clark, 1963).

Collateral Effects of Token Programs

A plethora of studies on token programs in the behavioral literature demonstrated the power of systematic, extrinsic consequences as the critical component in classroom management. As a result, many behavior analysts became interested in the collateral effects of this intervention. What ancillary effects might occur in conjunction with the administration and exchange of tokens? Of particular impact was a study by Mandelker, Brigham, and Bushell (1970). These researchers investigated the effects of a token delivery system on the behavior of the individual who administers the tokens—the teacher. While using a group of three male and three female kindergarten students as the recipients of the tokens, these researchers observed and analyzed the teacher's rate of social contacts with her students as the program was in progress.

Six students were instructed in handwriting as the study progressed across forty days. During nine twenty-minute baseline sessions (one session per day) the frequency of teacher social contact with various students within the group was recorded. Social contact was operationally defined as "a verbal statement directed to a child: (1) by name, and/or (2) while in face-to-face orientation with the child, and/or (3) while touching or looking at the materials in front of the child" (Mandelker et al., 1970, p. 169). The teacher was asked to carry on class in the same manner as she had previously. During this time all six children were socially contacted by the teacher at about the same frequency. The teacher contact per child averaged between ten and twenty occurrences per session over the nine baseline sessions.

Subsequently, during the six days of the first treatment phase, the children were divided into two groups of three. Group A then received tokens for correct writing responses throughout each twenty-minute session. The teacher could provide each student with up to ten tokens during the twenty minutes. Group B was noncontingently given ten free tokens at the beginning of the lesson but otherwise treated in the same manner as during baseline. Both groups exchanged tokens for various toys, activities, or food at the end of the period. From onset of this treatment those students who received tokens contingent on correct writing responses concurrently received an increased number of social contacts from the teacher. Those three students who had obtained ten free tokens at the beginning of the lesson actually obtained slightly fewer social contacts from their teacher than they had during baseline. Group A averaged around twenty-five contacts per session per child, whereas group B gradually dropped to about ten contacts by the end of the first treatment phase.

In the next eight-day phase of the study the contingencies were reversed. For eight sessions Group B now received up to ten tokens for correct writing responses, whereas Group A obtained ten noncontingent tokens at the beginning of the lesson. Frequency with which the teacher performed social contacts was reversed. The members of Group A now averaged about ten contacts per twenty-minute session, while the three children in Group B received between seventeen and thirty contacts per child on various days.

Once again a reversal was performed. For eight days Group A received tokens contingent on correct writing responses and Group B obtained their ten tokens at the beginning of the session. As in previous phases, tokens were exchanged for backup reinforcers at the end of the period. Again, a reversal of the teacher's social interactions took place. Group B received only about ten to fifteen teacher contacts per child, whereas Group A's rate of teacher contact increased to about twenty per child. Administering tokens was having a significant effect on the teacher's likelihood of verbally contacting the students who were receiving tokens contingent on correct responses. Furthermore, this was occurring at the social expense of those students who obtained free tokens.

In the final nine days of the study both groups received tokens contingent on correct writing responses; and both groups received approximately the same number of teacher contacts per child. In general, however, there was no average increase in the rate of both groups' social interaction with the teacher over the baseline rate. When both groups were exposed to the contingency of receiving tokens only when they made correct writing responses, both groups averaged about fifteen to twenty contacts per child with the teacher. No group differentiation in the rate of social contact could be detected.

Throughout the course of this investigation teacher contact with the students coincided with the experimental contingencies. As tokens became a requirement for improved writing behavior in a particular group, the frequency of the teacher's contact with the students in that group escalated. When both groups were simultaneously exposed to this same experimental manipulation, the rate of the teacher's social interactions was nearly consistent with the baseline rate. The authors point out that "while most of the changes in the amount of contact with the two groups was accounted for by the token component, there were small but systematic changes in the non-token contacts as well" (Mandelker et al., 1970, p. 171).

The authors speculate as to the underlying cause of this phenomenon, suggesting that there are two distinct possibilities. One, the acquisition and accumulation of tokens in each individual's cup maintained a form of discriminative control over the teacher's "attending behavior." This, they suggest, could be further investigated by using nontransparent cups as the token receptacle. Second, and perhaps a more likely possibility, the delivery of tokens contingent on correct responses increased the rate of accurate writing behavior. As they point out, "a greater number of correct responses would provide more opportunities for the teacher to contact the children with praise and additional tokens" (Mandelker et al., 1970, p. 174). Unfortunately this feature was not measured during the course of the study.

The authors suggest that because the teacher's rate of social contact increased with the concurrent administration of contingent tokens, the use of a token system has inherent heuristic value for teacher training. However, the data from this study seem to indicate that this is only true when part of a small group is placed on a token contingency to the exclusion of the rest of the group. When the whole group was simultaneously exposed to contingent tokens, there was no obvious change in the rate of teacher social contact over baseline rate. The rates for both baseline and contingent tokens to both groups appear to fluctuate between about twelve and twenty teacher contacts per session per child.

A "Token Helper"

By the early 1970s many behavior analysts were trying to find new ways to get teachers involved in using token programs. It had become increasingly obvious that these systems were helping students to perform better in class and that teachers were also benefiting from them. The question then became one of how to best provide the inexperienced teacher with the necessary skills to implement these behavioral techniques.

At about the same time modeling had become popular as an instructional and vicarious reinforcement procedure for children (Bandura, 1965). So it is not surprising that these newly investigated modeling/instructional methods were soon tried on teachers. Ringer (1973) was one of the first to study the use of a "token helper" as a model for the instruction of the necessary skills in the administration of a classroom token economy.

To accomplish this process, the modeling of token administration procedures was performed within the confines of a regular fourth-grade class of thirty-seven pupils. Of these thirty-seven students ten (five male and five female) were selected as targets for observation on the basis of having displayed especially high rates of off-task, disruptive, inappropriate classroom behaviors. However, all students in the class were exposed to the same classroom contingencies regarding the acquisition of tokens and backup reinforcers.

The experimenter in this study doubled as the "token helper." This "token helper" modeling system was intended to investigate three concurrent variables: the reduction of disruptions by particularly rowdy children, the effects these reductions might have on peers who interacted with the disruptive students, and a determination of the extent to which the teacher might be able to learn the principles and techniques associated with the running of a token management system by watching and interacting with the "token helper." Thus three dependent variables were measured: percentage of time-sampled intervals of inappropriate behaviors of targeted students, percentage of peer reactions to the inappropriate behaviors of targeted students, and frequency of teacher commentary contingent on student behaviors. The teacher comments were contingent on two kinds of student behavior: appropriate and inappropriate.

Students were observed during two separate periods of forty consecutive school days. Period 1 was devoted to essay writing and period 2 was used for instruction and drill in spelling and language exercises. The design of this experiment used the two separate periods to full advantage by implementing a multiple baseline, in which baseline observations continued in period 2 while treatment variables were instated in period 1. This process permits greater assessment of internal validity, as potentially confounding artifacts relating to history, maturation, testing, etc. are controlled.

Although baseline (no treatment) conditions were in effect in both periods (ten days), the targeted students averaged approximately 65 percent (with 20 percent variations) of the observed intervals involved in some form of inappropriate behavior. Peer responses to these targeted students averaged about 35 percent (with about 10 percent to 15 percent variations).

During the next ten days baseline conditions continued in period 2, and in period 1 the "token helper" system was implemented. In period 1 each student in the class was given a small card that was divided into twenty squares. The token helper/experimenter moved throughout the classroom randomly praising and initialing squares of the students who were behaving appropriately (i.e., either academically engaged or involved in some form of teacher-authorized activity).

In most school systems a visit to the principal's office is not necessarily construed as a desirable event. However, in this experiment the contingencies were arranged such that the principal praised each successful child's achievement and stamped the student's completed card with the school's emblem. Three to six periods were usually required for the students to obtain initials in all twenty squares.

The author notes that although no direct "hands-on" administration of tokens was performed by the teacher during this condition, she was encouraged by the helper/experimenter to praise students' good behavior at every opportunity. Furthermore, the teacher and helper/experimenter discussed the classroom management and reinforcement procedures on alternate days.

All students in the treatment condition demonstrated an immediate and consistent reduction in the frequency of inappropriate classroom behaviors and peer reactions to inappropriate behaviors. When the token helper condition was in effect for period 1, inappropriate behaviors dropped from 65 percent during baseline to approximately 20 percent. Peer consequences of classroom behaviors followed the same trend. During this time in period 2 the baseline condition was still in effect and no reinforcement procedure was operating. Both the average level of the targeted students' inappropriate classroom behavior, as well as peer reactions to such behaviors, remained high and variable, roughly 60 percent and 40 percent, respectively. This contrasts dramatically with the same children's behavior in period 1, when the experimental contingencies were in effect.

In the next ten days of the experiment the token helper system was implemented in period 2 after the teacher described in detail the requisite student behaviors related to earning tokens (initialing of cards). As a result, period 2 saw an immediate deceleration (to below 20 percent) of classroom disruptions and other inappropriate behaviors. This coincided with a highly correlated reduction in peer responses to these episodes. Also, in this phase of the experiment a reversal of contingencies was instituted in period 1 such that students were returned to baseline conditions. This resulted in an immediate acceleration of inappropriate behaviors (to about 50 percent of the observed intervals) during period 1, a rate not quite as high as had been witnessed during the first baseline condition. This was correlated with accelerations of peer responses to these disruptions.

In the last ten days of the experiment, reversals were again performed during both periods. For the first five days of period 1 the teacher was phased into the process of administering the token system. This required that she share the responsibility, with the helper, for initialing the students' cards. Gradually she performed more and more of this procedure independently. By the sixth day she was operating entirely alone and the helper/experimenter was no longer in the classroom. After class, however, the experimenter coached the teacher on proper techniques for providing reinforcement.

For the first five days of this phase the targeted inappropriate behaviors almost disappeared (at or below 20 percent). However, with the removal of the token helper from the classroom scene, for the remaining five days, a gradual increase in disruptions occurred. It is apparent from the data that the teacher had not incorporated all of the proper procedures related to the token reinforcement system. Inappropriate disruptions and rule violations jumped to a fluctuating 30 percent to 40 percent of the observed intervals. Peer reactions to these episodes closely approximated these levels. In period 2 or the same days the token system was withdrawn. Predictably, disruptions increased to near baseline levels (bouncing from 20 percent to 60 percent).

During all interventions and reversals a record of student-directed teacher commentary was maintained. The author points out that

> during the Baseline of Period I, 173 teacher remarks contingent upon inappropriate pupil behavior were recorded. The number dropped to 22 during the token phase, increased again to 59 during the withdrawal of tokens, and was reduced to five in the final phase. In Period II, there was a slight reduction from baseline levels of 80 and 42 during the first and second 10 days, respectively, to 34 in the token phase. During the no-token phase of Period II, 129 teacher remarks following inappropriate pupil behavior were recorded. (Ringer, 1973, p. 675).

Thus we see a somewhat predictable relationship between the frequency of teacher commentary on student behavior and the implementation of a token system. It is apparent that the token system reduced the frequency of student inappropriate behavior. As such, it was not necessary for the teacher to provide negative verbal responses to the students during the token phases. When the token system was not in effect the teacher tended to use negative verbal statements to control inappropriate classroom behavior.

The fact that the teacher's ineffective attempts to manage the class with verbal statements negatively covaried with the use of the token reinforcement contingencies, and the fact that student inappropriate behaviors began a gradual acceleration when the teacher was put in total charge of the token administration seem to indicate a lack of acquisition of necessary and sufficient behavior management skills on the part of the teacher. However, this should not be surprising. The design of this study probably did not permit adequate training for the teacher. During the first thirty days of this experiment the teacher's role was essentially a passive one. She carried on instruction while the token program was instated and reversed by the experimenter during both periods. There were only five days during which the teacher had an opportunity to run the program and receive ongoing instruction from the experimenter/helper. After that she was left on her own for the remaining five days of period 1. During these days the experimenter only coached her after class. Perhaps it was anticipated that the modeling and limited after-school coaching by the experimenter/helper should have been sufficient to allow the teacher to carry on the program independently. But teachers, as well as students and the rest of us, require detailed training to learn complex new skills. Had this teacher received a longer hands-on instructional phase of actually administering the token program, and received ongoing feedback as to errors and correct interactions with students, it seems likely that she could have maintained the level of classroom behavior seen in the earlier phases of the experiment.

Counselors or Teachers

Even though the literature in the 1970s was replete with elegant examples of the efficacy of behavioral procedures applied to the classroom, school personnel were, and still are, beleaguered by claims from a variety of competing schools of thought. An article by Marlowe, Madsen, Bowen, Reardon, and Logue (1978) addresses a somewhat popular, but infrequently published, controversy over the issue of alternative strategies to behavioral intervention. For many years there has been a running debate as to the efficacy of behavior analysis as compared with client-centered therapy (Rogers, 1969; Truax & Mitchell, 1971). At this stage in the development of behavioral technology it is still assumed by many teachers and administrators that both approaches have their own advantages and disadvantages, and that both can be used to the students' betterment.

The task of client-centered therapy is described by its proponents as follows. If the disturbed client (student) is provided unconditional positive regard through rapport with a warm, genuine, empathic, reflective therapist, eventually the client (student) will gain insight into the underlying causes of his or her behavior, and make alterations accordingly.

Behavioral and client-centered counseling techniques were tested within the confines of a public high school, using twelve male seventh-grade students as participants. These students were selected on the basis of having exceptional histories as discipline problems. Dependent variables relating to discipline were recorded by interval observations of the subjects' on- and off-task behavior during the fifth period of each school day. In the same observational intervals teacher behaviors were recorded as to demonstrations of "(1) academic approval, (2) academic disapproval, (3) social approval, (4) social disapproval, (5) a mistake or inappropriate use of one of the above four behaviors, or (6) no approval or disapproval behavior observed'' (Madsen & Madsen, 1974; cited in Marlowe et al., 1978, p. 55). These dependent variables were later analyzed in terms of their relationship to the frequency of the targeted students' on- and off-task behaviors. As stated by the authors, ''the purpose of the present study was to ascertain whether different types of counseling outside the classroom, or teacher approval within the classroom, with the counselor serving as a behavioral consultant, would be more effective in changing the students' inappropriate classroom behavior'' (Marlowe et al., 1978, p. 54).

The study used six successive experimental conditions with three separate groups of four subjects. These experimental conditions consisted of first baseline, counseling, counseling plus teacher attention, counseling plus teacher attention plus token reinforcement, second baseline, and teacher attention plus token reinforcement. Subsequent to the first ten days of baseline observation the subjects were matched and divided equally into the three groups so that there were equal representations and frequencies of off-task behaviors among all groups. One of each of the three groups was then randomly assigned to behavioral counseling, client-centered counseling, or no form of counseling. It is important to note that the counselor in this particular study had unique qualifications and was able to provide services to both experimental groups. He had received training at the master's level in the theory and practice of both client-centered therapy and behavior analysis.

All three groups demonstrated exceptionally high rates of off-task behavior during the first ten-day baseline condition. The behavioral counseling group averaged 54.8 percent. The client-centered counseling group averaged 59.2 percent, and the no-contact control group averaged 55.3 percent.

In the following phase of the experiment (eighteen days) the various forms of counseling were conducted. This consisted of eight separate days during which thirty minutes of either behavioral or client-centered counseling was performed. According to the authors, the behavioral counseling used a multifaceted instructional approach. This consisted of ''approval for positive behavior, ignoring inappropriate behavior, and setting specific and measurable goals'' (Marlowe et al., 1978, p. 56). This group was taught how to self-correct when acting inappropriately in class and how to self-reward appropriate on-task behaviors. The authors note that there was a strong emphasis on the instruction for taking responsibility for one's own actions.

In this same phase of the experiment the client-centered counseling group was provided a ''warm, friendly relationship, maintenance of respect for the students' ability to solve their own problems, and acceptance of the students'' (Marlowe et al., 1978, p. 56). The authors indicate that the primary focus of this type of therapy consisted of the students obtaining ''insight'' into the nature of their inappropriate behavior. The control group received no form of intervention or counseling during this time and essentially continued under baseline conditions.

Both of the above processes sound very ambitious and noble, but most behaviorally oriented psychologists may be tempted to anticipate that *their* strategies would prove overwhelmingly superior. However, the data do not substantiate a great deal of difference among the three groups during the first counseling condition. The off-task behavior of the behaviorally counseled group dropped 6.8 percent and the client-centered counseling group dropped 2.2 percent. However, the no-contact control group actually increased their average level of off-task behaviors by 10.7 percent during this condition. Still, since none of these changes are very different from baseline frequencies, one must conclude that, at least within the limits of this study, counseling, of any form, had only limited success.

During the next (five-day) teacher attention condition both the behavioral and the client-centered counseling continued according to the previous design, but a more critical program was instated in addition to these out-of-classroom interventions. This condition provided for the teacher's standard form of classroom control to be terminated while she implemented the simple strategy of socially and differentially reinforcing appropriate classroom behavior and rule following. The teacher emphasized the importance of following five rules:

1. If you need to talk, talk softly;
2. Sit quietly;
3. Raise your hand to get the teacher's attention;
4. Be prepared—bring pencil and notebook; and
5. Use the hall pass only in an emergency. (Marlowe et al., 1978, p. 56)

But as important as providing rules, *teacher attention* was also given to various students who behaved in accordance with the five provisions. Students who violated the rules were generally ignored.

Although the various forms of counseling in the previous condition appeared generally ineffective, contingent teacher attention proved to be a strong and immediate source of behavior change, even for these junior high, lower socioeconomic, behaviorally disordered students. With the implementation of this procedure all three groups, independent of counseling or no-contact conditions, began to behave differently. The behavioral counseling group dropped from an average 48.0 percent off task, in the previous phase, to 9.9 percent. The client-centered counseling group fell from a previous off-task level of 57.0 percent to 29.3 percent but even more impressively the no-contact control group demonstrated even slightly lower levels of off-task behavior than the client-centered counseling group. This group, which had received no form of counseling therapy, dropped from a previous off-task average of 66.0 percent to 25.3 percent, four percentage points below the client-centered counseling group. Although these data are perhaps not strong enough to indicate that client-centered counseling interferes with the reduction of off-task behaviors, it should be noted that such ''insight''-oriented interventions appear somewhat irrelevant in terms of producing observable behavior change.

In the fourth (seven-day) phase of this experiment all of the previous interventions were maintained, and token reinforcement was added to the other concurrent treatments. Both counseling groups continued their out-of-class sessions and the teacher continued providing contingent attention to all students in all groups. In conjunction with teacher attention the students now received tokens on each occasion that social reinforcement was provided. Each token was backed up with quarter segments of doughnuts or one-ounce portions of soda to be provided on Friday afternoons. Thus all students, during this phase, were given a "concrete" form of reinforcement contingent on their appropriate classroom behavior. As in the previous experimental phase, nonviolent off-task behaviors were generally ignored. This produced an immediate further reduction in off-task behaviors in all three groups. The behavioral counseling group fell to an average of 2.1 percent off task. The client-centered group dropped to 18.5 percent. The no-contact control group averaged 19.6 percent.

In the fifth phase all groups were returned to baseline conditions for four days. As might be expected, this produced a sharp upward swing in the frequency of inappropriate behaviors. Off-task averages jumped to 36.9 percent, 48.2 percent, and 38.6 percent for the behavioral counseling, client-centered counseling, and no-contact groups, respectively. The teacher found this trend so alarming that she requested that students be allowed to return to the previous reinforcement contingencies.

In the final phase of the experiment all groups were returned to teacher attention plus token reinforcement contingencies. Predictably, all groups demonstrated an immediate and significant transition in frequencies of off-task behaviors. These targeted behaviors fell to 2.9 percent, 10.0 percent, and 7.5 percent for the behavioral, client-centered, and no-contact groups. Thus it would appear that although the behavioral group generally performed somewhat better than the other two groups under all treatment conditions, there was not a great difference among the groups while the reinforcement contingencies were under direct teacher control. The authors note, however, that behavioral counseling might have performed slightly better because they were more prepared to receive the implementation of the teacher-controlled classroom management programs. In this regard they document the statistical comparisons among the three groups:

> The behavioral counseling group had a tendency to reduce its inappropriate behavior sooner and more durably than either the client-centered counseling or no-contact control group. Statistical analysis (chi-square approximations following Kruskal-Wallace analysis of ranks) indicates that, during the treatment conditions, the behavioral counseling group was significantly lower in off-task behavior than either the client-centered or no-contact control groups, chi square (10DF) = 3.50, $P < 0.05$. (Marlowe et al., 1978, p. 58)

The authors also explicitly describe the progression of the client-centered counseling group:

> Counseling did not decrease mean inappropriate student behavior when compared to initial observation (57.0 percent for counseling versus 56.4 percent for baseline); however, when the teacher attention variable was included during counseling plus teacher attention, inappropriate behavior (student off-task) dropped 36.7 percent. When token reinforcement was added to counseling plus teacher attention, the mean off-task behavior dropped from 21.3 percent to 13.4 percent. (Marlowe et al., 1978, p. 59)

Social and token reinforcers presented by the teacher in class were the primary source of behavior change. When teacher approval rates under various conditions were analyzed, it was found that the social approval, rather than academic approval or disapproval, was more consistently associated with decreases in student off-task behaviors. It was found that only 17 percent of all teacher approval related to academic performance. All other teacher social reinforcement was contingent on improved social responses of the students.

Frequently educators claim that a student's poor attitude or poor self-concept is the problem that must be addressed. Yet client-centered and other forms of insight-oriented interventions, which are primarily aimed at changing attitudes and self-concept, are not likely to affect student behaviors in the classroom. For that matter the lack of change resulting from behavioral counseling suggests that *talking* about *behavior* is similarly ineffective. *Doing* something about *behavior* is best accomplished by doing something constructive about the environment in which it occurs. Improvement in this case was closely tied to a well-designed classroom token system.

The data above demonstrate that using tokens in the administration of classroom management can be helpful for teachers who have difficulty in changing their in-class verbal behavior. The authors describe the role of tokens in the program above and provide a good general explanation as to why they are effective: "Token reinforcement may serve as a catalyst to accelerate decreases in inappropriate behavior similar to behavioral counseling. The tokens increased the approval ratio and one of their most important functions is probably to serve as reminders to the teacher to give approval" (Marlowe et al., 1978, p. 64).

IMPROVING TEACHER VERBAL BEHAVIOR

Many teachers believe that classroom management techniques are superficial and too highly structured for their personal teaching styles. Some of the same teachers find it difficult to provide their students with a positive and enjoyable learning environment. Much of the dialogue between teacher and student may primarily consist of teacher work directives or punitive reprimands. In such classrooms teacher positive comments may only infrequently be paired with students' on-task behaviors.

Another study that further demonstrates the catalytic quality of token systems for classroom teachers was provided by Breyer and Allen (1975). These authors point out that not all public school teachers are entirely enthusiastic about implementing behavioral techniques. Occasionally some even voice opposition to reinforcement procedures. As most school psychologists are all too well aware this description pertains to more than a few classroom teachers. Ironically this problem even relates to teachers who say they will try a recommended management strategy. Unfortunately there is not always a good match between the verbal behavior, which predicts a behavioral change on the part of the teacher, and the actual performance of the required behavior. In particular, many teachers find it difficult to praise students for performing approximations of improved academic and social behavior. Some of these teachers seem to have lost the "capacity" for positive reinforcement, and what little control they exert over their classes is maintained by threats and punishment. The question then becomes one of how to develop systems that remediate teachers' behavior in conjunction with their students' behavior. Breyer and Allen's (1975) study is a classic example of this circumstance. These authors conjectured that token programs seem to increase the chances of teachers monitoring their own in-class behavior. They and others have speculated that such "self-monitoring appears to be associated with increases in the rates that teachers praise pupils" (Cooper, Thomson, & Jackson, 1970; Thomas, 1971). Breyer and Allen's (1975) research evaluated the effects of a token economy on the rate of positive and negative teacher comments toward students. These data were analyzed in conjunction with the effects such comments had on the rates of student inappropriate behaviors.

According to the authors, the investigation was carried out within a "transitional" second-grade class of fifteen behaviorally disordered students who had well-established repertoires of poor social and academic functioning. These students were described as so severely disordered as to be unable to benefit from regular education. Their teacher was evidently of the "old school," and was not particularly amenable to novel interventions. Dependent variables in this study described not only the classroom rates of student on-task behavior, but also the correlated frequencies of the teacher's positive and negative verbal commentary during each observational session.

During the ten-day baseline, data were collected during a forty-eight-minute reading period. Initial observations indicated a serious problem. The teacher was found to be ten times more likely to use negative verbal control than she was to provide praise or other positive comments. In fact, on five of the ten baseline days, there were no documented instances of any positive reinforcement procedure. She averaged less than one praise statement per period during this phase of the study. In the same period she averaged more than 10 percent reprimands or punitive comments. These negative comments exerted only limited control. Classroom on-task behavior was 56 percent. The authors stated that "inappropriate behavior usually took the form of passive inattentiveness" (Breyer & Allen, 1975, p. 376).

For the next ten sessions the teacher was provided explicit instructions on the proper methods of verbal reinforcement. This included a list of diversified praise statements from Madsen and Madsen (1970) and a paper on classroom management by Breyer and Pollack (1971). She was asked to praise students' on-task behavior with three new comments a day, and to attempt a total of fifteen praise statements during the period. She agreed to attempt to lower the frequency of her reprimands. In addition, she was given detailed personal instructions on the theory and application of learning theory in the classroom. Feedback and examination of ongoing daily observational data was provided for fifteen to twenty minutes every other day. This is a somewhat detailed and exhaustive intervention in teacher instruction, and many teachers would have quickly benefited from such intensified tutoring and feedback. However, some teachers are more resistant to change. This teacher's frequency of negative comments during the ten-day *praise-and-ignore* phase of the experiment remained essentially unchanged. Her rate of positive comments accelerated slightly, to about 3.5 percent. The students were, evidently, not adequately impressed by this slight improvement. On-task data showed that students moved to a mean of only 64 percent. Furthermore, the authors point out that the teacher "reported considerable discomfort while using the suggested procedures and frequently expressed the opinion that she could not effectively motivate her class by using the techniques provided by the consultant" (Breyer & Allen, 1975, p. 376).

At the end of the ten-day *praise-and-ignore* phase the teacher was told that progress had been made in classroom behavior, but that it was possible to make further improvements by using a classroom token economy. In the next phase of the experiment a token system was implemented for nine sessions. This token system, like some previously described, did not require the actual delivery of three-dimensional items. Rather, a point system was used. The details of this system are best described by the authors:

> The teacher observed and scored each of the children for task-oriented behavior on a variable-interval schedule of 8 minutes. Task-oriented behavior included listening, seatwork, voluntarily reading aloud, or activities previously identified as appropriate by the teacher. She circulated among the students after every second interval and scored the number of points each child had earned for the two intervals. When she approached them, she was instructed to write the point total on tally sheets placed on each child's desk. (Breyer & Allen, 1975, p. 375–376)

The backup reinforcement menu for this point system was probably more complex than necessary. Again, the details are best described by the original authors:

> Each child could earn three points every time he was observed engaging in task-oriented behavior. It was also possible for a student to earn five points for satisfactory completion of daily assignments and three bonus points for producing a superior paper. These points could be redeemed at the "Good-Study Store" for prizes ranging in cash value from 5 cents to $1.50. Points had a sliding monetary value in relation to the cost of the items. Two points were redeemable for a penny for objects costing less than 25 cents. Prizes costing from 26 cents to 50 cents could be purchased at a ratio of three points for every 2 cents. Objects in the 51 cents to 75 cents range were sold at a ratio of four points for

every 3 cents. A penny per point was established as an appropriate ratio for prizes worth more than 75 cents. The children, therefore, could obtain more value for their points if they saved them for more expensive items. (Breyer & Allen, 1975, p. 376)

Although the teacher was encouraged to pair verbal praise with the delivery of tokens and to ignore disruptive behavior when possible, the authors specifically avoided the previous feedback to the teacher. It was the purpose of this phase to determine the effect of a token system operating independently of adjunctive in-class coaching by the consultant.

With the initiation of this system the teacher reported an immediate sense of comfort. She explained that she now felt that the emphasis of the program was on the students rather than on her. Her rate of positive comments accelerated, jumping from an average of about 3 percent to almost 8 percent. In this same phase her reprimands and general negative classroom commentary dropped from more than 9 percent in the previous phase to 5 percent. The students were also affected by the token system, and quite possibly the change in the teacher's verbal behavior. Student rates of on-task, appropriate behaviors jumped to a high of 86 percent and averaged 73 percent during the first nine days of the token economy condition.

When a reversal of contingencies was instated for five days both teacher and student behaviors deteriorated. During this phase the teacher was again coached on the proper methods of praising on-task behaviors while ignoring disruptions. The consultant provided fifteen to twenty minutes of feedback to the teacher on alternative days. With this previously attempted intervention teacher negative commentaries rose to an average of about 7 percent while reinforcing comments fell to about 2.5 percent. Students in turn demonstrated a quick response to her return to a punitive classroom orientation. On-task behaviors dropped to 63 percent. This was equivalent to the previous *praise-and-ignore* condition.

In the last ten days the token system was reinstated while the teacher feedback was terminated. Teacher and students immediately benefited. On-task behaviors returned to their previous average of about 74 percent as the teacher resumed her kinder mode of expression. Reprimands decreased to about 3.7 percent and her reinforcing comments increased to approximately 6 percent.

The authors point to some evidence of a significant systematic relationship between the teacher's negative verbal behavior and the students' level of on-task behavior. A Pearson Product Moment Correlation indicated a −0.66 correlation between these variables and a correlation of +0.84 between the teacher's positive comments and appropriate behavior.

The percentage of variations across the various conditions establishes the independent effects of the token system as it impacted both the frequency of teacher positive comments and the improvement in student on-task behaviors. However, this design does not permit an interpretation of a functional relationship between the teacher's commentary and student behavior. Although these variables probably interface at some juncture within the token system, their interdependencies can only be speculated. One explanation suggested by the authors is that improved student behavior allowed the teacher more opportunities for favorable comments. Alternatively, the teacher's increased reinforcement ratio may have promoted more appropriate behavior on the part of the students. More likely is the possibility regarding interaction of both these variables. As the authors point out, more data on this subject are still needed. However, it is unequivocally clear that the use of the token system improved both the classroom behavior and the teacher verbal reinforcement frequency.

It is important to add that for many teachers, a praise-and-ignore procedure is an eminently satisfactory intervention. A teacher who can consistently praise the students' on-task behaviors and appropriate social interactions, while ignoring behaviors that are incompatible with these, can probably bring his or her classroom under quick and effective control. Some teachers, however, are apparently unable to perform these operations without the use of a more concrete system, and some students may require tangible consequences. In such situations a token economy may provide the structure in which they and their students may operate more successfully.

Intrinsic Reinforcers

When token economies found their way into the public schools it was initially only with special populations. Typically, small classrooms within special education or a few students in regular classrooms were the only participants (O'Leary & Becker, 1967). Furthermore, in the early conception of token systems it was often believed that rather extravagant backup reinforcers were more effective than simple access to privileges, free time, or classroom activities (Wolf, Giles, & Hall, 1968). By 1972, the fourth year of the *Journal of Applied Behavior Analysis*, more extensive and less expensive systems were being investigated. McLaughlin and Malaby (1972) were among the first to attempt a classwide, regular education, cost-effective token system in the public schools. Their program was also unique in that data were collected throughout the course of an entire academic year.

This program was implemented and maintained by a teacher who was also the experimenter. However, extremely high reliability coefficients, obtained by impartial and naive observers, established the accuracy of measurement. All programming was conducted within the confines of a combination fifth- and sixth-grade classroom composed of between twenty-five and twenty-nine students. Dependent variables were all related to academic proficiency in the areas of spelling, language, handwriting, and math.

During the six-week baseline, standard public school educational practices were maintained. Students received letter grades for individual work and various tests. Discipline was maintained by keeping students after school, discussion with parents, and lecturing/scolding. This resulted in extreme variability of assignment completion in all four academic areas, ranging from 69 percent to 94 percent.

In the token 1 condition (about eleven weeks) a point system was introduced. Token reinforcement procedures involved giving points to students for assignment completion, accuracy, and an array of social and academic behaviors. Incomplete assignments were not provided partial credit. Assignments had to be entirely complete before grading for points. A listing of desirable behaviors is provided by the authors:

Behaviors	Points
Items performed accurately	6 to 12
Proper study behavior	5 per day
Provide animals with food	1 to 10
Provide animals with sawdust	1 to 10
Art activities	1 to 4
Attend to teacher presentations	1 to 2 per lesson
Extra credit	Assigned value
Neat school work	1 to 2
Home assignments	5
Proper notes	1 to 3
Appropriate lunch line behavior	2
Appropriate in cafeteria	2
Good noon hour behavior	3

Source: McLaughlin & Malaby, 1972, p. 264.

Fines were contingent on inappropriate behaviors. Token loss was contingent on the following undesirable behaviors (response-cost punishment procedure):

Behaviors	Points
Not completing assignments	Amount squared
Eating sweets in class	100
Inappropriate talking	15
Performing inappropriate physical activity	15

Fighting	100
Cheating on tests	100

Source: McLaughlin & Malaby, 1972, p. 264.

The author emphasized the intrinsic quality of backup rewards for these earned points. All activity reinforcers were available within the school and were generally activities that had previously been available to the students noncontingently. With the initiation of the token program the students voted on the determination of point cost for various activities on the reinforcement menu. Students exchanged points for the following items on a weekly basis:

Privilege	Price in Points Sixth	Fifth
Pencil Sharpening	20	13
Viewing animals	30	25
Carrying balls outdoors	5	3
Taking part in sports	60	40
Opportunity to write on board	20	16
Taking part in committee activities	30	25
Performing special jobs	25	15
Taking part in games	5	3
Playing records	5	2
Coming inside early	10	6
Looking at the gradebook	5	2
Performing special projects	25	20

Source: McLaughlin & Malaby, 1972, p. 265.

Particularly important is that assignments were made daily and completed by the next period. Students were responsible for grading their own work. At the end of each period, or the next day, students were individually awarded points on the basis of accuracy and completion. All points were recorded on the students' individual point sheets. The manner in which points were exchanged for backup reinforcers was especially well organized.

> Points were exchanged for privileges each Monday morning. A student was made banker for each of the privileges. Each banker subtracted the necessary number of points from a student's point total and initialed it. At the end of the period, he turned in a list to the teacher of the names of students who purchased privileges. This list enabled the teacher to control the use of privileges. (McLaughlin & Malaby, 1972, p. 265)

In the token 1 condition a number of changes occurred; with exception of math, variability of assignment completion was sharply reduced as completion rates generally improved. Completion rates for spelling, language, and handwriting generally fluctuated in the range of 80 percent to 100 percent. Math demonstrated less stability and erratically bounced between 60 percent and 100 completion.

In the following token 2 condition (about six weeks) the point-exchange days occurred on a variable schedule that approximated a variable-interval schedule of reinforcement. This was accomplished by exchanging points on a random schedule between 2 and 6 days, with an average payoff time of 4.25 days. The logic in this intervention was to attempt to use a schedule that would produce more consistent responding, one similar to an experimentally regulated variable-interval schedule. The results indicate that this schedule did indeed produce such a stabilizing effect in the work habits of the students. The authors indicate that in all four academic areas the students approximated 100 percent assignment completion.

To determine the degree to which this type of programming was directly responsible for the improved completion rates, students were subsequently exposed to a new contingency for the next eighteen school days. The token system for assignment completion was eliminated, and in its place was put a quiet behavior contingency. This condition emphasized the elimination of all extraneous noise from the classroom. Students were individually awarded points, exchangeable for the same backup reinforcers, for the maintenance of quiet behavior. Predictably the rate of assignment completion became highly variable and dropped dramatically, ranging from 69 percent to 99 percent.

In the final phase of the experiment a variable schedule of point exchange was again implemented for eleven days. This resulted in an immediate resumption to a near-stable 100 percent assignment completion rates in all four academic areas.

Some of the most important data from this study concern the differential effects this form of treatment had on students who previously had either high or low completion rates. Although a student with a history of high completion rates was minimally affected by this intervention, a student with demonstrable low and variable completion rates was maximally benefited. Under token system conditions the lower-performing students approximated the completion rates of higher-performing students. The authors close with a general description of their positive results:

The methods used in this study have definite practical implications for several reasons: (a) the back-up reinforcers were in the natural classroom environment and were cost-free, (b) the study took place in a typical classroom setting, (c) the number of students that received group contingencies was comparable in size with most classloads in a public school, (d) significant gains in academic completion were obtained without specially made assignments for individuals requiring programmed instruction, (e) the token economy was manageable by one teacher, requiring, on the average, some 20 minutes per week more than usual to record points, fines, privileges, etc. (McLaughlin & Malaby, 1972, p. 269)

Response Cost versus Reward

The previous study describes a token system in which points could be either earned or lost for specific behaviors. These contingencies existed concurrently for all students throughout the course of the entire study. However, there has long been the question as to which of these methods is more effective. Is it better to remove something known to function as a reinforcer from a student when inappropriate behavior occurs (response-cost punishment procedure), or to wait until she or he performs the correct behavior and use a reinforcement procedure? Both contingencies may aim for the same result, but the methods by which they are achieved are directly inverse.

Although reinforcement procedures are usually considered devoid of hazardous effects, punishment techniques, among which response cost must be included, have been associated with dangerous and deleterious side effects, including aggression, avoidance, and escape behaviors (Azrin & Holz, 1966). The question then arises as to whether teachers who use token economies in their classrooms might be better advised to use only reinforcement procedures and to avoid response cost. A study by Iwata and Bailey (1974) tested this question and provided interesting results. Of special importance were the pervasive outcome measures that took into account a wide variety of classroom variables relating to student academic productivity and achievement, off-task behavior, classroom rule violations, student satisfaction, and teacher positive and negative verbal behavior.

In their study Iwata and Bailey observed fifteen elementary school students from a special education class as they were exposed to a counterbalanced investigation of both response cost and reinforcement oriented token economies. The children had a mean age of ten years and a mean IQ of 70, and were described by their teachers as being moderately to highly disruptive and off task. The children were divided into two groups, and three of the most difficult children were selected from each group for observation and data collection. Dependent variables related to off-task behavior (not attending to academic materials for a period in excess of two seconds) and violations of classroom rules regarding staying seated, raising hands before talking, not disturbing others, and proper use of the bathroom. Arithmetic behavior of the entire class was measured daily for number and accuracy of math problems completed. Teacher behaviors were also recorded in terms of teacher approval (positive comments to individuals or groups) and teacher disapproval (negative verbal commentary).

After a four-week prebaseline period designed to accustom children to the recording procedure, a five-week baseline was conducted during the daily forty-minute math session. A variable-interval tone occurred every three to five minutes on ten occasions. No consequences were associated with the tone during baseline. Students were instructed to begin work independently in their arithmetic folders and to obey all classroom rules. With the presentation of the first tone they were to continue until four short tones were delivered at the end of the period. During this baseline period the six students on whom data were collected averaged between 30 percent to 32 percent off-task behavior with about 9 percent rule violations. The entire classroom of fifteen students averaged about twenty completed problems daily during this time, with nearly all of the problems performed correctly by all students. Data collected on teacher's approving comments showed that they occurred during less than two percent of intervals during all of baseline. Thus the teacher's verbal behavior was not considered to be serving a reinforcement function. Intervention for groups A and B were counterbalanced as follows. For group A (seven children) a reinforcement procedure was used for on-task behavior with no rule violations for the first eleven days, followed by a seven-day baseline period, and finally a ten-day response-cost contingency for off-task or disruptive behavior. The eight students in group B were exposed first to response cost, followed by a return to baseline, and finally a reinforcement procedure for on task and rule following. In the reinforcement condition students were individually provided empty cups into which tokens were placed contingent on on-task behavior during the interval just preceding each tone. Students who did not violate any classroom rules and who maintained on task were given up to ten individual tokens. Conversely, in the response-cost condition students were provided cups containing ten tokens at the beginning of the session. When a tone sounded a token was removed if, during the preceding interval, the student had demonstrated off-task behavior or rule violations. No explicit contingencies regarding academic achievement or problems completed were specified for either group. Students were initially told that they must earn (or keep) at least six tokens by the end of the period in order to obtain an edible treat. After six days of this arrangement the criterion for obtaining the back up reinforcer was changed to eight tokens. Furthermore, surprise days were promised. On unpredicted days three or four students with the highest number of tokens were given a "special bonus" (toys and candies). Thus, after obtaining extensive baseline data on a multitude of dependent variables, both response-cost and reward systems were alternately imposed on both groups, under the same classroom conditions. On the fifty-fifth session and for the next two days all students were given an opportunity to select the procedure (response cost or reinforcement) they preferred.

Both reinforcement and response-cost procedures produced an immediate drop in off-task behavior. It averaged about 10 percent while the criterion was held at six tokens and almost disappeared when the criterion was moved to eight tokens. Similarly, rule violations terminated almost entirely with the initiation of both systems. These variables both escalated back to initial baseline levels when the seven-day reversal was performed but returned to near nonexistent levels when the token procedures were reinstituted. Most notably, virtually no difference could be detected between effectiveness of the two systems with regard to both of these variables throughout the course of the experiment.

In the same vein, academic behavior was conspicuously but not differentially affected. Slight increases occurred in the number of problems completed while the token criterion was held at six, and the response-cost group appeared slightly more proficient. When the criterion was moved to eight tokens per day both response cost and reinforcement procedures resulted in an average of about fifty problems per session. Both groups dropped to near baseline levels with the reversal but returned to an average of about forty when the token contingencies were reinvoked.

Teacher verbal behavior might have been a particularly interesting variable in this analysis, but it did not, in fact, vary much throughout the course of the entire study. However, as previously indicated, this teacher was not outstandingly verbose under any conditions. Her approval statements occurred in only two percent more intervals in the reinforcement procedure than under baseline conditions. No changes were recorded during the response-cost phases.

One point of special interest relates to which type of contingency the students preferred. To assess this, the authors gave both groups an opportunity to select the type of token procedure they wanted for each of the last three days of the experiment (choice condition). According to the authors, "this phase showed no consistent pattern of preference toward either reward or cost. Over the 3 day period, four subjects consistently chose reward, five subjects consistently chose cost, and six subjects switched their choice at least once" (Iwata & Bailey, 1974, pp. 573–574). They go on to point out that

> one of the major objections to the use of response cost had been that it may lead to detrimental side effects, such as increased aggression or behavior that enables one to avoid or escape the cost condition. The present results failed to support either of these contentions. . . . Finally, data obtained from the Choice condition indicated that subjects found the cost contingency to be at least as "desirable" as the reward contingency, if not more so. Although more subjects chose reward on the first day, cost was chosen more frequently on both of the following days. (Iwata & Bailey, 1974, pp. 574–575)

The authors note that this particular use of response cost may have been less offensive than others. Tokens in the cost phase of this experiment had been given noncontingently at the beginning of each new session. In some studies (Boren & Coleman, 1970) response cost required the removal of tokens that had been earned previously for appropriate behavior. Under these conditions response cost was found to engender more negative behaviors.

Many of the components of this study were replicated and described in a one-page summary two years later. Hundert (1976) explored these contingencies with six elementary school children using a simple ABA design. Subjects were treated individually in a counterbalanced sequence such that (a) token reinforcement was provided for attending and correct arithmetic performance, (b) response cost was administered by removal of tokens for off task and arithmetic performance below a preset criterion, and (c) a combination of both contingencies. Although on task jumped from 29 percent to 85 percent and arithmetic problems from 6.4 percent correct to 11.4 percent correct during training, there were no detectable differences among the various procedural contingencies.

Improved Learning

It seems fairly well documented, at this point, that token economies can facilitate classroom management and that improved control of the classroom may enhance learning. However, what about the direct effects of tokens on learning? Does direct and immediate secondary reinforcement of academic behavior, by means of tokens, enhance the individual's learning? This is clearly a different kind of question from the kinds of questions asked in previously described research articles. Not only are we asking if token procedures create a climate in which learning can take place, but we are also asking if token reinforcement improves learning. To examine that issue, Lahey and Drabman (1974) investigated the use of direct token reinforcement on the retention of sight-word vocabulary in second-grade students.

In their study sixteen second-grade regular education students were observed under controlled conditions. In order to ascertain appropriate stimulus items during the first session, each child was required to view a large number of sight-word cards (Dolch, 1949). Cards that were not correctly read by each student were selected as practice items for that student until a total of thirty unique cards were obtained. Subsequently acquisition of the sight-word vocabulary was performed in basically the same manner for two groups (token and no-token) of eight children. Each acquisition session lasted until subjects could identify ten cards without error or until one hour had elapsed. During the first presentation of the stimulus cards the experimenters held each of the ten cards up for one second and pronounced it. Thereafter the subjects were required to identify the words independently; if the subject missed the word the experimenter pronounced the word correctly. Members of the one group received tokens immediately on correct identification of the sight-word cards as well as verbal feedback as to the correctness of their responses. Members of the other group merely provided the feedback. Subjects in the token group exchanged their tokens for pennies, at a rate of five tokens per penny, at the conclusion of each session. The no-token group received pennies at the end of each session based on the number of tokens earned by a yoked token subject.

Two retention tests were given to all subjects, the first at the conclusion of third acquisition session for each subject and the second two days later. During retention tests no tokens or verbal feedback were provided to members of either group. Retention tests included all thirty words. Thus the first retention test consisted of ten items learned on the same day, ten learned five days earlier, and ten learned seven days previous to the retention test. The retention test was replicated two days later. At this time learning had occurred for the three sets of words two, seven, and nine days previously.

The differences between the two groups in terms of speed of acquisition and in terms of retention were rather substantial. The no-token group required twice the number of stimulus presentations as did the token group. Using a simple *t*-test, the authors found that this difference was statistically significant; that is, there was less than a five percent chance that the difference in the learning rate was due to chance ($t = 2.30$, 14*df*, two-tailed). The token group outperformed the no-token group on both the first and the second retention tests.

The token group also showed greater improvement over the no-token group as the time since acquisition increased. The token group maintained an average of about eight out of ten correctly recalled words at short-, medium-, and long-retention intervals. The no-token group fell from eight out of ten at a short-retention interval to about four at medium and long intervals.

Lahey and Drabman provide an important concluding commentary:

> Fortunately, from the point of view of the development of a technology of education, the present results suggest that the same procedures that facilitate acquisition also facilitate retention. The significant interaction between tokens and retention interval is particularly important in this respect, as it suggests that the importance of token reinforcement increases as the length of the retention interval increases. (Lahey & Drabman, 1974, p. 311)

Composition

Although the objectives of instruction in reading are fairly well established, the objectives of instruction in writing skills are frequently less clearly defined. Many writing instructors seem to favor a somewhat random and spontaneous approach to the instruction of composition. Teachers frequently focus on correcting grammatical and punctuation errors and fail to reinforce clear and interesting presentations of ideas (Vargas, 1978). Alternatively, a behavioral analysis of composition might quantify certain dimensions of the written product and make potentially reinforcing consequences contingent on such production. Such an approach would permit a quantitative and, to some extent, a qualitative, examination of the writer's output. Under these conditions specific composition skills might be subjected to the same reinforcement contingencies as more traditionally taught academic skills, such as reading and mathematics.

A study of Brigham, Graubard, and Stans (1972) took just such an approach to the instruction of composition. These authors attempted to improve the writing skills of fifteen male members of a fifth-grade "adjustment class." Students had been placed in this restrictive environment because of academic failure as well as disruptive and inappropriate behaviors. The authors note that a broad range of specific writing topographies were available for analysis. These might have included proper word usage, diagrammatical productions, spelling, grammatical structure, etc. However, these authors selected number of words, number of different words, and the number of new words used in a particular story as their units of analysis. According to the authors:

> It was expected that positive changes in these components would increase the length of the stories (number of words), reduce the redundancy within the stories (number of different words), and increase the written vocabulary, possibly expanding the number of ideas in the stories (number of new words). Finally, if these objective components could be improved, the overall quality of the composition would also improve. (Brigham et al., 1972, p. 422)

Before the initiation of the investigation a well-designed and well-managed token economy was maintained in the classroom. Students were evidently acclimated to continuing variations of the ongoing point systems. The existing point program permitted them to earn a host of privileges and novel games and crafts. These same backup reinforcers were available when the composition program began.

In the first session of baseline the instructor simply directed the students to write a short story about anything they liked to do. The spelling of difficult words was aided by staff members who spelled any requested word on a separate card for the individual students. Length of these baseline compositions was not predetermined; however, starting and stopping times were documented, and no more than one hour was available during the writing periods. Subsequent to the initial baseline writing samples, each student was assigned to one of three groups of approximately equal writing skills. Tokens were made contingent on changes in each of the three dependent variables (total number of words per story, number of new words, and number of different words), one variable at a time. The reinforcement procedures remained in effect once they were introduced. However, each of the three groups began the various experimental conditions at different times as a separate group multiple-baseline design. Although group A only had two days of baseline observation, groups B and C had six and nine days, respectively. Succeeding conditions were introduced for each group at either three- or four-day intervals.

When the total number of words written was first introduced as a reinforceable behavior, students were simply told that they would receive 1 point for each word they wrote. Similarly, when the number of different words and the number of new words became reinforceable behaviors, these new contingencies provided for 2 and 3 points per word, respectively. The authors indicate that, at the time of this study's implementation, keeping a running record of novel words by each student presented a substantial scoring and recording chore. It is perhaps worth mentioning that this same type of record keeping could be easily accomplished today by using any one of several computerized word processing programs currently in popular use in most public school systems.

Results of this extensive investigation indicated quite clearly that all dependent variables were positively affected by the token reinforcement program. In all cases the predominant increases revolved around the total number of words written and the amount of time spent writing, which approximately doubled over the baseline compositions. However, the authors point out that there were also correlated increases in the number of different words and number of new words.

When 1 point per word written was introduced as a reinforcement contingency, the number of words written increased in all three groups. Based on the graphed data, it can be estimated that groups A and B increased in the number of words from an average of thirty during baseline to forty-five when points were contingent on the number of words written. Group C's average rose from thirty (baseline) to about ninety-five (ranging from 80 to 160). The number of new words and the number of different words also increased when the points were contingent on total number of words written.

With the introduction of the second concurrent contingency (2 points for new words) no significant increases in the total number of words occurred. More importantly, this coexisting contingency did not elevate the mean number of different words beyond the elevation that occurred when the first contingency went into effect. Baseline numbers of different words were approximately fourteen, twenty-one, and twenty-one per session, for groups A, B, and C, respectively. When the first contingency of 1 point per word was introduced, group A moved to about thirty-five different words, group B increased to about twenty-eight different words, and, with considerable variability, group C moved to around fifty different words per session. Offering 2 points for each different word coexisting with the previous contingency of 1 point per word, there was virtually no change in the mean number of different words for groups A and B.

In the same vein, providing 3 points for each new word caused no increases over the preceding mean numbers of new words used in the earlier and still active contingencies. During baseline group A maintained fourteen new words per session. Groups B and C showed some variability averaging about fifteen new words per baseline session. Offering 1 point per word increased new words for groups A and C. Group A averaged about twenty-three new words and group C averaged about twenty-eight new words under the 1 point-per-word contingency. Group B showed no change. The explicit offering of 3 points for each new word in groups A and B did not produce any further change. The authors try to explain these somewhat paradoxical results:

> The procedures that were aimed at increasing the number of different words and the number of new produced equivocal results. The different-words and new-words contingencies had little overall effect on the performance of the students in Group A and B. The advent of the new-word contingency (three points for each new word) was followed by a jump in the number of new words for both A and B the first day of this condition.

However, (in) the next sessions the use of new words dropped off. Paradoxically, the contingency itself may have contributed to this decline because the students were observed spending more time looking at their word lists, apparently trying to come up with new words, rather than simply writing. While the new-word procedure did not yield a clear increment in the use of new words, new words were consistently emitted throughout the experimental manipulations. The students used a number of new words during the study, indicating that the stories were not simply repetitions of earlier stories. (Brigham et al., 1972, pp. 425–426)

The authors note that in addition to the straightforward use of word counts, a scoring system was used to assess the quality of writing in the students' stories. Five upper-division college students were trained to rate the stories on the following dimensions: "(1) Mechanical aspects; (2) Vocabulary, variety, and word usage; (3) Number of ideas; (4) Development of the ideas; (5) Internal consistency of the story. All dimensions were scored from 0 to 5" (Brigham et al., 1972, p. 424). The college students practiced judging until agreement occurred in the scoring of each dimension (about 1.5 to 2 hours for each judge). After being typed exactly as originally written by the students, all stories were coded and randomly rated by the judges, who were not told the purpose of their evaluations.

As with the previously described measures of composition change, ratings given by judges improved at the point at which the contingency providing 1 point per written word was introduced. The authors indicate that, primarily as a function of judged improvements in vocabulary and mechanical aspects of writing, there were ratings between baseline and the number-of-words condition corresponding to the following means: A, 7.9 and 9.9; B, 7.7 and 10.0; C, 8.16 and 11.1. They go on to note that although ratings indicated little qualitative effect in the different-words condition, the new-words condition appeared to produce the greatest improvement in the judged ratings. Brigham et al. specify that under this condition subjects from group A obtained ratings as high as 13.0, 12.2, 9.3, and 13.0 compared with a previous high rating of 11.8. Similarly, group B showed high ratings of 12.5, 11.4, and 13.0 in this condition, as opposed to the previous high of 11.8. Increases in both the number of ideas and the development of ideas were primarily responsible for the improvement in rating during the new-words condition.

All changes were correlated with an increase in the amount of time spent writing. This began exactly when points became available for increased number of words and maintained throughout all phases of the experiment, independent of the condition or combination of conditions under experimental analysis. Subjects generally moved from about twelve minutes of on-task writing behavior during baseline to around fifteen to thirty minutes of on-task writing, fluctuating erratically throughout the remainder of the experiment.

The authors note that improvements in both the length and quality of writing occurred despite the fact that the total number of points that students obtained never increased over baseline conditions. It will be recalled that these subjects were operating under a token economy before the inception of the treatment conditions. Points given in these pretreatment conditions were provided for good work habits and various appropriate social behaviors. The authors note, quite correctly, that the improvements in writing occurred not as a function of increased amounts of reinforcement, but as a function of the changes in the reinforcing contingencies.

A Look Back

In this chapter we have seen that token programs are primarily effective because of the direct administration of secondary reinforcers to students' on-task behavior, as opposed to adjunctive effects derived from coincidental "educational structure," or "classroom rules" (O'Leary et al., 1969). Both Mandelker et al. (1970) and Breyer and Allen (1975) demonstrated that a teacher's rate of verbal praise is likely to increase when tokens are used. Ringer (1973) showed some limited and temporary improvement in a teacher's skill in administering a token program when a "token helper" was used as a model. Marlowe et al. (1978) compared the effects of teacher-run token economies with the effects of non-directive therapy on students' in-class behavior. McLaughlin and Malaby (1972) established the effectiveness of classwide token systems with reinforcers intrinsic to the classrooom. Response cost and token reinforcement are about equally effective in improving student behavior (Iwata & Bailey, 1974). Furthermore, it now appears likely that token programs may improve student recall of sight words (Lahey & Drabman, 1974) as well as provide a means whereby student compositions may be brought to a higher standard (Brigham et al., 1972). In closing this chapter and this book it might be interesting to look at the words of Kazdin (1982), who provides a retrospective and interesting overview of ten years of token economies both in and out of the public schools.

In 1972 Kazdin and Bootzin evaluated the token economy research as it pertained to a broad range of applied areas. At that time they described a number of important issues relating to the problems associated with the proliferation of token programs in human service and educational settings. In particular they identified "(a) maintaining behavior and ensuring generalization, (b) training staff to implement the token economy, (c) increasing client responsiveness to the contingencies, and (d) overshadowing client resistance to the program" (Kazdin & Bootzin, 1972, p. 432).

One decade later Kazdin (1982) again evaluated the token economy literature and restated many of the same concerns as well as mentioning emergent issues relating to the general effectiveness of this procedure. Note, however that many of his findings are based on research derived from mentally retarded populations and as such may not always adequately generalize to school populations. Kazdin reviewed progress since his previous paper and identified recent advances in the token economy research. He notes that from the beginning, there has always been a small portion of client population that appeared highly resistant to token economy procedures. Initially it was assumed that there might be some inherent quality that predisposed certain individuals to be unaffected by such reinforcers. But the evidence from a number of studies is contradictory on this point. Specifically Kazdin points out that although the extent of withdrawal and length of hospitalization were correlated with resistance to these procedures in some studies (e.g., Fullerton, Cayner, & McLaughlin-Reidel, 1978), they were correlated with improvement in others (Mishara, 1978). Other variables such as intelligence, sex, and age have also failed to demonstrate any consistent bias in favor of or in opposition to client's responsiveness to token economy contingencies (Moran, Kass, & Munz, 1977).

But here is where Kazdin applauds the research conducted since his previous article. It has become apparent that individuals who do not respond to a large-scale program are not necessarily inherently resistant. What has become obvious is that some individuals have a unique reinforcement history that makes them more resistant to typical reinforcement schedules and menus. Altering the contingencies in various ways may allow these individuals to respond positively to the program. Examples that Kazdin believes to be most consistently successful require a manipulation of the magnitude of reinforcers. The number of tokens earned, the value of backup reinforcers (Ayllon, Milan, Roberts, & McGee, 1979), and the use of reinforcer sampling (Ayllon & Azrin, 1968) are variables that frequently affect responsiveness in reluctant clients.

Kazdin indicates that reinforcer sampling is also a particularly effective strategy. This method bears a strong resemblance to what is often referred to as priming. Subjects are noncontingently permitted to sample the backup reinforcer previous to their exposure to the work requirement of the token economy. They are then more likely to respond to gain access to these backup rewards. Preselection of backup reinforcers, described in the study by O'Leary et al. (1969), has also proved helpful. To enhance probability of their responsiveness, subjects may be permitted to see and choose the available items on the reinforcement menu.

When token programs were viewed as an economic exchange system, Kazdin describes methods for which even more novel ideas were instituted. Such procedures as putting a ceiling on the number of tokens permitted in savings, increasing the cost per item of backup rewards, promoting sales with new and different items placed on the menu, instituting expiration dates on the sale of certain highly desired items, and even leveling fines for inappropriate behavior are tactics that have been found to improve the commercial and productive activity within various token economies (Hung, 1977; Milby, Clarke, Charles, & Willcutt, 1977; Winkler, 1973). Kazdin also recommends the use of peers to assist in the manipulation of variables. For example, Long and Williams (1973) found that a classroom management point system was more effective when the whole class earned points as a group versus when individuals earned their own points. Furthermore, it has been found advantageous to have peers help administer the actual delivery or removal of tokens (Phillips, Phillips, Wolf, & Fixsen, 1973).

As in all forms of behavioral intervention, response maintenance and transfer of training is still an issue. Kazdin indicates that token economies in the schools have proved robust with regard to transfer of training and generalization. In particular, Kazdin points to the overwhelming success of the behavior analysis follow-through program (Bushell, 1978). In this study the beneficial academic effects of a token system were still active two years after students left the program and entered classes that did not have the benefit of any form of token programming. Also, Heaton and Safer (1982) and Safer, Heaton, and Parker (1981) demonstrate that even junior high school students, when exposed to a rigorous token system, showed long-term reductions in suspension, grade failures, and expulsions. These students also demonstrated generally better classroom conduct and a lower dropout rate relative to a control group. Such outcomes demonstrate empirically that gains achieved by using token programs are not inevitably lost. However, such gains can be maintained only when programmers take into account the necessity of planned generalization procedures. If the beneficial effects are to endure, the later environments of students must provide the contingencies that maintain behavioral and academic advances. Kazdin suggests several strategies to increase the likelihood of transfer and maintenance of positive behaviors in new settings. They include the gradual elimination of the token system, using reinforcement procedures in a variety of settings, substituting everyday events such as praise and activities for tokens, gradually altering the schedule of reinforcement and delay of reinforcement to preclude an extinction process, and getting peers and clients themselves involved as reinforcing agents.

The fact that students can be "phased out" of a rigorous program and reintegrated into less structured environments in no way indicates that token programs can become less structured. On the contrary, token programs must maintain a high level of consistency throughout the course of treatment. Kazdin points out that one of the major problems in token program maintenance is ensuring the "integrity of treatment." By this he means that supervision of staff ensures that treatment is carried out and maintained as originally intended. He cites a long list of examples of programs that deteriorated when supervision terminated or was even partially reduced (Bassett & Blanchard, 1977; Scheirer, 1981). He cites a particularly disturbing report by Rollins, McCandless, Thompson, and Brassell (1974). These researchers developed several extensive and well-managed token programs in a number of elementary school classrooms. On termination of their study they concurrently removed all forms of data collection and on-site supervision, leaving the programs in the hands of school personnel. On returning one year later to collect follow-up data they found that the program had virtually disintegrated. Kazdin suggests that in the absence of adequate and continued data collection, token programs are likely to quickly deteriorate. He states that "with little or no feedback about direct execution of the program or its effects on client behavior, the integrity of treatment and the efficacy of the program are likely to be sacrificed" (Kazdin, 1982, p. 439).

To combat this most serious and pervasive problem, Kazdin recommends following the tactics of Rollins and Thompson (1978). These researchers adjusted and compensated for the previously described token program deterioration. Program monitoring, supervision, and evaluation were reinstituted by going back to these schools and instructing administrators and principals in the process of data collection and general behavioral techniques. Teachers were continually trained by these in-house administrator/supervisors and given feedback for continued improvement of their classroom behavior programs. Using this method, the school became semi-independent of the need for outside consultation. Kazdin notes that they maintained a consulting and advisory relationship with the extrainstitutional behavior analysts, but that the program carried on successfully in a semiautonomous fashion. This is an excellent and much needed system for many smaller school systems. However, within larger urban school districts the services of a behaviorally oriented school psychologist might be available. If this were the case, then even the need for consulting by "outside," extrainstitutional behavior analysts might be limited to the few cases in which unusual circumstances require a fresh view of the problem.

REFERENCES

Ayllon, T., & Azrin, N. H. (1968). *The token economy: A motivational system for therapy and rehabilitation*. New York: Appleton-Century-Crofts.

Ayllon, T., Milan, M. A., Roberts, M. D., & McGee, J. M. (1979). *Correctional rehabilitation and management: A psychological approach*. New York: Wiley.

Azrin, N. H., & Holz, W. C. (1966). Punishment. In W. K. Honig (Ed.), *Operant behavior: Areas of research and application* (pp. 380–447). New York: Appleton-Century-Crofts.

Bandura, A. (1965). Influence of model's reinforcement contingencies on the acquisition of imitative responses. *Journal of Personality and Social Psychology, 1*, 589–595.

Bassett, J. E., & Blanchard, E. B. (1977). The effect of the absence of close supervision on the use of response cost in a prison token economy. *Journal of Applied Behavior Analysis, 10*, 375–379.

Boren, J. J., & Coleman, A. D. (1970). Some experiments on reinforcement principles within a psychiatric ward for delinquent soldiers. *Journal of Applied Behavior Analysis, 3*, 29–27.

Breyer, N. L., & Allen, G. J. (1975). Effects of implementing a token economy on teacher attending behavior. *Journal of Applied Behavior Analysis, 8*, 373–380.

Breyer, N. L., & Pollack, B. (1971). Behavioral consultation within the existing public school system. *School Applications of Learning Theory, 4*, 2–13.

Brigham, T. A., Graubard, P. S., & Stans, A. (1972). Analysis of the effects of sequential reinforcement contingencies on aspects of composition. *Journal of Applied Behavior Analysis, 5*, 421–429.

Bushell, D., Jr. (1978). An engineering approach to the elementary classroom: The Behavior Analysis Follow Through project. In A. C. Catania & T. A. Brigham (Eds.), *Handbook of applied behavior analysis: Social and instructional processes*. New York: Irvington.

Cooper, M. L., Thomson, C. L., & Jackson, D. (1970). Effects of teacher attention on study behavior. *Journal of Applied Behavior Analysis, 3,* 153–157.

Dolch, E. W. (1949). *Basic sight vocabulary cards.* Champaign, IL: Garrard.

Fullerton, D. T., Cayner J. J., & McLaughlin-Reidel, T. (1978). Results of a token economy. *Archives of General Psychiatry, 35,* 1451–1453.

Heaton, R. C., & Safer, D. J. (1982). Secondary school outcome following a junior high school behavioral program. *Behavior Therapy, 13,* 226–231.

Hundert, J. (1976). The effectiveness of reinforcement, response cost, and mixed programs on classroom behaviors. *Journal of Applied Behavior Analysis, 9,* 107.

Hung, D. W. (1977). Generalization of "curiosity" questioning behavior in autistic children. *Journal of Behavior Therapy and Experimental Psychiatry, 8,* 237–245.

Iwata, B., & Bailey, J. S. (1974). Reward versus cost token systems: An analysis of the effects on students and teacher. *Journal of Applied Behavior Analysis, 7,* 567–576.

Kazdin, A. E. (1982). The token economy: A decade later. *Journal of Applied Behavior Analysis, 15,* 431–445.

Kazdin, A. E., & Bootzin, R. R. (1972). The token economy: An evaluative review. *Journal of Applied Behavior Analysis, 5,* 343–372.

Lahey, B. B., & Drabman, R. S. (1974). Facilitation of the acquisition and retention of sight-word vocabulary through token reinforcement. *Journal of Applied Behavior Analysis, 7,* 307–312.

Long, J. D., & Williams, R. L. (1973). The comparative effectiveness of group and individually contingent free time with inner-city junior high school students. *Journal of Applied Behavior Analysis, 6,* 465–474.

McLaughlin, T. F., & Malaby, J. (1972). Intrinsic reinforcers in a classroom token economy. *Journal of Applied Behavior Analysis, 5,* 263–270.

Madsen, C. H., Jr., & Madsen, C. K. (1970). *Teaching/discipline: Behavioral principles toward a positive approach.* Boston: Allyn & Bacon.

Madsen, C. H., Jr., & Madsen, C. K. (1974). *Teaching/discipline: Behavioral principles toward a positive approach.* Expanded 2nd edition for professionals. Boston: Ayllon & Bacon.

Mandelker, A. V., Brigham, T. A., & Bushell, D. (1970). The effects of token procedures on a teacher's social contacts with her students. *Journal of Applied Behavior Analysis, 3,* 169–174.

Marlowe, R. H., Madsen, C. H., Bowen, C. E., Reardon, R. C., & Logue, P. E. (1978). Severe classroom behavior problems: Teachers or counsellors. *Journal of Applied Behavior Analysis, 11,* 53–66.

Milby, J. B., Clarke, C., Charles, E., & Willcutt, H. C. (1977). Token economy process variables: Effects of increasing and decreasing the critical range of savings. *Behavior Therapy, 8,* 137–145.

Mishara, B. L. (1978). Geriatric patients who improve in token economy and general milieu treatment programs: A multivariate analysis. *Journal of Consulting and Clinical Psychology, 46,* 1340–1348.

Moran, E. L., Kass, W. A., & Munz, D. C. (1977). In-program evaluation of a community correctional agency of high-risk offenders. *Corrective and Social Psychiatry, 23,* 48–52.

O'Leary, K. D., & Becker, W. C. (1967). Behavior modification of an adjustment class: A token reinforcement program. *Exceptional Children, 33,* 637–642.

O'Leary, K. D., Becker, W. C., Evans, M. B., & Saudergas, R. A. (1969). A token reinforcement program in a public school: A replication and systematic analysis. *Journal of Applied Behavior Analysis, 2,* 3–13.

Phillips, E. L., Phillips, E. A., Wolf, M., & Fixsen, D. (1973). Achievement place: Development of the elected manager system. *Journal of Applied Behavior Analysis, 6,* 541–561.

Ringer, V. M. J. (1973). The use of a "token helper" in the management of classroom behavior problems and in teacher training. *Journal of Applied Behavior Analysis, 6,* 671–677.

Rogers, C. R. (1969) *Freedom to learn: A view of what education might become.* Columbus, OH: Charles E. Merrill.

Rollins, H. A., McCandless, B. R., Thompson, M., & Brassell, W. R. (1974). Project success environment: An extended application of contingency management in inner-city schools. *Journal of Educational Psychology, 66,* 167–178.

Rollins, H. A., & Thompson, M. (1978). Implementation and operation of a contingency management program by the elementary school principal. *American Educational Research Journal, 15,* 325–330.

Safer, D. J., Heaton, R. C., & Parker, F. C. (1981). A behavioral program for disruptive junior high school students: Results and follow-up. *Journal of Abnormal Child Psychology, 9,* 483–494.

Scheirer, M. A. (1981). *Program implementation: The organizational context.* Beverly Hills, CA: Sage.

Thomas, D. R. (1971). Preliminary findings on self-monitoring for modifying teaching behaviors. In E. A. Ramp & B. L. Hopkins (Eds.), *A new direction for education: Behavior analysis* (pp. 102–114). Lawrence: University of Kansas Press.

Tiegs, E. V., & Clark, W. W. (1963 Norms). Manual, California Achievement Tests, Complete Battery. Monterey: California Test Bureau.

Truax, C. B. & Mitchell, K. (1971) Research on certain therapist interpersonal skills in relation to process and outcome. In A. E. Bergin & S. L. Garfield (Eds.), *Handbook of psychotherapy and behavior change.* New York: Wiley.

Vargas, J. S. (1978). A behavioral approach to the teaching of composition. *The Behavior Analyst, 1,* 16–24.

Winkler, R. C. (1973). An experimental analysis of economic balance, savings and wages in a token economy. *Behavior Therapy, 4,* 22–40.

Wolf, M. M., Giles, D., & Hall, R. V. (1968). Experiments with token reinforcement in a remedial classroom. *Behavior Research and Therapy, 6,* 51–64.

10

Group-oriented Contingencies

The procedural variations between what are commonly known as token economies and what are now being described as group-oriented contingent reinforcement programs may be slight; however, the variables that ultimately affect behavior may be very different. Token economies are typically designed so that relations between behavior and consequences are entirely individualized. Each individual receives his just reward independent of behaviors of other class members. The student who is operating under token reinforcement contingencies is working for himself or herself only.

The procedures that are usually associated with group contingencies may be designed to affect the same types of behavior as token economies (compliance and productivity or disruptive behavior), but all members of the group gain or lose based on some group criterion. Thus, in a given group contingency program if Johnny gets out of his seat without permission, the whole class may suffer the loss of a point that would have been exchanged for backup reinforcers. In group contingencies individuals who "help" or "hurt" the progress of the group can be considered "hero" or "villain." Under these conditions students provide their own social contingencies (group pressure) that may enhance the reinforcement or punishment process.

CATEGORIES OF GROUP-ORIENTED CONTINGENCIES

Litow and Pumroy (1975) recognized the three primary categories of classroom group-oriented contingency programs: dependent, independent, and interdependent. In the case of dependent group-oriented contingencies, a system is implemented wherein all members of the class are consequated, positively or negatively, depending on the behaviors exhibited by an individual or subgroup within the class. In such an arrangement an entire class may gain free time based on the improved math scores of a particular student. Litow and Pumroy indicate that such a program may indirectly control behavior of the whole class by increasing the chances that members may aid the individual or subgroup to perform the requisite behaviors.

Independent group-oriented contingencies require that each individual within the class is concurrently exposed to the same set of contingencies, but that the application of consequences occurs on an individual basis. This form of group contingency is actually more like token economies; however, within many token economies individuals may sustain special contracts for unique reinforcements. In the case of a group-oriented contingency each member of a class who completes a specified assignment or level of accuracy may gain independent access to the same reinforcer.

Interdependent group-oriented contingencies are the more commonly used and commonly understood form of group contingency. Such a system provides that all members of a group be concurrently exposed to the same response requirements. This may be typified by a contingency that specifies that every student within a class be required to reach a level of performance accuracy in order for the class, as a unit, to obtain free time. If any one member failed to reach the criterion, then the whole class would fail to earn the free time.

Within this system are subdivisions that need special consideration. Litow and Pumroy (1975) point out that three types of group performance levels are possible in this system. The most popular of these was just described, in which the whole class meets a common criteria. In addition, averaging of all performances, high performances, and low performances have been used (Hamblin, Hathaway, & Wodarski, 1971). They also describe a system in which group performances are judged in terms of a single randomly selected individual within the class or the performance of the single highest or lowest individual within the class (Drabman, Spitalnik, & Spitalnik, 1974).

Litow and Pumroy indicate that two basic subdivisions or groupings have been described in the literature or interdependent group-oriented contingencies. One system emphasizes the whole class acting as a single group (Andrews, 1970); the other divides the class into competing subgroups (Barrish, Saunders, & Wolf, 1969).

A DEPENDENT GROUP-ORIENTED CONTINGENCY SYSTEM

As previously suggested, dependent group-oriented contingency systems require that subgroups or individuals within a class perform to the level of a preset criteria in order to produce consequences for themselves in conjunction with their classmates. In this system it is anticipated that classmates will encourage the subject's productivity and perhaps even discourage behavior of the subject that is incompatible with producing the consequence. This form of group-oriented contingency was demonstrated in a study by Coleman (1970). This author went to great lengths to obtain subjects who demonstrated extremely disruptive classroom behavior. Four subjects, from different classrooms, were chosen by computerized analysis of teacher ratings from all the disruptive students within a total school district. Target behaviors were talking out, out-of-seat behavior, and increasing on-task behavior (attending to written materials or the teacher).

After ten days of baseline observation subjects were individually given a pretraining session in which a classroom situation was rehearsed where the subjects received an M&M after each ten seconds of continuous academic behavior. The subjects were then told that this same program would be transferred to their classrooms but that the candy would be shared equally with their classmates.

In the classroom setting an unobtrusive observer controlled a radio-operated counter that was clicked (advanced) at the end of intervals averaging 10 seconds during which the subject had maintained on-task behavior. The class was told that the student was working for all of them in that each time the counter clicked, another piece of candy was earned, to be shared with all at the end of class. After four treatment sessions this contingency was reversed, and all reinforcement and experimental manipulations were terminated for a period of six sessions. Subsequently the treatment procedures were reinstated for five sessions. Finally, the subjects were each informed that they were to continue being monitored for good work, but that the machine that clicked and notified them of their progress was to be removed. However, they were still to be observed and they were still to earn points that were exchanged for candy for general consumption. The condition was maintained for only two sessions.

In the case of all four subjects, in all four separate classes, the target behaviors followed the experimental manipulations almost perfectly. During the ten days of baseline all subjects demonstrated extreme off-task behaviors. Out-of-seat and talking-out behaviors ranged from 50 percent to 100 percent of the intervals, while on-tasks fluctuated from near zero to about half the observed intervals. With the introduction of the treatment program, on task jumped to almost 100 percent for all four subjects and, necessarily, the talking-out and out-of-seat behaviors fell to near zero. This trend was reversed when the experimental contingencies were temporarily removed. On reinstatement of the experimental contingencies the appropriate on-task behaviors were resumed. With the removal of the radio-operated feedback device there was no visible change in the students. However, all subjects had been told that their behavior was still being monitored and that they were still earning points and candy for themselves and the class. No doubt this program was making these students very popular with fellow classmates.

The program described by Coleman (1970) meets the basic requirements for a dependent group-oriented contingency system in that the behavior of single students determines the acquisition of reinforcement for their respective groups. This is a powerful system for influencing student behavior, one that is relatively simple to operate and that has immediate positive effects in a classroom environment.

CONTRASTING INTERDEPENDENT AND INDEPENDENT GROUP-ORIENTED CONTINGENCY SYSTEMS

The question arises as to whether interdependent (everybody's behavior) or independent (individual's behavior) contingency systems are most effective in reducing disruptive behavior and facilitating on-task behavior. One study by Long and Williams (1973) addresses this issue directly. Using a class of seventh-grade, highly disruptive, academically deficient subjects from an inner-city metropolitan area, these researchers manipulated group-oriented contingencies in both math and geography classes in a multiple-baseline and reversal design.

Subjects displayed outrageous levels of disruptive and other off-task behaviors during both baseline and subsequent phase during which structured lessons were implemented and classroom rules were stated daily. These two phases were contrasted by arranging a multiple baseline in which baseline was conducted in math for nine sessions followed by nine sessions of math in which structured lessons were instituted and classroom rules were read aloud to the class by the teacher. Baseline data were taken in geography for those eighteen consecutive days. Thus the effects of providing structured lessons and stating classroom rules could be contrasted with previous days of baseline in math and concurrent days of baseline in geography. Group means of appropriate classroom behavior for the first nine days, when structured assignments and specific rules regarding proper classroom behavior were added in math, no decrease in the frequency of disruptions or improvements in appropriate behavior occurred. In fact, group data reveal a slight decrease in appropriate conduct during this period. Not until the interdependent group-oriented contingency system was instituted did there occur any change in student conduct. This was instated in the third nine-day phase when the teacher announced:

> For the next few days you will be able to earn certain privileges by helping to make a better classroom. By obeying the class rules, you can earn 18 minutes of free time each day. However, the free time can only be earned if every student cooperates. Each time any student violates a rule, I will flip (demonstrates) one of these cards, and the entire class will have one less minute of free time. (Long & Williams, 1973, p. 467)

During this nine-day period, when group-contingent free time was instituted in math, a dramatic transition in behavior became apparent. Appropriate behavior in math averaged 80 percent, but the corresponding percentage of proper conduct in the structured lessons of geography remained at about 31 percent. In the fourth phase this interdependent group-oriented contingency was withdrawn from math and instituted in geography. Appropriate behavior decreased an average of 30 percent in math, but on-task/appropriate conduct increased 43 percent during the same nine days of group-contingent free time in geography.

At the fifth stage of the research an independent group-oriented contingency system was invoked and contrasted with the interdependent system. Individualized contingencies were instituted in math while geography reversed to use of structured lessons and rules. However, the comparison and contrast are not without methodological flaws. Although the contingencies were changed from group to individual consequences, the means whereby points were maintained in class were also switched from a response-cost procedure, in which students lost points for misbehavior, to a reinforcement procedure. The possible significance of this change is given little attention in the analysis. Rather, the authors primarily attribute the effects of treatment to moving from a group contingency to individualized contingencies:

> Individually contingent free time was implemented via a point system in which each student had to earn a minimum of 12 from a possible 16 points before being permitted to participate in free-time activities. Students earned two points for each preparatory behavior (i.e., being present, ready to start lessons at the sounding of the tardy bell, and bringing appropriate materials). Two additional points were awarded during each of three variable time intervals in which a student remained in his seat and worked quietly. A kitchen timer was used to signal the three times intervals, which ranged from 1 to 10 min. Four required points for engaging in free time were earned by completing the assignment. The behaviors for which students could earn points were intended to reflect the rules specified during structured lessons. (Long & Williams, 1973, p. 468)

Students were individually penalized, by fining of earned points, for off-task behaviors and failure to work quietly. Nevertheless this represents an entirely different mode of operation from the response-cost program previously used during group contingencies.

This individually contingent free time procedure was initiated during math, while geography class was maintained on structured lesson, and resulted in math class returning to the previous high levels of appropriate behavior seen during group-contingent free time. Subjects averaged 76 percent appropriate behavior in math, while the structured lessons provided during geography averaged only 26 percent proper conduct.

In the sixth phase individually contingent free time was removed from math class and structured lessons were instated. Simultaneously the individualizing reinforcement procedure was initiated in geography class. Appropriate behaviors in geography quickly escalated to 70 percent but predictably dropped to 43 percent during the structured lessons given during math time. After this phase math students were given points for staying on task, but these points were not backed up with individual or group free time. Geography class was again returned to structured lessons. As a result, both classes demonstrated low levels of appropriate behaviors. When points alone were given in geography the same null effect occurred.

The series of reversals and multiple-baseline measures in math and geography demonstrated that both individually earned and group-contingent free time had a pronounced effect on appropriate classroom conduct. The use of structured lessons and the daily stating of classroom rules obviously do not go far toward producing well-behaved students. What is not clear is the contrasting effects of individual- versus group-oriented contingent free-time. This comparison is difficult to make because group contingency phases used a response-cost procedure, while individually contingent phases used a positive reinforcement procedure. This contamination interferes with a functional analysis of the comparative effectiveness of group-contingent and individually contingent free time. A clear and parsimonious interpretation of this study would have been easier had the authors simply maintained a response-cost format throughout all phases of the experiment. Nevertheless the authors proceed with a concluding description:

> The group approach did maintain slightly higher levels of appropriate behavior and greater day-to-day stability within and between subjects. Also, the group procedure made fewer demands on the teacher's time and seemed to be a simpler procedure to implement. Under the group contingent free time, for example, the teacher had merely to censor one student and the others behaved more appropriately. (Long & Williams, 1973, p. 471)

AN INTERDEPENDENT GROUP-ORIENTED CONTINGENCY SYSTEM

One of the first significant studies of an interdependent group-oriented contingency program was described by Barrish et al. (1969). At that time the intricacies and ramifications of this type of program were not adequately appreciated. However, the extent to which group-oriented contingent reinforcement could engender peer pressure on the behavior of individuals would be documented and recounted over the next two decades. The Good Behavior Game would become one of the most frequently described classroom management procedures ever to hit the behavior analysis literature. From 1969 to 1987 there are six separate studies that describe direct replications and variations of this program. There are at least another fifteen that are indirectly related to the original work done by Barrish et al. (1969), and this is only within the pages of the *Journal of Applied Behavior Analysis*. Although reasons for the popularity of this type of programming are numerous and multifaceted, the following three are most salient:

1. Group contingencies are simple for the teacher to operate and they usually require little in the way of instruction or modeling for the teacher.
2. These programs are amazingly powerful, as they can take full advantage of a very strong reinforcer, peer pressure.
3. The positive results of this type of intervention can be seen almost immediately. These programs really work, and they work quickly.

THE GOOD BEHAVIOR GAME

In the original 1969 production of Barrish et al.'s Good Behavior Game the initial classroom circumstances were typical. The authors noted that seven of the students had records of serious disruptions and classroom violations but that a "behavior management plan" had been in effect. The management plan had primarily consisted of the teacher repeatedly informing the students of the classroom rules regarding proper conduct. Apparently the students were not adequately motivated by this form of "behavior management."

Barrish et al. unobtrusively observed all twenty-four students in this classroom through ten sessions in both math and reading. Inappropriate talking-out behavior occurred during 96 percent of the observed intervals. Out-of-seat behavior occurred during 82 percent of the intervals. After baseline a multiple baseline and series of reversals were implemented in the experimental analysis of several contingencies. Initially, in math only, the class was divided into two teams of twelve players. It was explained by the teacher that when any member of a team was seen violating classroom rules, that person would cause his team to receive a mark. At the end of the math period the team with the fewest marks would be the winners. In the event that both teams received less than five marks, both teams would win concurrently.

Barrish et al. viewed the reward system in this program as a particularly important element. Previous classroom management programs, documented in various psychology journals, had indicated that a problem often occurred in either the teachers' ability to provide social reinforcement (Hall, Panyan, Rabon, & Broden, 1968), or the simple availability of adequate reinforcement menus. Barrish et al. believed that this particular type of classroom management program, which appealed to a sense of competition and an esprit de corps, permitted a reinforcement procedure that made use of opportunities intrinsic to the classroom environment. Winners of the day's Good Behavior Game were permitted to "(1) wear victory tags, (2) put a star by each of its members' names on the winner's charts, (3) line up first for lunch if one team won or early if both teams won, and (4) take part at the end of the day in a 30-min free time during which the team(s) would have special projects" (Barrish et al., 1969, p. 121). Losers of the day's game were required to continue working during the last half hour of the day, while the winners were enjoying their special projects. If one or both teams received fewer than twenty marks in the course of an entire week, then they were permitted to go to recess four minutes early each day. As one can easily see, all of these reinforcers are intrinsic to the school environment, do not require the social skills of a gregarious teacher, and, most notably, appeal to the competitive dispositions of many students. Furthermore, the contingencies were necessarily arranged so that both teams could win most of the time; and that is precisely what happened.

The data that describe the first experimental intervention during six days of the math period are most remarkable. Talking out immediately dropped to a median 19 percent of the observed intervals, and out-of-seat behavior dropped to 9 percent. The concurrent multiple baseline verified the internal validity of this intervention. During reading periods, which occurred on the same days, both dependent measures remained at baseline levels. After a four-day reversal of contingencies, whereby the game was withdrawn during math but instituted during reading, further validation of the independent effects of this program was established. Baseline rates for talking-out and out-of-seat behaviors were recovered during math periods, but the data during reading periods revealed that the game produced an immediate reduction and continued low level of inappropriate behavior. Both talking-out and out-of-seat behaviors during reading stayed below 20 percent during this phase of the study.

In the fourth phase of the study the game was implemented in both math and reading. Predictably the disruptive behavior rates during reading continued at a very low level, and math was once again conducted in a classroom nearly devoid of inappropriate talking or walking about the room. Between the sequential series of experimental reversals and the use of a multiple baseline showing that the effects occurred only in the target subject areas, there appears little doubt that the drastic change in student behavior was primarily a function of the game.

Important to remember is that this game can and should be arranged so that both teams win most of the time. In this experiment both teams won the game in more than 82 percent of the periods played. Yet at any given time during the operating of the game the disruptive behavior of particular students was punished by its causing their team to receive a mark. This mild form of punishment evidently carried with it rather strong peer pressure to cease and desist. Thus the teacher was exempted from her previous obligatory administrations of punishment and scoldings.

The authors do mention that two students proved to be rather bad sports during the game and actually appeared to try to gain social reinforcement by sabotaging their own teams. In order to terminate this antisocial behavior these students were simply removed from their teams and earned individual marks that detracted from their own individual free-time period.

No attempt was made to isolate particular components of the game that may have been most influential in terminating classroom disruptions. The authors state that "an analysis of exactly what components contributed to the effectiveness of the procedures is left to future research" (Barrish et al., 1969, p. 122). The authors go on to say that "it may follow that an understanding of the mechanisms of the game, e.g., peer competition, group consequences vs. individual consequences, etc., together with research designed to enhance the significance of winning with privileges, could lead to a set of effective and practical techniques of classroom behavior management based on games" (Barrish et al., 1969, pp. 123–124). Rarely has a concluding plea for future research resulted in such overwhelming and enthusiastic follow-up.

THE FIRST REPLICATION

Three years after the Good Behavior Game was first reported the first replication appeared in print. Medland and Stachnik (1972) produced a variation of the same group contingency with certain technological innovations and the same powerful effects. Using essentially the same set of game rules used in Barrish et al.'s original procedure, Medland and Stachnik (1972) reorganized a typical reading group of twenty-eight fifth-graders into a series of electronically controlled game conditions.

For purposes of both observation and game procedures, the class was divided into two fourteen-member teams. The study was divided into six separate phases, consisting of baseline (1), game (1), baseline (2), rules, rules + lights, and game (2).

during five forty-minute baseline (1) sessions it was observed that both teams had an exceptionally high rate of disruptive, out-of-seat, and talking-out behaviors. Baseline levels vacillated from a team rate of 200 episodes of such behaviors per session, to as low as only about 15 for one team on a particularly good day. However, graphs of baseline (1) data indicate averages of about 75 to 100 episodes of the target behaviors per session.

With the introduction of game (1) electronic contingencies took over. It was explained to the class that the two teams were now competing for free time. Competition was made possible by way of electronic feedback, which provided the whole class with cues regarding how well they were performing. Each time any member of either team was out of his or her seat, talking out, or causing any form of disruption they would cause their whole team to earn a mark. Marks against the teams were constantly monitored and posted by means of red and green lights stationed at the front of the class. These lights were controlled by college student observers with a control box at the rear of the room. The following rules were provided to the class:

> The green light means that "all is well" and the red light means that "someone has made an error and the team should be careful." (The red light went on for 30 seconds when a target behavior occurred and stayed on for 30 seconds after the last error, at which time the green light was switched back on.) (Medland & Stachnik, 1972, p. 47)

At the end of the forty-minute reading period the team with fewest marks won the game for that day, and thus received free time. This free time consisted of three minutes of extra morning recess time and extra activity time on a weekly basis if a team made less than twenty marks during the whole of a given week. Any individual who was especially disruptive, or who intentionally attempted to sabotage his own team, was removed from the game for a period of one day.

Although these reinforcers may seem rather meager compared with those used in the original Barrish et al. study, they were evidently sufficient to motivate these subjects. The authors point out that there was an immediate and dramatic transition in the students' frequency of performing all target variables. Groups 1 and 2 showed an immediate and consistent 99 percent and 97 percent reduction, respectively, in talking-out, out-of-seat, and disruptive behaviors. This near-zero level was maintained by both teams throughout the ten-day course of game (1).

The surprising outcome of this study was the rather limited change in target behaviors on reversal to baseline contingencies during baseline (2). Group 1 returned to only 33 percent of the frequency of inappropriate behaviors that occurred during baseline (1). Group 2, however, moved back to 82 percent of its baseline (1) rate of target behaviors. The authors point out that the last five sessions of baseline (2) showed continued acceleration in these variables. They therefore speculate that longer reversal might have eventually found both teams operating at higher rates before a stable state was achieved.

Despite the fact that rules had been previously introduced as part of the total treatment package in game 1, they were individually reinstated after baseline (2). For five consecutive sessions classroom rules were read to the students. This was not done in order to isolate the solitary effects of classroom rules as independent of other treatment variables. The authors state that this type of methodology "allows for the assessment of component control after their association with the game and its extra-recess and free-time contingencies" (Medland & Stachnik, 1972, p. 50). As a measure of the extent to which the components of a treatment package may operate after reinforcement procedure is withdrawn, such a tactic is quite reasonable. During this phase groups 1 and 2 dropped 24 percent and 38 percent respectively, when compared with the last five sessions of baseline (2). It is unlikely, however, that such a reduction would have occurred were it not for the previous association of these classroom rules with the total game (1) contingencies.

In this same vein, the next phase of the experiment, which involved the simultaneous instating of rules + lights, is also somewhat equivocal. In this phase the previous classroom rules were again described to the class on a daily basis; furthermore, the lights that had been used in game (1) as a form of group feedback were once again reinstated. However, in this phase, no backup consequence was associated with the feedback provided by the lights or the correlated appropriate behavior of the students. Group 1 inappropriate behavior dropped 80 percent and group 2 fell 94 percent of the previous baseline (2) level of target variables. Group rates of disruption, talking-out, and out-of-seat behaviors were once again at near-zero during the reading period. When game (2) was finally reinstated during the last five days, little further change was apparent, but there was little room for further improvement.

Quite obviously the stimulus cues associated with game 1 reinforcement contingencies carried over the conditions that did not include reinforcement. As the authors note, "the Rule + Lights phase may have exerted control for a long period of time, the duration of which may be determined by characteristics of the game presentation—a short game phase may not foster a strong and lasting Rule + Lights phase, etc. Many other related and interesting questions remain" (Medland & Stachnik, 1972, p. 50). Indeed, many "other related and interesting questions" were pursued and answered in the following years.

RELATED AND INTERESTING QUESTIONS

In the closing comments of the original (1969) version of the Good Behavior Game it was noted by Barrish et al. that no attempt was made to isolate the particular components of the game that may have been most influential in terminating classroom disruption. Barrish et al. had indicated that mechanisms regarding peer competition, group consequences versus individual consequences, and the variables relating to increased significance of winning might all be critical components of the game. However, this detailed analysis was left to "future research." In 1973 the future research arrived by way of Harris and Sherman, who analyzed many of these same variables. Specifically, the consequences of winning the game, criteria for winning, feedback to the class, dividing the class into teams, and the effects of the game on academic performance were all studied. Thus two of the three variables that had been recommended by Barrish et al. were analyzed. Furthermore, the role of feedback in this process, as originally investigated by Medland and Stachnik (1972), was reexamined.

Harris and Sherman (1973) used essentially the same dependent variables as did Barrish et al. These consisted of classroom disruptions in the form of talking-out and out-of-seat behaviors and general inappropriate off-task responses.

Students from a broad spectrum of elementary education served as subjects. The details can best be described by the authors:

> Children within two classrooms, a fifth grade and a sixth grade, were observed. In the fifth-grade classroom, which contained 22 children, daily observations were initially taken during two 30-min math periods. Later in the study, daily observations were also taken during 30-min science and spelling periods, and a reading period, which varied in length from 60 to 100 minutes. In the sixth-grade classroom, which contained 28 children, daily observations were taken during one 30-min math period and one 30-min English period. Typically, children in both classrooms received individual assignments at which they worked the observation periods. (Harris & Sherman, 1973, p. 406)

As in most variations of the Good Behavior Game, each class was evenly divided into opposing teams. The object of the game was as in previous studies. A list of classroom rules was both described by the teachers and put on the classroom boards. It was made clear that individuals who violated these rules would cause their respective teams to get marks. The team with the fewest marks would win. However, if the fifth-grade team made less than five total marks per period, they would win regardless of the other team's total. In the sixth-grade an automatic win required that no more than four marks be acquired. The total number of criterion marks doubled when the game was played during two consecutive periods. Thus both teams could win simultaneously if they both stayed below the specified ceiling. Members of the winning team(s) were permitted to leave school ten minutes early. A losing team, however, continued working on regular class assignments until the usual dismissal time.

During five sessions of baseline both forms of disruptive behavior occurred at an exceptionally high rate. Talking out was observed to occur at nearly 100 percent of the observed intervals and out-of-seat behavior averaged more than 50 percent. When the Good Behavior Game was introduced in Math II period alone, both rates fell below 15 percent. No change was seen in the Math I period, but this session was still operating according to baseline contingencies during the first five days after baseline.

This circumstance was reversed in the next five sessions. The game was played in Math I but not in Math II. Not surprisingly, disruptions tracked the experimental contingencies. Talking-out and out-of-seat behaviors resumed baseline levels in Math II and fell to less than 15 percent in Math I. When the game was instituted in both math sections for five days, the disruptions dropped below 10 percent in both groups concurrently.

The power of the game's contingencies to control student behavior was further established during the remainder of the first phase of the experiment. The game was introduced in reading, spelling, and science. This represented a total of five academic periods in which it was being played during the school day, for a total of 100 days. The game procedures were left intact during this period, and all forms of overt disruptions were virtually eliminated. The authors note that both teams won the game on 121 of the total 133 days in which these standard game conditions were in effect. Yet none of this is remarkable, since the spectacular effects of the Good Behavior Game on classroom behavior had, by this time, already been well established in the literature. The unique value of this study is the experimental analysis of the effects of various components of the game. Specifically, the effect of removing the early dismissal reinforcer was examined.

In the first phase of this investigation the game was not played in either English or math for five days. As one would expect, disruptions escalated to baseline levels. This represented about 80 percent and 75 percent of the observed intervals documented as involving talking out and about 60 percent and 45 percent out-of-seat behavior for math and English, respectively. In the next five days the game, minus the early dismissal contingency, was introduced in English but not math. With "winning" now the only consequence of good behavior, talking-out and out-of-seat disruptions dropped to about 40 percent and 25 percent in the English periods. Baseline levels of behavior continued in math, where the game was not in effect. As the authors point out, the game without the activity consequence had some positive effect but not as much as when the winning team was allowed to leave school ten minutes early.

Next the game was moved into the math period and removed from English. This caused an immediate reversal of levels of inappropriate behaviors in both classes. English sessions showed disruptiveness occurring at about 75 percent and 45 percent of the intervals, and math periods witnessed a reduction of about 50 percent and 40 percent from their former rates of talking-out and out-of-seat disruptions. This finding is somewhat consistent with the findings of the previously cited study by Medland and Stachnik (1972). The reader will recall that in that study classroom rules and a light feedback system operated independent of activity consequences. Again, it must be pointed out that this is not as substantial a reduction as had been seen when winning the game had been backed up by the more tangible consequence of early dismissal.

In the next set of experimental conditions the criterion number of marks permitted in order to be assured of the privilege of going home ten minutes early was systematically manipulated. During this phase of the study math and English periods were not contrasted. First, both periods were given a ceiling of eight marks for their respective teams in order to be assured of getting to go home early. This criterion was lowered to four marks for the next five days, returned to eight for the next five days, and finally returned to four. Both talking-out and out-of-seat behaviors varied with the stringency of the criterion. The mean daily percentage of intervals scored for talking out moved from about 10 percent to 5 percent in math and from 20 percent to 10 percent in English when the criterion was reduced from eight to four marks. When criteria were alternated between eight and four at five-day intervals, approximately the same results occurred. Out-of-seat behaviors followed the same pattern. Fairly low levels of about 10 percent talking-out and out-of-seat behaviors were seen when the criterion was eight. At a criterion of four these disruptions decreased still further to about five percent in both English and math. Approximately the same percentages were replicated when the contingencies were subsequently repeated at five-day intervals. It is apparent from these data that the teams' disruptive behavior tracked the contingencies. The students tended to go "as far as the law would allow" and still win the game, thereby earning permission to go home ten minutes early.

Next the effect of conspicuous visual feedback was investigated. Previously each time any member of a team performed a disruptive behavior, this transgression was made public by the teacher's placing a mark on the blackboard. In the next phase no such feedback was made available to the students.

The first five days of this condition were the same as the last five of the previous condition. Feedback was still provided. Both math and English periods had team limits of four marks to earn automatic access to early release from school. The data for this phase are roughly the same as for the previous five days. Talking-out and out-of-seat responses are both below 10 percent of the observed intervals in both classes. When the feedback was removed there was no apparent change in the frequency of these behaviors.

At this point the researchers totally removed the game from both classes. The inappropriate behaviors jumped back to baseline levels. Both classes now talked during 80 percent of the intervals of observation, and during 50 percent of those intervals at least one person was out of his or her seat. After five days of such pandemonium the researchers returned both classes to game conditions. The ceiling for automatic winning was set at four, but no form of visual feedback was provided by the teacher. That is, she simply did not keep a public tally of marks as she had in the past. Independent of feedback, the students in both periods demonstrated an almost complete reduction in disruptive behaviors.

The feedback, marks on the board, suppressed misconduct, of course, because of its systematic relation to the backup consequence of staying in school the whole day. The fact that low rates of disruptive behavior were maintained when no immediate consequence occurred suggests that the disruptive acts themselves may have become functional as conditioned punishers as they had previously been associated with marks on the board and loss of free time. Each succeeding act would have the effect of an added mark (possibly each further decreasing the probability of disruptive behavior).

Examination of the distribution of disruptive behavior across sessions when the early dismissal contingency was in effect would be informative. If the first four disruptive behaviors occurred early in the session, then only the last mark was functioning as a discriminative stimulus to avoid further disruptions. If the marks received during the contingency phase were distributed so the intervals between consecutive marks became longer as the session progressed, each mark would show increasing functional control over disruptive behavior as suggested at the end of the previous paragraph.

The somewhat surprising results of this study lead to several questions. How soon can the teacher-delivered conditioned punisher be removed? Is it necessary? If "the limit" is higher than ten or twelve disruptive behaviors, will the marks become more important, since it would be harder for the students to discriminate nearing the limit? Are the students counting the disruptive behaviors? If so, does the stated number, at each point, function as a discriminative stimulus (S^{Δ}) to avoid responding disruptively?

Next the researchers analyzed the effect of consequating the whole class as one unified group in contrast to the standard procedure of dividing the class into teams. The sixth-grade class was first returned to baseline conditions in both English and math. After the frequency of disruptive behaviors returned to baseline level, the game was reinstated with the following change. Instead of playing the game in teams, dismissal time for the whole class was made contingent on the behavior of all students. A class ceiling of eight marks for the two sessions was specified as the limit. If more than eight marks were recorded the opportunity for early dismissal was automatically lost.

During this condition disruptions approached the level that had occurred when the class had been divided into two teams. Talking-out and out-of-seat behaviors dropped back to below 10 percent in math. However, somewhat more talking was noted during the English period, where an increase of about 30 percent was recorded. This may be partially accounted for by what is sometimes referred to as a doomsday contingency. In this circumstance the experimental contingency did not permit opportunity to avoid loss of early dismissal after a specific number of violations had occurred. A class that obtained a ninth mark across the two periods had nothing more to lose in the event that additional marks were accumulated. That is, they had already lost their early dismissal privilege (doomsday) and further effort could not retrieve it.

Although data were obtained on the effect of the Good Behavior Game on academic performance, a relatively small proportion of the total intervention time was used to analyze the game's effect on this variable. In two separate fifth-grade math periods students were first returned to baseline conditions. Student performance was similar in the two periods in terms of percentage of problems correct, correct problems per minute, and incorrect problems per minute. When the game was introduced in the Math II period for five days, but not the Math I period, an obvious difference in performance resulted. Not only did disruptive behavior immediately terminate in the Math II period, but concurrently the percentage of correct problems was approximately 10 percent higher, the number of incorrect problems per minute decreased by comparison to Math I, where classroom disruptions were still high, and the number of correct problems per minute stayed about the same. As the game was removed from Math II and instated in the Math I period for five days, a reversal of effects was seen. Disruptions escalated in Math II, whereas Math I was now about 8 percent superior in terms of percentage correct and also showed a comparative reduction in the number of incorrect problems per minute. However, correct problems per minute stayed constant throughout all conditions of this phase of the experiment. As the authors note:

> In the present study, reduction of disruptive behavior seemed to produce somewhat higher accuracy. However, the improved accuracy was a result of a lower rate of incorrectly answered problems, rather than a higher rate of correctly answered problems. Thus, the combined results of previous studies and the present one have not indicated a consistent or strong relationship between performance on academic materials and attention, study, and disruption behaviors. (Harris & Sherman, 1973, p. 416)

This was a particularly exhaustive and important study on group contingencies within the Good Behavior Game. Therefore, some recapitulation is probably in order. Generally it can be said that many components of the game were found to have an effect on behavior somewhat independent of the others. The limit set on the number of marks allowed seems to be a rather important variable. As the limit increases and decreases, so does the number of classroom disruptions. Conspicuous visual feedback may be unnecessary and has been shown to be so after the contingency between behavior and winning (by itself or as a means of earning early dismissal) has been established and when the limit can be easily tracked by students. Concrete consequences for winning each game may not always be necessary. In fact, data seem to indicate that the competition factor alone may be sufficient to induce students to play the game with some level of enthusiasm. Dividing the class into competing teams is also somewhat questionable. Students appear to be as well behaved when consequated as a class as when competing against one another on two teams. However, one element of this class contingency must be considered. It is likely that if the class, as a unit, obtains a number of marks in excess of the ceiling that allows access to the group reinforcer, all further effects of the game are negated for the day. That is, the "doomsday" effect comes into play; the students have nothing to lose by additional misbehaving.

It would appear that the Good Behavior Game provides teachers and students with a quieter and less distracting classroom. In such an environment some students will tend to perform slightly better academically. However, the contingencies in this classroom management program have not been directed toward positive consequences for improved academic performance. Therefore, one should not expect that students in such a program would spontaneously show significant academic improvement.

CONCERNS AND COMPARISONS OF THE GAME'S EFFECTS

By the mid–1970s the Good Behavior Game was beginning to gain some measure of popularity in many school districts. Warner, Miller, and Cohen (1977) noted that the game had given rise to certain ethical and professional questions. Was the game so effective and easy to use that teachers might inadvertently use the procedure at the expense of the students' welfare? They questioned whether the use of social competition in the game might have deleterious effects on peer relationships. However, this issue was never tested in their experimental procedures.

In their briefly described study, comparisons were made in a counterbalance design using two fourth-grade classes and two fifth-grade classes, each of which contained twenty-five students. They compared two methods of classroom management: the Good Behavior Game and the teacher attention method. Unfortunately the particular procedures involved in the implementation of the teacher attention method were not adequately described. Presumably this technique involves the teacher providing special social reinforcement for on-task behavior. Although both methods were found to be effective, results of the study indicated that the Good Behavior Game was easier to implement and more satisfying to the teachers and provided better control of the class than the teacher attention method.

Although no evidence was provided for their speculations, the authors suggested that peer pressure and potential resentment might be eliminated if classroom rules were stated positively. They also suggested, without supportive data, that long-term positive effects might be enhanced if the Good Behavior Game were gradually faded out in favor of the teacher attention method.

IN THE LIBRARY

As noted by the concluding speculations of the study above, there is probably no good reason classroom rules could not be stated positively as well as negatively. It is quite conceivable that positive phraseology might even give some students a better "feeling" about playing the Good Behavior Game. On the other hand, there had been no real evidence, as of 1981, that such terminology makes a great deal of difference either way. In a study conducted by Fishbein and Wasik (1981) the use of positive rules became a significant component of their version of the Good Behavior Game in a library setting.

Using a class of twenty-five fourth-grade elementary students who had been referred to the school psychologist by the librarian as displaying intolerable rates of noise and disruption, these authors devised a series of experimental reversals of contingencies in a multiple-baseline design. Data were collected every Wednesday, for thirteen weeks, in both the library and in a regular education comparison class. No form of intervention was ever performed during the comparison class time. Target behaviors in this study included rates of on-task (task-relevant behaviors), off-task (irrelevant behaviors), and disruptive behaviors (disturbing other students). Data were obtained by having the observers scan the classroom and library at the end of two-minute intervals.

Baseline was conducted during the first four sessions in these environments, and it was found that on-task behavior averaged 73 percent, off-task averaged 9 percent, and disruptive behavior averaged 18 percent in the library. The comparison class demonstrated similar levels of on-task, off-task and disruptive behaviors during this time.

When intervention was initiated in the library setting for three sessions, a number of innovative tactics were used. Not only were the rules stated positively in this game, but they were at least partially conceived and decided on by the class. Furthermore, rather than giving marks (associated with the loss of privilege) for disruptive behavior (punishment procedure), points were given contingent on positive, on-task behavior (reinforcement procedure). At various times during the library period the librarian would take note of the activity of the members of both teams. If the respective members were properly engaged in library-related activities, she would award members a team point. If some member of a team was not obeying the rules, no point would be awarded. In order to win the game it was necessary for a team to obtain at least three out of four possible points. Of course, if both teams received this number, then both teams won concurrently. Winning teams obtained access to reinforcement in the regular education classroom, where during the last ten minutes of the afternoon, winners were permitted either to work on a special art project or to listen to a story read by their regular classroom teacher.

The effect of this intervention was immediate and conspicuous. The percentage of on-task behavior increased by an average of 21 percent over baseline data. Off task decreased by 5.7 percent and disruptive behaviors dropped by 16 percent. The authors note some slight simultaneous improvement in the regular classroom, but this is not apparent from a casual inspection of their graphs.

Subsequently, in order to gauge the effect of the regular classroom teacher's reinforcement strength, the game was played without the previous reinforcement procedure for a period of two weeks, although the librarian did verbally commend winners of the day's game during this time. This verbal reinforcement procedure was not as effective without the consequence provided by the regular education teacher. In this condition all target behavior quickly resumed baseline levels in both classes. The authors note that the librarian was somewhat disconcerted by this regression and apparently requested that the reinforcment component be reinstated.

When the regular classroom teacher resumed her role as provider of consequences, the game once again became an effective means of improving library behavior. All target behaviors resumed the previous levels obtained during the initial intervention. The authors indicate a concurrent, but limited, improvement in the comparison class setting. They suggest that even though this procedure was used only in the library, it may have positively affected the student's behavior in other locations.

In conclusion the authors state:

> Although not experimentally tested, it is possible that student involvement in designing rules and stating rules in positive terms may provide additional benefits when compared to standard game procedures. Benefits may include increased student motivation to behave appropriately, less resentment among class members, and increased teacher attention for positive behavior. Improvement in the comparison setting may have been influenced by the use of the classroom teacher in delivering reinforcers, but the effect of this procedure was not empirically evaluated. (Fishbein & Wasik, 1981, p. 93)

In point of fact, this study did not compare any of the variables above with standard game procedures. None of the arrangements regarding positively stated rules, rules that were devised by the class members, and the administering of points based on good behavior were compared or contrasted with the traditional, standard game procedures. The data from this study do not suggest that the new procedures produced better effects than standard game procedures. Thus any speculations regarding improved effects of these ''positive'' procedures are essentially gratuitous. However, the fact that these slightly altered procedures do provide positive effects leads to an important question for future research. It would be interesting and important to know whether positive versus negative rules, class-determined versus teacher-determined rules, and the giving of points for good behaviors versus the giving of marks for inappropriate behaviors produced significantly different results. Perhaps these variables will be contrasted at some point in future research.

THE GAME'S EFFECTS ON STUDENTS FROM ANOTHER CULTURE

The game was next investigated in terms of its effects on students from another culture; and it was performed in total disregard of any of the more positively oriented variables previously described by Fishbein and Wasik (1981). But the game, even with its traditionally competitive and somewhat negative feature of giving marks for off-task and/or disruptive behavior, was seen by the authors as a positive intervention strategy when compared with the typical classroom management procedures used in a developing country.

The following study was conducted in order to test the social validity of behavioral classroom techniques. Although few people would doubt that the results of behavioral experiments derived from strict laboratory conditions are generalizable to all parts of the world, there has long been the suspicion that applied behavioral strategies and techniques may not be applicable to Eastern and Third World cultures (Badri, 1978; Saigh & Khan, 1982; Watts, 1973). According to the authors:

> In view of the drawbacks that have been associated with negative classroom environments (Skinner, 1968), and since a positive model of behavior management had not been field-tested in the area, the specific purpose of this investigation was to determine the efficacy and social validity of the Good Behavior Game (Barrish, Saunders, & Wolf, 1969) in the Sudan. (Saigh & Umar, 1983, p. 339)

The researchers made a special attempt to obtain a class of students who were representative of the mainstream Sudanese public school population. In this effort they chose a second-grade class in which disruptive behavior was similar to that of other elementary Sudanese classes. The authors indicated that 80 percent of the students' parents were totally illiterate and that seventeen of the twenty students spent approximately twelve hours per week working with their families on cotton farms. This is quite typical of many Sudanese families. But these students represent a segment of a very rural and perhaps semiprimitive culture, one that is unlikely to share the ideals and mores of mainstream America. It is important to note that up to this point in time, the Good Behavior Game had only been used with students who were very much a part of our American culture. Is it possible that the game's effectiveness had thus far been enhanced, or perhaps mitigated, by idiosyncracies of our highly industrialized and competitive Western culture?

In order to make this study consistent with most of the previous American investigations of the Good Behavior Game, Saigh and Umar performed the experimental operations with the same time parameters and same target variables typically used. The collection of data was held to one regularly scheduled fifty-minute period, and the target variables consisted of the usual talking-out, out-of-seat, and general physical disruptions. After the experimenter interviewed Sudanese educators, parents, and each student regarding reinforcement preferences, it was determined that many of the items on the reinforcement menu might be very much the same as those originally used by Barrish et al. (1969). It was determined that such rewards as free time, victory tags, and placing of stars next to the names of winners on a "victory chart" maintained a certain level of "cross cultural utility." In addition, the authors used "letters of commendation" attesting that the students performed in an "exemplary manner." Such letters were thought to be held in special regard by the families of the Sudanese students.

The authors of this study took special care not to contaminate dependent variables by (a) the conspicuous presence of observers and (b) selection bias. In order to allow the students to adapt to the presence of the observers, before the collection of baseline data the observers sat unobtrusively in the fifty-minute class for a period of one week. Teams A and B were arbitrarily determined so as to provide five boys and five girls on each team. Statistical tests confirmed that frequencies of disruptions by the two teams, before the manipulation of independent variables, were similar, which added to the internal validity of the study.

During six sessions of baseline the teacher maintained her usual methods of classroom control, primarily scoldings and spankings. In addition, each day she posted and read aloud a list of undesirable, prohibited behaviors. The occurrence of these target behaviors were recorded at thirty-second intervals throughout the course of the study. Baseline intervals of aggression, seat leaving, and talking out averaged 8.5 percent, 9.6 percent, and 12 percent respectively.

The teacher instated the contingencies of the Good Behavior Game for the next six sessions. She told the class that they were to be divided into teams and that students who violated classroom rules would earn marks against their teams. The team with the fewest number of marks would win daily and weekly prizes. Daily winners received victory tags and stars next to their names on the victory chart. In addition they obtained a full thirty minutes of free time at the end of daily recess during which they were free to engage in such activities as sports, stories, or art activities. Weekly winners, those teams with twenty-five or fewer marks, received letters of commendation to parents. However, the authors do not describe any contingencies whereby both teams could have concurrently won the game on the same day. This is slightly inconsistent with the manner in which the game is usually played. Nevertheless, with the implementation of the Good Behavior Game the usual transitions in student behavior became immediately apparent. Intervals during which aggression, out-of-seat behavior, and talking out occurred dropped to 3.5 percent, 1.7 percent, and 4.7 percent, respectively.

The entire game, rather than just the reinforcement contingencies, was removed during the next six sessions. Data show a jump to 6.6 percent for aggression, 8.7 percent for seat leaving, and 9.4 percent for talking out. These target variables were near the level as had occurred during the initial baseline period.

When the game was reinstated from the remaining six sessions the target variables all dropped back to the low levels previously seen during the first administration of the game. Aggression, seat leaving, and talking out averaged 1.9 percent, 4.7 percent, and 2.9 percent, in that order. It was noted by the authors that a terminating series of statistical tests showed no significant differences between the target behaviors of male and female subjects. Team A won on seven days and team B won on five days, but both teams received letters of commendation to their parents at the end of each week during which the game was played.

The authors conclude that "it is felt that a considerable degree of support for the cross-cultural utility of the game was established'' (Saigh & Umar, 1983, p. 343). In addition, personal interviews with parents, principals, and participants indicated that all were very much impressed and pleased with the results of the experiment. The authors note that although the results of this experiment may not be surprising to American psychologists, they may have a dramatic impact on the educational foundations in the developing African culture where behavioral technology is neither widely understood nor appreciated.

REINFORCEMENT, RESPONSE COST, AND COMBINATIONS OF BOTH

There has long been the question as to whether it is more effective to remove a reinforcer from a student when he or she demonstrates inappropriate behavior (response cost, a punishment procedure), or to wait until the student performs the correct behavior and then provide a desirable consequence (reinforcement procedure). Both contingencies may aim at the same topography, but the behavior being focused on is different. Because that issue has been brought up in this chapter the following study will be here reported.

Hundert (1976) compared the two kinds of contingencies with six elementary school children, using a simple ABA design. Subjects were treated individually in a counterbalanced sequence in which (a) token reinforcement was provided for attending and correct arithmetic performance, (b) response cost was administered by removal of tokens for off-task and arithmetic performance below a preset criterion, and (c) a combination of both contingencies was used. Although subjects jumped from 29 percent on task and 6.4 correct problems during baseline to 85 percent on task and 11.4 correct problems during training, there were no detectable differences among the various procedural contingencies. However, because this investigation did not take into account the effects of group-oriented contingencies on student competition and peer pressure to achieve, one cannot generalize the results of such positive and negative systems to group programs such as the Good Behavior Game.

GROUP-ORIENTED CONTINGENCIES UNDER THE CONTROL OF CLOCK-LIGHT FEEDBACK

Another study that investigated the separate effects of classroom rules, rules in conjunction with feedback, and a package consisting of rules + feedback + consequences for adhering to classroom rules was conducted by Greenwood, Hops, Delquadri, and Guild (1974). This study also investigated a gradually lengthened postponement of reinforcement, and the use of teacher praise as part of the treatment package.

Three teachers and their respective first- (A), second- (B), and third- (C) grade classes of twenty-eight, twenty, and twenty students participated. Intervention was conducted in upper- and lower-level reading groups and during math period.

Implementation of this group-oriented contingency system differs from most with regard to the feedback apparatus that monitored moment by moment on-task behavior. This mechanism is described by the authors as a "modified version (Cobb & Hops, 1973) of Packard's (1970) clock-light apparatus" (Greenwood et al., 1974, p. 415). Because much of the research hinges on the use of this device a further description is warranted:

> The present model consisted of an ordinary nightstand alarm clock (Westclox, 115 V ac, 60 cy) and a 15-W white light connected in a series circuit with a hand-held remote switch. The white light was screwed into a plastic base and placed in a section of the room visible to the entire classroom. The switch was connected to the apparatus via a 15-ft cord allowing teacher movement about the room. (Greenwood et al., 1974, p. 415)

This clock was used throughout four of the five phases of the experiment to determine the proportion of time the students in the three classes spent behaving appropriately. At the beginning of a session the correct time was noted on the board and the clock was set at 0. As soon as all members of the class were properly engaged in academic activity the clock (and a light) were activated. If one or more members of the class became disruptive, off task, or inappropriate in any fashion, the clock and the light were switched off by the teacher. The clock was reactivated as soon as all students resumed appropriate behavior. End-of-session time was noted on the board. Thus, after each session, it was easy to calculate the proportion of time in which the whole class was behaving appropriately by dividing the amount of time shown on the clock by the total time for the session and then multiplying by 100. This percentage score was graphed on a daily basis and used as one of the dependent variables.

Teacher-delivered social consequences constituted the other dependent variable. Positive teacher social consequences were scored as correct if they occurred within five seconds of a student's behavior and were correctly related to the student's actions. Such teacher responses as smiling, touching, and talking to the students in a nice way were all counted as positive if they were contingent on appropriate student behavior. Incorrect teacher social consequences occurred when either the teacher praised inappropriate behavior or indulged in any negative response (reprimands, threats, etc.) toward one or more students irrespective of whether the students were behaving poorly.

Experimental sessions occurred during upper- and lower-level reading periods and the math period in all three classes. The treatments were initiated with a two-day delay between classes in a multiple-baseline design. This experiment involved a total of approximately thirty consecutive experimental sessions with a follow-up occurring about three weeks after the last session.

Baseline lasted from seven to twelve sessions, depending on the length of the baseline period scheduled for each class. During this phase the clock-light was placed on the classroom wall, but students were not told its purpose. As previously described, teachers used the apparatus to record the percentage of appropriate behavior. Levels of appropriate behavior were calculated at 47.0 percent, 60.1 percent, and 29.7 percent for classes A, B, and C, respectively.

The first treatment phase lasted for six sessions and primarily consisted of the teacher posting and reading classroom rules. In addition, an experimental consultant modeled the correct rule-following behavior and then had the class members demonstrate following the rules appropriately. The consultant spent the remainder of that period informing students as to whether they were correctly following the rules. The authors note that this introduction of classroom rules produced no significant changes in appropriate behaviors in any of the three classes. One class actually displayed a slight drop in the percentage of targeted behaviors.

During the next nine to ten sessions rules + feedback were introduced as a joint experimental manipulation. Feedback was provided by the clock-light and bar graphs placed on the board. The teacher explained the relationship between the clock-light and the students' following of the classroom rules for proper conduct. She indicated that so long as all members of the class were academically engaged or otherwise conducting themselves appropriately, the clock and light would remain on. If, however, any student violated a rule, the light and clock would be terminated until they were again in compliance with the class. At the end of the period the teacher graphed, on the board, the percentage of appropriate behavior that had been timed for that period. In this phase, classroom B improved to a level slightly above baseline, the other two classes displayed no demonstrable changes in the average percentage of target behaviors.

In the next thirty-four to thirty-six sessions the complete package, consisting of rules + feedback + group and individual consequences, was implemented. This fairly complex arrangement involved both the coaching of teachers and the use of consequences for group behavior.

Teachers were individually instructed and given feedback from a consultant as to the proper method of providing social reinforcement to students who were on task. Furthermore, teachers allowed class members to vote for particular reinforcing activities (free time, games, etc.) to be contingent on the class surpassing its previous average level of appropriate behavior. These reinforcers became immediately available after each session was over. The students were encouraged to applaud themselves when they succeeded in reaching the criterion percentage, and the teacher praised their achievement. On occasions when the class failed to reach criterion, the teacher announced their obtained percentage of group on-task behavior, and moved to the next scheduled activity.

The authors arranged for a gradual increase in the criterion for earning the activities the students chose, as they describe below:

> The reinforcement schedule was changed to establish maintenance of the acquired behaviors in the following ways. First, the scores in the reading periods I and II were combined, requiring an overall score of 80 % to meet the criterion for the entire class. Thus, reading was now tallied and reported by the teacher as a single session. Secondly,

> a delay in the group consequence was introduced. Each class was now required to meet the criterion (80%) for two of the next three consecutive sessions (alternating mathematics and combined reading session). When this was achieved, the criterion increased systematically in a step-by-step fashion. As success was achieved at each level, the criterion shifted upwards from three of four consecutive sessions at 80%, then four of six, six of eight, eight of 10, until a maximum of 10 of 12 sessions delay in the group consequence was attained. (Greenwood et al., 1974, p. 419)

The authors point out that when a class did not meet the preset criterion, they were recycled back to a lower level. This whole process produced a gradual thinning of the reinforcement schedule with the purpose of enabling the student to learn to behave appropriately independent of all tangible reinforcement.

It is precisely at this point in the experimental manipulations that a transition in target behaviors became apparent. Classrooms A, B, and C jumped to 81.2 percent, 84.6 percent, and 74.2 percent, respectively, and maintained a stable steady state for the last twenty-five sessions. In a follow-up of four sessions, which occurred three weeks later, these levels maintained at 86.3 percent, 76.5 percent, and 75.0 percent. These high levels were obtained despite the fact that all experimental materials, including the clock-light, rules, and contingent tangible reinforcers, had been removed from the classroom. During this phase the teachers' primary intervention strategy was the simple use of contingent verbal praise for students who displayed academic achievement and/or who demonstrated academic engagement or appropriate conduct. The program, with all experimental manipulations and apparatus, had been successfully faded while the students continued to benefit from the intervention.

From baseline through rules and rules + feedback all three teachers maintained relatively high rates of incorrect social contact and low rate of correct social contact. However, when the total package, which included rules + feedback + group and individual consequences, was presented, there was an almost immediate change in the percentage of appropriate classroom behavior. When this step was initiated, praise rates jumped from three to eighty times higher. Concurrently, incorrect teacher social contact was almost totally eliminated during the package intervention phase.

Before the package intervention system, teachers were given instructions on how to increase their rates of individual and group praise. Furthermore, the teachers themselves were praised for accomplishing this. Two of the three teachers maintained high rates of correct social consequences, and all three continued to abstain from indulging in incorrect social consequences, even during the follow-up. As the authors state, "comparing teacher social consequences during the rules plus feedback condition to the entire package condition suggested that the teachers' use of correct consequences was under consultant instructional and reinforcement control" (Greenwood et al., 1974, p. 422).

The authors point out that these results concur with those of Madsen, Becker, and Thomas (1968) and O'Leary, Becker, Evans, and Saudergas (1969) in that classroom rules without consistent social consequences for violation of or compliance with rules are an insufficient means of controlling classroom behavior.

CONTROL OF "CLASSROOM ATTENTION"

In many of the previous studies that have investigated the effects of group-oriented contingent reinforcement the dependent variables have typically consisted of frequencies of inappropriate behaviors that interfere with classroom productivity. Dependent variables have most often been described as disruptive behaviors, off-task behaviors, talking-out behaviors, and out-of-seat behaviors. In a study conducted by Packard (1970) the emphasis was on the more positive, if not easily documented, target behavior of classroom attention. Packard paraphrases Skinner (1968), noting that "attending is one of several behaviors traditionally identified with thinking, but technically precurrent to it, which must be analyzed and taught as such" (Packard, 1970, p. 27).

A definition of attention was necessarily confined to student topographies These included correct body positioning relative to the academic task, absence of inappropriate vocalizations, and following teacher instructions. Although these behaviors were being adequately performed by all students, classroom attention was considered to be maintained. The method by which classroom attention was recorded bears some resemblance to the manner in which Greenwood et al. (1974) measured appropriate conduct:

> The observations and recording were carried out simultaneously by the teacher and the experimenter. The teacher used a stopwatch (during baseline) or a timer-light device. A Cramer 1/100-sec timer, housed in a 3 in. by 5 in. (7.5 by 12.5 cm) metal box, with a silent, single-throw mercury switch, was on the teacher's desk, a red light (40 w) on a flat 3 in. by 3. in. (7.5 by 7.5) wooden stand was placed either on the teacher's desk or on a portable stand, but always positioned to be prominent to the students. The timer was connected to a wall socket and the light to the timer. When the switch was flipped up, the timer began running and the light went out; when the switch was flipped down, the timer stopped (without resetting) and the light went on. The experimenter sat to the side, near the front of the room with a panel of four Cramer 1/100-sec. timers, each operated by a silent, single-throw mercury switch. (Packard, 1970, p. 15)

The teacher activated the timing mechanism only when all students were attending; in the event that one or more students failed to meet the criteria for attending, the teacher switched off the timer and the red light was illuminated. Although the whole class was measured and consequated by the teacher, only four randomly selected students within the four elementary classrooms served as primary subjects in this standard reversal-of-treatments design. Interventions occurred during thirty minutes (daily) of introduction to reading in kindergarten, thirty minutes (three days a week) of reading-group period in third grade, fifty minutes (three days a week) of reading in fifth grade, and fifty minutes (3 days a week) of social studies in sixth grade.

Six experimental conditions were instituted across thirty-two consecutive school days. During the first five days of baseline observations the teachers and experimenter both used a stopwatch to calculate attending behaviors. The teachers measured their whole class as a unit. Concurrently, the experimenter observed and recorded only the four randomly selected students in each class. During this baseline period the classes were instructed in the exact same format as had existed before the experimenter's arrival. All four classes primary subjects demonstrated considerable variability in their daily attending. However, classroom attention as recorded by the teachers and the attending behavior of the four primary subjects in each class as recorded by the experimenter were highly correlated. During the first five days all four classes demonstrated amazingly low levels of on-task behavior. Percentages averaged between 0 percent and about 35 percent for the class as a whole. The four primary subjects in each class demonstrated much greater variability but generally followed the same trend toward erratic and low levels of attending to academic tasks and teacher instructions. When the timer-light apparatus was introduced during the next two sessions, but not explained to the class, no systematic changes in target behaviors occurred.

At the beginning of the next phase (instructions only) the teachers provided their classes with an explanation as to the purpose and operations of the clock-light device. Teachers described the classroom behaviors that would keep the timer on and the light off. Apparently only the fifth-grade class was impressed with this mechanism. For a time this class showed a significant improvement in attending. However, this improvement was short-lived, and by the fifth session of this phase their level of attending had declined to baseline level.

In the following treatment phase of the experiment (reinforcement 1) reinforcement procedures were introduced in all four classes. Reinforcement in kindergarten was primarily related to access to various free-time activities. In grades three, five, and six points were provided that were later exchanged for normally unavailable privileges. These were described as gaining access to a private study booth or typewriter, helping the teacher, or permission to play with various games or art activities.

An important variation in this reinforcement menu was the development of the list of reinforcing activities and their various point costs by the students themselves. Also important to note is that although the classes received points or access to free time as a group, the distribution of points was administered individually. In fifth and sixth grade three points per student were provided. In third grade tokens were used initially but later changed to points. In kindergarten direct access to play was made available. The specific manner in which criteria for access to backup activities were established is best explained by the author:

This criterion also varied from class to class, since it was established at a slightly higher value than the performance that each class had previously demonstrated during the baselines and Instructions Only phases. A bonus of two extra points or tokens (or, for the kindergarten, 5 min extra of activity) was contingent on the class exceeding the criterion by 5% or more. These two criterion numbers for normative and bonus performance were written on the board at the beginning of each reinforcement session. (Packard, 1970, p. 18)

The teacher then provided the class with feedback by writing the percentage of total points and resulting consequences on the board. Upon the class reaching the specified percentage in three prior sessions, the criterion for succeeding sessions was raised by five percent. Packard also notes that when criteria were exceeded by more than five percent, the following session's requirements were raised to the nearest five percent. Thus a gradual shaping process was constantly in effect.

In most classes points were not administered immediately; distribution was typically accomplished at the end of the day. However, the students were immediately told whether or not they had reached the criterion for that day. In contrast, kindergarten children usually were given access to free play as soon as possible after reaching the day's goal. All individually measured students in all four classes quickly accelerated attention to levels between 90 percent and 100 percent. Two of the classes averaged around 70 percent and two classes attended at approximately 80 percent during this first phase in which a reinforcement procedure was used. This is a most impressive transition from baseline and instructions only phases that averaged between 0 percent and 35 percent. The author describes the immediate beneficial effects of this intervention as "fairly constant between classes and for all individual children" (Packard, 1970, p. 23).

Fifth-grade and sixth-grade classes were subjected to a seven- and five-day reversal, respectively. Teachers in both classes simply told their students that they would no longer receive points for keeping the clock running and light off. They also indicated that they expected students to behave in the appropriate manner that they had demonstrated while being rewarded for attending. As is often the case, instructions as to how to behave appropriately, independent of contingent consequences, had little effect on behavior. Both classes demonstrated a gradual regression toward baseline levels of attention. The deceleration curves in both classes seem to indicate that before long the instruction only condition would result in classes returning to baseline levels of attending.

Without waiting out the complete regression to baseline attending, these classes were returned to the previous reinforcement schedules for the remainder of the study. With this reinstatement individually monitored students demonstrated an immediate return to the high levels seen in the first reinforcement phase (90 percent to 100 percent attending). Likewise, the teachers' data indicated that both classes improved to around 80 percent attending behavior.

In kindergarten another change took place that temporarily reduced that class's group level of academic engagement. The teacher determined that the class was ready to start working in small reading groups while the rest of the class worked independently. This evidently produced some temporary disorientation in some students. The class as a whole, as well as individually monitored students, displayed a drop in attending for about five days. This proved to be only a temporary effect, however. By the sixth session these students were all operating at their previous high levels of attending (90 percent to 100 percent for the four primary subjects and at about 70 percent for the teacher's observations of the class as a whole).

It is quite clear from the discrepancies above that the teachers' ongoing measurement of classroom attending behavior was not perfectly consistent with the observations made by the experimenter. However, the experimenter restricted his observations and recordings to four primary subjects within each class. Not all members of the class would necessarily be expected to act exactly the same as any particular four students. In general, however, there was a consistent and strong correlation (averaging about .95) between the teacher recordings and those of the experimenter. Furthermore, it is apparent that the teachers' determinations as to when students were adequately attending to task related closely enough to the students' actual behavior to allow accurate differential reinforcement and punishment by means of the timer and red light. The authors thus determined that teachers' assessments served as adequate and reliable indices to allow them to control behavior with the clock-light apparatus.

PROCEDURAL VARIATIONS IN GROUP CONTINGENCIES

Many procedural variations of group-oriented contingencies have been examined in the series of studies reported above. The final study combines many of the procedures and examines their effects in a single experiment. Following Litow and Pumroy's (1975) description of procedural variations that are possible in group-oriented contingency systems, Speltz, Shimamura, and McReynolds (1982) conducted an experiment that compared and contrasted the academic and social effects of many of these variations.

Four girls and eight boys (seven to ten years old) from a special elementary learning disabled class served as subjects. The twelve subjects were divided into four groups of three. Based on exceptionally low performance, one subject in each of these groups was selected as a target subject. After two phases of baseline four treatment conditions were presented to each group in a random sequence in a Latin square design (Fisher & Yates, 1955).

During the first baseline phase (eight days) all subjects stayed in their own classrooms and worked on math worksheets. The four target students all performed at levels approximating ten to twenty-five correct math problems per work period. The number of positive social interactions between members of the groups and the number of positive (or even neutral) social interactions aimed at target students remained low (less than 10 percent) during this time. In the second baseline phase (four days) students were divided into their respective groups and placed in a separate experimental classroom where they worked in groups of three (one target and two others) at small tables. The number of correct math problems and social interactions performed during these ten-minute periods remained consistent with the first baseline sessions.

Subsequently a Latin squares design selection of group-oriented procedural variations was initiated. In what Speltz et al. (1982) refer to as the *individualized contingency*, which lasted for six days, the contingencies were the same as those Litow and Pumroy (1975) described as an independent group-oriented contingency system; that is, each student simply received 1 point for each correctly solved problem on his or her worksheet. No student's earnings were affected by the performance of members of their group. Teachers and experimenters left the room during the ten-minute work sessions. However, student behaviors were monitored and later analyzed by means of an unobtrusive videotape.

Points for correctly solved problems were backed up by items from a menu of privileges, games, and unique activities to be selected and exchanged on Friday afternoons. Three of our target students within each group demonstrated a 20 percent to 30 percent improvement in the number of correctly solved problems with the implementation of this contingency between behavior and consequences. However, no consistent improvement over baseline can be seen in the graphs depicting group social interaction or social interactions directed at the target subjects within each group.

A different phase of the experiment, called the *all-member group contingency* (six days) is similar to Litow and Pumroy's (1975) interdependent group-oriented contingency. This phase actually provided for a variation of this procedure in which the "students received points for average number of correctly completed problems in the group during the work session" (Speltz et al., 1982, p. 536). The total correctly solved problems during the ten-minute period were divided by the number of students in the class. Each student received a share of the average number of points acquired by the group. In terms of both group and individually targeted student productivity and social interaction, the effects of this arrangement did not differ strikingly from the effects of the *individualized contingency*.

The *unidentified responder group contingency* (six days) can be exactly paralleled with a second variation of the interdependent group-oriented contingency described by Litow and Pumroy (1975). This contingency stipulated that the number of points provided to the group would be determined by the number of accurately completed problems of a randomly selected student. Again, there was no significant group or individual trend associated with the implementation of this system. However, all of the procedures above showed significant improvements in targeted behavior over both baseline observations. Yet none of the graphs of the procedural variations described thus far show any systematic or group variations among themselves in terms of the number of problems completed or improved social interactions, and no statistically significant effects for any of these contingencies were found.

However, one procedural variation, *the identified responder group contingency* (six days), did produce a substantial increase in two of the four targeted subjects' academic completions as well as the number of positive group social interactions and positive social interactions directed toward the targeted subjects in each group. This procedure was essentially the same as Litow and Pumroy's version of a dependent group-oriented contingency system. Here the identified target students were publicly responsible for the acquisition of points for the entire group. The contingency between the behavior of one student and points for the group clearly produced social interactions often referred to as peer pressure. The authors offer some important observations regarding this particular procedural variation:

Among the more efficient group contingencies, there is much to recommend the use of the identified responder procedure when low-performing students are the targets of intervention. Two of the three lowest performing students in the class during the baseline (Students 6 and 12) achieved their highest average performance during the identified responder contingency. Another low-scoring target student (Student 9) also performed at a relatively high level during this procedure. Target students rated identified responder contingency highest in terms of acceptability and , in three of four student groups, this procedure produced higher levels of positive social interaction than the other contingencies. (Speltz et al., 1982, pp. 542–543)

The authors close by noting that some investigators have expressed concerns regarding potential emotional/behavioral problems resulting from strong peer pressures when group contingencies are used in classrooms. Seemingly the most potentially hazardous among all procedural variations would be the identified responder contingency (or dependent group-oriented contingency system), in which one child bears the burden of acquiring reinforcement for the whole group. The authors note that in this study, the subjects were unaware that their behavior was being recorded and that no increase in negative social interactions appeared in the various contingency conditions. In fact, even during the identified responder contingency "not a single instance of negative behavior was directed at these children" (Speltz et al., 1982, p. 543). They also point out that all children, in all four groups, performed at their highest academic levels when operating under the influence of one or another of the group contingencies as opposed to the individualized contingency (independent group-oriented contingency system). This is, according to the authors, a most important finding when one considers the response cost to teachers when they operate according to demands inherent in individualized contingencies.

REFERENCES

Andrews, H. B. (1970). The effects of group contingent reinforcement on student behavior. Unpublished doctoral dissertation, University of Tennessee.

Badri, M. B. (1978). *The dilemma of Muslim psychologist*. London: Prentice-Hall.

Barrish, H. H., Saunders, M., & Wolf, M. M. (1969). Good behavior game: Effects of individual contingencies for group consequences on disruptive behavior in a classroom. *Journal of Applied Behavior Analysis, 2,* 119–124.

Cobb, J. A., & Hops, H. (1973). Effects of academic survival skill training on low achieving first graders. *Journal of Educational Research, 67*, 108–113.

Coleman, R. (1970). A conditioning technique applicable to elementary school classrooms. *Journal of Applied Behavior Analysis, 3*, 293–297.

Drabman, R., Spitalnik, R., & Spitalnik, K. (1974). Sociometric and disruptive behavior as a function of four types of token reinforcement programs. *Journal of Applied Behavior Analysis, 7*, 93–101.

Fishbein, J. E., & Wasik, B. H. (1981). Effect of the good behavior game on disruptive library behavior. *Journal of Applied Behavior Analysis, 14*, 89–93.

Fisher, R., & Yates, F. (1955). *Statistical tables for biological, agricultural and medical research*. Edinburgh: Oliver & Boyd.

Greenwood, C. R., Hops, H., Delquadri, J., & Guild, J. (1974). Group contingencies for group consequences in classroom management: A further analysis. *Journal of Applied Behavior Analysis, 7,* 413–425.

Hall, R. V., Panyan, M., Rabon, D., & Broden, M. (1968). Instructing beginning teachers in reinforcement procedures which improve classroom control. *Journal of Applied Behavior Analysis, 1,* 315–322.

Hamblin, R. L., Hathaway, C., & Wodarski, J. S. (1971). Group contingencies, peer tutoring and accelerating academic achievement. In E. A. Ramp & B. L. Hopkins (Eds.), *A new direction for education: Behavior analysis* (Vol. 1, pp. 41–53). Lawrence: University of Kansas.

Harris, V. W., & Sherman, J. A. (1973). Use and analysis of the "Good Behavior Game" to reduce disruptive classroom behavior. *Journal of Applied Behavior Analysis, 6,* 405–417.

Hundert, J. (1976). The effectiveness of reinforcement, response cost, and mixed programs on classroom behaviors. *Journal of Applied Behavior Analysis, 9,* 107.

Litow, L., & Pumroy, D. K. (1975). A brief review of classroom group-oriented contingencies. *Journal of Applied Behavior Analysis, 8,* 341–347.

Long, J. D., & Williams, R. L. (1973). The comparative effectiveness of group and individually contingent free time with inner-city junior high school students. *Journal of Applied Behavior Analysis, 6,* 465–474.

Madsen, C., Becker, W., & Thomas, D. (1968). Rules, praise, and ignoring: Elementary classroom control. *Journal of Applied Behavior Analysis, 1,* 139–150.

Medland, M. B., & Stachnik, T. J. (1972). Good-behavior game: A replication and systematic analysis. *Journal of Applied Behavior Analysis, 5,* 45–51.

O'Leary, K. D., Becker, W. C., Evans, M. B., & Saudergas, R. A. (1969). A token reinforcement program in the public school: A replication and systematic analysis. *Journal of Applied Behavior Analysis, 2,* 3–13.

Packard, R. G. (1970). The control of "classroom attention": A group contingency for complex behavior. *Journal of Applied Behavior Analysis, 3,* 13–28.

Saigh, P. A. & Khan, S. (1982). Token reinforcement in a Pakistani classroom. *Journal of Social Psychology, 118,* 11–16.

Saigh, P.A., & Umar, A. M. (1983). The effects of a good behavior game on the disruptive behavior of Sudanese elementary school students. *Journal of Applied Behavior Analysis, 16*, 339–344.

Skinner, B. F. (1968). *The technology of teaching*. New York: Appleton-Century-Crofts.

Speltz, M. L., Shimamura, J. W., & McReynolds, W. T. (1982). Procedural variations in group contingencies: Effects on children's academic and social behaviors. *Journal of Applied Behavior Analysis, 15,* 533–544.

Warner, S. P., Miller, F. D., & Cohen, M. W. (1977). Relative effectiveness of teacher attention and the "good behavior game" in modifying disruptive classroom behavior. *Journal of Applied Behavior Analysis, 10,* 737.

Watts, A. W. (1973). *Psychotherapy east and west*. London: Penguin.

Glossary

Avoidance: Behavior that occurs because in the past it has had the effect of precluding onset of a stimulus event. Sometimes the behavior is limited to specific situations. A student might perform on-task behaviors in the presence of a particular teacher if such work prevents scolding that otherwise occurs.

Chaining: An extended series of stimulus → response sequences in which stimuli act as cues to initiate the next response in the chain of behavior. This is maintained by the reinforcement of the last response in the sequence.

Consequence: Any change in the environment immediately after a response.

Contingency-shaped behavior: Behavior shaped and maintained by contingencies into which the behavior enters. Some behavior is reinforced, other behavior punished or extinguished. Discrimination and generalization occur when consequences occur for responding on some occasions but not on others. Behaviorial units emerge through selection by consequences and are maintained as long as consequences support them. The individual does not need to, and often doesn't, know what he is doing or why he does it.

Dependent variable: The events being studied in any science. Informally, the effects in cause/effect systems. Some dimension of behavior is always the dependent variable in behavior analysis because behavior is what is to be understood, explained, modified, or predicted.

Deprivation: The withholding or absence from the environment of stimulus events that would function as reinforcement. The duration of deprivation usually increases the reinforcing value of that which is unavailable. This is especially true of primary reinforcers. Deprivation of food, water, and sexual contact increases the likelihood of any behavior that has produced them in the past.

Differential reinforcement of other behavior (DRO): Reinforcement is contingent (dependent) on any behavior that is occurring at given intervals so long as the behavior is incompatible with an undesirable target behavior. This schedule is designed to eliminate undesirable behavior by strengthening incompatible behavior. Sometimes the incompatible behavior is required to occur for the entire interval for reinforcement to occur. For example, a student may typically go no longer than about five minutes without indulging in some inappropriate conversation with a neighbor. A DRO 5′ would require that the student remain quiet for a period of five minutes in order to obtain reinforcement. Later DRO schedules might require 8′, 10′, and, eventually, 20′ of behavior *other* than talking.

Discrimination: The selective control over responding that is acquired by particular stimulus configuration. Discrimination is a function of a specific reinforcement history. If reinforcement is provided *only* when responses occur in the presence of a particular stimulus configuration (occasion), then such occasions will reliably evoke the behavior.

Discriminative stimulus: Any stimulus event or configuration that reliably occasions (evokes) a behavioral unit because such behavior has produced reinforcement on similar occasions in the past. Students will say "here" when their name is called if they are counted as present only if they do so. The sound of their name is a discriminative stimulus for "here."

Escape: Behavior that occurs in the presence of an ongoing aversive stimulus because it has terminated that stimulation in the past. Simply put, the aversive stimulus is escaped.

Extinction procedure: The allowing of a response to occur repeatedly and "die out" by ensuring that no reinforcing consequence follows.

Extinction process: The decrease in frequency of a specific behavior that occurs when that behavior fails to produce reinforcing consequences (*see* Spontaneous recovery).

Fading: The gradual removal of conspicuous cues associated with a stimulus that is eventually left as the sole discriminative stimulus. Under most conditions the fading procedure is designed so the behavior continues to occur reliably to cues as they become increasingly subtle.

Fixed-interval schedule of reinforcement (FI): A reinforcement schedule in which a consequence is delivered after the first response that occurs after a specified interval of time, beginning with the previous reinforcement (or task beginning). In a fixed-interval schedule a specific and consistent amount of time must elapse after which the first response emitted results in reinforcement. Students on such a schedule perform in much the same manner as those on fixed-ratio schedules. They develop a time discrimination and respond infrequently just after reinforcement; however, as the time for reinforcement draws near the rate of work tends to accelerate. If a teacher sets a clock at five-minute intervals and only rewards students who are still working at the close of each interval, this would constitute a fixed-interval 5′ (FI 5′).

Fixed-ratio schedule of reinforcement (FR): A reinforcement schedule in which a consequence is delivered each time a specified number of responses have been emitted. The number of responses required is constant from one delivery to the next. For example, a child may be given a token on completion of every tenth math problem he completes. This would be referred to as a fixed-ratio 10 or FR 10. In an environment in which doing math is the only operant behavior that produces reinforcers, a certain pattern of responding would become apparent after a short while. After each token delivery the child would probably pause briefly before initiating any additional problems. This temporary delay in responding is called the post reinforcement pause. After this short rest we may see the child begin slowly and gradually to work faster and faster until completion of his next set of ten problems. At this time we would again expect to see some delay in performance after the administration of the token. After a short pause we would again see the child resume problem solving, his behavior tracing the same pattern until the token again is awarded. This is the usual pattern associated with FR schedules, although seldom is such a pattern seen in the natural environment, since other operant behavior is usually concurrently reinforceable.

Independent variable: The events manipulated to study their effects on the dependent variable. In applied behavior analysis the independent variables are usually consequences of behavior and the occasions on which behavior occurs.

Operant: Behavior that operates on or results in a change in the environment.

Primary reinforcers: Stimulus events produced by behavior that ensure survival, either of individuals or of a species. Some primary reinforcers are food, water, warmth, sexual stimulation.

Prompt: A stimulus that is added to an occasion to ensure that a response will occur on that occasion. The prompt is gradually faded out so that the occasion will come to function as a discriminative stimulus when it occurs without the prompt. If a child reading *sat* said "s" and hesitated for some time, the teacher might say "a," adding the imitative stimulus to the printed *a*. The child would repeat the "a," partially under stimulus control of *a* and partly under control of the teacher's voice. Eventually the printed *a* would function as the discriminative stimulus, as the teacher waits longer and longer to add the prompt.

Punishment procedure: Arranging the environment so that a specified behavior is followed by a stimulus event designed to suppress or decrease the frequency of that behavior.

Punishment process: A decrease in frequency of a behavior that results from a repeated previous response/consequence contingency.

Reinforcement procedure: Arranging the environment so that a specified behavior is immediately followed by a stimulus event designed to increase the frequency of that behavior on future occasions.

Reinforcement process: The increase in frequency of behavior that results from a repeated response/consequence contingency.

Response cost: A punishment procedure in which the behavior of an individual "costs" him something. A fine may be levied contingent on talking out, for example. Used in conjunction with a reinforcement procedure that provides ample reinforcement for desirable behavior, response cost often suppresses undesirable behavior. If reinforcement is too sparse, the loss of already short supplies may result in a kind of hopelessness. Too much behavior is required to get what is so easily lost.

Response generalization: The tendency toward producing responses that are variations of the response topography previously reinforced. If the reinforcement contingency respects the variations, the behavior may range in topography across time, drifting as far and only as far as reinforcement allows. Behavior that fails to meet the requirement for reinforcement will be extinguished and the drift is stopped.

Rule-governed behavior: Behavior evoked by a statement specifying the relations between responses and consequences is called "rule-governed." If such behavior is reinforced, stated rules become an important part of the environment that affects behavior. When behavior is governed by a rule, the behaver need not experience the environmental consequences named in the rule in order to learn. For example, a person who is told that smoking makes the possibility of his developing lung cancer more probable may stop smoking. Although he has never had lung cancer as a result of smoking, he may throw away his cigarettes. Sometimes such rule-governed behavior is highly desirable, but an informal survey of the effectiveness of such rules should suffice to reduce our confidence in the control they have over behavior.

Many people can recite a multitude of rules for appropriate behavior, but their behavior is not controlled by these rules. The rules that one learns must evoke responding before the individual's behavior can accurately be described as rule-governed. There are two primary points to be emphasized regarding the function of rule-governed behavior: (1) The rule describes contingencies of reinforcement that hold in the natural world—"Eating green berries will make you sick"—or the social world—"If you go into the street, you will be sent indoors for the rest of the day." Ordinarily the rule describes behavior, its antecedents and consequences. (2) The rule functions as a discriminative stimulus for the behavior described and usually will continue to function that way if the consequences are forthcoming as advertised. Once a person has learned to respond under stimulus control of a rule, the rule comes to control behavior that would seldom, if ever, evolve without it. The rule clarifies weak contingencies and provides a clear discriminative stimulus.

Satiation: The excessive availability of stimulus events that function as reinforcement. Satiation occurs when we have had too much of a "good thing." A great deal of food, drink, or sexual contact reduces the likelihood of behavior that will produce those kinds of stimulation. Primary reinforcers are especially likely to produce satiation, but sometimes conditioned reinforcers temporarily lose their value. The decreased rate of behavior that produces the reinforcer will eventually result in deprivation and the cycle will be repeated.

Schedules of reinforcement: Patterns of reinforcement delivery defined on the basis of time or number of responses between programmed deliveries.

Secondary reinforcers: Stimulus events that have acquired reinforcement value because of their association with primary reinforcers. As a function of this association, secondary reinforcers also increase the probability of behavior producing them. Typical secondary reinforcers include money, tokens, and most important in the acquisition of social behavior, praise and acknowledgment from others.

Shaping: The differential reinforcement of successive approximations of a target behavior. Behavior gradually changes as the criterion for reinforcement shifts in the direction of a new and different type of behavior, while unacceptable or previously reinforced behavior is ignored (extinguished).

Spontaneous recovery: The temporary increase in behavior that occurs some time after an extinction procedure has resulted in the elimination of the behavior. Continuation of the extinction procedure eventually results in extinction without spontaneous recovery.

Stimulus control: A consistent relation between a particular occasion and a response. Because reinforcement has followed, in the past, when the response has occurred, the occasion reliably evokes the response. As long as reinforcement occasionally occurs and motivational conditions are present (e.g., deprivation), the stimulus control relation remains quite constant.

Stimulus generalization: The tendency to respond to variations of discriminative stimuli from the original training stimuli. Less precisely, the tendency to behave in the same manner under new conditions.

Time out: The removal of a person from an environment in which his behavior can produce reinforcement. When behavior produces reinforcement in a given set of circumstances, then we speak of this removal of the person from the situation as time out from reinforcement. Note that this is not the same as putting someone into an aversive location. The location of time out is not so critical as the fact that reinforcement was available in the environment at the time the individual was removed. Under such circumstances behavior that was taking place previous to time out is less likely to occur in the future. Thus time out can be used as a means of reducing the frequency of inappropriate behaviors.

Variable: Any empirical event that can vary in some way. Behavioral events may occur or not occur; they may drag out or occur snappily; they may occur immediately after a cue is given or after a time lag. Environmental events may occur or not occur as well as vary along many dimensions. Light may be bright or dim, sound pitched high or low. Tokens may be delivered or not.

Variable-interval schedules of reinforcement (VI): A reinforcement schedule in which a consequence is delivered after the first response after some fluctuating but average length of time has elapsed. For example, in a variable-interval 5′ (VI 5′) schedule a token would be delivered after the first response occurring after varying lengths of time that approximate five-minute durations. One interval during the schedule might be only three minutes long, another might be seven minutes. The average would equal five minutes. Students reinforced on such fluctuating schedules tend to work continually, since reinforcement may occur at any moment. In the laboratory, variable-interval schedules do not produce quite as high a rate of performance as a variable ratio; however, the difference in a classroom setting may be only slight.

Variable-ratio schedule of reinforcement (VR): A reinforcement schedule in which a consequence is delivered after a continually varying number of completed tasks or responses. The exact number of required responses will constantly change but will always average a specified number. For example, a variable ratio 5 (VR 5) will require between one and ten or twelve responses, but on the average the token will be delivered after five responses. Such a schedule results in more consistent and more frequent responding. As soon as the consequence is produced, responding begins again and occurs at a steady high rate.

Bibliographic Essay

The articles compared and contrasted in this text are those that were judged as the best at describing the current state of behavioral technology in school psychology. While there are numerous journals dealing with educational matters, there are surprisingly little scientific data of immediate usefulness to those people charged with dealing with students on a daily basis, namely, teachers, school psychologists, and counselors. The purpose of this text is twofold: to bring together in one place as much of this kind of data as possible, and to provide a conceptual framework in which the various studies reported can be understood in relation to one another. For this reason research published in the *Journal of Applied Behavior Analysis* (*JABA*) is heavily represented in the text.

JABA has addressed the issues of classroom token economies, group-oriented contingencies, hyperactivity, behavioral contracting, shy and withdrawn behavior, self-management, and the general features of classroom management, all within a coherent conceptual framework. In 1968, in the very first article of the fledgling journal, Hall, Lund, and Jackson described the "Effects of Teacher Attention on Study Behavior." This began a long and highly acclaimed series of scholarly presentations of applied behavioral research in the classroom. Almost every issue of *JABA* has contained some direct or indirect reference to the application of scientific methodology in an educational environment. In the present text over 400 authors' investigations are compared and contrasted. About 90 percent of this research is derived from the *Journal of Applied Behavior Analysis*.

Studies from the *Journal of the Experimental Analysis of Behavior, Behavior Research and Therapy,* the *Journal of Abnormal and Social Psychology,* the *Journal of Abnormal Psychology*, the *Child Study Journal, Behavioral Engineering,* and perhaps to a greater extent, *Exceptional Children* account for other portions of the applied research reported in this text. These journals have long and distinguished histories of scholarly publication. However, they are either primarily devoted to basic research, or they represent a broad range of approaches having no common conceptual core. Thus the combined requirements of empirical data, research immediately applicable in the school setting, and a consistent conceptual framework resulted in the preponderence of studies from *JABA*.

If there has been any criticism of *JABA* from the psychological community it has been related to the experimental design characteristics typical of research reported in the journal. The *Journal of Applied Behavior Analysis* has, most often, published research involving small numbers of subjects, although various large group studies do appear occasionally. While arguments can be made for alternative research strategies, a design that allows extended observations across time is of great practical importance in research designed to have applicability outside the research setting. Teachers and others working in schools must have techniques that work with individual students. If we learn that under certain conditions a large number of students, on the average, behave slightly better or learn slightly more, we may wish to instate those conditions. But that doesn't help school personnel to deal effectively with those students not helped by the introduction of a variable. The single-subject design, typical of behavior-analytic basic research, is a strategy that stresses identification of all the kinds of variables relevant to changes in behavior. The kinds of relationships that universally obtain between creatures and the world that they live in are explored by closely examining those relations over long periods of time. The strategy has been enormously successful, producing basic principles that are then studied, by applied researchers, as they occur in the world outside the laboratory, and with the purpose of making a difference that is of significant value to the consumer.

The *Journal of Applied Behavior Analysis* has provided an outlet for an extremely useful form of applied research that might have been unreported otherwise. As a result the advantages of analyzing detailed changes in the behavior of single subjects have become apparent. The fact that individuals demonstrate varying degrees of latency, duration, and frequency of behaviors as they are exposed to similar treatments has not interfered with rigorous interpretations of data. Use of various research designs, such as multiple baseline and reversal of treatments, allows individual variations to be observed even as they exemplify general learning processes. *JABA* has emphasized this type of research to the advantage of its audience—providing school psychologists, classroom teachers, administrators, professors, and students planning careers in education with an increasingly sophisticated array of procedures that work in educational environments.

We believe that these school personnel will find the research reported in this book of immediate and lasting use because it demonstrates socially significant changes in behavior in school settings and makes clear the kind of procedures that produce those changes.

Author Index

Subject Index

About the Authors

H. A. CHRIS NINNESS is Supervising School Psychologist, Denton ISD, and Adjunct Professor of School/Child–Clinical Psychology at the University of North Texas. He has contributed articles to *Behavioral Engineering* and *Child Study Journal*.

SIGRID S. GLENN is Assistant Professor and Director of the Center for Behavior Studies at the University of North Texas. She is the coauthor of *Introduction to the Science of Psychology* and *Introduction to Behavior Analysis and Behavior Modification*. Her articles have been published in *Biological Psychology*, *Behavior Research of Severe Developmental Disabilities*, *The Behavior Analyst*, and *Behavior Analysis and Social Action*.